# Jane Austen's England

# Jane Austen's England

ROY and LESLEY ADKINS

VIKING

VIKING
Published by the Penguin Group
Penguin Group (USA) Inc., 375 Hudson Street,
New York, New York 10014, USA

USA | Canada | UK | Ireland | Australia | New Zealand | India | South Africa | China

Penguin Books Ltd, Registered Offices: 80 Strand, London WC2R 0RL, England
For more information about the Penguin Group visit penguin.com

First published in Great Britain as *Eavesdropping on Jane Austen's England* by Little, Brown,
an imprint of Little, Brown Book Group

Published by arrangement with Little, Brown Book Group

Map illustrations on pages viii, ix, x and xi by John Gilkes

Library of Congress Cataloging-in-Publication Data

Adkins, Roy (Roy A.)
Jane Austen's England / Roy and Lesley Adkins.
pages cm
Includes bibliographical references and index.
ISBN 978-0-670-78584-1
1. England–Social life and customs–19th century. 2. England–Social life and customs–18th century.
3. Austen, Jane, 1775-1817. 4. England--In literature. I. Adkins, Lesley. II. Title.
DA533.A35 2013
942.07–dc23
2013016959

Printed in the United States of America
1   3   5   7   9   10   8   6   4   2

*To Anne and David Barclay*
*For their friendship, support and encouragement*

# CONTENTS

———•◆•———

*England with the main place-names mentioned*

# Jane Austen Territory

Kingsclere •

Farnborough
Basingstoke • Fleet •
Ashe • • Deane Odiham Aldershot •
• Steventon

Andover • Whitchurch

Alton •
Chawton •
• Stockbridge

• Alresford • Selborne
• Winchester

Romsey Petersfield •
•
• Eastleigh
• Bishops Waltham
• Fordingbridge Southampton Horndean •
Cadnam • Wickham •
• Lyndhurst
Fareham • Havant •
• Ringwood
• Brockenhurst
Gosport •
Lymington • The Solent Portsmouth

ISLE OF WIGHT

English Channel

0        5        10        15 miles
0    5    10    15    20 kms

*Map showing the main places in Hampshire, where Jane Austen lived*

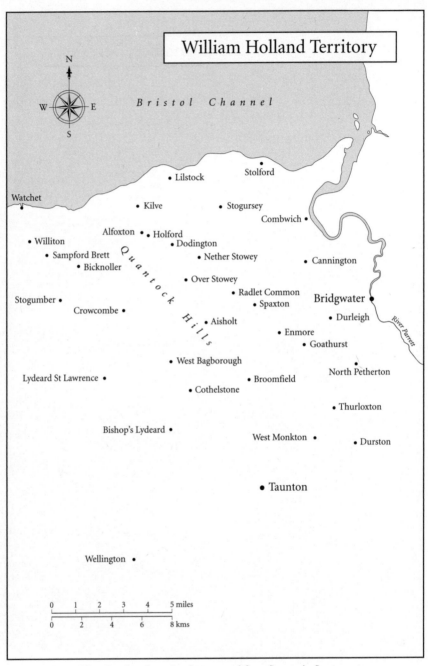

*Map showing the main places around Over Stowey in Somerset,*
*where William Holland lived*

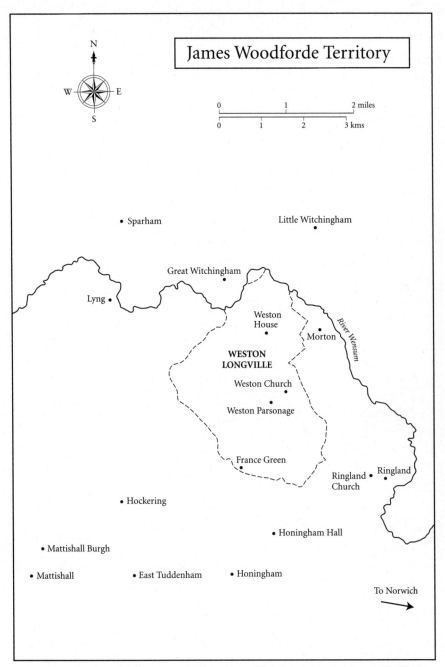

*Map showing the main places around Weston Longville in Norfolk, where James Woodforde lived for many years. The parish boundary is shown as a dashed line*

*The counties of England and Wales in 1809, with major place-names and mail coach routes. The English counties (as spelled on the map) are: 1. Northumberland; 2. Cumberland; 3. Durham; 4. Yorkshire; 5. Westmoreland; 6. Lancashire; 7. Cheshire; 8. Shropshire; 9. Herefordshire; 10. Monmouthshire; 11. Nottinghamshire; 12. Derbyshire; 13. Staffordshire; 14. Leicestershire; 15. Rutlandshire; 16. Northamptonshire; 17. Warwickshire; 18. Worcestershire; 19 Glocestershire; 20. Oxfordshire; 21. Buckinghamshire; 22. Bedfordshire; 23. Lincolnshire; 24. Huntingdonshire; 25. Cambridgeshire; 26. Norfolk; 27. Suffolk; 28. Essex; 29. Hertfordshire; 30. Middlesex; 31. Surrey; 32. Kent; 33. Sussex; 34. Berkshire; 35. Wiltshire; 36. Hampshire; 37. Dorsetshire; 38. Somersetshire; 39. Devonshire; 40. Cornwall*

*A 1797 map of London showing Covent Garden, the British Museum and the Foundling Hospital on the west side, extending to Whitechapel Road and Mile End on the east. Southwark lies to the south of the River Thames*

Detail from a 1797 map of London, with Holborn running from east to west, St Giles on the left and Fleet Street, Strand and Covent Garden at the bottom

*Detail from a 1797 map of London, with (from left to right) Blackfriars Bridge, Ludgate Hill, St Paul's cathedral, Bethlem Hospital and the Royal Exchange (the Bank of England is adjacent)*

# INTRODUCTION

———◆———

# KNOW YOUR PLACE

One does not love a place the less for having suffered in it, unless it has been all suffering, nothing but suffering.

*Persuasion*, by Jane Austen

The *place* is an austere, wartime England. In the north Hampshire village of Steventon, Jane Austen was born in December 1775, and just 12 miles away in the cathedral city of Winchester, she died in July 1817. Such a short distance separates her birth and death, yet during her lifetime of forty-one years she travelled more than most women of this era, westwards as far as Dawlish in Devon, eastwards to Ramsgate in Kent, southwards to Portsmouth and probably as far north as Hamstall Ridware in Staffordshire.[1] England was the only country she knew, and for most of her adult life, that country was at war. In fact, England was at peace for only twelve years and eight months of her entire life – a decade of peace was enjoyed from the end of the American Revolutionary War in 1783, with another brief interlude of peace between the ending of the Revolutionary Wars with France in 1801 and the start of the Napoleonic Wars from 1803, and then more permanent peace when the wars with France and America ended in 1815.[2]

Yet wartime England makes only a low-key appearance in Jane Austen's novels. George Wickham, the villain of *Pride and Prejudice*, is a lieutenant in the militia who is bought off with a commission in the regular army, while Fanny Price in *Mansfield Park* has a brother in the Royal Navy and a father who is a retired marine lieutenant. War forms a backdrop to the novels, but no fighting took place on English soil – men sailed away to war at sea or in other lands. Even so, military men, preparations for war and foreign prisoners-of-war were encountered everywhere, and the threat of invasion by the French generated immense unease and, at times, panic. With a strong and efficient British navy, the danger of invasion was in fact small, but public perception was different. Invasion scares helped to make the population tolerate relentless rises in taxes, much of which went on the wars and on the extravagant royal family. This was a time of glaring disparity between the immensely rich minority and the poor majority, who suffered from steep rises in the price of food and from falling wages. It is hardly surprising that a good deal of support was shown for the French Revolution when it began in 1789.

The ruling class and the Church of England dreaded such an uprising in which they might be stripped of power and even put to death if the country became a truly democratic state. The Reverend William Holland, a Somerset clergyman whose background and status were similar to that of Jane Austen's father, was forthright in his views about some of the lower classes: 'They expect to be kept in idleness or supported in extravagance and drunkenness. They do not trust to their own industry for support. They grow insolent, subordination is lost and [they] make their demands on other people's purses as if they were their own.'[3] Even so, he was broadly sympathetic towards the plight of the poor: 'I wish I could prevail on the farmers to sell their wheat to the parish at the rate of ten shillings per bushel and then keep the poor to their usual standard of allowance.'[4]

This was a period of drastic, sweeping changes that affected almost everyone and everything in England. The upper classes became fearful that the class structure was under threat, while the oppressed lower classes had to endure constant hardships. Although the poor were increasingly assisted by charities, such as the provision of free education and hospitals, they continued to be treated as an inferior part of society and were expected to know their place and show absolute deference towards their betters.

Despite some political protests and anti-royalist affrays, a French-style revolution never materialised. Instead, England experienced a revolution within industry and agriculture, with more efficient, often more scientific, production of food and manufactured goods. The people who did the hard work were at best regarded as just another factor in the economy, alongside raw materials, capital and land – those who had the least often lost the most, while the wealthy literally capitalised on the improvements. In both wartime and peacetime, Jane Austen's England was not a tranquil place. Hundreds of disturbances and riots were ignited by protests against industrial change, the enclosure of common land and, above all else, high food prices. One desperate mob at Brandon in Suffolk in 1816 gathered under the banner 'Bread or Blood' and threatened to march on London.[5]

Throughout Jane Austen's lifetime, King George III was on the throne. Only her last few years fall within the Regency period, when Prince George ruled as regent on behalf of his father, who was declared insane in 1811. When he died in 1820, the prince became King George IV, but immediately after his own death a decade later, historians, satirists and political commentators began to write about the evils of his regency and his reign as king. By the mid-nineteenth century the Regency period was recognised as an episode that had impoverished the nation at a time of war and damaged the influence of royalty through the lazy, self-indulgent and profligate life led by the Prince Regent. One saving grace was his patronage of art and architecture, creating a climate where all kinds of art, writing and music flourished. It was a world inhabited by poets such as John Keats, Samuel Taylor Coleridge and William Wordsworth, painters including John Constable, J.M.W. Turner and David Wilkie, and novelists like Jane Austen, Fanny Burney and Walter Scott.

Novels were in fact a fairly new art form in England that were able to develop from around 1700 once government controls over publishing had been relaxed. Being part of a family of avid readers, Jane Austen was well acquainted with the books being published,

and for the first half of her life she had access to her father's extensive library.[6] One trend was for Gothic novels of horror, suspense
and the supernatural, which flourished after the publication in 1764
of Horace Walpole's *The Castle of Otranto*. Subsequent successful
writers of this genre included Ann Radcliffe, William Beckford
and Matthew Lewis, while other novelists were drawn towards the
dilemma of young women finding suitable marriage partners, as in
Fanny Burney's first novel *Evelina*, published in 1778, which she followed by *Cecilia* (1782) and *Camilla* (1796). Maria Edgeworth also
wrote popular novels about English society, manners and marriage,
most famously *Belinda* in 1801. Such novels were treated with suspicion by many, an attitude that Jane Austen described with
amusement in her own works. In *Northanger Abbey* the narrator
criticises those who are embarrassed by novels: "'I am no novel-
reader – I seldom look into novels – Do not imagine that I often
read novels – It is really very well for a novel." Such is the common
cant. "And what are you reading, Miss – ?" "Oh! It is only a novel!"
replies the young lady, while she lays down her book with affected
indifference, or momentary shame. "It is only *Cecilia*, or *Camilla*, or
*Belinda*".'

Having moved to Ireland with her father in 1782, Maria Edgeworth
was better known for her four Irish novels, in particular *Castle
Rackrent* (1800). Other writers also ignored England and chose the
more romantic backdrops of Ireland, Wales, Scotland or the
Continent, such as the Spanish setting of Matthew Lewis's *The Monk*
(1796) and the French location for Ann Radcliffe's *The Romance of the
Forest* (1791), while her *Mysteries of Udolpho* (1794) took place in sixteenth-century southern France and Italy. It was Sir Walter Scott
who raised the status of historical fiction with his immensely popular Scottish tales, the first of which was *Waverley*, dealing with the
Jacobite uprising of 1745, an event still remembered by many when
Jane Austen was born. As she remarked to her niece Anna a few
weeks after its publication in 1814, 'Walter Scott has no business to
write novels, especially good ones. It is not fair. He has fame and
profit enough as a poet, and should not be taking the bread out of
other people's mouths. I do not like him, and do not mean to like

*Waverley* if I can help it, but I fear I must . . . I have made up my mind to like no novels really but Miss Edgeworth's, yours, and my own.'[7] Anna was currently immersed in writing a novel, some of which she had recently shown to her aunt.

An article in the *Edinburgh Magazine* in January 1799 examined why novels were so popular:

> we fly for relief from the sameness of real life to the composition called Novels. In them we find common things related in an uncommon way, which is precisely the remedy we have been seeking to vary our amuse-ments . . . It is this art of making much out of little that reconciles us to a course of novel-reading. We find how tame and insipid real life is; we awake in the morning, dress ourselves, go out shopping or visiting, and return in perfect safety to the same employment or amusements this day that we returned to yesterday, and which will probably engage our time to-morrow. It is not remarkable, therefore, if young and active spirits become tired of a routine so dull and unvarying, and are desirous of adventures which may distinguish them from the common herd of neigh-bours . . . Such are to be found in novels.[8]

In short, novels were considered as cheap escapism, the pulp fiction of their time, and not to be regarded as in any way realistic.

Jane Austen took a different direction, writing about what she observed of contemporary English society. She advocated authenti-city and so advised Anna to steer clear of Ireland in writing her own novel: 'you had better not leave England. Let the Portmans go to Ireland; but as you know nothing of the manners there, you had better not go with them. You will be in danger of giving false repre-sentations. Stick to Bath and the Foresters. There you will be quite at home.'[9] Her meticulous attention to detail is highlighted by another comment to her niece: 'Lyme will not do. Lyme is towards forty miles' distance from Dawlish and would not be talked of there. I have put Starcross indeed. If you prefer Exeter that must be always safe. I have also scratched out the introduction between Lord Portman and his brother, and Mr. Griffin. A country surgeon . . . would not be introduced to men of their rank.'[10] Other errors in

Anna's novel were also pointed out, such as the amount of time consumed by travelling: 'They must be two days going from Dawlish to Bath. They are nearly 100 miles apart.'[11]

The novels and letters of Jane Austen provide realistic glimpses into the way of life in England, even if the world she depicts is largely the privileged end of society. But in order to understand the context of her novels, the rest of the nation needs to be considered. England was highly stratified, and everyone knew their place or 'rank'. In 1709 Daniel Defoe roughly summarised the social strata as 'The great, who live profusely; the rich, who live plentifully; the middle sort, who live well; the working trades, who labour hard, but feel no want; the country people, farmers, etc. who fare indifferently; the poor that fare hard; the miserable, that really pinch and suffer want.'[12]

In the ensuing decades little had changed to alter his sketch of society. The bulk of the population comprised skilled and unskilled labourers, craftsmen, servants, apprentices, the unemployed, vagrants and criminals. Even these lower ranks had subtle gradations, and social mobility was rare. Anyone's hopes of bettering themselves might well be frowned upon by the ranks above, and William Holland certainly took a sceptical view of his servant's aspirations: 'Robert borrowed my horse to go to his brother's wedding. He is [to be] married to a farmer's daughter which has turned poor Robert's head and he begins to think that both he and his family in a short time must rank with the principal men in the kingdom.'[13]

Apart from this strict social ranking, a person's place in society was frequently influenced by their wealth. An increase in wealth could improve status, but would not erase memories of humble beginnings, as Holland revealed in a comment about a local man, Andrew Guy, 'alias squire Guy, a rich old widower ... the son of a grazier [who reared cattle] lifted up to the rank of gentleman, but ignorant and illiterate'.[14] Nor could money alone bridge the gap between the elite and the working majority, as many newly prosperous merchants and manufacturers discovered. They would never be fully accepted, and the best hope was for their children to marry 'above their station', something that nevertheless carried a stigma. In the novels of Jane Austen, wealth and income often form part of a character's description, and in *Persuasion* a rich bride is described as a 'very low woman' because, despite her wealth, 'her father was a grazier, her grandfather a butcher'.

England itself measures roughly 360 miles north to south and 330 miles east to west at its widest extent. Jane Austen's England was not an overcrowded country – in 1801 the entire population was approximately that of London today. Even though London was the largest city in Europe, most people at that time still lived and worked on the land. To the residents of London, the city seemed vast, prompting the politician George Canning to lament that it was possible to lose close acquaintances for days on end.[15]

There were pronounced regional differences and much variety in the way people lived – more so for the poorer classes who relied on local resources than for wealthier people who could afford to do or buy whatever they wanted. In the closing years of the eighteenth century, the insurance businessman Sir Frederick Morton Eden carried out a remarkable survey, which was published as *The State of the Poor*. In it he included a wide range of prices for common items across the country, such as potatoes selling at 1 shilling the bushel in Petersfield, Hampshire, 2 shillings and 8 pence in Winslow, Buckinghamshire, and 3 shillings in Brixworth, Northamptonshire.[16]

Fundamental changes were taking place in the very appearance of the countryside, as hedges, walls and fences sprang up to mark the boundaries of newly enclosed fields, while new turnpike roads and canals carved fresh lines across the land. The open landscape that had existed since before medieval times was fast evolving into the chequered pattern of fields still seen in some places today, or else was being devoured by rapidly expanding industrial towns such as Birmingham and Manchester. As William Blake saw it, 'England's green and pleasant land' was in grave danger from 'dark Satanic mills'.[17]

This place of radical change is the real England of Jane Austen and the subject of this book. We wanted to show how the mass of ordinary people, our ancestors, lived and fitted into her England. It used to be fashionable to trace your ancestry back to royalty, even if on the wrong side of the sheets, but even the most humble or most nefarious ancestors are just as interesting. They all had a part to play in shaping events and influencing history. Without them, history is nothing.

We used a similar approach for *Jack Tar: The Extraordinary Lives of Ordinary Seamen in Nelson's Navy*, in which we charted the everyday details of what it was like to be a seaman rather than a high-ranking officer. The period we chose for *Jack Tar* was roughly 1771 to 1815, from when Horatio Nelson first joined the navy as a captain's servant to a decade after his death, when peace finally came. This coincided with Jane Austen's lifetime, and so we hope that *Eavesdropping on Jane Austen's England* will provide a fascinating contrast and give a flavour of life on land two centuries ago.

When encountering a remote era of history, such as Roman or medieval times, it is not surprising to find an alien world, but life in Georgian England was also very different to the world of the twenty-first century. The basic amenities that we take for granted, like electricity, a water supply and sewerage, were non-existent or just being introduced, so that simply keeping warm, clean and free from hunger entailed laborious, time-consuming and inefficient tasks. Steam engines were transforming some industries, but travel relied on horsepower, manpower or windpower. If someone went away for several years, perhaps serving in the Royal Navy, they might not be recognised on their return, because there were no photographs to refresh memories.

Even walking the streets in bad weather was a different experience, since few buildings had guttering. Instead, roofs overhung the walls so as to throw rainwater away from the foundations. Naturally, people kept close to the walls for shelter, under the overhang – the eaves – and caught snatches of conversation from within as they passed. In a similar way to this eavesdropping, we have caught snatches of the lives of Jane Austen's contemporaries from the writings they left behind. Our book is a snapshot of her era, reflecting the variety of life at that time. It is not a narrative of events, but of people's daily lives. We have opted for a loose chronological thread, running from marriage (the main theme of Jane Austen's novels) to the birth of babies, progressing through childhood, domestic work, religion, occupations, entertainment, travel, illnesses and finally death and burial.

We have relied upon the words of people who lived at that time, recorded in documents such as letters, diaries, travelogues, accounts of criminal trials and newspapers. The spelling in these eyewitness accounts has occasionally been corrected and the punctuation and style sometimes modernised, particularly the tendency to use dashes instead of full-stops, ampersands (&) instead of 'and', and upper-case letters for the start of many words. Most quotations have been only slightly altered, if at all, and the words and meaning have not been changed.

Personal letters and diaries were rarely intended to be published, but were written for the information and enjoyment of one or two people, or at most a family and their descendants, as William Holland revealed in January 1801: 'I began reading my diary to my family from its commencement and shall continue to do so as far as the last year goes.'[18] His extensive diaries allow us to become acquainted not just with him and his family in the Somerset parish of Over Stowey and beyond, but also with his overworked servants and the local people including various paupers, labourers and tradesmen. Only an abridged selection of these diaries has ever been published,[19] and so the full, original manuscript diaries provide a fresh window on English life, rather like the diaries of the Reverend James Woodforde. Six years younger than Holland, he was an unmarried clergyman from Ansford in Somerset who spent much of his working life on the other side of England, in his Norfolk parish of Weston Longville. Although classically educated, Woodforde turned his back on such learning after leaving Oxford university, and instead filled his diaries with extraordinary details about everyday life. We have made use of the complete text of his extensive diaries that have been so ably transcribed over the years by the Parson Woodforde Society, superseding the edited extracts published decades ago.

In northern England, from Wigan to Liverpool, through the Lake District and Yorkshire, Nelly Weeton provides another perspective on life at that time. She was clearly very intelligent, but her potential was stifled by poverty and her low-class status as a governess. Nelly's letters and diaries are filled with comments that were often as satirical and perceptive as those of Jane Austen herself. Numerous other voices are heard in this book, including Sarah and William Wilkinson, whose mundane letters to each other (while he was at sea) convey valuable insights into daily life, while the writings of foreign visitors such as the American Benjamin Silliman and the German Carl Moritz provide an outsider's viewpoint. Such documents take us right to the heart of Jane Austen's England, allowing us to eavesdrop on what people thought and discussed among themselves – the very words of those who lived two centuries ago.

In her novels Jane Austen brilliantly portrayed the lives of the middle and upper classes, but barely mentioned the cast of characters who constituted the bulk of the population. *Mansfield Park* was started in 1811 and published in 1814, and her account of how the Price family lived at Portsmouth is the closest she came to portraying the lower classes. It would be left to the genius of the next generation, Charles Dickens, to write novels about the poor, the workers and the lower middle classes. Born in Portsmouth in 1812, before most of Jane Austen's books had even been published, Dickens was sent to work in a factory in London at the age of twelve and came to rely on writing to earn money. Looking back to the time of the French Revolution, his novel *A Tale of Two Cities* starts with the celebrated words: 'It was the best of times, it was the worst of times, it was the age of wisdom, it was the age of foolishness, it was the epoch of belief, it was the epoch of incredulity, it was the season of Light, it was the season of Darkness, it was the spring of hope, it was the winter of despair.' This is a succinct summary of Jane Austen's England, on which we are about to eavesdrop.

A chronological overview of the main historical events is given on p. 347, including some key events of Jane Austen's lifetime. For more about this book, see our website www.adkinshistory.com.

————— ·◆· —————

# ONE

# WEDDING BELLS

It is a truth universally acknowledged, that a single man in possession of a good fortune, must be in want of a wife.

*Pride and Prejudice*, by Jane Austen

On a bitterly cold Norfolk morning in January 1787, Parson James Woodforde left the comfort of his rectory at Weston Longville and rode on horseback over a mile and a half along a muddy lane until he reached the imposing church of St Peter in the village of Ringland.[1] Because its vicar was away, he had been asked by the parish officers to perform an urgent marriage ceremony – for the customary fee of 10 shillings and 6 pence. Inside this medieval church, the spectacular nave roof enhanced the impressive setting for the wedding, but it was not a day for joy and celebration, as Woodforde noted in his diary: 'Rode to Ringland this morning and married one Robert Astick and Elizabeth Howlett by licence ... the man being in custody, the woman being with child by him. The man was a long time before he could be prevailed on to marry her when in the church yard; and at the altar behaved very unbecoming.'[2]

Standing in the numbing cold before the altar, poor Elizabeth surely dreaded the prospect of being saddled with this man. Although his only alternative was to return to gaol, Robert proved highly reluctant to marry and almost needed to be dragged to the altar. His crime was not premarital sex, but causing a penniless woman and baby to be a burden on the parish, and as a result he was forced into marriage. Under the Bastardy Act of 1733, unmarried pregnant women were taken before the magistrate by the parish overseers of the poor and forced on oath to name the father – or alleged father. The named man then had the dubious choice of paying the parish for the upkeep of the child, marrying the woman (unless he was already married) or a spell in prison. If he ran away, a reward might be offered for his recapture. Nine days after Robert and Elizabeth's forced marriage, John Hammonway in Northumberland escaped from prison, and the *Newcastle Courant* carried a detailed description of the offender:

### COUNTY OF NORTHUMBERLAND

*Made his Escape over a wall, in a yard joining to the House of Correction, at Morpeth, on the 3rd of Feb. instant* [1787], JOHN HAMMONWAY, late of the town and county of Newcastle upon Tyne, nailer, was committed for bastardy.– The said John Hammonway is about 23 years of age, five feet five inches high, slender made, swarthy complexion, short black hair, dark-brown sully eyes; had on, when he escaped, a dark-blue coat, flowered cotton waistcoat, leather breeches, with metal buttons.

Whoever will secure the said John Hammonway, and give notice to John Doxford, Keeper of the said House of Correction, shall receive a reward of TWO GUINEAS, to be paid by JOHN DOXFORD.[3]

Forced marriages were commonplace, but the unmarried Parson Woodforde disliked them intensely: 'It is a cruel thing that any person should be compelled by law to marry ... It is very disagreeable to me to marry such persons.'[4] He himself conducted several such weddings at his own church in Weston Longville. 'I walked to church this morning between 10 and 11 o'clock,' he recorded some years later, 'and married by licence, one Daniel Tabble of Ling [Lyng] and Anne Dunnel of Weston, a forced match, she being very near her time, and he under custody of the parish officers ever since yesterday morning. I recd. of the officers for marrying them 0.10.6, being the usual fee for marrying by licence here.'[5] Anne gave birth two months later.[6] These weddings were a far cry from the romantic notion of courtship, love and marriage that form the essence of Jane Austen's fiction.

Marriage based on love and on freedom of choice was becoming more common, and from the later eighteenth century romantic novels such as *Evelina* by Fanny Burney and *Belinda* by Maria Edgeworth confronted such issues, to be followed a few years later by the novels of Jane Austen. For many, though, particularly if accustomed to wealth, such an approach to marriage was totally impractical. A husband with a respectable income or a wife with a generous dowry was still extremely desirable, if not an absolute necessity, and the conflict between marrying for love and marrying for money and social advantage is a common element in Jane Austen's writing. In *Northanger Abbey* she parodied novels such as Ann Radcliffe's Gothic romance *The Mysteries of Udolpho*,[7] and when Isabella's impecunious brother John wants to marry her friend Catherine, she is pleased that Catherine is not interested, 'for what were you both to live upon, supposing you came together? You have both of you something [some income] to be sure, but it is not a trifle that will support a family nowadays; and after all that romancers may say, there is no doing without money.'

A good number of parents arranged marriages to ensure that their children were securely established in life, and girls from wealthy families were provided with dowries, or 'portions', to make them attractive to male suitors. In Jane Austen's novel *Sense and Sensibility*, Edward Ferrars is to marry the wealthy Miss Morton, and on learning that his older brother Robert is also contemplating her, Elinor Dashwood says: 'The lady, I suppose, has no choice in the affair.' Elinor's own brother is puzzled by her reaction: 'Choice! – how do you mean?'

Wealth was the key factor. Happiness was of secondary importance. For the upper classes, marriage was essential for the provision of legitimate heirs and for the survival of estates, fortunes and families, but for women of all classes marriage was crucial, because ways of supporting themselves were severely limited, resulting in the obsession with pairing off daughters with suitable men. For Mrs Bennet in *Pride and Prejudice*, 'The business of her life was to get her daughters married.'

It was customary to marry within the same social class – because of hypocrisy and snobbery, marrying into a different class was problematic. It was frequently acceptable for a wealthy man to maintain a mistress of low rank, but he was despised and even shunned if he had the temerity to marry her. In 1810 Nelly Weeton was working as a governess at Dove Nest, a house near Ambleside in the Lake District. The previous year her wealthy employer, Edward Pedder, had married his dairymaid, as Nelly told her unmarried friend Bessy Winkley: 'if you knew the sorrow that person must undergo who marries above herself, you would never be ambitious to marry out of your own rank; people call it doing well; they are most egregiously mistaken. Let the husband be ever so kind, it cannot compensate for the numberless mortifications a woman so raised must endure. Those married people have the greatest chance of being happy whose original rank was most nearly equal.'[8]

Originally from Lancashire, Nelly's parents were both dead, and her younger brother Tom was a lawyer. She was forced to work because she had little money and at the age of thirty-three was still unmarried. A few months later, she elaborated on the former servant girl's family:

Mrs. P. [Pedder] has a brother and sister ... the sister keeps her father's house, working in the fields, on the peat moss, or her father's house, as occasion serves. What a difference in the situation of the two sisters! The one with her father wishes much to emerge from her present obscurity; but her father, an honest, warm-hearted, affectionate parent, sensibly says 'there is more happiness in his humble situation, than where there is more bustle, show, and finery'; he thinks his eldest daughter might do just as well, or better, in marrying a farmer, as the youngest has done in marrying a gentleman. 'People,' he says, 'do not always do well that marry so much above them, for they only get despised and abused by their fine new relations.'[9]

Finding a suitable marriage partner could prove stressful, since there were insufficient numbers of eligible men to go round, particularly with so many fatalities and injuries in the wars. Accurate figures are impossible to calculate, but throughout the Napoleonic Wars the combined casualties in the army and navy were on average about twenty thousand a year, and many thousands more were engaged in fighting overseas. Some eligible bachelors inevitably preferred the freedom of the single life, and countless young working men were prevented from marrying by restrictions such as apprenticeship contracts. Matchmaking and courtship therefore provided admirable material for Jane Austen's fiction.

The most effective way for the middle and upper classes to meet prospective partners was at the various balls that were so frequently held in both public and private venues, but courting couples were expected to behave formally, even when greeting each other in public. In *Sense and Sensibility*, Elinor hears Willoughby using Marianne's first name and so assumes they are to be married: 'in his addressing her sister by her Christian name alone, she instantly saw an intimacy so decided, a meaning so direct, as marked a perfect agreement between them. From that moment she doubted not of their being engaged to each other.'

When a woman married she passed from the control of her father, who 'gave her away' at the wedding to the control of her husband. Her property became her husband's, despite his promise in the marriage ceremony, 'with all my worldly goods I thee endow'. As a wife, she could not legally own land or have a separate source of income, unless set out in a specific contract – the marriage settlement. Such a settlement might entitle her to receive the interest from her dowry in her lifetime and to bequeath the dowry to her children or use it as income if her husband died. Otherwise, she effectively had no legal status, and any children belonged to her husband.

The law governing marriage was Lord Hardwicke's Marriage Act of 1753, which decreed that after 25 March 1754 marriages were valid in law only if they had been advertised by banns or sanctioned by a special licence and were conducted by an Anglican clergyman in a church. Marriages also had to be recorded in a register. A marriage conducted in any other way was not legal, and the person performing it was guilty of a felony and liable to transportation. The Act also advised that the ceremony should take place in the church of the parish where the bride or groom resided, but this was not essential for the marriage to be valid. The main intention of the Act was to prevent clandestine or irregular marriages and to prevent minors from marrying without parental consent – something that was of considerable consequence to the upper classes, who feared wealthy heiresses marrying impoverished husbands.

This Act was the first statutory law to require a formal marriage ceremony. Before 1753 all such matters were in the sole control of the Church of England, with the single requirement that the marriage should be conducted by an Anglican clergyman. Other requirements such as banns were not then essential, so all kinds of rapid and irregular marriages had been valid in law, and various places became notorious for the availability of pliable clergymen willing to perform clandestine marriages. Many churches in London conducted such weddings, mainly of Londoners, but some accepted outsiders as well. Weddings also took place at the Fleet prison, which claimed to be outside the jurisdiction of the Church. It was a prison for debtors whose inmates invariably included some clergy, and marriages performed there were called 'Fleet marriages'. Most nonconformists, or dissenters, believed that marriage was not a religious ceremony, but for purposes of legality their marriages before and after the 1753 Act tended to be in parish churches, whereas Jews and Quakers, exempt from the Act, were allowed to marry according to their own customs. Not until 1837 could couples legally marry in register offices, or in their own chapels if a civil registrar was present.

After 1754 it was still possible to have a discreet wedding in a parish where neither bride nor groom was known, and for rapid marriages couples fled across the border to Scotland where the laws were much less restrictive. For those complying with the law, banns were called in the parish church of both parties on three consecutive Sundays or holy days in order to publicly proclaim the intended marriage. This allowed anyone to raise objections – something that happened in January 1791 at Weston Longville, as Parson Woodforde noted: 'One Bush of this parish (whose daughter's banns were published last Sunday) came to my house this evening to forbid the banns, the man being found out to be a very infamous character.'[10] Five days later, he added: 'Brown (whose banns were forbid last week by the girl whose name is Bush) called on me this morning and I returned him the half crown that I recd. last Sunday sennight [seven nights ago] by my clerk for publishing the banns that day.'[11]

For anyone with an urgent need to marry or who did not wish banns to be proclaimed in public, the more expensive option was to obtain a licence, for which an 'allegation' had to be sworn, usually by the groom, giving details of the couple and assurances of no impediments to the marriage. Normally, common licences were issued by archbishops, bishops and some archdeacons, or by clergy in certain parishes and officials acting on their behalf. A marriage was then permitted to take place within the jurisdiction of the person issuing the licence, in one of the parishes named on the licence, but the requirement to be married in a named parish was often ignored. The wedding could take place later that day, but usually happened the day after. In August 1788 Woodforde conducted such a ceremony: 'About 11 o'clock this morning I took a walk to Weston Church and there married by Licence Jas. [James] Herring of Norwich to Miss [Elizabeth Ann] Peachman of this parish, for which I recd. of Mr. Herring 2.2.0 which I think very handsome of him.'[12]

Parental consent was required for anyone under the age of twenty-one marrying by licence, but minors could marry by publication of the banns, though parents were at liberty to object. The age of consent was fourteen for boys and twelve for girls, but most did not marry until their early twenties, even if they were betrothed at an earlier age. Apprentices were not permitted to marry, so many young men married late, in their mid- to late twenties. Richard Cureton, on becoming an apprentice in London in 1783, had to sign an indenture stating that during the seven years of apprenticeship he would 'not commit fornication, nor contract matrimony'.[13]

For rich and poor alike, a church was the venue for weddings. By today's standards most were low-key affairs, with few guests and moderate expenditure on wedding clothes and celebrations. 'Smock weddings' were a peculiar type of ceremony at which the bride was married naked – although usually she was barefoot and *en chemise*, wearing only a shift ('chemise'), smock or sheet for propriety. The point was that if she brought no clothes or property to the union, the husband-to-be was thought not liable for any debts she might have. Such weddings, randomly reported, occurred mainly in the eighteenth century, particularly for widowed women whose deceased husbands had left debts.

One Derby newspaper in September 1775 chose to run a story about a marriage that had taken place over a hundred miles to the south: 'Thursday se'nnight was married by licence, at Bishop's Waltham, Winchester, Mr. Richard Elcock, bricklayer, to Mrs. Judith Redding, who, to exempt her future husband from the payment of any debts she might have contracted, went into one of the pews in the church, and stript herself of all her cloaths except her shift, in which only she went to the altar, and was married, much to the astonishment of the parson, clerk, &c.'[14] A few years earlier, a similar wedding took place at St Michael's church at Ashton-under-Lyne in Lancashire: 'On Thursday last, was married, at Ashton-under-Lyne, Nathaniel Eller to the widow Hibbert, both upwards of fifty years of age; the widow had only her shift on, with her hair tied behind with horse hair, as a means to free them both from any obligation of paying her former husband's debts.'[15]

It was sometimes wrongly supposed that a smock wedding enabled a bride to retain her own wealth if her husband-to-be had debts. In December 1797 such a wedding was held at St Philip's parish church (now the cathedral) in Birmingham, with several newspapers reporting that the bride wore nothing (possibly not even a chemise) so that the creditors of her debt-ridden new husband could not seize her property:

> There is an opinion generally prevalent in Staffordshire, that if a woman should marry a man in distressed circumstances, none of his creditors can touch her property, if she should be *in puris naturalibus* [stark naked] while the ceremony is performed. In consequence of this prejudice, a woman of some property lately came with her intended husband into the vestry of the great church of Birmingham, and the moment she understood that the

Priest was ready at the altar, she threw off a large cloak, and in the exact state of Eve in Paradise, walked deliberately to the spot, and remained in that state till the ceremony ended.[16]

For the wealthier classes, a wedding was an opportunity to flaunt status and the latest fashions, as happens in *Sense and Sensibility*. With the marriage of Miss Grey to Willoughby being imminent, Elinor 'could soon tell at what coachmaker's the new carriage was building, by what painter Mr Willoughby's portrait was drawn, and at what warehouse Miss Grey's clothes might be seen'. The wealthy wore fine clothes for weddings, with white chosen for the bride and sometimes for the bridesmaids as well. Most people, including the brides, simply wore their Sunday best or something that could be subsequently used for that purpose. The bride's wedding clothes were secondary to her trousseau, for which she might be given household linen, items of clothing and other articles for her new life. In *Mansfield Park*, Jane Austen wryly says of the wedding between Maria Bertram and Mr Rushworth: 'It was a very proper wedding. The bride was elegantly dressed; the two bridesmaids were duly inferior; her father gave her away; her mother stood with salts in her hand, expecting to be agitated; her aunt tried to cry; and the service was impressively read by Dr Grant.'

At the wedding that he conducted by licence in August 1788 between James Herring and Elizabeth Peachman, Woodforde was impressed by everything:

It was a smart genteel marriage, 2 close carriages with smart liveries attended. Sheriff Buckle of Norwich and Mr. John Herring who was Sheriff of Norwich the last year and his son, old Mr. Peachman, Mrs. John Herring, Mrs. Forster of this Parish, and a very pretty young lady very neatly dressed, and attended as a bride maid and whose name was Miss Wingfield were at the ceremony. The bells rang merry after. Mr. Buckle, Mr. Herring and son and old Mr. Peachman returned with me on foot from Church to my house and eat some cake and drank some cyder &c. Mr. Peachman pressed me much to dine with them but I was not well enough to go into company.[17]

Rather than riding in a carriage, most people walked to church, and it was customary for flowers, herbs and rushes to be strewn along the route or at the church porch. A poem published in 1796 by Henry Rowe, rector of Ringshall in Suffolk, alludes to this practice:

> The wheaten ear was scatter'd near the porch.
> The green broom blossom'd strew'd the way to church.[18]

For the lower classes, wedding ceremonies were simple. In November 1810 the Reverend William Holland of Over Stowey in Somerset described the marriage of two of his servants:

> I went to church and married my servants Robert Dyer and Phebe [Phoebe Symons], and I trust they will be happy in each other and I gave them and their friends a dinner on the occasion and they are to continue with me as servants till Lady [Day] next ... Dyer desired me to publish the banns now and they were to be married about Christmas. I answer'd if the banns be publish'd, 'tis best marrying immediately, and they took my advice. My wife [Mary] is to take Phebe with her to Bath where we mean to go if it please God after Christmas and Dyer will stay in the house to take care of things here.[19]

All weddings were morning events, since canon law decreed that they could be solemnised only between 8 a.m. and noon – a rule that held until 1886. Particular times of the year (especially Lent) were traditionally avoided, and Sundays could be a nuisance. Holland certainly grumbled in October 1800: 'Had a wedding, but the clerk did not give me notice of the same the day before which made me very angry. Indeed Sunday is a bad day for these things, as it hurries me and I can scarce get myself ready for prayers.'[20]

The oldest customs, survivals from antiquity, were the wedding cake and the ring that was given to the bride during the ceremony. 'The Wedding Ring is worn on the fourth finger of the left hand,' according to the antiquary and clergyman John Brand, 'because it was antiently believed ... that a small artery ran from this finger to the heart.'[21] Because the dissection of human bodies had disproved this fact, he added, 'though the opinion has been justly exploded by the

Anatomists of modern times'.[22] He also mentioned that some wives never removed their wedding ring: 'Many married women are so rigid, not to say superstitious, in their notions concerning their wedding rings, that neither when they wash their hands, nor at any other time, will they take it off from their finger, extending, it should seem, the expression of "till Death us do part" even to this golden circlet, the token and pledge of matrimony.'[23]

Brand was fascinated by old customs and folklore, and when conducting weddings in London and in Newcastle, he had observed the tradition of saluting the bride: 'It is still customary among persons of middling rank as well as the Vulgar, in most parts of England, for the young men at the marriage ceremony to salute the Bride, one by one, the moment it is concluded. This, after officiating in the ceremony myself, I have seen frequently done.'[24] For those who could afford to pay the ringers, a wedding was often marked by a peal of bells, and in the church of the Holy Trinity at Kendal, Westmorland, one bell bore the inscription:

> In wedlock bands,
> All ye who join with hands,
> Your hearts unite;
> So shall our tuneful tongues combine
> To laud the nuptial rite.[25]

After the event, a meal might be laid on, and being a morning ceremony, a wedding breakfast was most common. More elaborate celebrations could continue the whole day, perhaps with a dinner and a supper, along with music, dancing, games and sports. Then as now, the wedding cake was an important element of the ceremony and was subsequently distributed to family and friends, something Jane Austen mentioned when writing to her sister Cassandra in 1808: 'Do you recollect whether the Manydown family send about their wedding cake? Mrs Dundas has set her heart upon having a piece from her friend Catherine, and Martha, who knows what importance she attaches to this sort of thing, is anxious for the sake of both, that there should not be a disappointment.'[26]

Customs varied across the country, and in northern England the cake was broken up over the bride's and groom's heads or scattered into the crowd. Elsewhere, the traditions relating to the ring and the cake were linked when pieces of cake were passed through the ring and thrown over the heads of the newly-weds, or placed beneath the pillows of young people to induce prophetic dreams of lovers and marriage. Henry Rowe wrote that after the bells rang out for the married couple, the cake was passed through the ring:

> The wedding cake now thro' the ring was led,
> The stocking thrown across the nuptial bed.[27]

There were many local variations of the old custom of throwing the bride's stocking. In one, the married couple sat up in bed and the bridesmaids sat at the end of the bed, with their backs to the couple. They then threw the stockings over their shoulders, and whoever managed to hit the bride would soon be married themselves.

The next day, most married couples began their everyday life together. No modern concept of a 'honeymoon' then existed – the term still referred to the month after the wedding. Rich newly-weds might make an extended tour, usually in Britain as the country was so often at war. The couple rarely went away alone, but were accompanied by friends, relatives and, of course, servants. The less well-off settled for whatever they could afford, perhaps staying with relatives for a week or two, while the lower classes had little or nothing in the way of a holiday, most returning to work the next day. Unless it was a royal or aristocratic wedding, in which case the newspapers would report the event at length, a modest notice might appear in a local newspaper. One from the *Derby Mercury* in June 1802 is typical: 'Married ... Sunday se'nnight, Mr. James York, chymist and druggist, to Miss Weston, both of Nottingham.'[28] These notices were more common after 1800, though still confined to the middle and upper classes.

Less welcome to the families involved were sensational newspaper accounts of elopements, as in February 1815 when the *Western Luminary* reported:

ELOPEMENT.– Another fashionable couple have eloped, it is supposed from the neighbourhood of Bristol. They arrived at Stourbridge about half-past six o'clock on the morning of Saturday se'nnight, in a post-chaise and four, and stopped at the Talbot hotel, where they changed horses. The Lady must have emerged in great haste from her bed-chamber, having no covering but a flannel petticoat and a great coat. They wished to purchase a bonnet in that town; but did not procure any other covering for the damsel until they reached Penkridge. They gave the different post-boys a 1*l.* [£1] note each, and proceeded northward from Stafford, for that celebrated spot, Gretna Green. The parties were unknown.[29]

In novels such as Jane Austen's, the heroines are invariably concerned with relationships and about overcoming impediments to those relationships. Had she been writing some decades earlier, clandestine marriages might well have featured, but as they were now illegal, elopement was the solution where a couple was desperate to marry without parental consent. The Bennet family in *Pride and Prejudice* is dismayed to discover that young Lydia has run off with Wickham. In a letter, Lydia describes her happiness: 'I am going to Gretna Green . . . for there is but one man in the world I love, and he is an angel . . . I can hardly write for laughing.' Wickham actually has no intention of marrying, and they are eventually tracked down in London.

Villages just over the Scottish border were favoured locations for couples fleeing from England to be married, and the best known was Gretna Green, some 10 miles from Carlisle. In a letter to Bessy Winkley written at Dove Nest in the final days of 1809, Nelly Weeton described how her employer had eloped: 'Mrs. Pedder was a dairy maid at Darwen-Bank, Mr. P's house near Preston [Lancashire], when he fell in love with her. Her father heard of the connexion and fearing his daughter might be seduced, sent for her home. He lives near-by here. Mr. P. followed her, took her off to Gretna Green and married her . . . She is not eighteen yet . . . Mr. P. is a little man of about 34.'[30]

Scottish marriage law required only a declaration before witnesses, a role performed by various Gretna Green inhabitants, including

Joseph Paisley, who was a farmer, fisherman and smuggler. For sixty years from 1753 he officiated as Gretna Green's parson. He was known as a blacksmith, though according to his successor Robert Elliott, he 'only acquired that name from his quickness in uniting eloping parties, for the common saying there was, "strike the iron when it is hot, Joseph".'[31] Robert had become acquainted with Paisley in 1810 and took over his business three years later. He left his version of the marriage ceremony:

It is very simple. The parties are first asked their names and places of abode; they are then asked to stand up, and enquired of if they are both single persons; if the answer be in the affirmative, the ceremony proceeds.

Each is next asked:—'Did you come here of your own free will and accord?' Upon receiving an affirmative answer the priest commences filling in the printed form of the certificate.

The man is then asked, 'Do you take this woman to be your lawful wedded wife, forsaking all other, [and] keep to her as long as you both shall live?' He answers 'I will.' The woman is asked the same question, which being answered the same, the woman then produces a ring which she gives to the man, who hands it to the priest; the priest then returns it to the man, and orders him to put it on the fourth finger of the woman's left hand, repeat these words, with this ring I thee wed, with my body I thee worship, with all my worldly goods I thee endow in the name of the Father, Son, and Holy Ghost, Amen. They then take hold of each other's right hands, and the woman says 'what God joins together let no man put asunder.' The priest says 'forasmuch as this man and this woman have consented to go together by giving and receiving a ring, I, therefore, declare them to be man and wife before God and these witnesses in the name of the Father, Son, and Holy Ghost, Amen.'[32]

The upper classes set great store by the legalities of marriage, but the lower classes were rarely worried by such niceties, and many couples simply lived together rather than pay fees to marry in church, particularly after the 1753 Act made the less costly clandestine marriages illegal. Some only married once the woman was pregnant. There were alternative, cheaper methods of marrying, mainly comprising informal declarations, but although acceptable by custom they were not actually legal. Few poor people could afford to elope to Gretna Green unless they were marrying someone wealthy, but the clergy could make life difficult for those living together without marrying.

William Holland kept a close eye on what was happening in his Somerset parish of Over Stowey, and in October 1800 one couple felt obliged to marry: 'It seems the persons were but lately come into the Parish and they had lived together before and they brought a bouncing child to be christened the very day of their wedding. I gave them a good jubation [severe rebuke], and told them that had I known there were such people in my Parish I would not have suffered them to have remained long in that situation. This they were aware of, so came to be married.'[33]

While unmarried couples were censured, single unmarried women like Nelly Weeton were pitied, because with their limited options in life they most likely faced penury unless they had a private income. They had long been referred to as 'old maids', a disparaging term for spinsters unlikely ever to marry.[34] The poet and biographer William Hayley wrote a substantial work on old maids. For an unmarried woman from a good family, he said,

> it is probable, that after having passed the sprightly years of youth in the comfortable mansion of an opulent father, she is reduced to the shelter of some contracted lodging in a country town, attended by a single female servant, and with difficulty living on the interest of two or three thousand pounds, reluctantly, and perhaps irregularly, paid to her by an avaricious or extravagant brother, who considers such payment as a heavy incumbrance on his paternal estate. Such is the condition in which the unmarried daughters of English gentlemen are too frequently found.[35]

After her father died in 1805 such was the condition of Jane Austen herself, and she would remain single for the rest of her life. In her novel *Emma*, published a decade later, she has Harriet express her horror that her friend Emma might never marry:

'But still, you will be an old maid! And that's so dreadful!'

'Never mind, Harriet, I shall not be a poor old maid; and it is poverty only which makes celibacy contemptible to a generous public! A single woman, with a very narrow income, must be a ridiculous, disagreeable old maid! The proper sport of boys and girls; but a single woman, of good fortune, is always respectable.'

This was fiction, but Jane Austen said something similar when writing to her niece Fanny Knight in March 1817: 'Single women have a dreadful propensity for being poor, which is one very strong argument in favour of matrimony.'[36]

The same point was made by Nelly Weeton to her brother Tom a few years earlier, in 1809, after he accused her of having the ideas of an old maid. She hinted that she might soon be married, but only 'to avoid the finger of contempt, the smile of ridicule. If it were not for that, I am too happy to wish for any change.'[37] She added: 'An old maid is a stock for everyone to laugh at. Every article of dress, every word, every movement is satirized. Boys play tricks upon them, and are applauded. Girls sneer at them, and are unreproved. Upon my word, I think I will write an essay upon the pitiable state of old maids for some Magazine or Paper.'[38] Her hints at marriage were not then realised, but in 1814 she wed the Wigan widower Aaron Stock, a cotton manufacturer. The following year a daughter Mary was born, but it turned out to be a desperately unhappy and violent marriage that ended in a deed of separation in 1822.[39]

It was not easy to end unhappy marriages – and just about impossible for women, short of deserting the husband, murdering him or waiting for him to die. There was no divorce law before 1857. Instead, couples could obtain an annulment or separation through the ecclesiastical courts, which was costly. A divorce could then be sought by private Act of Parliament, which ensured that inheritance and legal heirs were safeguarded. Such a process was prohibitively expensive, and between 1700 and 1857 only around three hundred such Acts were passed, almost always undertaken by the husband, virtually never by the wife, who usually had no wealth to bequeath and no funds to secure an Act of Parliament. It was customary that the mother lost custody of (and usually all contact with) her children.[40]

General William Dyott's wife, when an invalid in Bath in 1814, asked him for a separation, having fallen in love with someone else. Two years later, when he was fifty-five, his bill was passed, as he described:

> The second reading of the bill for the divorce in Parliament was fixed for the 7th of the month, when it was necessary for me to attend. Nothing was more kind than the exertion of Lord Lauderdale in carrying the bill through the House of Lords; the third reading having taken place in the House of Commons on the 2nd July and was passed in the House of Lords the next day previous to Parliament being prorogued. Thus ended the most melancholy event, which deprived my children of a mother and me of a wife.[41]

Dyott never remarried, and he and his children never saw or heard of his wife again until she died in 1841, six years before his own death.[42]

Most people could not afford to involve lawyers, and so many suffered terrible marriages instead. Women could not even divorce on the grounds of cruelty, since a man was allowed to beat his wife and ill-treat her, unless his behaviour was judged as life-threatening. Because this was difficult to prove, the law usually sided with the husband, sometimes showing a surprising leniency towards the guilty party. At Winchester in 1796 William Gamon received a mild sentence after being found guilty 'for ill-treating, and threatening to murder Hannah Gamon, his wife, and for refusing to ... appear at the next General Quarter Sessions'.[43] As punishment, he was bound over to keep the peace for three years. Many, probably most, cases of husbands abusing their wives never even came before the courts.

One way of ending a wretched marriage was for a husband to sell his wife – regarded as the poor man's divorce. Some sales were by consent of the wife, but at other times they were carried out against her will. Leading a wife to a public place with a rope tied round her neck and then selling her, like an animal at a market, was thought – wrongly – to be a legal and binding transaction, transferring the marriage to somebody else. Commentators considered wife-selling a barbaric practice, but it persisted to the late nineteenth century, and John Brand noted: 'A remarkable superstition still prevails among the lowest of our Vulgar, that a man may lawfully sell his wife to another, provided he deliver her over with a halter about her neck. It is painful to observe, that instances of this occur frequently in our newspapers.'[44]

Many such sales were to pre-arranged buyers, but they still needed to be carried out in a public place, as one newspaper reported in January 1790: '*Another Bargain and Sale of a Wife.*—A Man in the Neighbourhood of Thame, in Oxfordshire, two or three Years ago, sold his Wife for *Half a Guinea*; and his Neighbours telling him that the Bargain would not stand good, as she was not sold in public Market, he last Tuesday led her seven Miles in a String to Thame Market, and there sold her for Two Shillings and Six-pence, and paid *Four-Pence Toll*.'[45]

The *Morning Post* newspaper described another incident in January 1815 at Maidstone in Kent, after one man, John Osborne, realised it was not market day:

> the auction was removed to the sign of the coal-barge, in Earl street, where she was actually sold to a man named William Serjeant, with her child for the sum of one pound: the business was transacted in a very regular manner, a deed and covenant being given by the seller, of which the following is a literal copy:—
>
> 'I, John Osborne, doth agree to part with my wife, Mary Osborne, and child, to William Sergeant, for the sum of one pound, in consideration of giving up all claim whatever: wherunto I have made my mark as an acknowledgement.
>
> 'Maidstone, Jan. 3, 1815. X'
>
> This document was witnessed in due form, and the woman and child turned over to the buyer, to the apparent satisfaction of all parties; the husband expressing his willingness to take his spouse again at any future period.[46]

A woman being widowed could result in her sinking into poverty, because property and wealth usually passed to male descendants or relatives. Remarriage was therefore desirable, and in December 1808 Jane Austen wrote to Cassandra from Southampton: 'Lady Sondes' match surprises me, but does not offend me; had her first marriage been of affection, or had there been a grown-up single daughter, I should not have forgiven her; but I consider everybody as having a right to marry once in their lives for love, if they can, and provided she will now leave off having bad headaches and being pathetic, I can allow her, I can wish her to be happy.'[47] Mary Elizabeth Milles had entered into an arranged marriage in 1785, becoming Lady Sondes, but Lord Sondes died in 1806, and she was now remarrying for love.

Forty-nine-year-old Welshman William Jones was vicar at Broxbourne in Hertfordshire, then a peaceful country village a few miles north of London. He noted in his diary: 'Many mothers have I heard warn their dear daughters against "hateful matrimony," yet few, very few daughters have I known inclined to listen to the warning.'[48] He believed that daughters were in part encouraged by widows who remarried time and again: 'They will ... try the experiment for themselves!—&, with the less apprehension, when they observe widows, (even their own Mothers ...) adventure a *second*, & perhaps a *third*, time.'[49]

For many, whether in happy or unhappy relationships, marriage was an end to childhood and the start of adulthood and running a household. For young women it most likely meant years of child-bearing, which was considered to be the very purpose of a Christian marriage. Jane Austen, in almost her last letter to her niece Fanny, warned her not to worry about getting married too soon, because 'by not beginning the business of Mothering quite so early in life, you will be young in Constitution, spirits, figure and countenance'.[50] Given the likelihood of at least one partner succumbing to an early death through disease, accident or childbirth, many marriages did not survive for long.

# TWO

———— •◆• ————

# BREEDING

If tenderness could ever be supposed wanting, good sense and good breeding supplied its place.

*Mansfield Park*, by Jane Austen

Some years before her daughter Jane was born, Mrs Cassandra Austen wrote to her sister-in-law: 'My sister Cooper has made us a visit . . . Her boy and girl are well, the youngest almost two years old, and she has not been breeding since, so perhaps she has done.'[1] The word 'breeding' had two meanings – on the one hand, education, manners and respectability; on the other, the reproduction of children, which may sound strange today when applied to humans rather than birds or animals. In an era without effective contraception, breeding could be never-ending. In February 1798 the newspapers announced one mother's latest birth: 'On the 21st ult. Mrs Banting, of Little-Rissington, near Stow-on-the Wold, Gloucestershire, was safely delivered of a daughter, being the thirty-second child by the same husband.'[2]

A few months later, Jane Austen wrote to her sister Cassandra: 'I believe I never told you that Mrs. Coulthard and Anne, late of Manydown, are both dead, and both died in childbed. We have not regaled Mary with this news.'[3] Mary, the wife of their brother James, was due to give birth, but the family shielded her from these tragedies, a reminder of the dangers of childbirth. The next day Jane had pleasing news: 'I have just received a note from James to say that Mary was brought to bed last night, at eleven o'clock, of a fine little boy, and that everything is going on very well.'[4]

A good marriage was measured by a couple's ability to produce children, which for many women meant a succession of pregnancies unless they were unfortunate enough to die in the process. Maybe this influenced Jane Austen to remain single, preferring not to face the constant possibility of death and referring instead to at least one of her books as 'my own darling child'.[5] For the upper classes and royalty a male heir (or more than one, as a spare, in case of death) was essential, given that property and the family name descended via the male line. In 1809, on a visit to her former home village of Upholland in Lancashire, Nelly Weeton heard about the scale of preparations for the birth of the first child of Mr and Mrs Bankes at nearby Winstanley Hall,[6] a Tudor mansion on the edge of Wigan:

> She [Mrs Bankes] had been married eleven or twelve years, I think, and had never been in the family way before ... When her pregnancy was announced, it occasioned great joy at Winstanley, and great preparations were made. It was determined upon that the child should positively be a son. Malt was procured for brewing ale, to be drank when he came of age. The caps and other garments were all ordered, and made in the boyish forms; not so much as a *single one* for a girl. For the child and for Mrs. B. upon the occasion, between 5 and £600 worth of linen were purchased, £400 worth of which came from London. Alterations were made in the house, partitions taken down, and rebuilt for the accommodation of a couple of nurses ... She had scarcely been allowed to stir during the whole time of her pregnancy, not so much as to reach a chair nor shut a door; nor to remove from one room to another without one or two assistants, for fear of a miscarriage.[7]

During pregnancy, there was a superstitious dread of omens that might affect the fate of the baby. The physician Hugh Smith was scathing about such beliefs and related the story of when one pregnant woman, 'a lady of quality', suffered convulsions:

When her ladyship came a little to herself, she cried out, 'The black cat! the black cat!' . . . the servants diligently searched for the object; when in a tub, placed to receive the rain water, near her ladyship's dressing-room window, poor puss was discovered. This sight so terribly affected the lady, that her fears were ever uppermost, and she was miserable until the time of her delivery . . . she was fully persuaded that her child's face would be like this black cat's.[8]

Her fears were unfounded, and she was 'brought to bed of a lovely boy without either mark or blemish'.[9]

Women due to give birth were treated like invalids and confined to the house. During this period of 'confinement' or 'lying-in', they were expected to stay indoors, preferably in bed, for up to six weeks after the birth. The same terms were also used for the entire pregnancy, as was the expression 'in for it', which Jane Austen put in a letter to Cassandra in January 1801: 'So Lady Bridges, in the delicate language of Coulson Wallop [MP for Andover], is in for it!'[10] This was her first child, a son born five months later, called Brook-William Bridges.

In readiness for the birth, one tradition required the husband to provide a cake and a large cheese, which John Brand described:

It is customary at Oxford to cut the cheese (called in the North of England, in allusion to the mother's complaints at her delivery, 'the Groaning Cheese') in the middle when the child is born, and so by degrees form it into a large kind of ring, through which the child must be passed on the day of the christening. In other places the first cut of the sick Wife's cheese (so also they call the Groaning Cheese) is to be divided into little pieces, and tossed in the midwife's smock, to cause young women to dream of their lovers. Slices of the first cut of the Groaning Cheese are in the North of England laid under the pillows of young persons for the above purpose.[11]

Most women gave birth at home; only the poorest went to a hospital or the workhouse. Poor married women in London had access to charitable lying-in hospitals that had been established from the mid-eighteenth century. Other towns and cities were slow to follow, though at Newcastle-upon-Tyne one was founded in 1760, while at Manchester a lying-in charity was established in 1790 by Charles White.[12] Working-class women rarely had the luxury of preparing for a birth, but worked as long as possible. Those with access to a hospital were admitted during the last month of pregnancy and remained there for a while after the birth.

Around 5–7 per cent of children were illegitimate, a figure that had been rising steadily since the early eighteenth century and would reach a peak of about 7 per cent by the early Victorian period, before falling again in the late nineteenth century. However, the numbers of illegitimate children were probably under-reported, and so the percentage may be a little higher. Describing Upholland during her visit in 1809, Nelly Weeton complained: '[it] is, if possible, more licentious and more scandalous than when I lived in it; such numbers of unmarried women have children, many of whom one would have thought had years, discretion, sense, and virtue to have guarded them'.[13]

Unmarried mothers-to-be were not well treated. In Norfolk in November 1794 Parson Woodforde was unhappy to learn about his servant: 'My maid Molly has declared herself with child, more than half gone. Molly is with child by one Sam. Cudble, a carpenter of the parish of Coulton, and he says that he will marry her. The man bears a fair character. However, in her situation, it is necessary for me to part with her as soon as possible. To morrow therefore I intend at present to dismiss her. She is a very poor, weak girl, but I believe honest.'[14] Being unmarried himself, Woodforde was obliged to dismiss Molly to avoid scandal and so sent her away the next day:

After breakfast, I talked with Molly, paid her three quarters of a year and one months wages, which amounted in the whole to 4.7.0 and after packing up her things, about one o'clock she left my house, and walked off for Coulton [Colton] where she is to be at Cudble's father's, till such time that they are married. She says that Cudble made not the least objection to marrying her, she foolishly denied being with child till the middle of last week, and then obliged to, the work becoming too much for her present situation. I don't think that she is far from lying-in by her appearance. For my own part, I have long thought her breeding.[15]

Molly, who was actually called Mary Woods, did marry Samuel Cudble, and their daughter Elizabeth was born on Christmas Eve 1794. Sadly, Elizabeth died on Christmas Day 1810, just sixteen years old.

Stillbirths and premature births were feared by all classes, and in October 1798 Jane Austen wrote to Cassandra from Steventon: 'Mrs. Hall, of Sherbourn, was brought to bed yesterday of a dead child, some weeks before she expected, owing to a fright. I suppose she happened unawares to look at her husband.'[16] Parson Woodforde noted when the squire's wife went unexpectedly into labour one summer afternoon in 1783:

> Nancy [his niece] and myself dined and spent part of the afternoon at Weston House with Mr and Mrs Custance . . . Whilst we were at dinner Mrs Custance was obliged to go from table about 4 o'clock, labour pains coming on fast upon her. We went home soon after dinner on the occasion . . . After supper we went up to Mr. Custances to enquire after Mrs Custance who was brought to bed of a fine girl about 7 o'clock and as well as could be expected.[17]

The next day Woodforde baptised the baby at Weston House: 'I walked up to Mr Custance's this morning soon after, named the little girl by name Frances Ann[e], and a very pretty infant she is.'[18] Since the baby had arrived earlier than anticipated, this was a precautionary measure in case she did not survive to be christened in church, though Frances actually lived to beyond her ninetieth birthday.

Two years later, in July 1785, Woodforde recorded another premature birth: 'I was sent for to go to Weston House to name a child of Mrs. Custance's who was brought to bed this afternoon about 2 o'clock. I therefore walked up directly to Weston House and named the child by name Mary Anne, the smallest infant I think I ever had in my arms. The child came 10 weeks before its time, therefore afraid that it would not live.'[19] Mary Anne survived just seventeen weeks.

Childbirth traditionally involved only female friends and family to assist in the birth and possibly a paid midwife – someone possessing experience, though no formal qualifications. When educated surgeons became involved in obstetrics, as 'man-midwives' or 'accoucheurs', they replaced some of the female midwives. In London the radical Francis Place, by trade a breeches maker, related: 'After the birth of our first child [in 1792] . . . we employed a medical man in good practice, he had two guineas for his first attendance and a guinea for each of the succeeding two. The guinea was always carefully saved and immediately paid.'[20]

Man-midwives transformed childbirth, making use of the recently invented forceps and scientifically researching, debating and publishing on aspects of pregnancy. The most famous man-midwife was the Scottish anatomist William Hunter, at whose anatomy school in London deceased women in various stages of pregnancy were dissected. After years of work, he published *The Anatomy of the Human Gravid Uterus Exhibited in Figures* in 1774, containing for the first time life-sized images of the developing foetus.

In this era before anaesthetics, antibiotics or any understanding of infection, giving birth was hazardous and painful. Most mothers suffered at least one miscarriage or stillbirth, and many died of complications during labour or afterwards from sepsis (usually called 'puerperal fever').[21] Those in the lying-in hospitals were at particular risk of bacterial infection, which could spread rapidly. Jane Austen in *Northanger Abbey* made Catherine Morland's mother more robust: 'She had three sons before Catherine was born; and instead of dying in bringing the latter into the world, as anybody might expect, she still lived on – lived to have six children more – to see them growing up around her, and to enjoy excellent health herself.'

For women who experienced complications in childbirth, the only option was a caesarean section, but surgeons were reluctant to attempt this procedure. The first operation in which the baby survived, though not the mother, was performed in London in 1774 on Elizabeth Foster. When twenty-four-year-old Elizabeth Sedgley had married Joseph Foster at St Andrew's church, Holborn, in April 1759, she was 'perfectly strait, very thin, and measured five feet four inches'.[22] A succession of children and deteriorating health followed. 'When in labour of her eighth child,' the physician William Cooper related, 'she was a patient of the lying-in charity, for delivering poor married women at their own habitations, to which I am one of the physicians. The attending midwife, therefore, after waiting a proper time, sent for me on December 18, 1770.'[23] Elizabeth was in such a bad state that Cooper removed the foetus by an embryotomy.

For the next two and a half years she was helpless, with severe curvature of the spine, 'scarce ever able, without assistance, even to turn herself in bed'.[24] Yet in this state her husband impregnated her twice more, the first time leading to a miscarriage. By the next pregnancy, 'she measured only four feet four inches; and she generally stooped so very much, especially lately, as to appear to be little more than three feet high'.[25] In mid-August 1774 Elizabeth was ready to give birth and in such severe pain that Cooper persuaded John Hunter (brother of William Hunter) to come to her home in Robinhood Court, close to St Andrew's church, and perform a caesarean. 'During the whole of the operation,' Cooper recorded, 'the poor woman behaved with remarkable patience and fortitude.'[26] Without anaesthetics she was, of course, fully conscious. The next day she died and two days later was buried in St Andrew's churchyard.[27] Incredibly, the baby girl, Sarah, survived and was baptised at the same church in July the following year.

It was the surgeon James Barlow from Blackburn in Lancashire who performed the first caesarean in England where the mother survived. She was forty-year-old Mrs Jane Foster, a mother of several children from the village of Blackrod near Wigan. Some months earlier, she had been attended by Charles White of Manchester and Mr Hawarden from Wigan after falling beneath a cart and fracturing her pelvis.[28] Not long afterwards, she became pregnant again, and when she went into labour in late November 1793, it was realised that the pelvic injury made giving birth impossible. Barlow was consulted, and he recommended a caesarean, even though 'of the nine or ten instances then on record, in which that operation had been performed in this country, not one had furnished a voucher for its success'.[29] Mrs Foster refused to give consent, but relented on the fifth day of labour. The baby was pulled out dead, but the woman survived and lived another three decades.[30]

Barlow later discussed the case with Charles White, the celebrated man-midwife and former pupil of William Hunter in London. In 1773 White had advanced the understanding of caesareans and other aspects of childbirth when he published *A Treatise on the Management of Pregnant and Lying-In Women*. With old traditions difficult to eradicate, he warned: 'The nurses in London are a numerous and powerful body, and an attempt to reform their ancient customs might be looked upon as an open attack upon them, and an actual declaration of war.'[31]

Meanwhile, their practices were killing women, and he advocated that mothers-to-be should give birth naturally, with minimal interference from midwives or instruments, and that they should be clean and not remain stationary in bed. In his opinion, 'The thick fustian waistcoats and petticoats usually worn during the lying-in, are much too warm.'[32] He disagreed with the old customs that were intended to prevent women from catching cold:

> As soon as she is delivered, if she is a person in affluent circumstances, she is covered up close in bed with additional cloaths, the curtains are drawn round the bed, and pinned together, every crevice in the windows and door is stopped close, not excepting even the key hole, the windows are guarded not only with shutters and curtains, but even with blankets, the more effectually to exclude the fresh air, and the good woman is not suffered to put her arm, or even her nose out of bed, for fear of catching cold.[33]

One of White's recommendations was for increased ventilation, so that the 'lying-in chamber should in every respect be as sweet, as clean, and as free from any disagreeable smell, as any other part of the house'.[34] In most cases the bedroom where the birth occurred was anything but sweet and clean. Women traditionally recovered in overheated, airless rooms, which was no doubt true for Mrs Austen when her daughter Jane was born on 16 December 1775, at the start of a severe winter.

Before 1800 around 1.5 per cent of mothers died in childbirth, but where White worked, in Manchester, the situation was much improved, with a mortality rate of less than 1 per cent. The details he gave of one woman who became ill after giving birth must have been typical of paupers across the country:

MARY LORD of Manchester, a poor woman aged 31, was delivered on the 25th of May 1772, in the morning, by a midwife in the neighbourhood. She had an easy labor ... her third lying-in ... [but] she gradually grew worse till I first saw her, which was on the fourth day in the evening ... The whole family lived in the same room in which she lay, being the only one they had; it was very warm, having a large fire in it, and smelt very disagreeably. I desired the fire might be lessened, and more air let into the room, accordingly the window was set open and remained open all night. She had scarcely sitten up in bed since her delivery, but had lain in a horizontal position all the time. I advised her to sit up frequently in bed, and to get out of it once every day, to put on clean linen ... On the fifth day the room was much cooler, and did not smell so disagreeably ... On the sixth day all her complaints were vanished.[35]

The wealthy were not immune from death in childbirth. Despite the lavish arrangements for the birth of the first child of Mr and Mrs Bankes at Winstanley Hall, both mother and baby died, even though the renowned Charles White attended. Nelly Weeton described what happened: 'Dr. White from Manchester resided in the house upwards of three weeks before Mrs. B's confinement ... After suffering a most severely painful time, a *son was born*, but heir only to the grave, for it was dead. The mother survived little more than a week – and died too; few more beloved or more lamented, she was so kind to her servants, so charitable to the poor.'[36]

Another eminent man-midwife was Edward Rigby of Norwich, and he and his wife Anne had twelve children. Two were twins, a girl and a boy born on 1 August 1804, and four were quadruplets, three boys and a girl, born on 15 August 1817. This remarkable event was reported in the newspapers: 'BIRTHS EXTRAORDINARY – The Lady of Edward Rigby, Esq. M.D. of Norwich, was safely delivered of three sons and a daughter. Mrs. R. is as well as usual so soon after childbirth; and the children are all alive and hearty. Before the birth of these little ones Dr. R. was the father, by his present wife, of eight most lovely and healthy children, the two eldest of whom are twins.'[37] Tragically, all the quadruplets died, the girl surviving the longest, for almost three months.[38]

Multiple births were rare, and such babies stood little chance of surviving. For the village of Selborne in Hampshire, close to the Austens, the curate Gilbert White compiled a statistical analysis of its population. The period 1720 to 1780, he said, saw just under a thousand baptisms, including 'Twins thirteen times, many ... dying young'.[39] Any exceptional birth was worthy of comment, as in January 1789 when the *New Exeter Journal* mentioned the arrival of triplets: 'Tuesday the 6th instant the wife of Richard Hannaford, of South-Brent, in the county of Devon, was delivered of three fine girls, all of whom are likely to do well.'[40] The more mundane births of prominent citizens were also announced in the local newspapers. As with all such news, the name of the mother was traditionally ignored, as in the *Hull Packet* in October 1801, which reported: 'BIRTH. Lately, at Everingham, near Pocklington, the lady of M. Constable, Esq. was safely delivered of a daughter.'[41]

It was not unusual for fathers to be absent from home when their children were born, and it took some time for the news to reach William Wilkinson, at sea in the navy, that he was a father. Finally he held the letter that his sister-in-law Fanny Platt had excitedly written from their lodgings at Kensington in London, a few hours after his daughter's birth. 'Heartily do I wish you were now here,' she said, 'that we might congratulate with each other on the happy arrival of your little daughter. It was born at 17 minutes past 9 o'clock this 9$^{th}$ day of Nov$^{br}$ [1807].'[42] Fanny next gave William an affectionate description: 'the precious Babe, it is, I think, the loveliest little creature I ever saw. Its eyes are dark and beautifully bright, its nose and chin we all agree in our opinion as to their being exactly like your own. It has a pretty little head with a good bit of hair, which is very dark. It is in good health and so plump you cannot think.'[43] Fanny's use of 'it', not 'she', was commonplace when speaking of infants and would not have appeared uncaring. William was extremely happy, and early the next year he wrote to his wife: 'in my Prayer Book (which I keep in my desk) I have your hair, Baby's and a piece of my own. I cut mine off the other day to see the contrast. They are all in a small piece of fine India paper … and they do look very pretty, yours light, mine dark, and Baby's between both.'[44]

For those who could afford it, a wet-nurse might be hired, a centuries-old tradition but an alien concept today and one that could be detrimental, even fatal, to the health of the newborn infant. Wet-nurses were usually married working-class women, capable of producing milk, perhaps having just lost a baby or recently weaned their own child. Some worked continuously for years. They took over the care and feeding of newborn babies, primarily from middle- and upper-class families. All too often, babies did not stay with their mothers, but were transferred to the homes of wet-nurses, especially if those women lived in the countryside rather than the less healthy town.[45] There is no conclusive evidence about Sarah Wilkinson's newborn daughter, but Fanny told William that 'We have a nurse who thoroughly understands her business',[46] implying that a wet-nurse was employed.

Various taboos deterred mothers from breastfeeding, such as the belief that they should be churched first as they were unclean from having given birth; that their first milk, the colostrum, was harmful; or that babies should be purged for a few days after birth with liquids such as wine, sugared water, or butter and honey. However, physicians and midwives were gradually realising the benefits of breastfeeding right from birth. In the late eighteenth century the employment of wet-nurses began to decline, and the increase in breastfeeding led to a drop in the mortality rate of newborn infants. Georgiana, Duchess of Devonshire, decided to breastfeed her daughter 'Little G' because the wet-nurse was a drunk, but she was criticised by the family as they believed it would prevent another pregnancy, and Georgiana's duty was to produce a male heir.[47]

Some women did not breastfeed for other reasons, such as husbands forbidding the practice, or because of physical problems and illness. The Exeter physician Hugh Downman was a pioneer in understanding how infants should be nursed, unfortunately setting down his recommendations in a lengthy, albeit well-received, piece of blank verse, *Infancy*, published in six books from 1774. For mothers unable to breastfeed, he advised choosing a wet-nurse in the countryside:

> Far from the bounds
> Of the rank city, let some trusty mind
> Explore the straw-rooft cott; there, firm of nerve
> Her blood from every grosser particle,
> By hardy labour, and abstemious fare,
> Sublimed; the honest peasant's mate shall ope
> Her hospitable arms, receive with joy
> The infant stranger, and profusely yield
> Her pure balsamic nurture to his lip.[48]

Tight clothing, especially stays, hindered breastfeeding, according to Charles White: 'This dress by constantly pressing upon the breast and nipple reduces it to a flat form ... and the nipple is buried in the breast. By being constantly kept in this position, it contracts adhesions; it is prevented from coming out ... The tightness of the stays is alone sufficient to do much harm, but they are also, often made hard and unpliable by packthread and whalebone, which must greatly increase the mischief.'[49] Working-class women, he observed, were better at breastfeeding, because many did not wear stays: 'Hence it will appear evident why women of rank, and those in the middle stations of life meet with difficulty in giving suck to children ... why hard working, labouring women, who are obliged to go very loose about their breasts generally make good nurses, and that too with very little trouble.'[50]

Distress in weaning, it was recommended, could be lessened by administering laudanum or alcohol. Once babies were weaned, they were fed with a semi-liquid pap, which, as the man-midwife and surgeon William Moss explained, 'is composed of bread and water boiled and sweetened with brown sugar; to which is, sometimes, added a small quantity of milk: or; oatmeal and water, in the form of thin water gruel, with the same additions'.[51] From the late eighteenth century various types of feeding vessels were used, including animal horns, spoons, boat-shaped sucking bottles and upright pots with spouts, but sterilisation was unheard-of.

Some children were breastfed by their mothers and then handed to foster-parents after weaning. This is how Jane Austen and her siblings were brought up, fostered for several months (possibly by a woman called Bessy Littleworth) until deemed old enough to return home. In November 1772 Mrs Austen told her sister-in-law Mrs Walter: 'My little boy [Henry, born in June 1771] is come home from nurse, and a fine stout little fellow he is, and can run anywhere, so now I have all four at home, and some time in January I expect a fifth.'[52] This fifth one would be Cassandra.

In June 1773 Mrs Austen wrote: 'I suckled my little girl thro' the first quarter; she has been weaned and settled at a good woman's at Deane just eight weeks; she is very healthy and lively.'[53] Deane village was 2 miles from their parsonage at Steventon, and years later James Austen-Leigh, the nephew of Jane and Cassandra, mentioned this peculiar start to their lives:

Her [Jane's] mother followed a custom, not unusual in those days, though it seems strange to us, of putting out her babies to be nursed in a cottage in the village. The infant was daily visited by one or both of its parents, and frequently brought to them at the parsonage, but the cottage was its home, and must have remained so till it was old enough to run about and talk ... It may be that the contrast between the parsonage house and the best class of cottage was not quite so extreme then as it would be now, that the one was somewhat less luxurious, and the other less squalid.[54]

Writing in the Victorian era, he was perplexed by the concept of babies from the middle class or above being raised by their social inferiors.

Another custom that now seems strange or superstitious was that of 'churching'. A woman who gave birth was considered by many to be spiritually unclean and was supposed to be confined until her churching ceremony a few weeks later, when she left home for the first time to go straight to church and be ritually cleansed. Although sanctioned by a passage in the Old Testament,[55] this was a contentious issue within the Church, variously condemned as a relic of the Jewish religion or as a Catholic rite. It remained a widespread practice, probably bolstered by superstitions about women being dangerous and bringers of bad luck after childbirth until such ritual cleansing had taken place. The Church explained the ceremony as one of purification or of thanksgiving for the birth.

Both Parson Woodforde and William Holland regularly churched women. On one occasion, Holland recorded a conversation with a Mr Hurley: 'A civil man but an odd spoken one and an Anabaptist. His wife desired to be churched by me. Yes returned I, if you bring your child to be christened, otherwise not, for why should a person be indulged with the offices of the Church in one case who despises them in all other cases?'[56] The actual ceremony varied from place to place, but was primarily a blessing. While in Lincolnshire in 1791, the traveller John Byng witnessed such a service: 'In the church, this evening, were two women church'd by the clergyman . . . in the space of two minutes: which office I did not know could be thus huddled over, privately, in a church?'[57]

Inevitably, the parson charged a fee, but Woodforde frequently returned the money to poor women, particularly ones with large families. He routinely performed this rite, as in March 1787 when 'I read prayers, preached and churched a woman this morning at Weston Church – gave the woman her <sup>d</sup>6 [sixpence] . . . very soon after I mounted my horse and went to Witchingham, and there read prayers, churched one woman . . . Recd. for churching the woman at Witchingham 0: 0: 6.'[58] And a week later: 'I read prayers and preached this afternoon at Weston C[hurch]. Also churched 2 poor women . . . I gave the two poor women the churching fee.'[59]

Most children were baptised in church soon after birth, and so mothers waiting to be churched could not attend. The baptism ceremony, the sacramental rite admitting an individual to the Christian Church, included naming the child, as it still does today. Although births were not registered, baptisms had to be recorded in parish registers.[60] Private baptisms at home also took place, particularly where the baby was too ill to be brought to church. Having privately baptised baby Frances in June 1783, Woodforde performed a church baptism for her three months later: 'I walked to church this morning between 11 and 12, and publickly baptised Mr Custance's little maid by name Frances Anne. Lady Bacon and Lady Beauchamp stood Godmothers, and Mr Custance stood proxy.'[61] He also baptised illegitimate ('spurious') children privately, as in December 1786: 'I privately named a spurious child of one Mary Parkers this morning by name John. The fathers name I could not get intelligence of.'[62]

William Holland lamented the plight of one destitute pregnant girl who had been forcibly returned to her home parish of Over Stowey: 'A worthless girl in the poor house is in a sad state. She has begun to be in labour but when it will end is a melancholy consideration. She was brought home to the parish by an order with every kind of disease about her, the child they say is already dead. She at times suffers a great deal and has neither comfort nor a word of pity from any one around but indeed medical assistance she has.'[63] The next morning he was taken aback:

> While I was at breakfast this day the sad young woman whom I spoke of the day before was brought to bed of a fine girl to the astonishment of everyone for it was supposed that the child was dead. It was brought to me while I was at breakfast to be baptised and so I left breakfast and went to the kitchen, and poured water on its face and baptised the child but the mother had the itch and many other bad disorders [so] that I did not care to handle it much.[64]

The baby did not survive, and Holland was called on to bury her one week later.[65]

It was rare to give babies more than one name, and so Jane Austen and most of her contemporaries had no middle name. William Wilkinson's new baby had two names – Sarah Frances, after her mother Sally and her aunt Fanny, the popular pet-names for Sarah and Frances. In *Northanger Abbey* Isabella and Catherine become such good friends that 'They called each other by their Christian name, were always arm in arm when they walked.' Unless they were very close, it was customary to address most people by their title and surname, and because of such formality Jane Austen was frustrated at being ignorant of the Christian name of a woman she knew only as Miss Wapshire from Salisbury, who was soon to be married. 'I wish

I could be certain that her name were Emma,' she told Cassandra; 'but her being the eldest daughter leaves that circumstance doubtful.'[66] In upper-class families, it was usual to call the eldest unmarried daughter 'Miss', so those who did not know the family well might be unaware of her Christian name, which was the case here. In fact, she was Mary Wapshare, and on 12 December 1800 she married the widowed naval captain Sir Thomas Williams in Salisbury Cathedral.

Names were chosen for being traditional, for their biblical associations, for being names of royalty or perhaps those of dead siblings. They tended to perpetuate long-established family names ranging from the plain Jane to the uncommon Cassandra. In June 1783 Woodforde recorded: 'I privately named a child this morning of Dinah Bushell's by name Keziah, one of Job's daughters names ... I privately named a child of Brands of East Tuddenham, by name John this afternoon.'[67] For boys, common names included John, James, George, Joseph, Richard, Thomas and William, while Anne (or Ann), Sarah, Susan, Jane, Elizabeth, Mary and Hannah were popular names for girls. When commenting on a novel written by her niece Anna, Jane Austen said: 'I like the scene itself, the Miss Lesleys, Lady Anne, & the music, very much. Lesley is a noble name.'[68]

In January 1807 Jane Austen wrote to Cassandra from Southampton: 'I cannot yet satisfy Fanny as to Mrs. Foote's baby's name, and I must not encourage her to expect a good one, as Captain Foote is a professed adversary to all but the plainest; he likes only Mary, Elizabeth, Anne, &c. Our best chance is of "Caroline", which in compliment to a sister seems the only exception.'[69] This was Captain Foote's second marriage, to Mary Patton, having divorced his first wife. Shortly afterwards, at Southampton, the baby was in fact baptised as Elizabeth.

Babies, both male and female, were traditionally immobilised from birth in tight swaddling bands of cloth, in the mistaken belief that this prevented crooked limbs, a condition that was actually rickets caused by vitamin D deficiency. In order to minimise soiling by urine and faeces, the baby might not be completely swaddled, and periodically the cloths were removed for drying or washing. In a treatise on caring for babies, published in 1781, William Moss advised against tight swaddling: 'In dressing a new-born child ... great care ought to be taken that no part of the body or limbs be tight bound, or closely confined by rollers or any part of the dress . . . children thrive much better without it, and are much more likely to be free from deformity.'[70]

By the 1790s the practice of swaddling was on the decline. Instead, babies were dressed in gowns or tunics, and all wore bonnets or caps, so that in *Emma*, 'Mrs Weston, with her baby on her knee . . . was one of the happiest women in the world. If any thing could increase her delight, it was perceiving that the baby would soon have outgrown its first set of caps.' Moss recommended 'foundling dresses':

> The number of PINS used in the dress of a child is sometimes very great; but when *tapes* or *strings* can be substituted for them, they are much preferable. The *foundling dresses*, so called from being first invented at the *foundling* hospital, for the sake, no doubt, of convenience and dispatch, are come much into use. They draw and tye with strings, and are otherwise so contrived, that very few pins become needful in putting them on . . . the risque of pricking and wounding the tender bodies of children is avoided.[71]

Mass-produced safety-pins were as yet unknown, so these garments developed by London's Foundling Hospital were the best option. When babies were ready to crawl they progressed from long gowns to short clothes, and so when Cassandra was almost six months old in 1773, Mrs Austen noted that 'she . . . puts on her short petticoats to-day'.[72] Some babies may have had clouts or diapers (strips or squares of linen cloth) wrapped round them – the word 'nappy' was not then used – also fastened with pins or ties. Impoverished families might have used rags, but the amount of laundry needed would have made this burdensome.

Neither toilet training nor diapers figured in childcare and midwifery manuals, suggesting that most babies soiled their bedding or gowns. All Moss says is that babies 'ought to be dry and clean; for which purpose it will be necessary to renew and change them very frequently'.[73] Had they worn diapers, babies would probably have suffered much more than the occasional soreness mentioned by him: 'A child will sometimes have his backside red, inflamed, and sore, by the frequency and sharpness of his stools ... Take of, *extract of lead*, and *brandy*, each thirty drops; put them into a small vial with four ounces (or eight tablespoonful) of water. With a little of this, aired by the fire in a teacup, let the parts be bathed, once or twice a day, with a soft linen rag.'[74]

There was no tradition of babies being given soft toys and other playthings apart from rattles. Instead, they were sedated with proprietary soothers, especially Dr Godfrey's Cordial. Such concoctions contained opium, morphine and a mercury compound like calomel and were widely advertised, as in the *Derby Mercury* for March 1775:

> The Original GODFREY'S GENERAL CORDIAL, is a Medicine which answers to its Name, having a general Tendency to the curing [of] Diseases ... This CORDIAL is of the greatest help to weakly Women, when they are with Child, to prevent Miscarriages ... Also it's of excellent Use for young Children that are weakly and restless, and breed their Teeth hardly; and for those that are inclined to the Rickets, &c.[75]

Moss was especially critical of such medication:

> There are a number of quack medicines imposed upon the public under various titles, as Godfrey's cordial, &c. &c. ... but as their compositions are as mysterious and difficult to discover as their good qualities, nothing more can be said in their favour ... There is a *drug* however upon which, it is well known, their chief efficacy depends; and that is, *opium*; hence it happens they all have a stilling or sedative power ... I have known Godfrey's cordial given to children, successively for months, with no other design ... than keeping them quiet in the nights ... The abuse of spiritous liquors, and quack medicines of the opiate or composing kind, may be observed to happen most frequently ... with children who are nursed [away] from home.[76]

Child mortality was high, and particularly with the scant knowledge of hygiene, young babies were especially vulnerable to gastro-intestinal disorders as well as untold infectious diseases. In London, the baby Sally Wilkinson initially thrived and was doted on by her parents, but at the age of ten months she fell sick. William learned from his wife that after showing signs of recovery, his daughter was again unwell: 'she has not kept her food so well on her stomach. Last night I was told to get some sago powder and give her some port wine in it which I did and gave her some of the wine in the same arrowroot ... and once or twice today I gave her a little savoury biscuit rather too soon after taking the stuff with the wine in it that it made her so sick which with the little fever the wine occasioned alarmed me a little.'[77] This medical advice came from Mr Thomson, the doctor who had delivered the baby, but his remedies were proving harmful. A few days later her mother Sarah wrote:

> She has taken two or three doses of physic ... for Mr T said her bowels were in a bad state and must be thoroughly cleansed before she would get better. Which of course must be the case. Last night she got into a nice perspiration which I hoped would do her a wonderful deal of good. She is, dear creature, very weak this morning ... Mr T has ordered her asses milk and today he said she was to take some gravy that ran out of roast beef or mutton which she has done and sucked some beef.[78]

One week later, on 25 September 1808, their brother-in-law James Brothers broke tragic news to William:

> It is with much pain I am obliged to acquaint you with the little baby's death. She died this morning between 10 and 11 ... There was one comfort, if in such a case such a thing is possible, that she did not any of the time appear to suffer from pain, but her death seemed to be occasioned by gradual weakness. Sally and Fanny are as you may well suppose in great affliction, but yet I am happy in telling you, they bear it, considering how much their distress must be heightened by your absence, better than I could have supposed.[79]

It was rare for any family not to suffer the death of at least one child. In his commonplace book, Matthew Buckle recorded intricate details of his family tree, in which we see that his relatives and ancestors experienced numerous tragedies. At the age of forty-two in

February 1803, Buckle married his wife Hannah, who would give birth to seven children in the space of thirteen years. Their first, an unnamed daughter, was born on Christmas Eve 1803 and died 'one week and five days' later. The next child was Louisa, born in 1804, followed by Emma in 1807, Frances in 1809, Eleanor in 1811, Mary in 1814 and finally a boy, Christopher, born in 1816.[80] Keeping track of families was important. In 1782 Carl Philipp Moritz, a twenty-six-year-old German pastor, teacher and prolific writer, was travelling for seven weeks through England, mainly on foot. At Nettlebed in Oxfordshire he attended a church service: 'The prayer-book, which my landlord lent me, was quite a family piece; for all his children's births, and names, and also his own wedding-day, were very carefully set down in it.'[81]

Lack of proper information made it impossible to be certain about the size of England's population, and commentators gave opinions based on imprecise figures obtained from records such as local surveys, assessments of houses for the window tax and on the Bills of Mortality – tallies of the number of burials and causes of death compiled by parish clerks in London and elsewhere, originally to monitor the spread of plague. Records of baptisms and burials did not give a true picture, and some were convinced the population was getting smaller, even though places like London were expanding. In 1783 Dr Richard Price calculated that the population of England and Wales was five million maximum: 'Let ... the number of houses in England and Wales be called a million, and the number of people will be four millions and a half, or five millions at most.'[82] London's expansion, Price believed, was due to mass immigration from the surrounding countryside: 'The more London increases, the more the rest of the kingdom must be deserted; the fewer hands must be left for agriculture.'[83] He was partially correct, because there was massive movement into cities and towns, especially of families seeking work in the new factories, boys bound as apprentices and girls looking for positions as servants.

The first proper national census of Great Britain took place on 10 March 1801, though the information requested was limited – mainly the number of people, including children, in each household, their occupations and the number of inhabited and uninhabited houses. In the town of Falmouth in Cornwall, 465 houses were occupied by 947 families, and the population comprised 3684 people – 1466 males and 2218 females. Cornwall was an agricultural and mining county, but because Falmouth was a port, only 25 were employed in agriculture, with 626 in trade, manufacture or handicraft and 3053 in the general category of 'All other persons not comprized in the two preceding classes'.[84]

The 1801 census demonstrated that England's population was actually expanding rapidly and exceeded 8,300,000 – far more than previously reckoned.[85] In the 2011 census London alone had nearly 8,200,000 people, but in 1801 it was the largest city in Europe with barely a million inhabitants. The next largest places in England in 1801 were Manchester (still a town, not a city) and Liverpool. Both were expanding rapidly. Manchester's population had risen to nearly 95,000 from just over 27,000 in 1773, and Liverpool had nearly 83,000, having risen from 34,000 in 1770.[86] By 1801 one in seven of the population lived in large towns, which meant that the vast majority of people were still in rural areas.

In 1811 the census revealed that the population of England had increased by more than a million, to almost 9,500,000, and by then London had over a million inhabitants.[87] In May of that year, forty-four-year-old Louis Simond, a Frenchman who had gone to America before the Revolution and was now a successful New York merchant, commented on London's expansion:

> We have spent a few days with some of our friends in Hertfordshire, 20 miles north of London. For half that distance you travel between two rows of houses, to which new ones are added every day ... London extends its great polypus-arms over the country around. The population is not increased by any means in proportion to these appearances, only transferred from the centre to the extremities. This centre is become a mere counting-house, or place of business.[88]

What is not apparent in census information is the origins of people, such as that of the black population, which in some places was so small that their presence was noteworthy. In 1808 Silvester Treleaven related how the people of Moretonhampstead in Devon reacted joyfully to the wedding of a black servant: 'Married with licence Peter the black servant to General Rochambeau to Susanna Parker. The bells rang merrily all day. From the novelty of this wedding being the first negro ever married in Moreton a great number assembled in the church yard, and paraded down the street with them.'[89] Some prejudice certainly existed on a personal level, such as that revealed by William Holland, who wrote in his diary in January 1805:

I met young [Brian] Mackey, who is come to see his father … This young man is his son by a negro woman, and has had from the father an excellent education, and is in [holy] orders and has two livings, and is in good circumstances. Pity that he should suffer his father to feel distress in his latter days. But he is so far from assisting him that in all his visits he is drawing money from him and plundering him and I fear now poor Mrs. Mackey [his stepmother] will be left without a shilling. I am not very partial to West Indians, especially to your negro half-blood people.[90]

The fact that 'young Mackey' had received an Oxford education and was parish priest of Coates in Gloucestershire is some indication that black people from a wealthy background were not necessarily handicapped by their colour.[91]

Holland's dislike of Mackey was possibly influenced by his conviction that this ungrateful son was treating his father badly, although he did hold strong opinions about anyone he perceived as different. A Welshman himself, from Llanelian in Denbighshire, Holland described the Somerset people he lived among as 'of a large size and strong, but in my opinion very slow and lazy and discontented … and very much given to eating and drinking'.[92] He was repeatedly dissatisfied with the work done by his servants, referring to one of them in his diary as a 'strange nog-headed blockhead' – 'nog-headed' was Anglo-Welsh dialect for 'wooden-headed'.[93]

Prejudice and suspicion towards foreigners were widespread, though people were also wary of anyone from different parts of

England. The Irish and the Jews were generally more reviled than enemy nations like France. There was an ever-growing Irish population, who were flocking to places like Manchester to work in the textile industries or migrating to London to work mainly as unskilled labourers. By 1780 there may have been as many as 23,000 Irish in the capital,[94] and the main Irish quarter was the parish of St Giles, a desperately overcrowded area known as the Rookery. When being questioned in 1816 about the inhabitants, one Irish teacher, Thomas Augustine Finnegan of the St Giles's Irish Free School in George Street, was not complimentary about his fellow countrymen. He reckoned that the children were 'most depraved; they are exposed to every species of vice with which the streets abound; they generally associate with gangs of pickpockets', and as for the parents, they were 'very dissolute, generally; on Sundays particularly they take their children with them to public-houses, and the children witness the scenes of riot and sanguinary conflict that happen among the parents in the streets.'[95]

Hostility was likewise suffered by the Jews. In 1796 the magistrate Patrick Colquhoun wrote: 'It is estimated that there are about twenty thousand Jews in the city of London, besides, perhaps, about five or six thousand more in the great provincial and sea-port towns ... Educated in idleness, from their earliest infancy, they acquire every debauched and vicious principle which can fit them for the most complicated arts of fraud and deception.'[96] According to Francis Place, such prejudice was rife: 'It was thought good sport to maltreat a Jew, and they were often most barbarously used, even in the principal streets ... I have seen many Jews hooted, hunted, cuffed, pulled by the beard, spit up [upon], and so barbarously assaulted in the streets, without any protection from the passers-by or the police, as seems ... almost impossible.'[97]

Prejudice against gypsies was universal, even though for the middle and upper classes the idea of a gypsy lifestyle often seemed romantic, and gypsy characters figured in popular plays, while gypsy dress was adopted for fancy-dress balls and sometimes influenced high fashion. However, gypsies themselves were regarded as thieves and swindlers. They, and anyone consorting with them, often fell foul of the vagrancy laws, which carried penalties of whipping, imprisonment and transportation.

Gypsies were also frequently blamed for the abduction of children. In June 1802 the *Morning Post and Gazetteer* carried a story about a young girl 'in most wretched attire', who had been found near Lewisham in Kent. She said that 'she was the daughter of a Captain Kellen, of the Marines, at Plymouth; that about seven months ago, being sent a small distance out of the town, on some business for her parents, she was met by a gang of gypsies, consisting of five men and six women who seized her, and forcibly carried her away'.[98] A band of gypsies was arrested, and the continuing story made good copy, but a week later the same newspaper admitted they were innocent:

> This tale of wonder, at length, proves to be a gross imposition, on the part of the girl, almost in every respect, and that the account given by the gypsey, of meeting her on Kennington Common, is true ... Andrew Dew, a serjeant of marines belonging to the Plymouth Division, stated, that he well knew the girl ... he remembered her in January last at Stonehouse Barracks near Plymouth, selling apples and nuts for her mother; that he had lately seen her father, who informed him the girl had absconded from them soon after January.[99]

The gypsies were released, and the girl 'was sent to the House of Correction, until her place of legal settlement can be ascertained. She is very little, and plain in person, and cannot be above eleven or twelve years of age, though she says she is seventeen.'[100]

Unwanted children, usually of paupers or unmarried mothers, might be abandoned in public places like a market square or church porch, making them the responsibility of the parish, which had to care for infants born or abandoned within their boundary whose relatives were unknown. Some of these foundlings were looked after in the workhouse, while others were boarded out to poor women or widows who were paid, but the mortality rate was exceptionally high. This was one reason why in 1741 Thomas Coram had opened the London Foundling Hospital, England's first home for abandoned children and, from 1801, for illegitimate children as well.

Some unmarried mothers were so desperate and ashamed that they murdered their children or left them to die. Others tried to abort the foetus, such as by inserting a wire or knife into the uterus or by ingesting some potion that was poisonous to the foetus in order to induce a miscarriage. Midwives were well aware of the best abortifacients, recommending ergot, rue, penny royal, tansy and savin. When living in Upholland, Nelly Weeton wrote of one attempted abortion: 'Mary Downall is in a poor state of health … I am afraid she took something when pregnant of her little girl intended to fall on the child, and it has light on herself. She has looked a bad colour ever since.'[101]

For those women who needed to hide their pregnancy and who could afford to pay, discreet services were available. One London business advertised on the front page of a West Country newspaper in 1803:

PREGNANT LADIES, whose situation requires a temporary retirement, may be accommodated with an Apartment, in an airy situation, to Lye-in, agreeably to their circumstances, their infants put out to nurse, and taken care of. Tenderness, honour, and secrecy, have been the basis of this concern for many years.—Those regardless of reputation will not be treated with.

Apply to SYMONS, late Dr. WHITE, No. 4, London-House-yard, St. Paul's Church-yard.[102]

There was no contraception for married women apart from sexual abstinence or breastfeeding, and on average they had six to seven live babies. After Sophia Deedes gave birth to her eighteenth child, Marianne, Jane Austen wrote to her niece Fanny: 'I wd recommend to her and Mr. D. the simple regimen of separate rooms.'[103] In fact, Mrs Deedes would give birth to yet another child. It was deemed morally unacceptable for married women to use artificial contraception, though some undoubtedly tried methods like inserting a natural sponge soaked in lemon juice or vinegar. There was a thriving market for condoms (also called 'cundums', 'armour' or 'preservatives'), which were primarily for prophylactic purposes, worn by men using prostitutes to guard against disease or with mistresses to guard against pregnancy. Made from animal intestines, condoms had a hand-sewn seam at one end and were secured by a silk ribbon. They could be washed out and reused. The term 'armour' was defined in a contemporary dictionary of slang as 'to make use of Mrs. Philips's ware. See C—D–M', and 'cundum' was defined as:

> The dried gut of a sheep, worn by men in the act of coition, to prevent venereal infection ... These machines were long prepared and sold by a matron of the name of Philips, at the Green Canister, in Half-moon-street, in the Strand. That good lady having acquired a fortune, retired from business, but learning that the town was not well served by her successors, she, out of a patriotic zeal for the public welfare, returned to her occupation; of which she gave notice by divers hand-bills, in circulation in the year 1776.[104]

Mistresses were kept mainly by married and unmarried men of the upper class and gentry, who could afford the costs. Parson Woodforde met one such mistress in mid-May 1777: 'Mr. Custance [Press Custance, the squire's brother] called on me this morning to go a fishing. We rode down to the river [Wensum]. Mr. Custances mistress a Miss Sherman and one Sandall an oldish man a broken gentleman and who keeps a mistress also tho' he has a wife living, went with us on horseback.'[105] Despite being a clergyman, he made no comment in his diary about the Christian morality of gentlemen keeping mistresses.

Two years earlier Woodforde had seen a play at Covent Garden in London and afterwards noted: 'I met many fine women (common prostitutes) in my return home [to his inn] and very impudent indeed.'[106] Men of all classes resorted to prostitutes, of which there was no shortage, particularly in London and in seaports like Portsmouth and Plymouth. A directory to Covent Garden prostitutes, *Harris's List*, was published annually from 1757 until 1795 when the publisher was jailed for a year for indecency. Appearing around Christmastime, it reputedly sold up to eight thousand copies annually in brothels, taverns and even reputable bookstores.[107] Its entries gave clues as to why the women were prostitutes – some had escaped from abusive husbands, while others were abandoned mistresses. Their rates ranged from a few shillings to a few guineas, and one of the cheaper prostitutes in Harris's 1789 directory, charging one guinea, was Miss Pheby Cambell from Norfolk, evidently seeking a better life in the city:

> Miss Pheby C—mb—ll, No. 9, Holland Street, near Wardour Street . . . About the month of May or June, this young lass arrived in town from Norfolk, unhackneyed in the Cyprian Game [prostitution], she now treads the common path . . . Her age is now only twenty one, and she is both good tempered and able to sing an excellent song, no one can imagine so many shillings badly spent in her company.[108]

Young women flocked to the cities to find work as servants and to seek their fortune, but very often turned to prostitution, especially if they were abused by their employer and then thrown out when pregnant. 'Mr. Meyrick . . . is said to have seduced the servant girl of the house where he lives,' Nelly Weeton wrote from Liverpool in 1809. 'He is so much disliked in many respects, that whether the report be true or false, people seem determined to believe it.'[109] The Newcastle seaman George Watson certainly believed the prostitutes at Portsmouth to be seduced and abandoned women:

> This is always a stirring place, and particularly so in war time, owing to its being such a rendezvous for his Majesty's ships, and transports, for the same reason it is a place notoriously wicked young women flock here from all corners of our island, and some from Ireland, and live by prostitution, I mean women that are previously seduced, and cast upon the world, abandoned by the villains that caused their ruin: it would be absurd to suppose any truly modest girl, though brought to the greatest extremity of penury and want, would deliberately come hither to join herself to such an unblushing set of wretches as pervade the Point at Portsmouth, where a modest woman would be as hard to find as a Mermaid.[110]

Prostitution was not illegal, but when visiting Bath in the summer of 1779, Woodforde was concerned about the plight of two young women: 'After tea this evening I took a walk in the fields and met in my walk two girls, the eldest about 17, the other about 15, both common prostitutes even at that early age. I gave them some good advice to consider the end of things. I gave them o.1.o.'[111] In London a few years later, he went to a service at the Magdalen Hospital for Penitent Prostitutes: 'we took coach and went to Magdalen Chapel in St. Georges Fields being Sunday and heard prayers read and a sermon. Very excellent singing at Magdalen Chapel. The women had a thin green curtain before them all the time, one of them played the organ.'[112] The Magdalen Hospital had been established in 1758, and its chapel was a fashionable place to be seen on Sundays.

The preface to the 1789 edition of *Harris's List* claimed that prostitution prevented crime: 'What villainies do they not prevent? What plots, what combinations, do they not dissolve? Clasped in the arms of beauty, the factious malcontent forgets the black workings of his soul.'[113] Furthermore, it was stated, their earnings were beneficial to the community: 'The toyman, the mercer, the milener, the play, and opera, nay even the parish church (sometimes) is gladdened with the chink of their gold.'[114] This was special pleading to keep pimps and brothels in business. Life was wretched for women who ended up like those witnessed by Francis Place near his house at Charing Cross in London: 'Along the front of Privy Gardens [now Whitehall near Downing Street] ... there was an old wall ... At night there were a set of prostitutes along this wall, so horridly ragged, dirty and disgusting that I doubt much there are now any such in any part of London. These miserable wretches used to take any customer who would pay them twopence, behind the wall.'[115]

Too often young prostitutes were servants abandoned by men like Charles Fothergill, a younger son of a successful Yorkshire family involved in farming, the law, medicine and manufacturing. His father manufactured ivory products such as combs and toothbrushes, but Charles had literary ambitions. Having already squandered a legacy and fallen into debt, in 1805 he was in Yorkshire collecting material and subscribers for a proposed natural and antiquarian history of the county that he had decided to undertake. His private diary reveals that during his excursions, he preyed on several young women, with little thought for the consequences. He stayed several times at the White Swan inn at Middleham in the Yorkshire Dales, where that August he was drawn to a servant girl 'J . . . ' – probably Jane – whose 'temperament was very warm and easily worked upon: I succeeded quite as far as I wished this evening'.[116]

The next evening he tried his luck once more: 'It was dark when I got to the inn again: successful with my nymph; partly make her promise to admit me. In the middle of the night I rise and grope my way to her room; find another girl sleeping with her . . . I stay about two hours and spend the time in great part as I had wished.'[117] Fothergill related similar incidents, as in October: 'From my going to bed 'till 4 o'clock in the morning I enjoyed my nymph tho' my pleasure was not a little damped by occasional qualms of conscience on her account.'[118] Without reliable contraceptives, what was for Fothergill a bit of fun with an unmarried servant girl may well have ended in pregnancy for her, with its devastating consequences.

Although prostitutes and mistresses were tolerated by much of society, homosexuality and bestiality were feared, abhorred and illegal. In the summer of 1810, William Holland was utterly shocked to learn that his manservant George had committed bestiality, which was a capital crime. He spoke to George, telling him that he had to leave: 'he cried most bitterly and it indeed affected me very much. I then told him that I hoped what had passed would sink deep into his heart and that he would fall down on his knees and pray to his God (whom he had most grievously offended) that he might repent of his great wickedness . . . I paid him his wages and he left me overwhelmed with tears.'[119] A few days later, Holland met his friend the Reverend John Mathew of nearby Kilve and apologised for cancelling an invitation. The reason, he explained, was having to dismiss his servant. When he told him the details, Mathew was sympathetic:

He approved of all I had done yet was in doubt (he said) on account of the effect it might have on society, whether I should have him go off

48

without prosecuting him. I answer'd that as soon as I came to the knowledge of the business I discharged him, but (wretch as he was) and horrid as the deed was, I felt a disinclination to hang him. Well (he returned), you have got rid of him. Perhaps it is as well.[120]

——————•◆•——————

# THREE

# TODDLER TO TEENAGER

... she was moreover noisy and wild, hated confinement and cleanliness, and loved nothing so well in the world as rolling down the green slope at the back of the house. Such was Catherine Morland at ten. At fifteen appearances were mending ... Her love of dirt gave way to an inclination for finery.

*Northanger Abbey*, by Jane Austen

Walking was one early challenge for a toddler, but the initial steps may well have been a bruising experience without the protection of fitted carpets that are commonplace in today's homes. Various devices to help young children walk included harnesses for support and trolleys they could grasp, the ancestors of modern babywalkers, but by the early nineteenth century medical opinion was turning against such aids. 'Before infants attempt to walk alone,' one writer recommended,

they should first learn to crawl: by feeling the want of their legs, they will gradually try to use them. With this intention they might be placed on a large carpet, and surrounded by toys: here they will busily employ themselves, move and extend their limbs, or roll about to reach their playthings ... While in the nursery, they may be taught to rise from the floor, by laying hold of chairs; and, if occasionally supported under the arms, they will easily learn to stand erect; but they should never be raised up by one arm only.[1]

This was good advice for families who could afford carpets, nurseries and toys, but irrelevant to those poorer families who, through lack of resources, allowed their children to fend for themselves.

Babies who had wet-nurses learned their first words with these women and were influenced by their way of speech. Likewise, live-in servants contributed to a melting-pot of language, with people of contrasting levels of education and manners of speech in the same household for toddlers to copy. Regional accents and dialect were very distinctive two centuries ago, and even dialects of adjoining counties were noticeably different. When Elizabeth Ham's family was living in Weymouth, Dorset, where her father ran a brewery, one brother stayed with relatives in neighbouring Somerset, causing her to comment: 'My brother William ... spoke broad Somerset.'[2]

Accents from other regions were not encountered every day. When men from all parts of the country were brought together on board naval or merchant ships, the diversity of dialect was striking. Going to sea for the first time, the young seaman Robert Hay was amazed by 'all the provincial dialects which prevail between Landsend and John O'Groats'.[3] During his travels through England each summer, John Byng was irritated rather than charmed by the different ways of speaking. 'I enquired if the river was navigable to this place,' he noted at Ringwood, Hampshire, in 1782, 'but could not explain myself, till a man told me I certainly meant *navigal* and that it was not.'[4] He was impatient not just with regional accents, but with the manner of speaking, as in the Midlands (near Castle Donington) seven years later: 'The slowness of answer in this county is very irritable; when I stop to ask the plainest question, as the name of our road to, any village, they being [begin] with "Why as to that" "Let me consider" "You seem to be out of your way" "And so I was saying". Here I ride off; for life were not long enough to hear them out.'[5]

In 1805 the twenty-five-year-old American Benjamin Silliman arrived in England to further his studies in science. He had initially read law at Yale College and then studied chemistry and natural philosophy – in time he would become a foremost figure in science. On his return to America in 1806, he published detailed observations and impressions of his travels, including his thoughts on language. In May 1805 he had been at Tideswell in Derbyshire, virtually the centre of England. 'They speak the language with many peculiarities of pronunciation,' he noted, 'and with a considerable number of words which we never hear in America.'[6]

A few months later, he visited Cambridge university, where he was informed that as he spoke the English language so perfectly, he could not possibly have been educated in America. He thought this was an inexcusable error on the part of supposedly educated people: 'They ... know that the Anglo-Americans speak the English language; but they imagine that it is a colonial dialect, with a corrupt and barbarous pronunciation, and a vocabulary, interspersed with strange and unknown terms of transatlantic manufacture.'[7]

Silliman reckoned that Americans had the advantage, as everyone there could understand each other, whereas the 'provincial dialects ... render the language of the common people of one county in England in a considerable degree unintelligible to those of another, even of the country gentlemen'.[8] He himself was usually taken for a Londoner: 'a well-educated American may travel from London to John a Groat's house [Scotland], and thence to the Land's-end [Cornwall], and every where pass for a Londoner; this is the universal presumption concerning him'.[9]

Adam Walker, a travelling lecturer and writer, described the dialect of his home county:

A speciment of the Westmoreland Dialect I shall give in one of that Country's Riddles:

> I went toth' wood an I gat it,
> I sat me doon en I leakt at it;
> En when e saa I cudn't git't,
> I teakt heam we ma.

Made in English thus:

I went to the wood, and I got it,
I sat me down and I look'd at it;
And when I saw I could not get it,
I took it home with me.

It is perhaps unnecessary to say, that the solution is, 'a thorn in the foot.'[10]

The accents of boys sent away to boarding schools or perhaps to sea would have become diluted, though even as an adult Nelson was said to have retained his 'true Norfolk drawl'.[11] Jane Austen and her siblings must have learned to speak with a north Hampshire accent, but through education, travel and socialising, they most likely dropped the use of dialect words. Adam Walker was of the opinion that dialects were becoming less distinctive, something he blamed on the influence of increasing numbers of people travelling round England. In 1791 he described the situation in northern England: 'I could once have traced the exact extent of the various dialects of England, and had them coloured in a map. I traced the limits of the Saxon burr (or what is called the Newcastle burr) from Haddington in Scotland to Chester-Le-Street in the County of Durham, and made its western boundary the mountains that divide Northumberland from Cumberland. This singular croak is produced by pronouncing the r with the middle of the tongue instead of the tip.'[12]

Also in 1791 John Walker brought out a dictionary, partly in an effort to improve pronunciation. It became influential, particularly with the middle classes – what Beau Brummell was to high fashion, Walker was to spoken English. The dictionary included a section on the pronunciation faults of Londoners, such as 'Not sounding h where it ought to be sounded, and inversely' and 'Pronouncing w for v, and inversely'.[13] His examples highlight how language has changed over two centuries, since he advised that h should be silent in words like 'humour' ('umour) and 'hospital' ('ospital), whereas h, he said, should be clearly pronounced in a word like 'whet' to distinguish it from 'wet'. In his advice not to confuse w and v, he pointed out that many Londoners pronounced words like 'veal' and 'vinegar' as 'weal' and 'winegar' and conversely pronounced words like 'wine' and 'wind' as 'vine' and 'vind'. Despite his efforts, wide variations persisted in the way English was spoken.

George III was in fact the first Hanoverian monarch to speak English as his main language, declaring to Parliament after ascending to the throne in 1760: 'Born and educated in this country, I glory in the name of Briton.'[14] The upper classes adopted affected forms of talking, which was mocked by Jane Austen in *Northanger Abbey*, where the heroine, Catherine Morland, says, 'I cannot speak well enough to be unintelligible', to which the well-read young clergyman, Henry Tilney, replies, 'Bravo! – an excellent satire on modern language.'

Having learned to walk and talk, children would have learned games and played with different toys, which all too often meant improvising with available materials; anything from words to water. In October 1808 Jane Austen's nephews George and Edward were staying with her at Southampton, while in mourning for their recently deceased mother. 'George is almost a new acquaintance to me,' Jane wrote to Cassandra, 'and I find him in a different way as engaging as Edward. We do not want amusement; bilbocatch, at which George is indefatigable, spillikins, paper ships, riddles, conundrums, and cards, with watching the flow and ebb of the river, and now and then a stroll out, keep us well employed.'[15] Those traditional games, now regarded with nostalgia, included seeing whose handmade paper ships sailed furthest before sinking. In bilbocatch, or 'cup and ball', a ball was caught in a cup of wood or ivory, while in spillikins, a bundle of thin sticks was spilled on to a table, and players tried to pick up a stick without disturbing the rest.

Other toys included marbles and the spinning top or whipping top: 'Boys have different kinds of tops, some which are kept up by whipping, some made to spin by winding string round them ... It is curious, too, to observe the humming top, the sound occasioned by the wind rushing into the hole, which there always is on one side of these tops.'[16] The Reverend Holland remarked on his convalescent son playing with such a toy: 'Little William whipping his top in the passage for he must not stir out as he has taken physick.'[17] On another occasion he noted: 'Mr. Blake call'd here about his son Johnny, but he permitted him to continue with William till the evening and they have been playing and jumping, and flying a kite and at marbles and various things.'[18] Holland doted on his young son, born when he was fifty-one and his wife forty-seven, and left a vivid account of him in his diary.

More and more toys were available for wealthier parents to purchase, some of which served moral or educational purposes, such as geographical jigsaw puzzles. There were also increasing numbers of books for children, some to entertain and others evangelical in tone. Newspapers carried advertisements for such books, and one in the *Northampton Mercury* in April 1772 announced: 'Books for the Instruction and Amusement of Children, Printed for T. CARNAN and F. NEWBERRY, junior, at No. 65, in St. Paul's Church-Yard, London.'[19] The long list included *Tom Thumb's Folio*, *The London Cries* and *Nurse Truelove's Christmas Box*, all priced at one penny, while for sixpence *The History of Little Goody Two-shoes* and *Fables in Verse, by Abraham Aesop, Esq.* were offered. Collections of nursery rhymes were also sold cheaply in little books. Children often learned nursery rhymes from their parents, but new rhymes such as 'There was an old woman who lived in a shoe' and 'The Queen of Hearts' were composed throughout the eighteenth and into the nineteenth centuries.

Young girls were expected to play with suitable toys like dolls, and Elizabeth Ham remembered once being left alone with a friend: 'We were so absorbed in our interesting occupation, making a frock for the doll from a piece of *real India* gingham, that we took no note of the fire.'[20] The fire dwindled to nothing, their candle was accidentally extinguished, and they were left terrified in the darkness until the adults returned. Often, though, girls preferred boys' toys and games, and as a five-year-old in rural Somerset in the 1780s, Elizabeth had freedom to play:

When not in school I ran wild with my playmate. The unoccupied saw-pit made a delightful house; then in the summer we could play under the bridge on the turnpike road. The little clear stream was then so shallow as to leave a gravelly strand by which we could pass from one flowery meadow to the other without being seen from the road. There was one field where in haymaking time we had a delightful hidden bower round the bole of a large tree that grew out of a double hedge. We always ran home after the load of hay that we might ride back to the field on the empty wagon.[21]

Some girls may have yearned for boyish pursuits, but to modern eyes the young boys of the time resemble girls in contemporary illustrations, because they wore dresses or tunics, making it difficult to deduce a child's sex. In an Old Bailey trial in 1811, relating to the abduction of a three-year-old boy, his clothes and those of his five-year-old sister were described: 'The boy had a white frock, black skirt, a blue pinafore, and black half boots; the little girl, she had a light buff-coloured frock on, a black skirt, a dark coloured pinafore, and half boots.'[22] Boys' hair could be shorter, but in this case it was 'turned up on the right side; his hair rather wanted cutting'.[23]

When they were about four or five years of age, in what was sometimes a formal ceremony to mark the transition from babyhood into boyhood, boys were breeched. They gave up dresses and instead wore breeches and short jackets. Girls likewise lost their freedom. Their skirts became longer, more like women's clothing, and they were fitted with whalebone stays to ensure a good figure, though this practice was waning. When Elizabeth Ham was nine or ten years old, her wild childhood days ended:

I was at this time a little rustic, uncouth child ... The first reformation made in my appearance was effected by a staymaker. I was stood on the window-seat, whilst a man measured me for the machine [stays], which, in consideration of my youth, was to be only what was called half-boned, that is, instead of having the bones placed as close as they could lie, an interval the breadth of one was left vacant between each. Notwithstanding, the first day of wearing them was very nearly purgatory.[24]

If their clothing was at times akin to purgatory, some of the punishments meted out to children for wrongdoing seem brutal. In May

1803 Holland noted his six-year-old son's misbehaviour: 'William saying his lesson to his Mama but he has been very unruly and I have been obliged to strap him.'[25] Four months later he pilfered nectarines and peaches from trees in the garden. 'I gave my boy two or three straps,' his father recorded, 'but as he told the truth and promised never to do the like again I did not chastise him any further.'[26]

Cases of extreme cruelty to children were not tolerated, though. In 1814 one couple from the Yorkshire village of Cottingham were prosecuted for such an offence:

> At the late Quarter Sessions at Beverley, the following case of cruelty came before the court:– *George Clarke*, and *Elizabeth*, his wife, were indicted for an assault on their servant, a boy of eight or nine years age. The parties were chimney sweepers at Cottingham, and had bought the child of a travelling tinker for 6s. and a pair of shoes ... Several witnesses deposed to seeing the boy tied up in a stable by both his wrists, and there suffered to hang for a long time ... Another mode of treatment ... consisted in tying his leg to a horse's leg – by this means preventing both from making their escape. As the horse moved for the sake of pasture, he dragged his companion after him; and by these and other means his back was dreadfully bruised and lacerated. Both defendants were convicted; the husband was sentenced to imprisonment and hard labour for one year, and the wife for one month.[27]

This abused boy may not have been the tinker's son, but a stolen child, because when babies and young children were seized, they were almost impossible to locate. *The Times* mentioned one such kidnap: 'This being the first day of May [1799], Mrs MONTAGUE will give her annual entertainment of roast meat and plum-pudding to the Chimney-sweepers of the Metropolis, in the court-yard of her house in Portman-square, in commemoration of discovering her child among them long after it had been trepanned [stolen] away.'[28] Elizabeth Montagu was a wealthy widow who gave annual feasts for the chimney boys, but the kidnap tale was a myth – her only son had died at the age of sixteen months.[29]

Children were stolen for various reasons, such as by couples desperate for a family, to be used as cheap labour on land or at sea or even for selling into slavery. In June 1789 *The Times* described an abduction in Lambeth:

> A fine little boy, the son of an eminent tradesman, was taken from the gate of the garden, to which he had walked, and which unfortunately happened to be open. He was about three years of age. The woman who committed this theft was seen by several persons on the Black Friars Road, with the Child on her back crying bitterly, and being better dressed than it could be supposed she was able to afford, she was questioned by several people whose it was.[30]

The woman had a convincing story, claiming the boy was 'a Mr Smith's in the Temple [London], who with his wife were gone on faster than she could walk, on account of the rain'.[31] Thirty minutes later, the boy was missed: 'the usual enquiries were made in the neighbourhood—but without success, and the Child is probably lost for ever ... What makes this peculiarly distressing, is, that the poor little boy was an only son, and at the death of his Grandfather will become entitled to an Estate of *fourteen hundred pounds* per annum, in Yorkshire.'[32]

Such crimes were so heinous, *The Times* suggested, that the pillory was insufficient punishment – the death penalty was needed. Gypsies and other itinerant people were the prime suspects: 'Persons have been dispatched to all places where it is probable these thieves dwell, and hand bills distributed among the Gypsies in the vicinity of London; and an application made to the King of those gangs, offering a large reward for the Child.'[33] It was the newspaper's belief that a market for stolen children existed, especially babies, who were intended for slavery or prostitution: 'The general opinion is, that those Children are sent down into a cheap part of the Country, and reared to about nine years of age, when they are shipped off, and sold to the Barbary States, who are excellent customers for the females in particular, if there be any signs of growing beauty.'[34]

Another London abduction was that of Thomas Dillone, the three-year-old son of a warehouseman in Thames Street. On 18

November 1811 his mother left Thomas and his sister Rebecca with Mary Cox, a fruiterer in St Martin's Lane. While Mary was busy with other customers, a woman purchased some apples and then enticed both children away. 'I ran to the door, and the children was not there,' Mary reported. 'I ran half-way up St. Martin's-lane; I called Beckey, Beckey, they did not answer; I returned down to No. 11, to the yard, and called, Beckey. I did not find them there. I did not think of their being stolen away; I ran down to the wharf, and as I was crossing of Swan-lane, I saw the little girl returning with a penny plumb cake in her hand, and an apple.'[35]

The woman who had taken Thomas was a Mrs Magnes, and that same night 'she left town [London] for Gosport [Hampshire], with the boy, having *rigged* him out according to the taste of her husband, with a new dress, and a black hat and feather'.[36] Her husband Richard had recently returned home after a long period of absence while serving as a gunner in the Royal Navy. He was desperate to meet his son Richard for the first time – a son that his wife had invented to please him. He was overjoyed to see Thomas Dillone, believing him to be his son, but back in London the parish churchwardens distributed notices offering a hundred-guinea reward for the child's return, which led to the deception being uncovered in late December.

In rural Somerset, William Holland was struck by the idea that 'In London tis the practice to teach children to mention their names and the street they live in, which is a good method lest by some accident or other they should run out or be lost in the croud that pass along constantly.'[37] He was therefore pleased that his young son William could state where he lived in the local dialect: 'tis to Overstowey near Bridgewater Somersetshire'.[38] William was using the common West Country construction 'it is to' rather than 'it is at'.

A few days afterwards Holland noted: 'My little boy [is] saying his lesson to his Mama in the study by my elbow, he spells well and will read very soon, not much above three years old, he is a quick child.'[39] When he was abducted, Thomas Dillone had been the same age and was wearing a frock, as he was too young to be breeched. Once they were breeched, boys of the middle class and above started their education. Most began with reading and were then taught writing, and by the time he was six years old Holland's son was learning both skills: 'After breakfast I had William up to write and his Mama heard him read.'[40] Education, particularly the ability to read and write, was a prized asset that was passed on to other family members – parents taught their children, who in turn helped each other.

Either at school or at home, children were taught to write on slates with soft slate pencils or else they made their first letters in sand, progressing when older to paper, pencils and pen and ink. Slates and pencils were also used for rough notes and drawing, something that William Jones kept to hand: 'I frequently have a slate and pencil by my bed-side, and when I wake, at perhaps far too early an hour to rise, I scribble down any thoughts or reflexions which present themselves to my mind.'[41] Black lead pencil production was initially a cottage industry, based around Keswick in the Lake District, the only place in Europe with deposits of solid graphite. The graphite core of pencils used on paper is still called 'lead', because it was originally thought to be a type of lead. In the late eighteenth century a Frenchman, Nicolas Conté, invented a pencil with a lead made from a mixture of crushed graphite and clay. Pencils were relatively expensive, usually sixpence each, and they were bought singly, as in December 1800 when Holland wrote in his diary: 'I walked to [Nether] Stowey, bought a pencil and returned.'[42]

Pen and ink had been used for centuries, and for children and adults alike the technology had hardly changed. Quill pens, usually made from goose or similar feathers, were the norm, although pens with metal nibs were making an appearance. Whatever the kind of pen, it needed constant dipping into an inkwell, and after writing about a dozen lines, nibs of quill pens needed trimming with a small knife – giving us the term 'penknife'. Writing to his wife Sarah from HMS *Minotaur* when moored in Yarmouth Roads, William Wilkinson commented: 'I am obliged to borrow this ink and paper, and am writing with the back of the pen.'[43] This was one way of prolonging the use of a quill pen rather than trimming it.

Because quill pens wore out, there was a perpetual market for goose feathers. Many came from a traditional production area in the Lincolnshire Fens, which one visitor there described:

The geese are plucked five times in the year; the first plucking is at *Lady-Day*, for feathers and quills, and the same is renewed, for feathers only, four times more between that and *Michaelmas*. The old geese submit quietly to the operation, but the young ones are very noisy and unruly. I once saw this performed, and observed that goslings of six weeks old were not spared; for their tails were plucked ... to habituate them early to what they were to come to. If the season proves cold, numbers of geese die by this barbarous custom.[44]

Ink could be bought in shops, but many households made their own. In 1805 a mineral agent called William Jenkin wrote down his recipe:

¾ lb. of Alleppo Galls – bruised (but not small)
4 oz. of Clean Coperas – 4 oz. of Gum Arabick
1 oz. of Roche Allum –
Put the above in 3 quarts of rain water; shake it often for about 6 or 7 days.[45]

Aleppo galls were good-quality oak galls that formed a substance which etched the ink into the paper, while the other ingredients provided extra colour and diluted the mixture. To stop the ink from smudging, it could be dried quickly with blotting paper.

While parchment or vellum was preferred for some official documents, paper was used for most other purposes. It was manufactured by hand, largely using finely shredded rags. This produced a paper that was much more durable than modern types made from wood pulp. Paper was sold in several grades from very fine to coarse, and it varied in colour (the whiter the better) and price. Hot-pressed paper was finished by being rolled between heated rollers, resulting in a higher-quality paper with a smoother surface. In 1775 Parson Woodforde noted: 'For a quire of paper of a man at the door, pd. 0.1.0',[46] and over a decade later he paid the same in a shop for 'a quire of black edg'd letter paper'.[47] A quire was a bundle of twenty-four sheets, and two quires cost roughly a week's wages for a housemaid, far more expensive than paper today.

Well-to-do young boys might start their education at home,

taught by their parents, as with young William Holland, or tutored by a governess, alongside any sisters. Next, they might attend a small private school or academy. In 1782, when Carl Moritz was travelling through England, he visited one such establishment:

> I found means to see the regulation of one seminary of learning, here called an academy. Of these places of education, there is a prodigious number in London and its vicinity; though, notwithstanding their pompous names, they are, in reality, nothing more than small schools, set up by private persons, for children and young people ... From forty to fifty pounds [per annum] is the most that is generally paid in these academies ... It is, in general, the clergy, who have small incomes, who set up these schools both in town and country.[48]

This is precisely what Jane Austen's father George did for several years at the Steventon parsonage, where he taught reading, writing and the classics to his own sons (but not his daughters) alongside a handful of fee-paying pupils, some of them boarders.

Older boys could next attend a local grammar school, most of which had been set up after the dissolution of the monasteries as charitable endowments by wealthy benefactors, teaching Latin grammar to the virtual exclusion of anything else so as to enable pupils to enter Oxford or Cambridge University where Latin was also predominant. By the late eighteenth century many of these schools also taught ancient Greek and subjects like mathematics and literature, as well as oratory and team sports such as cricket. Some grammar schools were founded even earlier, in the medieval period, including Winchester College (1382) and Eton College (1440), which was granted a monopoly 10 miles around Eton 'so it may excel all other grammar schools ... and be called the lady mother and mistress of all other grammar schools'.[49]

Almost every English town had an endowed grammar school. They were open to the public with a public management, unlike privately run schools. However, the landed elite in particular chose to send their sons as boarders to a select number of these public grammar schools, notably Eton, Harrow, Winchester, Westminster, Rugby,

Charterhouse and Shrewsbury, and in England the term 'public school' came to describe, bizarrely, such exclusive, private, fee-paying boarding schools for the privileged minority. When on his walking tour of England, Moritz found himself at Eton:

> I passed Eton College, one of the first public schools in England ... I suppose it was during the hour of recreation, or in playtime, when I got to Eton; for I saw the boys in the yard before the college, which was inclosed by a low wall, in great numbers, walking and running up and down. Their dress struck me particularly: from the biggest to the least, they all wore black cloaks, or gowns, over coloured clothes; through which there was an aperture for their arms. They also wore, besides, a square hat, or cap, that seemed to be covered with velvet ... They were differently employed: some talking together, some playing, and some had their books in their hands, and were reading; but I was soon obliged to get out of their sight, they stared at me so, as I came along, all over dust, with my stick in my hand.[50]

Connections with influential people were needed to get children into these public schools, and William Holland was thrilled when, in 1808, his ten-year-old son William was accepted by Charterhouse in London: 'He was nominated by Mr Windham [an Eton-educated politician] by the application of my good friend Mrs Benwell and Mrs Windham both which ladies I was well acquainted with in my younger days ... It is a Glorious Act and deserves to be recorded, this has settled the education of my son William for the time to come and [I] hope it will be the foundation of his future advancement in this life.'[51] As well as admitting fee-paying scholars, Charterhouse accepted poor boys, primarily the sons of impecunious gentlemen. That same year his friend Mrs Penelope Benwell (née Loveday) became Mrs Hind when she married John Hind, vicar of Findon in Sussex – her previous husband was the Reverend William Benwell, who had died in 1796.

A few years later, in 1813, Holland was even happier on hearing from the Dean of Christ Church, Oxford, who promised

> a studentship ... for my son as soon as he can arrange matters for that purpose ... so this is an important thing indeed. He is sure of patronage

of the Dean, and studentships are in fact fellowships, they succeed to [church] livings ... and all this I have gained through my very valuable and zealous friend Mrs. Hind and not only this but his appointment to the Charter House was through the same channel. Mrs. Hind was the first mover, and her cousin Mrs. Wyndham [Windham] took it up.[52]

While boys might be sent to school, girls were generally taught at home – if at all – by governesses or by their mothers, who might themselves have received minimal education. In the summer of 1812, Nelly Weeton moved to High Royd in Yorkshire as a governess for the Armitage family. In a letter to a friend, she described her status:

A *governess* is almost shut out of society; not choosing to associate with servants, and not being treated as an equal by the heads of the house or their visitors, she must possess some fortitude and strength of mind to render herself tranquil or happy; but indeed, the master or mistress of a house, if they have any goodness of heart, would take pains to prevent her feeling her inferiority. For my own part, I have no cause of just complaint; but I know some that are treated in a most mortifying manner.[53]

As a child, Nelly's own desire to learn had been stifled, even though her widowed mother was running a school in Upholland:

my mother continually checked any propensity I shewed to writing or composing; representing to me what a useless being I should prove if I were allowed to give up my time to writing or reading, when domestic duties were likely to have so frequent a call upon me. 'It is very likely, my dear girl,' she would often say, 'that you will have to earn your livelihood, at least in great measure; and a wretched subsistence do they obtain who have it to earn by their literary abilities! Or should you become a wife, think in what a ragged, neglected state your family would be if you gave up much of your time to books.'[54]

In Somerset, Holland grumbled about one educated girl, Elizabeth Poole: 'This little girl is very clever and learns surprizingly and writes Latin letters but I should not like any woman the better for understanding Latin and Greek. All pedantick learning of this kind makes them conceited. I do not approve of the manner of boys in petticoats.'[55] The same age as his son William, the two children enjoyed playing together whenever she was visiting her uncle Tom Poole at nearby Nether Stowey. A few years later, when she was fourteen, Holland elaborated: 'She has a thirst after knowledge of every kind to the greatest degree. She has made great proficiency in Latin and Greek and is making the same advance in French and Italian ... It is a pity she was not a boy for then such studies would turn to better account ... I know not where this will end but is not a likely mode to get her well married.'[56]

Holland's own daughter Margaret was given a basic education at home, with private tutors for music and French, but she never married. In spite of her education, Elizabeth did marry in 1825, at the age of twenty-eight, becoming the wife of John Sandford, Archdeacon at Wells in Somerset.[57] In Nelly Weeton's view, women deserved equal opportunities: 'Why are not females permitted to study physic, divinity, astronomy, &c., &c., with their attendants, chemistry, botany, logic, mathematics, &c. To be sure the mere study is not prohibited, but the practise is in great measure. Who would employ a female physician? who would listen to a female divine, except to ridicule? I could myself almost laugh at the idea.'[58]

Young ladies were expected to become accomplished with practical skills. Education for girls was viewed as a luxury, though by Jane Austen's childhood there was an increasing number of fee-paying 'dame schools' for young girls and boys. The standard of such establishments varied hugely. Many were run by older women like Nelly's mother, who lacked qualifications and could not earn a living any other way. The term 'dame' was a respectful way of addressing these women, who might have no claim to rank other than schoolmistress.

At the age of seven Jane Austen was sent away to Oxford with her sister Cassandra and her cousin Jane Cooper to be taught by a private tutor.[59] In the summer of 1783, after the tutor and her pupils moved to Southampton, all three girls fell ill with typhus, and Jane Austen nearly died. She and her sister recuperated at home and then joined their cousin in 1785 at the Reading Ladies' Boarding School, but were removed at the end of the following year, putting a stop to their tuition. By the time Jane Austen was eleven years old, her formal education was over.[60]

If educating females was considered pointless, educating the poorest in society, both boys and girls, generated real fear that it might encourage bloody revolution, as in France, or, at the very least, a lack of deference to the elite. This opinion was not universal, and many charity schools for the poor had long been established by the Society for the Promotion of Christian Knowledge. With the rapid population growth and movement into towns, increased worries about the lack of schooling for poor and destitute children led to the formation of many more charity schools and Sunday schools. Some were free of charge, others charged a penny or twopence weekly.

In the early years of the nineteenth century nonconformist churches actively set up Sunday schools and charity schools. The main group of nonconformist schools were the British Schools, established by the British and Foreign School Society, in which Joseph Lancaster was especially prominent with his Lancasterian system of schools. Following this nonconformist lead, the Church of England – through the National Society for Promoting Religious Education – began to found schools of its own for the poor that became known as National Schools and in which the clergyman Andrew Bell played a leading role.[61]

While touring the Midlands in 1790, John Byng expressed his prejudice against schools for the lower classes: 'I have met some of the newly-adopted Sunday-schools today, and seen others in their schools; I am point blank against these institutions; the poor shou'd not read, and of writing I never heard, for them, the use.'[62] In July 1802 William Holland took an opposite view, in support of the local Sunday school at Over Stowey, convinced that it could teach the poor to be good Christians and know their place:

We had some talk about Sunday schools yesterday. Mr King [a wealthy physician] thought that they did harm, that plowmen were better without learning. I answered that I could not think that the teaching them of their duty could do any harm; obliging children to go to Church, teaching them to read and say their Catechism, to give them some sense of Religion and a due subordination to their superiors must be of some service in these times.[63]

Five years later the Cornishman Davies Giddy, Member of Parliament for Bodmin in Cornwall, spoke during a House of Commons debate about the Parochial Schools Bill, which attempted (but failed) to make all parishes provide free education for the labouring poor. A renowned scientist, Giddy had himself received a privileged education, but he was unconvinced about mass education:

> it would ... be found to be prejudicial to their morals and happiness; it would teach them to despise their lot in life, instead of making them good servants in agriculture, and other laborious employments to which their rank in society had destined them; instead of teaching them subordination, it would render them factious and refractory ... it would enable them to read seditious pamphlets, vicious books, and publications against Christianity; it would render them insolent to their superiors.[64]

Despite such opposition, goodwill increased towards charity schools, and in Cornwall in 1811 contributions were sought for a Sunday school at Wheal Alfred, which the mineral agent William Jenkin outlined:

> Captains [of mines] John Davey and Samuel Grose (the two principal agents in Wheal Alfred Mine) having observed the profligacy [lack of decency] of the Children of many of the Labourers in that Mine, – and particularly of those who cannot read – have begun a Sundays School and have from 250 to 300 Boys and Girls under their care. But finding the expense of Books and rewards for the meritorious to be too heavy for them, they are under the necessity of soliciting the aid of those Gentlemen who are interested in the Mine, and of others who may feel disposed to assist such a praiseworthy undertaking ... W. H. Hore [Hoare], a banker in London, is amongst the list of subscribers with a £5 donation. The number of Men, Boys and Girls employed in the Mine is about 1000.[65]

Most charity schools were obsessed with religious teaching and moral improvement, though children did acquire elementary literacy skills. James Lackington was born in Wellington, Somerset, in 1746, the eldest of a family of eleven children. He was apprenticed to a shoemaker in Taunton at the age of fourteen, later moving to Bristol and in 1773 to London. Taught to read by the Methodists, he became obsessed with books, and with a legacy of £10 from his grandfather and a loan of £5 from the Methodists, he established what became a thriving bookselling business. His was a rare success story. Most lower-class children never realised their potential, as was the case with Thomas Carter, who worked as a tailor in often wretched circumstances. His autobiography, published in 1845, reveals a highly intelligent man, trapped by poverty.[66]

In 1816 witnesses before a Parliamentary Select Committee testified that education was improving the general behaviour of 'the lower orders' in London. Henry Althens described the East London Auxiliary Sunday School Union Society, which had ten Sunday schools teaching nearly 1300 children: 'First, they are taught to read, and our main object is to teach them to read the Bible, and we exhort them to attend to all the moral duties of life. Our chief object is to convey religious instruction to the children, believing that to be the foundation of all moral good.'[67] Writing was taught only in the evenings, as a reward, more often to boys than to girls, who were considered better suited to needlework.

It was reckoned that about half of all children in England received no education at all, not even at Sunday schools, which gave children an opportunity for education on their one day off work. The concept of teenagers, a time of adolescence, did not exist until the twentieth century. Females of teenage years were either working, seeking husbands, or both, but rarely being educated. Charity schools taught boys until they were fourteen, the usual age to start an apprenticeship, though many went to work before then: the poorer the family, the shorter the childhood. By thirteen or fourteen, if not sooner, childhood for the majority was over. Only a privileged few, like William Holland's son, remained in education.

For boys of the upper and middle classes who did not prolong their education, joining the Royal Navy was a popular next step. Nelson joined as a captain's servant in 1771 at the age of twelve, but some boys were even younger. Jane Austen had two brothers, Francis (Frank) and Charles, who joined the navy. Francis attended the Royal Naval Academy at Portsmouth from the age of twelve and joined his first ship two years later, while Charles went to the same Academy in 1791 at the same age and joined his first ship three years later. Jane had four other brothers. The oldest, James, went to Oxford University and then became a clergyman. George, a sickly child who suffered from fits, was looked after by foster-parents, funded by the Austens. Edward was adopted by distant cousins, Thomas Knight and his wife, and inherited a fortune, while Henry, Jane's favourite brother, had a varied career. After Oxford University, he joined the militia and later became an army agent and a banker, but after his bank failed, he too went into the Church and spent the rest of his life as a clergyman.

Most poor children needed to start earning money as early as possible, because their meagre wages were essential to their family's survival. In 1816 Frederick Augustus Earle, a clerk in London's parish of St Giles, reckoned that countless young girls were prostitutes. The previous week about thirty had been arrested, and 'several of them were very young, two or three of them not above thirteen or fourteen years of age'.[68] Even younger children were put to work in various manufacturing trades and as labourers, while others were apprenticed, bound by indenture, usually for seven years, which meant that the parents, the parish or a charity had to pay for them to learn a trade.

Rules governing apprentices were strict. When fourteen-year-old Richard Cureton of Bow Lane off Cheapside in London became apprenticed on 5 August 1783, he was bound for seven years to William Wakelin, a girdler (who made ceremonial girdles). The official indenture, written on parchment, gave a list of rules to which the apprentice had to agree, including:

> He shall do no damage to his said Master nor see to be done of others, but that to his power shall let, or forthwith give warning to his said Master of the same. He shall not wast the goods of his said Master nor

lend them unlawfully to any. He shall not commit Fornication, nor contract Matrimony within the said Term. He shall not play at Cards, Dice, Tables, or any other unlawful Games whereby his said Master may have any loss with his own goods or others during the said Term, Without License of his said Master; he shall neither buy nor sell. He shall not haunt Taverns or Playhouses nor absent himself from his said Master's service day nor night unlawfully: But in all things, as a faithful apprentice he shall behave himself towards his said Master and all his during the said Term.[69]

Richard's fee of £10 was paid to Wakelin by a charity administered by the Merchant Taylors' Company that gave money for apprenticing poor children.[70] In return, Wakelin was expected to ensure that the apprentice was 'taught and instructed the best way and manner that he can, finding & allowing unto the said Apprentice sufficiant Meat Drink Apparel Lodging and all other Necessaries according to the Custom of the City of London, during the said Term'.[71] Five years after finishing his apprenticeship, Richard was married to Frances Carter, but died in 1804 at the early age of thirty-five, a year after his only child Joseph was born. In 1817 Joseph was apprenticed at the age of fourteen to a fishing-rod and tackle maker. He himself had nine children, and direct descendants today live in Canada and the USA.

Innumerable apprentices, bound to a skilled master, learned a valuable trade, but others suffered seven years of virtual servitude. Children of destitute families were compulsorily apprenticed by the parish as allowed by the Poor Law, usually in lower-status positions like servants or agricultural labourers. If they could be apprenticed outside the parish, so much the better, because responsibility for them was then transferred to their new parish. Any child living in the workhouse or whose parents received poor relief could be apprenticed in this way. Mines regularly took children from local workhouses, while countless children from London's workhouses ended up in northern textile mills. Until 1814, when compulsory apprenticeships were abolished, it was an offence to run away, and notices in the newspapers warned about such culprits. Two apprentices in a cotton spinning mill fled in May 1793:

# TWO RUNAWAY APPRENTICES

ABSCONDED from LITTON MILL, near *Tideswell*, in the County of *Derby*, on Tuesday morning the 14th of May Instant.

DAVID POWELL, about 13 Years of Age, fair Complexion, and light Hair; had on a light Cloth Coat and Breeches, or else a Fustian Coat and Breeches.

Also, MARY BEDINGFIELD, about 14 Years of Age, dark Complexion, and dark Hair, and has remarkably thick Lips; had on a blue Gown, green stuff Petticoat and black Hat.

Whoever will apprehend the said Apprentices and give information thereof to Messrs. Needham, Frith, and Co at Litton Mill aforesaid, shall receive ONE GUINEA Reward, and be paid all reasonable Expences.[72]

A few years later, around August 1799, an orphan called Robert Blincoe was sent to Litton Mill from London's St Pancras workhouse. Believed to have reached the age of seven, he was bound as an apprentice for fourteen years. He survived the ordeal, though he lost a finger and was left with crooked legs. As he explained, 'I got deformed there; my knees began to bend in when I was fifteen ... a very little makes me sweat in walking; I have not the strength of those who are straight.'[73] In 1833 he gave evidence to the Select Committee on the employment of children in factories. When asked if he would send his own children to such a mill, he replied:

No; I would rather have them transported. In the first place, they are standing upon one leg, lifting up one knee, a great part of the day, keeping the ends up from the spindle; I consider that that employment makes many cripples; then there is the heat and the dust; then there are so many different forms of cruelty used upon them; then they are so liable to have their fingers catched and to suffer other accidents from the machinery; then the hours is so long, that I have seen them tumble down asleep among the straps and machinery, and so get cruelly hurt.[74]

Questioned about this cruelty, he said:

I have seen the time when two hand-vices of a pound weight each, more or less, have been screwed to my ears, at Lytton mill in Derbyshire. Here are the scars still remaining behind my ears. Then three or four of us have been hung at once on a cross beam above the machinery, hanging by our hands, without shirts or stockings. Mind, we were apprentices, without father or mother to take care of us ... we used to stand up, in a skip, without our shirts, and be beat with straps or sticks; the skip was to prevent us from running away from the strap.[75]

Litton Mill was far from exceptional. Throughout England the textile industry relied on unskilled child workers. Four different threads were manufactured that could be made into fabrics – these were silk, wool, linen (from flax) and cotton threads. Silk, the finest of threads and used for sewing and weaving, depended on the labour of children because their small and dexterous fingers could handle the threads more efficiently. In 1800 the antiquary Richard Warner, who was a curate at Bath, visited a silk-spinning factory in a nearby Somerset village:

A little silk manufactory enlivens Maiden-Bradley, established by Mr. Ward of Bruton, about nine miles from this village. Fifty-three children great and small, are employed in spinning two of the fine filaments, as produced by the worm, together; this work is carried to Bruton, when, with the assistance of ingenious machinery, the silk thread for use is made ... The children employed (who begin working before they are six years of age) earn wages proportioned to their expedition and ability; the youngest make about three half-pence or two-pence per day, and the most experienced half-a-crown or three shilling per week; but for this they are expected to work from five o'clock in the morning till six at night![76]

Warner was obviously concerned about the long working hours, and in 1816 during a parliamentary debate on children working in cotton factories, Sir Robert Peel stated that 'little children of very tender age were employed with grown persons at the machinery, and those poor little creatures, torn from their beds, were compelled to work even at the age of six years, from early morn till late at night–a space of per-haps 15 to 16 hours!'[77]

Children in agriculture also worked excessively long hours. Some were hired as farm servants, usually on a yearly basis, for indoor and outdoor labour, while others were apprentices, bound to the farm for several years as unpaid hired hands, receiving board and lodging in return. Mrs Mary Rendalls described being apprenticed at the age of eight or nine, in about 1811, to Thomas Nicholls, a small farmer at Lower Woodrow near Brampford Speke in Devon:

When I was an apprentice, I got up as early as half-past two, three, four, or five, to get cows in, feed them, milk them, and look after the pigs. I then had breakfast, and afterwards went into the fields. In the fields I used to drive the plough, pick stones, weed, pull turnips, when snow was lying about, sow corn, dig potatoes, hoe turnips, and reap. I did everything that boys did. Master made me do everything ... My mistress was a very bad temper; when bad tempered she treated me very ill; she beats me very much; she would throw me on the ground, hold me by the ears, kneel upon me, and use me very ill; I used to scream. This has happened several times a week ... My master beat me, and I went to my father's house. My father was afraid to let me stop, as he might be summoned, as I was an apprentice.[78]

Some of the most physically exhausting work of all was in the mines, both underground and on the surface. In 1841 shocking evi-dence was collected for a parliamentary commission on the conditions then being suffered by children, though older miners reck-oned it had actually been far worse several decades earlier. When they were children, many had started work at six or seven years of age, some even younger. Their first job would be to open and close the heavy wooden tunnel doors. In Cumberland in 1813, the traveller and writer Richard Ayton went down the William Pit near Whitehaven, a coal mine that extended under the sea. He was horrified at what he saw:

a number of children ... attend at the doors to open them when the horses pass through, and ... in this duty are compelled to linger their lives, in silence, solitude, and darkness, for sixpence a day. When I first came to one of these doors, I saw it open without perceiving by what means, till, looking behind it, I beheld a miserable little wretch standing without a light, silent and motionless ... On speaking to it I was touched with the patience and uncomplaining meekness with which it submitted to its horrible imprisonment, and the little sense it had of the barbarity of its unnatural parents. Few of the children thus inhumanly sacrificed were more than eight years old, and several were considerably less, and had barely strength sufficient to perform the office that was required from them. On their first introduction into the mine the poor little victims struggle and scream with terror at the darkness, but there are found people brutal enough to force them to compliance, and after a few trials they become tame and spiritless, and yield themselves up at last without noise and resistance to any cruel slavery that it pleases their masters to impose upon them. In the winter-time they never see day-light except on a Sunday, for it has been discovered that they can serve for thirteen hours a day without perishing ... As soon as they rise from their beds they descend down the pit, and they are not relieved from their prison till, exhausted with watching and fatigue, they return to their beds again.[79]

Ayton described what else he and his companion witnessed:

We traced our way through passage after passage in the blackest dark- ness ... Occasionally a light appeared in the distance before us, which did not dispel the darkness ... but advanced like a meteor through the gloom, accompanied by a loud rumbling noise, the cause of which was not explained to the eye till we were called upon to make way for a horse, which passed by with its long line of baskets, and driven by a young girl, covered with filth, debased and profligate [indecent], and uttering some low obscenity as she hurried by us. We were frequently interrupted in our march by the horses proceeding in this manner with their cargoes to the shaft, and always driven by girls, all of the same description, ragged and beastly in their appearance, and with a shameless indecency in their behaviour.[80]

At least there was standing room in this Whitehaven pit, because in many mines the coal was dragged or pushed along low passageways by 'hurriers', or 'drawers', crawling along on their hands and knees. This barbaric work was done by girls, boys and women (even when they were pregnant), wearing round their waist a belt from which a chain passed between their legs and was attached to the huge baskets or tubs. Years later Joseph Gledhill related his first experiences down a coal mine in Yorkshire, in about 1798:

> I began life as a hurrier when I was between five and six years of age; I was a hurrier till I was 16 ... there was no such thing as rails upon the roads; we used to hurry then upon 'sleds', with a belt and chain, and with a pair of short crutches we held in our hands to enable us to hurry on our hands and feet; I remember at that time such things as crooked legs, but whether that resulted from the employment I cannot tell; they [the boys] worked then about 12 hours.[81]

Even before the steam engines and furnaces of the accelerating industrial revolution began to devour vast quantities of coal, a constant supply was required for open fires for cooking, as well as for heating water and keeping rooms warm. With so many domestic fires kept constantly alight or relit each day, smoke hung in the air summer and winter. All houses and many other buildings needed chimneys to allow the smoke from fireplaces and cooking ranges to be channelled outside, and an accumulation of soot caused chimney fires that could spread rapidly through buildings. To remove this danger, chimneys were cleaned about four times a year, but adults were too big for this job. It had to be done by boys and girls who would climb up the narrow flues, sweeping with a handbrush and using a scraper to dislodge compacted soot. The youngest climbing boys were made to seek work by 'calling of the streets', and the soot itself was a valuable commodity, sold to farmers as fertiliser.

Sweeping chimneys was hard, dangerous and claustrophobic. The choking black dust harmed the children's eyes and lungs, and like those employed down mines, climbing boys rarely washed, though some masters ensured they washed on Sundays. The chimney sweep David Porter, it was reported to Parliament in 1788, 'knows many instances of boys who have served four or five years without being at all washed'.[82] Because soot is a carcinogen, chimney sweeps were particularly prone to 'Sooty Warts',[83] which was cancer of the scrotum.

In 1802 the writer Samuel Pratt commented on the awful plight of these children: 'Where a chimney sweeper's boy is not regularly cleansed once a week, and is kept in filth and nastiness, he is often afflicted by violent itchings, which break out in small pimples, and soon become an ulcer, and ultimately end in an incurable cancer, the consequence of obstructed perspiration.'[84] He was saddened by three pitiful boys he encountered in London's St Martin's Lane:

> The three poor creatures immediately under my eyes, were melancholy both to see and to hear ... They were in their boyhood; the youngest six, the next seven, and the third told me he was 'past nine a little bit, and going on for ten.' They were all brothers, and apprenticed to a huge grim being, who soon after came up with them, damned the elder apprentice for leaving one of his brushes, with which he struck him on the shoulders.[85]

An Act of Parliament in 1788 had made it illegal to employ children under eight years of age, but this law was constantly ignored, particularly by sweeps using their own children. The three boys observed by Pratt were barely clothed, and the youngest was limping so badly that he begged his master to let him rest on the church steps:

> Rest, said the black man, that's a fine story indeed; I have two chimneys to sweep now before half past eight, in Covent Garden, and don't you hear St. Martin's is now striking seven, and there is one of the chimneys as crooked as a cork screw, that none but such a shrimp as you can crawl up. While he was growling out these words, he took up the child and slung him over his shoulder, just as he would have slung one of his sacks.[86]

A tradesman suddenly called out for a sweep, so he went inside to examine the chimneys, and Pratt seized the opportunity to question the boys:

> the elder apprentice who appeared to be in extreme ill health, told me in a fearful whisper, on my asking concerning his mode of living and labour,

that ... if he lived would rather be a shoe black or a galley slave than a chimney sweeper, especially to the brute who is gone into that house, for he not only almost starves but beats me and my brothers to death, though I have gone all weathers through my morning work for many years. I have nothing to sleep on but some of these sacks in a soot cellar, and what's worse, my master won't allow us to wash and tight ourselves up [free from rags] not once a month: so that I am quite sore with the clogged stuff that has almost eat into my flesh – only look, Sir, at these sore places and these great lumps.[87]

Effective alternative methods of sweeping chimneys, using long rods and brushes, without the need to climb chimneys, were being developed, but a reluctance to use them prevailed. Children were preferred, not just for sweeping but for ascending flues to extinguish fires. Some chimneys were so narrow that even a small child could become stuck. Before a parliamentary committee in 1788, James Dunn described what happened to him during one chimney fire:

he himself had been very ill-treated by his Master, having been bound Apprentice at 5 Years of Age, for 7 Years ... when he was about 10 Years old, he was sent up a Chimney which had been on Fire for 48 Hours ... during the Time he was up the Chimney, his Master came, and found Fault with him, in so angry a Manner, as to occasion a Fright, by which Means he fell down into the Fire [having reached the fire by ascending an interconnecting flue], and was much burnt, and crippled by it for Life.[88]

In early 1806, in what was then the western edge of London, one chimney of a well-to-do house leased by Richard Creed of Marsh and Creed navy agents was in need of cleaning:

a boy was sent up a chimney in the house of Mr. Creed, Navy Agent, No. 23 Hans Place, Knightsbridge. Being unable to extricate himself, he remained there for about half an hour, while a person went to fetch assistance. A hole was made through the brick-work, and the boy, at length, released. It appeared, that, in consequence of the unusual construction of the flue in one part, a vast quantity of soot had accumulated there, into which the boy had plunged, and was not able, probably from partial suf-focation, to get back again.[89]

James Dunn was by now a master sweep, working in the same part of London, but he was unwilling to deal with this particular chimney: 'So dangerous was the sweeping of this chimney considered, that James Dunn, chimney sweeper, No. 46, Hans Town, refused to let his apprentice ascend the flue'.[90] A few years later, in 1814, this same house at 23 Hans Place became the home of Jane Austen's brother Henry. 'It is a delightful place – more than answers my expectation,' Jane wrote that August, apparently oblivious of the wretched chimney boy's plight.[91]

The boy was lucky to be pulled out alive. An inquest in London in November 1810 heard that Lewis Realy, about eight years old, had suffocated in a similar accident. He 'was sent up a chimney in the house of Susanna Whitfield, in Little Shire Lane, Temple Bar. After ascending the first part of the flue, he came down, and objected to attempt climbing it a second time.'[92] Despite his terror, he was forced back up:

He remained in the chimney a considerable time, and then a boy (William Best) went up, and tried to pull him down by the legs; this not succeeding ... [he] ascended another flue, which communicated, but could not extricate Realy, though he received from him his cap and scraper. At a quarter past one, William Herring, a bricklayer, was sent for, who broke an opening into the flue, through which the body of Realy, then dead, was taken. The body, when extricated, was naked, and com-pletely jammed in the chimney.[93]

The writer of this report was indignant: 'When we assure our read-ers this is only one of many authenticated accounts equally dreadful, we leave it to them to reflect how much they are called on to mitigate, by every means in their power, the sufferings of these wretched chil-dren, by encouraging the use of mechanical means of sweeping chimneys.'[94]

Chimneys were of course swept all over England, not just in the great smoky cities. In rural Norfolk on 12 August 1797, James Woodforde had several chimneys cleaned: 'Holland the chimney sweeper swept my study chimney, parlour ditto – and the chamber chimneys, with kitchen and back-kitchen ditto – in all six. He had a new boy with him who had likely to have lost his life this morning at Weston House in sticking in one [of] their chimnies. I gave the poor boy a shilling.'[95] Campaigners had long tried to ban the use of climbing boys, and finally in June 1817 a Bill was passed, only to be thrown out in the House of Lords the following year. It was not until 1875 that the practice of employing climbing boys was banned.

# FOUR

———— ·◆· ————

# HOME AND HEARTH

She was then taken into a parlour, so small that her first conviction was of its being only a passage-room to something better.

*Mansfield Park*, by Jane Austen

William Pitt the Elder, who died in 1778, once declared: 'The poorest man may in his cottage bid defiance to all the forces of the Crown. It may be frail – its roof may shake – the wind may blow through it – the storm may enter – the rain may enter – but the King of England cannot enter! – all his force dares not cross the threshold of the ruined tenement!'[1]

While this centuries-old sentiment is normally expressed as 'an Englishman's home is his castle', the upper classes did live in country mansions and even occasionally real castles, with an army of servants to run the house and tend the grounds. By the time of the 1801 census, England had a population of just over 8 million living in a country of some 32 million acres – and about 80 to 90 per cent of this land was owned by the aristocracy or landed gentry.[2] Some of them had estates of thousands of acres, including large kitchen gardens, lawns, shrubberies and other landscape features, as well as orchards for fruit, woodlands for fuel, rivers and lakes for fishing, and huge swathes of land for farming and shooting wild animals and birds.[3] They received ever-increasing income from their tenant farmers, mines and other industrial concerns, as well as from urban developments.

It was accepted that respectable individuals could ask to view these lavish homes, and usually a small sum of money was handed to the gardener or housekeeper for their trouble. In Oxfordshire in July 1785, though, John Byng, the younger son of George Byng, 3rd Viscount Torrington, who would himself succeed to the title, was annoyed to be refused entry to the fourteenth-century Shirburn Castle:

> Our ride was to Wheatley, and, leaving the high road, to the village of Gt Milton ... thence over an openish country to Aisley ... cross'd many pasture grounds and much nasty country to Sherborne Castle, Ld Macclesfields seat, the object of our ride; but were refused admission, as his L'dship was at home. This is the second rebuff we have lately experienc'd, and which, after a tedious sultry ride of 16 miles, fretted us not a little: let people proclaim that their great houses are not to be view'd, and then travellers will not ride out of their way with false hopes.[4]

In *Pride and Prejudice*, when Elizabeth Bennet and her aunt and uncle are touring round Derbyshire, they visit Mr Darcy's house on his Pemberley estate: 'It was a large, handsome, stone building, standing well on rising ground, and backed by a ridge of high woody hills; and in front, a stream of some natural importance ... Elizabeth was delighted.' If the fictional Pemberley existed, it would now be considered a 'stately home', a term coined by Felicia Hemans in 1827 in a poem that begins 'The stately Homes of England, How beautiful they stand!'[5] While travelling from Slough to Bath in 1805, the American Benjamin Silliman noticed many such houses: 'Throughout our whole ride, at intervals of a mile or two, beautiful country seats adorned the road, and with their forests, their parks, their sloping fields, and their herds of deer, presented a most interesting succession of objects.'[6]

Many grand country homes and smaller houses were being constructed or rebuilt in what we today call the 'Georgian' style, such as Dodington House near Bath, a sixteenth-century manor house that was completely rebuilt over many years from 1796. Other older buildings were remodelled so that, certainly from the front, they appeared to conform to fashion. At Althorp in Northamptonshire, the original sixteenth-century house was greatly in need of repair by the 1780s, and so Lord Spencer brought in the architect Henry Holland. He transformed the external appearance of the house and went on to remodel some of the interior as well. The Georgian style of architecture, which evolved over a hundred years, was at its most developed form in Jane Austen's lifetime, influenced by classical Greek and Roman architecture and less heavily ornamented than earlier in the century. While the term Regency is now applied to architecture dating from about 1800 until about 1837, at the time it was of course regarded as modern.

Along with their servants, wealthy families moved 'up to' London from their country establishments, renting a house or staying in their own property for 'the Season', which coincided with parliamentary sittings. Benjamin Silliman explained that 'in England, *down* means *from* London, and *up*, *to* London: they speak of going down into the country, no matter in what direction. The Londoners talk of going down to Scotland. Is this a figure of speech unconsciously adopted because London is the great fountain supplying all the kingdom with streams of wealth and knowledge. Perhaps the country might dispute the claim.'[7]

For want of money, John Byng reluctantly worked in London from 1782 as a commissioner of stamps and was relieved to leave his employment each summer and travel round rural England, which he so loved. In August 1790, as he headed northwards to Biggleswade, Byng witnessed the annual desertion of the city: 'The roads are now crowded as London empties in August, and fills in February.'[8] In a guide to London published that same year, advice was given on renting houses: 'The dearest season is from Christmas to June, when families are in town and the parliament sitting; the cheapest, when families are out of town, and the parliament prorogued.'[9]

Even though the poor had to stay put, London did become visibly depleted, particularly during the summer when anyone who could afford to do so would abandon the stinking city. However, in August 1811 Louis Simond, on a tour of Britain, was actually surprised that 'London is less empty than we expected, and the wheels of numerous carriages are still rattling over the pavement of Portman Square, near which we occupy the house of an absent friend, obligingly lent to us.'[10]

Towns and cities across England were expanding rapidly, leading Horace Walpole in 1791 to comment: 'There will soon be one street from London to Brentford, ay, and from London to every village ten miles round! . . . Bath shoots out into new crescents, circuses, and squares every year: Birmingham, Manchester, Hull, and Liverpool would serve any King in Europe for a capital.'[11] The previous summer Miss Mary Heber of Weston Hall in Northamptonshire received a letter from a friend: 'We intend going to spend the day at Bath some day this week . . . imagine I shall scarcely know the place, there are so many new Buildings erected since I had the pleasure of meeting you there.'[12]

In places like London and Bath, many new houses were appearing, including grand terraces or squares with their mews buildings behind for carriages and horses. In June 1797 George MacAulay, a merchant and insurer, remarked on London's expansion: 'In the evening I walked sev'ral times round Finsbury Square, a place which now approaches nearly to the elegance of the Squares in the West. I remember it a place for rubbish, and not a House built!'[13] This square was where James Lackington had just established London's largest bookstore.

The fashionable Georgian architectural style was also adopted for the more humble terraced houses of the middle classes and even those of the better-off skilled workers, but the rapid expansion of towns resulted in poorly constructed houses. On the outskirts of London Simond watched brick terraces being built: 'their walls are frightfully thin, a single brick of eight inches, – and, instead of beams, mere planks lying on edge. I am informed, it is made an express condition in the leases of these . . . houses, that there shall be no dances given in them.'[14] Even so, he said, 'People live in the outskirts of the town in better air, – larger houses, – and at a smaller rent, – and stages [stagecoaches] passing every half hour facilitate communications.'[15]

Although England's population was a fraction of today's, living conditions were overcrowded by modern standards. Privacy was not valued so highly, and even families with modest incomes had live-in servants who needed basic accommodation. Simond gave a vivid description of a typical rented London terraced house 'of the middling or low kind':

> Each family occupy a whole house, unless very poor ... These narrow houses, three or four stories high,—one for eating, one for sleeping, a third for company, a fourth under ground for the kitchen, a fifth perhaps at top for the servants ... The plan of these houses is very simple, two rooms on each story; one in the front with two or three windows looking on the street, the other on a yard behind, often very small; the stairs generally taken out of the breadth of the back-room. The ground-floor is usually elevated a few feet above the level of the street, and separated from it by an area, a sort of ditch, a few feet wide ... and six or eight feet deep, inclosed by an iron railing; the windows of the kitchen are in this area. A bridge of stone or brick leads to the door of the house. The front of these houses is about twenty or twenty-five feet wide; they certainly have rather a paltry appearance,—but you cannot pass the threshold without being struck with the look of order and neatness of the interior.[16]

Filled with large families and several servants, such houses could be crowded, but nothing like the dwellings of the poor, who might not have servants but had numerous children who were squeezed into homes that often served as their workplace as well. Noisy, cramped conditions were the lot of most town dwellers, about which Jane Austen was sensitive in *Mansfield Park* when Fanny Price is back home in the tiny terraced house in Portsmouth: 'The living in incessant noise was ... the greatest misery of all ... Here, everybody was noisy, every voice was loud ... Whatever was wanted was halloo'd for, and the servants halloo'd out their excuses from the kitchen. The doors were in constant banging, the stairs were never at rest, nothing was done without a clatter, nobody sat still, and nobody could command attention when they spoke.'

In spite of his aristocratic background, John Byng was aware of problems faced by the lower classes. To him it made sense for every poor person to be housed in a cottage with some land attached. He outlined his vision of an ideal place to live:

> As for poverty, rags and misery they should not exist in my village; for the cottages should not be only comfortable and low-rented, but attached to each should be, at least, 2 acres of ground, which on first possession the hirers should find well cropped with potatoes, and planted with fruit trees;– teach them how to proceed, redeem the poor from misery, make a large public enclosure at the end of the village, for their cows, &c., and then poverty would soon quit your neighbourhood.[17]

This was Byng's dream, but the clergyman William Jones in 1802 made comments in his diary that were closer to reality: 'In most towns and villages the poor and indigent class, I fear, have very wretched accommodations. They are generally crowded together in dark courts and narrow alleys, in cellars, or in garrets; where damps, stagnated air, and accumulated filthiness, injure their health, and facilitate the progress of contagious diseases.'[18]

In 1816 a parliamentary committee heard evidence about the state of houses in streets close to Covent Garden, including Short's Gardens, 'occupied by poor room-keepers, generally with families, living in apparent wretchedness, unhealthy, filthy in their persons, their rooms, and their bedding; the staircases of the houses of course common to the numerous families which occupied them, and being common to all, appeared to be cleaned by none; the rooms in want of ventilation and white-washing.'[19] London was notorious for its warrens of alleyways and courts, the haunt of beggars and criminals, with squalid houses only a few streets from fashionable squares and their fine town-houses. Louis Simond was struck by the proximity of low and high life:

> We have in our neighbourhood one of those no-thoroughfare lanes or courts ... This one is inhabited by a colony of Irish labourers, who fill every cellar and every garret,–a family in each room; very poor, very uncleanly, and very turbulent. They give each other battle every Saturday

night . . . We should never have known that there were such wretches as these in London, if we had not happened to reside in Orchard Street, Portman Square, which is one of the finest parts of the town.[20]

Renting a home was far more common than owning one. In April 1808 Nelly Weeton decided to let out the house that she had inherited from her mother at Upholland in Lancashire: 'On Wednesday, I let my house to a Mr. Winstanley, a watch-maker, who I am told is very likely to pay his rent regularly. His wife and children are above the common order and not likely to injure the house. I mean to draw up a little agreement for him to sign; to leave the house in as good repair as he finds it; to pay half a year's rent on entering it &c. He is to pay eight guineas a year'.[21] The plan was to close her late mother's dame school that generated a modest income, move to cheaper rented lodgings and live off her small amount of capital and Mr Winstanley's rent, but first of all she needed to 'dispose of my furniture, pack up what I shall want, and whitewash the house'.[22]

Whitewash, a solution of lime and chalk mixed with other additives, was brushed on interior and exterior walls like paint. It took several days to set, forming a white surface that could be coloured with other substances; in some areas animal blood or vegetable dye was added to give exterior walls a pink colour. Whitewash was a cheap way of decorating rooms. More expensive options included textile hangings, wallpaper, painting and wainscoting. In 1817 William Holland was decorating parts of the vicarage at Over Stowey. His daughter's bedroom had wallpaper, but he hired a painter for some of the woodwork, inside and out: 'The painter from Stowey has been here and painted the outward gate green and the skirting boards along the passage and stairs a chocolate colour.'[23]

Wallpaper became especially popular with the middle classes from the late eighteenth century, and businesses based primarily in London would send out samples to customers far beyond the capital.[24] Local upholsterers usually sold wallpaper and advertised their wares in newspapers. In April 1789 the *Ipswich Journal* announced: 'John Sparrow, Upholsterer, Cabinet-maker, Appraiser, and Auctioneer, Buttermarket, Ipswich . . . has just laid in a fresh assortment of every article in the upholstery branch, particularly ... a great variety of elegant paper hangings, from 2½d. to 2s. 6d. per yard; every pattern sold at the London prices, and hung at a very low rate. Patterns sent to any distance.'[25]

The customer would select a wallpaper pattern and place an order for a number of rolls, just as James Woodforde did in 1785. He visited an upholsterer in Norwich to choose what to order for the Weston Longville parsonage, and when the paper arrived he and his niece did the work themselves: 'Nancy and self very busy most of the morning and evening in papering the attic chamber over my bedchamber.'[26] Whether one or two rooms were papered is unclear, but the job took them four days. The reason for middle-class people taking on such a task rather than hiring workmen or using their servants may have been the high cost of even the cheapest papers and the fear that a bungled job would waste a great deal of money.

In the summer of 1808, having let out her Upholland property, Nelly Weeton stayed with acquaintances in Liverpool until she found lodgings in an isolated house on the banks of the River Mersey, close to what is now the Wellington Dock:

I came here on the 18th of October, to a small, white, shabby-looking house, close to the sea shore, called Beacon's Gutter ... Edward Smith, his wife, and little boy (about 8 years old), compose the whole of the family, besides myself. Edward is in a tobacconist's warehouse, as a journeyman; his wife does nothing but take care of the house. In the summer they take in lodgers. They have, in general, very respectable families.[27]

Even a middle-class clergyman like William Jones could not provide for a growing family without sharing his home with lodgers, which he lamented: 'Though my wife often reminds me that I could not have *this* & *that*, without foreigners, and, now & then, threatens to put me on coarse fare and short allowance, when we have none of these inmates;– yet I cannot help thinking that I shall never truly enjoy my dear cottage, till it is clear of all but my own dear family ... If the taking of boarders enlarges my *income*, it most certainly curtails my *comforts*.'[28]

After one year, Nelly Weeton returned to Liverpool and then moved to the Lake District as governess at Dove Nest, a house overlooking Lake Windermere that was originally built for John Benson (who also owned Dove Cottage which he rented to William Wordsworth). Nelly's employer, Edward Pedder, was now renting Dove Nest, as she told her brother Tom: 'Mr. P. gives a hundred a year for the house and land. Estates here let and sell amazingly high.'[29] Two decades later the poet Felicia Hemans rented Dove Nest, which she described as 'a lonely but beautifully situated cottage on the banks of Windermere'.[30]

A familiar theme in Jane Austen's novels and letters is lack of security and tenure – something she experienced when her father died. Wives often had to vacate the marital home on their husband's death, and the families of deceased clergymen were particularly vulnerable. In June 1798 William Jones expressed sympathy for the plight of a fellow cleric's family: 'Poor Mr. Fowler is gone – he died about 11 o'clock last night … His poor wife and three unestablished daughters, (the youngest of them not very young), are, I fear, left in distressed circumstances. How must their hearts droop at exchanging their present large, convenient, beautiful house for a cottage! A rectory, or a vicarage house, is certainly but a caravanseray; for it frequently exchanges its inmates.'[31]

Because rents varied enormously, finding somewhere reasonable could be difficult. Sarah Wilkinson considered all kinds of accommodation in London in 1809 while her husband was away, serving in the navy: 'I was looking at some lodgings that were to let in Knightsbridge the other evening,' she told him. 'For a first floor 3 rooms and a kitchen thirty pounds; without the kitchen twenty five pounds, and another place with only two rooms on the floor twenty pounds per year.'[32] To consider a place without a kitchen might seem strange, but the urban poor were lucky even to share a kitchen, relying instead on street vendors and inns for cooked food if they had no fireplace. Two months later, William Wilkinson decided that they should rent a terraced house in east London. 'I think I see us now living in our house in Poplar Row,' he wrote, 'and sitting in the parlour in a winter evening, you and Fanny at your needle and myself reading ... We would let the first floor and one of the rooms upstairs.'[33] Not even a naval warrant officer could afford to rent a London house without subletting.

Finding a place to live was only the start, since many houses were let unfurnished. Ready-made furniture, both new and secondhand, could be bought, and in November 1789 Parson Woodforde purchased items from one of the cabinet makers on Hog Hill in Norwich: 'Bought this day of Willm Hart, Cabinet Maker on Hog Hill Norwich, 2 large second hand double-flapped mohogany tables, also one second hand mohogany dressing table with drawers, also one new mohogany washing-stand, for all which paid 4.14.6, that is, for the 2 tables 2.12.6, dressing table 1.11.6, mohogany wash-stand 0.10.6. I think the whole of it to be very cheap.'[34]

Furniture was also built to order. Designs would be agreed with the cabinet-maker, often with reference to one of the design books issued by fashionable London craftsmen. Thomas Chippendale was the first to publish such a book (*The Gentleman and Cabinet Maker's Directory*) in 1754, but by the end of the century George Hepplewhite's designs (published in 1788 as *The Cabinet-Maker and Upholsterer's Guide*) and Thomas Sheraton's four volumes of *The Cabinet Maker's and Upholsterer's Drawing Book* (published from 1791) were more in vogue. Less famous designers also issued catalogues. Cabinet makers would remodel furniture, making a piece more fashionable or turning it into something entirely different. This is what the Austens chose to do at Southampton. 'Our dressing table is constructing on the spot,' Jane told Cassandra in February 1807, 'out of a large kitchen table.'[35]

Most families owned very few items of furniture and could not afford to buy anything new. Travelling from Taunton to Bristol in 1810, soon after arriving in England, Louis Simond glimpsed inside several rural cottages which were modestly furnished: 'The villages along the road are in general not beautiful,—the houses very poor; the walls old and rough ... Peeping in, as we pass along, the floors appear to be a pavement of round stones like the streets,—a few seats, in the form of short benches,—a table or two,—a spinning wheel,—a few shelves.'[36]

The more expensive the house, the larger the rooms, the higher the ceilings and the more windows they possessed. Every house incurred a window tax, in two parts: a relatively low flat-rate tax (which in 1778 became a variable tax related to the value of the house) and a higher variable rate depending on the number of windows. The tax on windows was constantly changing, and the introduction of further taxes in 1784 may have prompted Woodforde to take action: 'Mr Hardy and boy fastened up 3 windows with brick for me.'[37] Blocking up windows was a common way of avoiding the tax – widely regarded as a tax on light and air. Woodforde, who ran a modest establishment, frequently noted what he paid, as in May 1788 when the taxes ranged from windows to servants:

| | |
|---|---|
| To J$^s$. Pegg [tax collector] this morning – Qrs. Land Tax | 3.0.0 |
| To D°. ½ years window tax | 2.13.3 |
| To D°. ditto house ditto | 0.1.9 |
| To D°. ditto male servant tax | 1.5.0 |
| To D°. ditto female Do | 0.10.0 |
| To D°. ditto horse tax | 0.10.0 |
| To D°. ditto cart Do | 0.1.0[38] |

Upper- and middle-class people such as Woodforde had leisure time because their household chores were done by servants. Without servants their lives would have been so very different. The lower classes had less time and energy because they had no servants – they *were* the servants. Jane Austen was accustomed to having servants, often mentioning them in her letters. In October 1798 she wrote to Cassandra from Steventon when one of them left: 'We do not seem likely to have any other maidservant at present, but Dame Staples will supply the place of one. Mary has hired a young girl from Ashe who has never been out to service to be her scrub, but James fears her not being strong enough for the place.'[39] She added: 'Earle [Harwood] and his wife live in the most private manner imaginable at Portsmouth, without keeping a servant of any kind. What a prodigious innate love of virtue she must have, to marry under such circumstances!'[40] Her tone is ironic, but in an era without electricity or labour-saving appliances, domestic chores were hard and time-consuming.

When a family's income was reduced, servants had to go. In *Sense and Sensibility* Miss Elinor Dashwood persuades her widowed mother to economise: 'Her wisdom ... limited the number of their servants to three; two maids and a man, with whom they were speedily provided from amongst those who had formed their establishment at Norland.'

By contrast, Nelly Weeton was not brought up with servants, but spent her time looking after her mother and their house. In her new role as governess at Dove Nest she took time to adjust to the wealthy household. 'At supper we had two servants in livery attending,' she confided to a friend, 'and some display of plate, silver nutcrackers, &c., and some things of which poor ignorant I knew not the use. I felt a little awkward, but as you may suppose, strove not to let it appear.'[41] In respectable households, manservants were expected to wear livery, usually a recognisable jacket and breeches. Because the lifestyle at Dove Nest was so different to what she had previously known, Nelly described the household to another friend: 'I found on my arrival here, an establishment of five servants (two men and three maids), a curricle, four or five horses, five or six dogs, two pigs, and a whole host of rats, too many to be counted.'[42]

Servants often found employment at hiring fairs, or were recommended by friends and family.[43] Many were hired for one year only and were at the mercy of their employers, who could dismiss them with bad character references or no references at all and abuse them without fear of reprisals. In 1777 a tax was imposed on manservants, which affected the numbers employed, and in 1785 a tax was also imposed on female servants but repealed six years later. It was customary to pay servants a sum of money on taking up their post, with the rest of their wages paid in arrears. In mid-January 1798 Woodforde was late paying his servants:

After breakfast I paid my servants their year's wages due Janry 5th 1798 as follows.

| To Benj. Leggatt, my farming man | pd. | 10.0.0 |
| To Bretingham Scurl, my footman | pd. | 8.0.0 |
| To Betty Dade, my house-maid | pd. | 5.5.0 |
| To Sally Gunton, my cook & dairy maid | pd. | 5.5.0 |
| To Barnabas Woodcock, my yard-boy | pd. | 2.2.0[44] |

Apart from these live-in servants, Woodforde also relied on his unmarried niece Anna Maria Woodforde, usually called Nancy or Miss Woodforde. Born at Ansford in Somerset in 1757, she went to live at the Weston Longville parsonage in Norfolk in 1779 and remained there for the rest of her uncle's life, becoming his house-keeper.[45] The wages of his servants were lower than those of agricultural workers, who usually earned £12 a year or more, or those of industrial workers, who almost always earned more than that, while wages of skilled craftsmen might be in the region of £20 or £30. Live-in servants did have board and lodging and received other extras, such as cast-off clothes and sometimes lengths of cloth for making their garments.

Nothing like a career structure existed, but a good servant might aspire to grander households, higher wages and perhaps a better position. In 1784 Woodforde lost one maid and immediately hired another:

> After dinner I paid Lizzy half a years wages due this day, and then dismissed her from my service, as she is going on my recommendation to Weston House. I gave her extraordinary 0.2.6. I paid her for wages 1.6.6. In the evening sent Ben with a market cart for my new maid who lives at Mattishall and she came here about 8 at night and she supped and slept here. Her name is Molly Dade about 17 years of age – a very smart girl and pretty I think. Her friends bear great characters of industry &c.[46]

This was a rise in status for Lizzy, because Weston House was the residence of Squire Custance, though this did not mean that conditions would necessarily be better. A few years later Woodforde noted: 'Great complainings at Weston-House. Servants complaining to their Master that they had not victuals enough owing to the house-keeper,

Hetty Yallop, keeping them very short.'[47]

Servants worked long hours and could be called upon at any time of the day or night. William Holland was extremely intolerant of anything resembling idleness and expected his servants to labour tirelessly. His diary is littered with complaints about his manservant Robert Coles, as in November 1799: 'Tis a difficult thing to get a servant that is worth any thing. He has some good qualities, but the bad ones outweigh them. His slowness and laziness and want of method puts me out of patience. When the year is out he must go.'[48] He obviously changed his mind, as Robert was kept on, though the circumstances of his eventual parting are unknown because the relevant volume of Holland's diary is missing.

Someone with only one or two small, sparsely furnished rooms to call their home might have no servants at all. Nelly Weeton remembered her old room at Upholland: 'A fire in my room on a cold winter's evening, was one of the greatest comforts I had during that long, dreary, solitary season; and many a snug sit have I had there, shut up in a box 7 feet by 9, with a bed, a chest of drawers, two chairs, and a wash-stand in it, (don't peep under the bed now!) with just spare room for myself and the fire, and a tea-tray put over the washstand to serve for a table.'[49]

Descriptions of the everyday contents of rooms, such as chamberpots hidden beneath the bed as Nelly alludes to here, are uncommon in letters and diaries because they were considered unexceptional, but the observations of travellers like Carl Moritz can provide fascinating glimpses of how people lived. He was struck by the bedding in England that was so different to his native Germany: 'The custom of sleeping without a feather-bed for a covering, particularly pleased me. You here lie between two sheets, and are covered with blankets, which, without oppressing you, keep you sufficiently warm.'[50] Feather beds in England meant mattresses to lie on, not quilts or duvets, and when travelling through Hampshire in 1782, John Byng criticised the Crown Inn at Ringwood: 'Of all the beds I ever lay in, that of last night was the very worst, for there could not be more than fifty feathers in the bolster, and pillow, or double that number in the feather-bed; so there I lay tossing, and tumbling all night, without any sleep, or place to lay my head upon, tho' I rowl'd [rolled] all the bolster into one heap.'[51]

Warm bedding was essential because houses were so cold and draughty, at the mercy of the weather, with ill-fitting doors and windows. All too often they were in some state of disrepair, especially with poorly maintained roofs. Following the Great Fire of 1666, thatched roofs were banned in London – tiles and slates had to be used instead. Elsewhere in England, roofing and other construction materials reflected local geology and the resources available, creating a distinctive character in each region. Many buildings outside London had thatched roofs of reed or straw, and in January 1784 Woodforde noted: 'I rejoiced much this morning on shooting an old wood-pecker, which had teised [teased] me a long time in pulling out the reed from my house. He had been often shot at by me and others ... For this last 3 years in very cold weather did he use to come here and destroy my thatch. Many holes he has made this year in the roof, and as many before.'[52]

Unlike modern heating that can be switched on or off, rooms were heated by inefficient open fires. In the summer of 1808, Jane Austen complained to Cassandra: 'What cold, disagreeable weather, ever since Sunday! I dare say you have fires every day. My kerseymere Spencer [woollen jacket] is quite the comfort of our evening walks.'[53] The winter cold could be dreadful, something that Woodforde described in January 1789 in Norfolk: 'I never felt the cold so much in my life before. It froze the whole day long within doors and very sharp ... The air very clear and very piercing.'[54]

It is difficult to imagine the temperature *indoors* being below freezing, but the 1790s saw particularly harsh winters, as Woodforde described in 1792: 'The most severe frost last night and this morning as I ever felt. The milk in the dairy in the pans was one piece of ice and the water above stairs in the basons [ceramic wash basins] froze in a few minutes after being put there this morn.'[55] Two years later the winter was even worse: 'Very severe frost indeed, freezes sharp within doors and bitter cold it is now. Two women froze to death Saturday last going from Norwich Market to their home.'[56] The next year, January 1795, was also bad: 'The frost ... froze last night the chamber pots above stairs ... The ice in the pond in the yard which is broke every morning for the horses, froze two inches in thickness last night, when broke this morning.'[57]

At the end of the decade, harsh winters were causing widespread problems, and Woodforde reported heavy snowfalls in February 1799:

> The weather more severe than ever with continued snow all last night and continued snowing all this whole day, with a good deal of wind which have drifted the snow in some places so very deep as to make almost every road impassable – in many roads 15 feet deep ... Such weather with so much snow I never knew before, not able to go to Jericho [the outside toilet]. Dreadful weather for the poor people and likewise for all kinds of cattle &c. &c. It is dangerous almost for any person to be out.[58]

Coal was the predominant fuel for households wherever it could be supplied cheaply by sea, rivers and canals. The growing canal network made coal increasingly available inland, as Frederick Eden recorded in 1795 in Louth, Lincolnshire, as part of his survey of the poor: 'Coal is now brought by a canal from the Humber to within ½ a mile of this town, which has considerably lessened the prices of fuel. It is hoped, that the introduction of coal will induce the inhabitants to desist from their ancient practice ... of using the dung of their cattle for fuel.'[59] Peat and turf were cut in some areas, something Eden observed at Orton in Westmorland: 'The fuel is principally turf, procured from the commons: coal must be brought 30 miles by land carriage.'[60]

Where coal was too expensive, wood was frequently burned, though gathering firewood was a constant struggle for the poor, especially when the common land was enclosed. Eden described how the children of poor agricultural labourers obtained their firewood at the village of Seend in Wiltshire: 'If the labourer is employed in hedging and ditching, he is allowed to take home a faggot every evening, while that work lasts: but this is by no means sufficient for his consumption: his children, therefore, are sent into the fields, to collect wood where they can; and neither hedges nor trees are spared by the young marauders, who are thus ... educated in the art of thieving.'[61]

In Over Stowey, Holland complained about some village children who 'have committed great depradations on my new hedges by drawing off the laid sticks. I must call them to account for this. There is wood sufficient on the hills [Quantocks], and yet these wretches prefer damaging the hedges of their neighbours to fetching it.'[62] In 1798 Dorothy and William Wordsworth were living at nearby Alfoxton House, while Samuel Taylor Coleridge ('a democratic libertine', according to Holland)[63] was at Nether Stowey – writing some of his best poetry. They often took walks together over the Quantock hills, gathering firewood as they went, as on one occasion when Dorothy recorded: 'Walked with Coleridge over the hills ... Gathered sticks in the wood.'[64]

In winter the fire was the focal point of any room – usually the kitchen in poorer households. With open fires used for cooking, smoke actually poured from the chimneys all year round. The black fallout from soot in the air and the pervading smell of coal smoke might diminish in towns in the summer, but it never disappeared. While in London in the summer of 1802, Dorothy Wordsworth was therefore surprised by the unusual distance they could see: 'The city ... made a most beautiful sight as we crossed Westminster Bridge. The houses were not overhung by their cloud of smoke, and they were spread out endlessly.'[65] In March 1810 Louis Simond gave a vivid description of the more normal winter smog:

It is difficult to form an idea of the kind of winter days in London; the smoke of fossil coals forms an atmosphere, perceivable for many miles, like a great round cloud attached to the earth. In the town itself, when the weather is cloudy and foggy, which is frequently the case in winter, this smoke increases the general dingy hue, and terminates the length of every street with a fixed grey mist, receding as you advance. But when some rays of sun happens to fall on this artificial atmosphere, its impure mass assumes immediately a pale orange tint ... loaded with small flakes of soot ... so light as to float without falling. This black snow sticks to your clothes and linen, or lights on your face. You just feel something on your nose, or your cheek,—the finger is applied mechanically, and fixes it into a black patch![66]

Smoke from open fires was also a nuisance indoors, and at Alfoxton Dorothy noted: 'The room smoked so that we were obliged to quit it'.[67] Woodforde had similar trouble: 'Very windy all the day, obliged to be in the parlour as our study smoaked so very much. Wind W.N.W.'[68] He had a running battle with this particular fireplace, commenting four years later: 'Had my study chimney-piece altered to day by Mr Hardy and to prevent its smoking, but am still afraid of it. This is, I believe the 4th time of altering it.'[69] Smoking chimneys were so common that specialist workmen, 'chimney doctors', offered to remedy such problems.

On cold, dark evenings better-off families would sit together in the parlour or drawing room with its comforting fire. The temptation to get close to the hearth meant that long garments easily caught alight, and newspapers were full of reports of women being burnt to death. This was a hazard that had no class boundaries, with rich women as much at risk as poor ones. Nelly Weeton was horrified to witness her ten-year-old pupil Mary Gertrude (Mr Pedder's daughter by his previous marriage) die at Dove Nest in February 1810:

I heard a scream. I ran instantly. I heard her scream again, and, opening the parlour door, met her running towards it, the flames higher than her head – What a sight it was! Without the loss of a moment, I flew into the servants' hall for the ironing blanket – it was washing week and I recollected seeing it there . . . I threw the blanket to the nurse, who was trying to extinguish the flames with her apron. While she was rolling her in the blanket, I ran again into the butler's pantry and servants' hall, to find some water to throw upon her, and cool the burning flesh. I could find no liquid of any kind.[70]

There was no water to hand because Dove Nest, like most houses, had no piped supply. When a house caught fire, little could be done, as on Easter morning in 1793 at Weston Longville, while Woodforde was conducting a service:

Before I got out of Church . . . heard that one of the widow's cottages on Greensgate, where poor old John Peachman and his wife lived, was burnt to the ground whilst we were at Church. The poor woman was at Church, and her husband gone to Lyng. It almost distracted the poor woman, having lost almost all that she had. The house was burnt down to the ground in about an hour. Poor John Heaver's house [adjacent] caught fire once or twice, and if it had not been for the kind assistance of neighbours, it must have been burnt.[71]

The need for efficient fire fighting and insurance against losses was made clear by the Great Fire of London and led to the formation of fire insurance companies such as the Sun Fire Office and the Royal Exchange. These companies operated their own fire brigades, and insured properties were identified by the fire marks of the companies on the front wall of the property – a lead or copper plaque with a readily recognisable design.[72] These fire brigades operated primarily in towns, where industrial and domestic buildings crowded together, increasing the risk of fire spreading. While a fire brigade's primary concern was dealing with insured buildings, it was in their interests to assist with nearby fires, and by the early nineteenth century the brigades from different insurance companies frequently cooperated.

Unattended candles was a common cause of fires, something that agitated Woodforde:

Ben [his manservant] went to help Stephen Andrews's men at harvest, came home in the evening in liquor ... I saw a light burning in Ben's room, upon that I walked up into his room, and there saw him laying flat upon his back on the bed asleep with his cloaths on and the candle burning on the table. I waked him, made him put out the candle and talked with him a little on it, but not much as he was not in a capacity of answering but little. I was very uneasy to see matters go on so badly.[73]

Although experiments were taking place with gas street lighting, it would be many years before homes had gas lamps. As with heating, no instant lighting system existed. Instead, candles could be lit with spills ignited from the hearth or from another burning candle, or else tinderboxes were employed. These metal or wooden containers held a flint, a firesteel and some combustible material (the 'tinder'), such as very dry cloth fibres, lichen or thin bark. The flint from the tinderbox would be struck against the firesteel to create a spark that ignited the tinder. It was then convenient to use matches, which were little pieces of card, rope or wood dipped in sulphur that caught fire easily.[74] A match would be lit from the glowing tinder to produce a flame that lit the candle. Lighted candles were carried in holders to avoid spilling the hot wax, but walking too fast with the candle or walking through a draught could easily extinguish the flame. Outdoors, candles were put into protective metal lanterns (or 'lanthorns') with pierced sides or panels of thin translucent horn or sometimes of glass.

Candles, made and sold by licensed chandlers, were heavily taxed, which encouraged their clandestine manufacture.[75] The best-quality ones were of beeswax – some were made from thin sheets of beeswax wrapped round a flax or cotton wick and others were laboriously manufactured as solid candles.[76] Such candles were favoured by the wealthy and the Church, and they were better for chandeliers (often called 'lustres') in public buildings like theatres, where the light would be reflected and magnified by the numerous pieces of glass ('drops'). Beeswax candles might also be mounted in candelabra or candlesticks, or fixed on wall brackets. Also of high quality were candles of spermaceti, a waxy oil from the head of sperm whales. Unlike beeswax candles, these could be made in moulds. Both beeswax and spermaceti candles burned slowly and brightly, producing little smoke or smell.

Louis Simond found the inns in southern England superior to those elsewhere in the country, but was annoyed to discover that 'wax-candles are forced upon the travellers, whether they choose or not this piece of luxury, for which 2s. 6d. a-night is added to the bill'.[77] He expected cheaper, everyday tallow candles, which were manufactured by repeatedly dipping a cotton or flax wick into hot animal fat, which hardened on cooling. These candles ('dips') yielded a poor flickering light and an unpleasant smell.

Tallow candles were also formed in metal moulds using superior mutton tallow rather than beef or pig, with some of their wicks dipped in wax, as seen in one London advertisement in 1807:

TALLOW CANDLES with WAXED WICKS –
In consequence of the Wicks of these Candles being coated with Wax,
These Candles have the following advantages:– 1st, They are seldom, if
ever, subject to what is called a thief in the candle:– 2ndly, They will not
gutter, except from bad snuffing, or carrying about:– and 3dly, They burn
longer and give a brighter light than the usual mould candles. Sold only
at the Candle and Soap Company's Warehouse, No. 182, Fleet-street, two
doors from Fetter-lane.[78]

Tallow candles burned at a lower temperature and produced a large
amount of hot fat, which could run down the sides, a process called
guttering. They needed thicker wicks, which tended to smoke and
could cause guttering when they became too long – something
described as a 'thief in the candle' because so much of the candle was
wasted. The wick was therefore trimmed or 'snuffed' with snuffers (a
type of scissors) while in use, without snuffing out the flame.

Poorer families could not even afford tallow candles, but might
make rushlights, which were not taxed. Writing at Selborne in 1775,
where he was curate, Gilbert White explained that after obtaining
rushes for the wicks, their outer coating was peeled off except for one
strip supporting the inner pith. After drying, the rushes were drawn
through waste cooking grease and fat:

A pound of common grease may be procured for four pence; and about six
pounds of grease will dip a pound of rushes; and one pound of rushes may
be bought for one shilling: so that a pound of rushes, medicated and
ready for use, will cost three shillings. If men that keep bees will mix a
little wax with the grease, it will give it a consistency, and render it more
cleanly; and make the rushes burn longer ... A good rush, which measured in length two feet four inches and an half ... burnt only three
minutes short of an hour: and a rush still of greater length has been
known to burn one hour and a quarter. These rushes give a good clear
light.[79]

White estimated that a farthing's worth of rushlights provided over
five hours of illumination. Because rushlights burned best at an angle

of about 45 degrees, they were placed in simple metal or wooden holders.[80]

Another simple centuries-old method of lighting was the open lamp – a shallow metal or ceramic container filled with oil in which a wick floated. Such lamps were practical in coastal areas where cheap fish oil was available, such as train oil from pilchards, but they generated more smoke and foul smells than candles. Towards the end of the eighteenth century the Argand lamp with a glass chimney was introduced, which used whale or vegetable oil as fuel. Visiting London in 1786, Sophie von La Roche was impressed by the new lamps: 'We finished the evening at tea investigating Argand lamps of all descriptions. Their advantage lies in a wick which burns around a tube fixed inside a glass funnel higher than the flame, with an air current beneath to prevent flickering and smoke. There is a paper screen on top.'[81]

Candles or lamps illuminated only small parts of rooms, but open fires were brighter, so that everyone congregated around the hearth for light as well as for warmth. In poorer households this was the kitchen fire. In all types of home, from the poorest to the aristocratic, cooking was done over open fires, and the Frenchman Louis Simond observed that 'an English cook only boils and roasts'.[82] At the most basic level, food was boiled in pots suspended over a simple fire, but wealthier families had an open range for cooking.[83]

Early open ranges had a freestanding grate – a container raised above the hearth, so that the ashes fell through and enabled the coal to burn efficiently. These ranges became more sophisticated, acquiring sides and backs, and any oven was built to one side with its own grate and flue. By the late eighteenth century ironfounders were developing integral ovens that took their heat from the open fire. As well as adjustable hooks for suspending pots over the flames, other accessories might be fitted to the grate, such as hotplates over part of the fire. Years later, Victorian cast-iron ranges had an integral oven, water heater with tap and hotplates, and the fire was fully enclosed.

The roasting of meat was not done in an oven. Instead, horizontal spits were placed in front of (not above) the open fire, and the juices and fat were collected in a pan underneath. These horizontal spits were turned by hand or by mechanical contrivances such as weight-driven jacks and smoke jacks (fitted inside a chimney so that they rotated by the hot smoke rising from the fire). Alternatively, clockwork bottle jacks might be suspended over the open range – the meat was hung from a hook, and the clockwork mechanism kept the meat turning while it roasted. The *Morning Chronicle* in 1807 advertised these cooking aids:

IMPROVED OECONOMICAL KITCHEN RANGES, &c.– At the London Patent Register Stove Manufactory, the corner of Brooke-street, Holborn, are finished and ready for the inspection of the Public, KITCHEN RANGES, from the latest improved principle, combining oeconomy with utility. Likewise, Smoke Jacks, which may be oiled by any servant, without going up the chimney.[84]

Such machines needed maintenance and repair, as Woodforde found with his weight-driven jack: 'Mr Symonds came here this afternoon and cleaned my jack and took away the compass wheel, as it required so large a weight to it and was always breaking the line. I hope now it will go better and with a less weight.'[85]

In better-off homes, cookbooks were increasingly used in the kitchen. Many were published during the eighteenth century, and the most popular ones remained in print for years, such as *The Art of Cookery Made Plain and Easy*, first published by Hannah Glasse in 1747. Aimed at households with servants, it was designed both for the servants and for the mistress of the house (so that she could direct them). Because Glasse was writing a book to be read by servants, she apologised to her lady readers for the use of simple language: 'my intention is to instruct the lower sort, and therefore [I] must treat them in their own way'.[86]

Glasse's cookbook contained a variety of household information, including all kinds of recipes, such as how to 'roast a pig' and 'make a currey the indian way', handy tips on how to 'keep venison or hares sweet, or to make them fresh when they stink' and 'how to keep clear from bugs'.[87] The latter process advised sealing the draught holes in the affected room and then fumigating it by burning brimstone on a charcoal fire, but after six hours, 'If you find great swarms about the room, and some not dead, do this over again, and you will be clear.'[88]

This and other popular cookbooks were reprinted, copied and plagiarised over many years, but they would have been of little use to working-class people, who subsisted mainly on bread, potatoes and cheese, with some vegetables, fruit and meat. The type of food varied across the regions of England, so that in Kendal in Westmorland in March 1795, Frederick Eden recorded: 'Oat-cake is the principal bread used by the labouring classes: the men generally eat hasty-pudding, or boiled milk, twice a day: the women live much on tea, but have, of late, discontinued the use of sugar. Potatoes are a general article for dinner: they are sometimes eaten with a little butter, and sometimes with meat.'[89] The poor were accustomed to buying grain in small quantities and having it ground at the local mill, or else they purchased flour direct from the millers. Mills, particularly windmills, were to be seen everywhere. When he arrived at Liverpool in 1805, Benjamin Silliman remarked: 'The city is surrounded by lofty windmills, which are among the first objects that strike a stranger coming in from the sea.'[90] They were so commonplace in the landscape that after one violent gale in Norfolk, Woodforde simply noted: 'Many windmills blown down.'[91]

The increase in population, bad harvests in the 1790s and the lengthy wars with France led to food shortages. Farmers made more profits by selling in bulk to the millers and by holding back their crops until prices rose. This withholding was made possible by the banks lending farmers money as a low-risk investment. Similarly, the millers increased their income by selling flour directly to the bakers. Inevitably, bread prices rose, and in November 1795 Eden noted at Hereford: 'The labouring classes, who usually bake their own bread, say, it is extremely difficult to procure a small quantity of corn from the farmer; and that the millers and mealmen buy it in large quantities, and exact a large profit from the consumer.'[92]

A few months before, the caricaturist James Gillray had lampooned William Pitt, the Prime Minister, for having advised people to eat meat rather than bread, a remark worthy of Marie Antoinette, demonstrating how little the politician knew about England's poor. Gillray's cartoon, 'The British butcher, supplying John Bull with a substitute for bread', depicted Pitt as a butcher, accompanied by a verse:

BILLY the BUTCHER'S advice to JOHN BULL.

Since bread is so dear, (and you say you must Eat,)
For to save the expence, you must live upon Meat;
And as Twelve Pence the Quartern you can't pay for Bread
Get a Crown's worth of Meat, – it will serve in its stead.[93]

Sporadic food riots were breaking out across England, but rather than loot, the mob used the threat of violence to force profiteers to sell their goods more cheaply. The tailor Thomas Carter recalled these wretched times of his childhood in Colchester, Essex:

The first [memory] is the great scarcity of wheat and other bread-corn during the year 1800. This to poor people was the source of much distress. My father's wages were but ten shillings and sixpence per week, and my mother's little [dame] school brought from two to three shillings more. With very little besides this scanty income, they had to provide for the wants of themselves and four children, while bread was sold at the enormous price of one shilling and tenpence for the quartern loaf. We were consequently forced to put up with very insufficient fare, and sometimes with that which was rather hurtful than nutritious.[94]

Unscrupulous bakers concealed cheaper, often harmful, additives in brown bread. Consumers therefore preferred white bread, but bakers could also adulterate this bread with chalk, alum or even bone-meal. Another ploy was selling undersize loaves, though authorities did try to prevent such abuses. News of the arrest and prosecution of bakers was always popular, as in London in October 1807: 'MARL-BOROUGH-STREET.– A Baker, of the name of Dix, who resides in High-street, Mary-le-Bonne, was charged by the Parish Inspectors with exposing a quantity of bread deficient by weight. A quantity of light bread was produced by the Officers, and there appeared in the whole a deficiency of 29 ounces, for which the Defendant was fined 7l. 10s.'[95]

Underhand tricks were likewise done with milk. In a survey of agriculture in 1806, John Middleton, a land surveyor, reckoned that over 8500 cows were kept for milk near London.[96] Farmers were paid for milking the herds by dairy retailers who, as he explained, diluted the milk:

Every cow-house is provided with a milk room ... mostly furnished with a pump, to which the retailers apply in rotation; not secretly but openly, before any person that may be standing by; from which they pump water into the milk vessels at their discretion. The pump is placed there expressly for that purpose, and it is seldom used for any other. A considerable cow-keeper in Surrey has a pump of this kind, which goes by the name of the *black cow* (from the circumstance of its being painted with that colour); it is said to yield more than all the rest put together.[97]

Matters were worse where no pump was provided,

for in that case the retailers are not even careful to use clean water. Some of them have been seen to dip their pails in a common horse-trough. And, what is still more disgusting, though equally true, one cow-house happens to stand close to the edge of a stream, into which runs much of the dung, and most of the urine, of the cows; and even in this stream, so foully impregnated, they have been observed to dip their milk-pails.[98]

The milk was next taken to the retailers' homes and left for a day, so that the cream rose to the surface to be skimmed off. The deteriorating milk was then sold as fresh, while the cream was sold separately or made into butter, particularly when the upper classes were in town: 'When the families of fashion are in London for the winter season, the consumption, and consequent deterioration, of milk, are at the highest. During the summer months, when such families are for the most part in the country, the milk may probably be of a better quality.'[99] Middleton rightly thought that the situation was scandalous: 'A cow-keeper informs me, that the retail milk-dealers are, for the most part, the refuse of other employments;

possessing neither character, decency of manners, nor cleanliness. No delicate person could possibly drink the milk, were they fully acquainted with the filthy manners of these dealers.'[100]

All kinds of other foods were adulterated, either by adding cheaper substances to increase profits, or else by freshening unfit food, such as sprinkling fresh blood over putrid meat. For the lower classes, the best meat they might eat was ham or bacon, but more likely the less popular parts of pigs or else rabbits and hares, sometimes obtained by poaching. Birds of all sizes were eaten by all classes, from larks and pigeons to pheasants, chickens and occasionally swans. In June 1808 Nelly Weeton received a gift from her brother Tom: 'My uncle is obliged to you for your present of rooks. As my uncle is so very fond of those little nick-nacks ... I took the liberty of presenting the two you intended for me, to him, so that the whole five composed a handsome pie for his dinner, and my Aunt's too.'[101] Rooks were a nuisance, but at least they were edible.

Other birds were often considered a delicacy. In 1788, when John Byng and a friend were exploring the Sussex downland around Hastings, they gathered ingredients for their dinner:

> After walking the beach, we ascended the steep hill ... searching many turf-traps set for wheat-ears [which nest in holes in the ground], when the custom is to leave a penny for every caught bird you take away. Within the castle, we seated ourselves for some time, delighted with the weather, the freshness of the sea-breeze and the cheerfulness of the scenery; till the shepherd came to survey his traps, when we paid him sevenpence for his capture of seven birds, whom we sat instantly to pluck in preparation of our dinner spit; and it wou'd have made others laugh to have seen us at our poulterers work; which, being finish'd, we hasten'd back to the inn [to have them cooked].[102]

Some cookbooks included recipes for preserving these birds: '*To pot wheatears*. Pick them very clean, season them with pepper and salt, put them in a pot, cover them with butter, and bake them one hour; take them and put them in a colander to drain the liquor away; then cover them with clarified butter, and they will keep.'[103]

Parson Woodforde enjoyed his meals and recorded numerous details about food in his diary. In January 1780 he ate some swan at a dinner with the squire:

We had for dinner a calfs head, boiled fowl and tongue, a saddle of mutton rosted on the side table, and a fine swan rosted with currant jelly sauce for the first course. The second course a couple of wild fowl called dun fowls, larks, blamange, tarts &c. &c. and a good desert of fruit after amongst which was a damson cheese. I never eat a bit of swan before, and I think it good eating with sweet sauce. The swan was killed 2 weeks before it was eat and yet not the least bad taste in it.[104]

Beef roasted on spits was so popular that the French nickname for the English was 'le rosbif' (roast beef), though mutton, lamb, pork and venison were likewise favoured. Most of the carcass was cooked, with nothing allowed to go to waste, as seen in cookbooks which had recipes for dishes like 'Ox cheeks, baked', 'Neat's feet, fried', 'Pigs feet and ears, to pickle', 'Lamb stones, fried' and 'Calves heads, in ragout'.[105] Various kinds of fish were consumed, and being cheap and plentiful, oysters were widely eaten by the lower classes.

Vegetables were frequently referred to as 'garden stuff', which most people with gardens grew. Virtually nothing was imported, but wealthy estates had hothouses (greenhouses) for delicate produce like grapes. William Holland with his manservant was constantly growing vegetables. 'Busy in my garden this day with Robert,' he noted in mid-March 1800, 'preparing ground for early potatoes.'[106] Four days later: 'Very busy with Robert in the garden, we sowed some onions and carrots',[107] then 'Five rows of peas put in this morning, and I myself raked the asparagus bed and howed the cabbage.'[108] Later that week he recorded: 'Robert ... sowed some turnap [turnip] seeds among the currant and gooseberry bushes.'[109] Salads largely comprised lettuce and cucumbers, with Holland commenting later in June: 'Robert busy in the garden. He manages a cucumber bed for me but brings it on very slow, and late, like himself, yet the plants look healthy. As to myself I regard cucumbers little, and only eat them stewed, and the dung of the bed serves afterwards for the garden.'[110]

Holland never mentioned tomatoes. Few people grew them, and like most vegetables including cucumbers they were cooked, a fortunate precaution considering that cesspit contents were spread as manure.

He also took pride in the rest of his garden, with its lawns, shrubs and flower borders, and Louis Simond certainly found English lawns attractive, as he noted in June 1810:

> The ground, ploughed and harrowed carefully, is either sown or sodded; rolling and mowing, and a moist climate do the rest, for there is nothing at all peculiar in the grass itself. The rolling is principally done in the spring ... The mowing, or rather shaving of this smooth surface, is done once a week ... The grass must be wet with dew or rain, and the scythe very sharp; the blade is wide, and set so obliquely on the handle, as to lye very flat on the sod. The rollers are generally of cast iron, 18 or 20 inches in diameter, and two and a half or three feet long, hollow, and weigh about 500 pounds, moved about by one man; those drawn by a horse are, of course, three or four times heavier.[111]

In Norfolk Woodforde was also obsessed with his garden, and in June 1794 he bought a new roller for £4: 'Sent Ben early this morning to Norwich with my great cart, after my new garden roller of cast-iron. He returned home with it before two o'clock ... It is a very clever roller and is called the ballance roller, as the handle never goes to the ground. It is certainly very expensive, but certainly also very handy.'[112]

Most fruit that was grown in people's gardens was cooked rather than eaten raw, and sweet boiled puddings were so popular with all classes that they were another characteristic of the English. Along with roast beef, plum (or 'plumb') pudding was a national dish, frequently appearing in satirical prints – 'plums' in these puddings meant dried raisins:

*A good plum pudding.*
TAKE a pound and a quarter of beef sewet [suet], when skinned, and shred it very fine; then stone three quarters of a pound of raisins, and mix with it; add a grated nutmeg, a quarter of a pound of sugar, a little salt, a little sack, four eggs, four spoonsful of cream, and about half a pound of

fine flour, mixing them well together, pretty stiff; tie it in a cloth, and let it boil four hours. Melt butter thick for sauce.[113]

Food was difficult to keep fresh. In order to survive the winter, fruit and vegetables were stored, but vermin, mildew and freezing weather were constant hazards. Caught by an unusually hard frost in December 1784, Gilbert White in Selborne recorded: 'We were much obliged to the thermometers for the early information they gave us; and hurried our apples, pears, onions, potatoes, &c. into the cellar, and warm closets; while those who had not, or neglected such warnings, lost all their store of roots and fruits, and had their very bread and cheese frozen.'[114] The dreadful winter of 1798–9 prompted Woodforde to despair: 'Scarce ever known such distressed times ... no vegetation, every thing almost dead in the gardens ... All kind of garden-stuff, except potatoes that have been well covered and in ground, are almost all gone dead; potatoes that have been dug up, tho' kept in house are allmost all froze and useless.'[115]

Meat and dairy produce could be kept cool in pantries and cellars, but in hot weather everything deteriorated rapidly, as White observed in the summer of 1783: 'from *June* 23 to *July* 20 inclusive ... the heat was so intense that butchers' meat could hardly be eaten on the day after it was killed'.[116] Even during normal summers meat did not remain fresh for long, and so animals were slaughtered close to markets in the heart of towns and cities, especially in London. Cattle were driven to fairs across England from as far afield as Ireland, Wales and Scotland, their hooves fitted by blacksmiths with iron shoes specifically for the lengthy journey. Such was the huge number seen at Wetherby in Yorkshire in the autumn of 1789 that the local newspaper commented: 'A greater quantity of Scotch and Irish cattle have passed through Wetherby turnpike-bar, this season, than the oldest person ever remembers to have seen – most of which were for the South-country markets. One drover in particular had near 1000 beasts, all Irish ones.'[117]

A lot of food could be preserved by smoking, pickling or salting, while fruit might be made into jams and meat potted to keep it longer. Ice helped to chill food and drinks and enabled iced dishes to be made, including ice creams and sorbets. When she was staying at Lyme Regis in September 1804, Jane Austen wrote satirically to Cassandra: 'Your account of Weymouth contains nothing which strikes me so forcibly as there being no ice in the town. For every other vexation I was in some measure prepared, and particularly for your disappointment in not seeing the Royal Family go on board ... but for there being no ice what could prepare me? Weymouth is altogether a shocking place.'[118]

The wealthy had ice-houses in their gardens, in which ice could be kept successfully for much of the year. In severe winters, servants and labourers obtained ice from frozen lakes, canals and rivers, piling it on sledges or carts and then taking it to these ice-houses. During mild winters, ice may have been obtained instead from whaling vessels.[119] Most ice-houses were brick-built, domed or arched structures, partly underground, and the ice was loaded through the roof or a doorway. Bundles of straw or reeds were placed on the floor and sides as further insulation, enabling the ice to remain frozen for months. One story amused the *Morning Post* newspaper in 1811: 'A well-known miser not having given an entertainment during a summer, and his ice-house remaining still quite full in the month of January, his steward asked him what he should do with all the ice? "Why!" replied Mr. B. "let it *be given to the poor!*"'[120]

Ice-houses were even constructed beneath London's streets, sometimes with disastrous consequences, such as in 1802 by St Mary le Strand church: 'A Confectioner, who rents a house directly opposite ... on the northern side of the Strand, some time ago formed a plan of making an ice-house directly in front, under the street ... The workmen then proceeded to excavate ... digging below the cellars of the neighbouring houses.'[121] The whole lot caved in and 'the three houses next to it were placed in the most imminent danger, the flagway and cellars having fallen into the excavation'.[122]

The wealthy might have had ice, but water itself was not widely drunk because palatable supplies were not readily available. Elizabeth Ham recalled that for supper at her boarding school at Tiverton in Devon, 'we had a little bit of bread with a little bit of cheese on it, and a little cider in a little mug. No one in these days ever dreamt of drinking water.'[123] Devon was a county that made prodigious quantities of cider, but the main drink in England was 'small beer', also referred to as 'small ale' or 'common beer'. Woodforde called it 'table beer', while strong ales were just 'beer' or 'strong beer'. Small beer was safer than water, and because of its low alcohol content, it was not intoxicating.

As well as making his own table beer, Woodforde also made mead: 'Busy most part of the afternoon in making some mead wine, to fourteen pound of honey, I put four gallons of water, boiled it more than an hour with ginger and two handfulls of dried elder-flowers in it, and skimmed it well. Then I put it into a small tub to cool, and when almost cold I put in a large gravey-spoon full of fresh yeast, keeping it in a warm place, the kitchen during night.'[124] The honey for the mead came from the beehives that both he and his niece Nancy kept. In January 1798 Nancy received a new swarm: 'Mr. Stoughton of Sparham sent Miss Woodforde to day a skep of bees by his farming man Jon. Springle who brought them all the way on foot and upon his head tyed up in a cloth. He was 4 hours almost coming from Sparham [about 4 miles away]. I gave the man a good dinner, some strong beer, and made him a present besides of half a guinea in gold 10.6.'[125]

Alcohol was popular and drunk to excess by many, but a class divide existed, because the poorest drank beer and spirits – but rarely wine. The tax known as excise duty, payable on all alcoholic drinks, was frequently increased to help fund the ongoing wars. This was a highly unpopular move with most consumers, such as the clergyman William Jones: 'Most men know when they have had too little wine, especially since Mr. Pitt has *poisoned* – *alias* – highly taxed – wine.'[126] Apart from home brewing, one way of avoiding tax was buying liquor from smugglers. Smuggling formed a nationwide industry operated by numerous gangs, such as those encountered by John Byng in August 1782 when travelling through the New Forest: 'I cross'd a black heath where I met two gangs of smugglers, whom I wonder'd not to have seen oftener in my ride.'[127]

Parson Woodforde constantly bought gin, brandy and rum, as on one occasion the previous year when 'Clerk Hewitt of Mattishall

Burgh called on me this even' by desire of Mrs. Davy to taste some smuggled gin which I tasted and he is to bring me a tub this week.'[128] With much else heavily taxed, smugglers supplied a range of goods, including tea, which Woodforde also purchased: 'Andrews the Smuggler brought me this night about 11 o'clock a bagg of hyson tea 6 Pd weight. He frightned us a little by whistling under the parlour window just as we were going to bed. I ... paid him for the tea at 10s/6d per Pd.'[129] He regularly recorded illicit purchases, as in his diary entry for 17 May 1780: 'I did not go to bed till after 12 at night, as I expected Richd. Andrews the honest smuggler with some gin.'[130] Ten days later he paid Andrews £2 10s for two casks, so avoiding around £3 in duty – at a time when his senior maid earned £5 11s 6d a year and his highest-paid manservant £10.[131] In September 1809 William Wilkinson, serving in the Royal Navy, warned his wife: 'Don't buy any more tea or sugar. I expect some from Guernsey, but say nothing about it for fear that it should be seized.'[132]

Better-off families kept their tea in special lockable tea-caddies to prevent it being pilfered by the servants. It tended to be used sparingly, so that it was made as a fairly weak drink, to which milk and sugar were added. Temperance campaigners advocated tea instead of beer, but others insisted that beer was more nutritious for working people on poor diets, as well as better value for money. While tea had filtered down to the working classes, coffee remained the preserve of the coffee house and the middle and upper classes. It was drunk at home less frequently than tea, and the quality was extremely variable, often being criticised for being too dark and burnt, though Carl Moritz found the opposite: 'I would always advise those who wish to drink coffee in England, to mention before hand how many cups are to be made with half an ounce, or else the people will probably bring them a prodigious quantity of brown water; which (notwithstanding all my admonitions) I have not yet been able wholly to avoid.'[133]

For those who could afford to eat well, breakfast was the first meal of the day, though a minimal affair, rarely more than toast with tea or coffee, while poorer households drank small beer. Often the toast was made during the meal by holding slices of bread in front of the fire on toasting forks. 'A breakfast is a comfortable meal when our little family assemble around the breakfast table in good spirits with a strong blazing fire,' William Holland wrote in February 1800.[134] His daughter Margaret usually prepared the family's breakfast, which they had in the study or the arbour outdoors when fine, and a few months later he noted: 'Margaret made breakfast in the study. My wife did not join us, tho Little William [did] and tho he had breakfasted before, [he] eat up a great quantity of toast, whey and curds and sugar.'[135]

On another morning, Holland grumbled: 'We did not breakfast before ten this morning ... I do not like this,'[136] and when Woodforde rose late after a rather late night, he observed: 'We breakfasted quite at a fashionable hour 11-o' clock.'[137] Holland preferred having breakfast fairly early, but the lower classes worked for several hours before they had anything to eat.

In Georgian times lunch hardly existed, although for those who breakfasted early, a small snack might be eaten. In towns many shops sold pies and pastries, while street sellers offered shellfish and other ready-to-eat items. Dinner was the main meal, eaten at any time in the afternoon between two and five o'clock. The timing of dinner was related to the hours of daylight, since the cooks needed to work in daylight, especially for formal dinners with guests where preparations could take hours. Dinnertime for the elite became later and later, and in contrast to the meagre breakfast, a formal dinner could be a dazzling array of food. The first course, served on the table all at once, had numerous dishes, and was followed by a second course with a smaller selection of meats and fish, along with savoury and sweet items. Finally, a selection of nuts, sweetmeats and occasionally fruit constituted the dessert course, at which point the servants withdrew.

When Woodforde entertained Squire Custance and other guests, he did his best to provide a suitable feast: 'I gave them for dinner, a couple of chicken boiled and a tongue, a leg of mutton boiled and capers, and batter pudding for the first course. Second, a couple of ducks rosted and green peas, some artichokes, tarts and blamange. After dinner, almonds and raisins, oranges and strawberries. Mountain and port wines.'[138] Even in more modest households, the hostess rose after the dessert course when guests were present and led the ladies to the drawing room, leaving the men to their own conversation for a while before they rejoined the ladies for tea or coffee.

An everyday family dinner was more restrained, and Woodforde routinely recorded meals such as 'Dinner calfs feet stewed, hash mutton &c'[139] or 'Dinner to day hashed calfs head and a loin of lamb rosted with stewed gooseberrries'.[140] For better-off people like Woodforde, even mundane dinners could be lengthy affairs, but most working people had no more than an hour's break for dinner, before continuing with their labours. Supper was the day's final meal and was usually something insubstantial.

Table manners were of importance to the higher classes, although the poorest were more concerned with survival than etiquette. In a book on manners, the Reverend John Trusler warned how to avoid appearing low class or impolite: 'Eating quick, or very slow, at meals, is characteristic of the vulgar; the first infers poverty, that you have not had a good meal for some time; the last, if abroad [dining out], that you dislike your entertainment: if at home [and eating slowly], that you are rude enough to set before your friends what you cannot eat yourself.'[141]

Some hosts did offer food that we would now discard, and just before Christmas 1778 Woodforde unashamedly set before his guests a dinner that included 'part of a ham, the major part of which ham was entirely eaten out by the flies getting into it'.[142] Even so, his guests also stayed for supper, and 'We were exceeding merry indeed all the night.'[143]

FIVE

## FASHIONS AND FILTH

I hope you saw her petticoat, six inches deep in mud, I am
absolutely certain; and the gown which had been let down to
hide it not doing its office.

*Pride and Prejudice*, by Jane Austen

Clothing for men and women changed markedly, in both styles and
fabrics, over Jane Austen's lifetime. Following the French Revolution
grotesquely elaborate fashions gave way to naturalistic styles, imitat-
ing the Classical world. Ladies wore simple gowns based on Greek
and Roman styles that were copied from the many archaeological
finds then being unearthed at places like Pompeii and Herculaneum.
Men's fashions were influenced by more practical military dress,
which resulted in sober clothing, more suitable for country life than
the extravagance of the urban fashions of the preceding period.
Advances in technology also saw the textile industry shifting into factories, so that many more clothes were made from new cotton fabrics
(using imported cotton-wool)[1] rather than the traditional woollen,
linen and silk fabrics.

In order to appear a gentleman, it was necessary to wear breeches
and stockings. Breeches ('culottes') were made of wool, linen, silk or
buckskin (a very soft leather), secured at the knee by ties, buckles or
buttons. They had a front opening covered by a flap, and could look
baggy, though buckskin ones fitted more snugly. Breeches were held

up not by belts but by leather braces or gallowses. The more comfortable pantaloons became fashionable, particularly with the influence of George 'Beau' Brummell; these pantaloons were longer than breeches and were tied or buttoned at the calf – the forerunner of full-length trousers. They were worn with shoes and stockings or else were tucked into boots.[2]

Stockings (hose) were secured beneath the knee by a ribbon or cord garter. For a muscular look, some men put artificial calves under their stockings, but this trend disappeared when pantaloons took over. Stockings were hand knitted from wool or woven in wool, cotton or silk. 'You have said nothing about how you pass your time or amuse yourself,' William Wilkinson wrote to his wife Sarah in December 1809. 'I should think you must be at a loss at times for something to do, tho' I suppose you nit [knit] a great deal now, and must have improved much. I never expect to have to buy any more worsted [woven wool] stockings.'[3] Prone to holes or to runs forming, stockings required constant mending, which made them uncomfortable, as Nelly Weeton warned her brother: 'I would advise you, my dear Tom, that you have the feet of your silk stockings lined with something soft when you put them on, or the darning will hurt your feet.'[4]

To prevent clothes being lost or muddled, they were sewn with identification marks, and at Northampton in April 1778 one thief made off with the clothing of an unnamed aristocrat:

> STOLEN, out of the George Inn Yard ... between Eight and Nine o'Clock on Saturday Evening ... A PORTMANTEAU, containing six Shirts, marked S. and a Coronet; six Pair of Silk Stockings, marked S. and a Coronet; Six Stocks, marked S. six Handkerchiefs, marked S. and a Coronet; three Shirts, marked I.H. three Stocks, marked H. two Pair of Silk Stockings, marked I.H. one Sky-blue Coat with gilt Buttons; and divers other Articles.[5]

Some breeches had a lining, known as drawers, that could be washed separately, with longer versions for pantaloons. Shirts and drawers were the male underwear of the day, though drawers were not universally worn. Shirts were longer at the back than at the front, with voluminous sleeves and an ornate cuff that had no holes for cufflinks. 'I would have completed the repair of your shirt,' Nelly told Tom, 'but had no cloth fine enough to make a new neck; and I did not know what to do with the ruffles, so I left them as they were. I have sent some wrist-bands which I stitched a few years ago for your old shirts. I fear they will be too strait; if not, they may be useful perhaps.'[6]

Shirts tended to be white in colour, shorter than nightshirts but similar in style. They were pulled on over the head and fastened with ties or buttons. The fastenings were concealed by a frill, often detachable, known then as a jabot or chitterlon. Above the jabot, a stiff stock covered the neck, or else a cravat was wound round and tied at the front.[7] In June 1810, when William Holland was sixty-four years old, he was lucky to escape severe injury or worse, as he explained:

> A bad accident had nearly happened to me last night as I was moving about the house with a candle in my hand to see all safe just before I went up stairs to bed. The point of my cravat caught fire and blazed immediately up to my chin and was going round my neck and to my shirt like wild fire. I holloed out and George [his servant] stood stupidly by me. Providentially however I seised the blazing cravat and all with both my hands and squeeze [squeezed] them hard and stifled the blaze almost instantaneously or I know not what might have been the consequence.[8]

Such ornate shirts were a sign of a gentleman, but instead of putting on a clean shirt, it was useful to have a false shirt front or dickey – defined in a dictionary of 1811 as 'a sham shirt'.[9] Two years earlier Nelly Weeton had noted that 'Mr. Chorley is quite a buck, and dashes away in his silk stockings, his Dickey and his quizzing glass [a single-lens glass held in the hand].'[10] Waistcoats were worn by men over their shirts, but when it became fashionable to have them fully buttoned up, frilly shirts were barely visible and so became less popular for daytime use.[11] In *Sense and Sensibility* Marianne Dashwood despises Colonel Brandon because 'he talked of flannel waistcoats; and with me a flannel waistcoat is invariably connected with aches, cramps, rheumatisms, and every species of ailment that can afflict the old and the feeble'. Flannel was a type of woollen fabric associated with keeping warm and protecting the infirm.

Gentlemen had their breeches and jackets made to measure by tailors. There was no concept of buying good-quality, ready-made clothes. Long jackets or coats, often dark blue, were worn over waistcoats and by 1800 they were 'cut-away' – short at the front with long tails at the back – while greatcoats provided even more protection against the weather. Short jackets known as spencers (after the 2nd Earl Spencer who started the trend)[12] became popular from the 1790s. This type of double-breasted jacket had no tails, though they were often put on over a traditional jacket with tails.

The poor wore whatever was affordable, either purchased second-hand or from slop-shops supplying new, cheap, ready-made clothes. Labourers preferred comfortable, hard-wearing garb, and in London the writer Samuel Pratt described one coal heaver who was wearing a 'coarse and heavy doublet [waistcoat] of many different coloured patches, formed of pieces of carpeting of brown sacking, and of yellow plush, all brought into the same sable [blackened with coal] uniform – his hose ungartered, his breeches knees unbuttoned, his shirt opened almost to the waist'.[13] Loose full-length trousers were the preserve of labourers and seamen.

When women got dressed, they first of all donned a shift or chemise,[14] which was a simple sleeved linen undergarment that reached just below the knees. It was put on over the head and secured at the neck with a drawstring or buttons. A similar longer garment was worn at night, with a cap. Over the shift went stays or a corset – a shaped garment with strips of pliable whalebone (baleen) or cane sewn into the fabric. Stays were wrapped round the upper torso and tightly laced at the back. They were lower at the front and usually had shoulder straps. Worn from childhood, stays kept the figure shapely and the waist tiny.

In May 1780 Parson Woodforde recorded that his niece Nancy 'had a new pr. of stays brought home this morn' by one Mottram a staymaker at Norwich. She paid him for the same 1.11.6. For his journey from Norwich to measure her she pd. 2.6.'[15] The style of stays changed with the fashion, but the physician Hugh Smith praised those women who stopped wearing stays, so 'giving themselves room in the waist'.[16] Young girls, he reckoned, 'were greatly injured by the stiffness of their stays, and by being laced so exceedingly close'.[17] By 1785 their popularity was declining, prompting him to add: 'We now rarely see ladies fainting in public places.'[18]

Also worn over the shift was an ankle-length waist petticoat, with a gown over the petticoat. Gowns had a bodice and a full-length skirt that was wide open at the front, revealing the often-matching petticoat – these petticoats were not underwear intended to be concealed. Since 1710 immensely wide, cumbersome hoop petticoats had been fashionable, supported on a framework of whalebone or lighter cane rods and wire.[19] The gown's skirt was sometimes bunched up at the rear, accompanied by a false rump called a bustle, which was a padded roll filled with cork or other stuffing. With artificial contrivances like the hoop and bustle, one poem in 1777 issued a mock warning to husbands of fashionable women:

> Let her gown be tuck'd up to the hip on each side;
> Shoes too high for to walk, or to jump;
> And, to deck the sweet creature complete for a bride,
> Let the cork-cutter make her a rump.
> Thus finish'd in taste, while on Chloe you gaze,
> You may take the dear charmer for life;
> But never undress her—for, out of her stays,
> You'll find you have lost half your wife.[20]

Hoop petticoats fell out of favour in the 1780s, though they persisted as court dress until the 1820s. In 1805 the young American Benjamin Silliman was amused at the sight of the nobility parading near St James's Palace for the king's birthday: 'The ladies wore hoop petticoats; the hoop was not a circle, but a large oval ... the ladies, as they passed through the crowd contrived to twist the whole machinery round, so as to bring the shortest diameter across the path ... it was no small achievement to deposit one of the ladies safely in her coach'.[21]

The new fashion was for round gowns, which had skirts completely encircling the body, so that petticoats were now more of an undergarment. By the 1790s the style of gowns was further transformed, with a slimmer, more naturalistic, classical shape, white or pale in colour. Sashes were tied round the waist or under the bust, and trains became fashionable, though mainly for evening wear. By about 1800 gowns had short sleeves and a short bodice – a low neckline and high waistline. With the constantly changing fashions, long and short sleeves went in and out of favour.

Fabrics such as fine muslins were initially imported from India, but the invention by James Hargreaves around 1767 of the spinning jenny enabled the production of greater quantities of cotton yarn for weaving into cloth, initially by workers in their homes, while Richard Arkwright's spinning frame, powered by water, produced stronger cotton yarn for the warp threads. From 1779 Samuel Crompton's spinning mule, driven by water and later steam, combined features from both inventions, enabling fine cotton thread to be spun in factories on a massive scale. These developments led to cheaper muslins and calicoes becoming widely available, and cotton surpassed silk, linen and woollen fabrics in popularity. By 1793 it was said that 'every shop offers British muslins for sale equal in appearance, and of more elegant patterns than those of India, for one-fourth, or perhaps more than one-third, less in price'.[22]

With these fine fabrics, gowns could be virtually transparent, and modesty was forsaken. At the end of 1799 *The Times* ridiculed such women's dress and the fashion for false bosoms:

If the present fashion of nudity continues its career, the Milliners must give way to the carvers, and the most elegant *fig-leaves* will be all the mode. The fashion of false bosoms has at least this utility, that it compels our fashionable fair to wear *something*. The stuffed bosoms of our females are at least *oeconomical* – they are made out of the old *Jean Debry* coats [no longer in fashion] of their husbands.[23]

William Holland was appalled by one woman's dress when he was dining at South Molton in Devon in September 1803: 'Captain and

Mrs Law, the gentleman handsome and of pleasing manners, the lady diminutive, affected and almost naked in her dress. It disgusts me much to see such conduct.'[24]

Undergarments were kept to a minimum beneath these thin gowns, and a shorter corset had replaced the restrictive stays. In mid-September 1813, when Jane Austen was in London, she wrote to Cassandra: 'I learnt from Mrs Tickar's young lady, to my high amusement, that the stays now are not made to force the bosom up at all; that was a very unbecoming, unnatural fashion. I was really glad to hear that they are not to be so much off the shoulders as they were.'[25] These new fashions proved rather chilly to wear, and invisible stockinette petticoats manufactured on a stocking loom were one solution, as advertised in the *Morning Chronicle* in 1807:

INVISIBLE PETTICOATS.– Mrs. ROBERT-SHAW informs the Ladies, that her Patent, Elastic, Spanish Lamb's-wool INVISIBLE PET-TICOATS, Drawers, Waistcoats, and Dresses, all in one, are now ready for their inspection – articles much approved of by every lady that has made trial of them, for their pleasant elasticity, softness and warmth; are found very convenient to ladies who ride on horseback.[26]

Because stockings were only knee high, women's thighs were bare beneath their gowns. They did not wear drawers until the early nineteenth century, when they apparently became acceptable after Princess Charlotte was seen wearing them. Previously, they were considered masculine and therefore immodest. Similar to men's drawers, the legs were fastened just below the knee.

Gloves were commonly worn in all weathers, not just for keeping warm, but thin gowns led to the fashion for enormous fur muffs and shawls. Men's coats, such as riding coats and spencers, were adapted for female use, and in his diary in June 1799 Woodforde wrote: 'Very cold indeed again to day, so cold that Mrs Custance came walking in her Spenser with a bosom-friend.'[27] He meant that she had a large handkerchief or scarf at her throat to keep her warm, a fashion that arose because of the low necklines and acquired the name 'bosom-friend'.

Pockets were sewn into the breeches, jackets and waistcoats worn by men. For women, large detached pockets, held in place by ties, could be worn under more substantial skirts and were used for items like coins, pocket watches and pocket books. Such pockets were impossible to wear with flimsy muslin gowns, and instead women carried small decorative bags or purses, frequently handmade, that came to be known as ridicules, reticules or indispensables.[28] These were the first handbags. In *Emma*, Emma herself 'saw her [Mrs Elton] ... fold up a letter ... and return it into the purple and gold reticule by her side'. These pockets and bags were vulnerable to theft, as a pickpocket or cut-purse might steal the entire pocket or purse, not just some of the contents. Folding fans were another essential fashion accessory, particularly in overcrowded, overheated environments like balls or theatres, and after one ball Jane Austen told Cassandra: 'I wore my green shoes last night, and took my white fan with me.'[29]

In fashionable circles, the term 'undress' referred to the more practical gowns worn at home in the morning, 'half dress' described smarter clothes worn during afternoon and evening visits, while 'full dress' involved more elaborate, formal garments worn to balls and other evening events. The upper classes followed fashions avidly, while the middle classes did the best they could, but rarely owned many outfits. At home most women wore an apron to protect their clothes, which were expected to last many years.

In his analysis of the poor in the 1790s, Frederick Eden noted the prices of ready-made clothes in slop-shops around London and how long they should last. For women, they included: 'A hat, the cheapest sort; (will last two years,) 1s. 8d ... Cheapest kind of cloak, (will last two years,) 4s. 6d.; Pair of stays, (will last six years), 6s. od.'[30] At Shrewsbury in Shropshire in November 1795 he listed the basic clothing doled out in the workhouse: 'A woman's dress, consisting of a bed-gown, 2 petticoats, linsey apron, shoes, 2 shifts, 2 pair of stockings, and a handkerchief, costs £1 7s. od. ... The women's cloaths are manufactured in the house, at 1s. 6d. a yard; except the flannel petticoats, which cost about 10d. a yard.'[31]

From what Carl Moritz observed during his travels, even the poorest strived to be modern: 'Fashion is so generally attended to among the English women, that the poorest maid servant is careful to be in fashion.'[32] Despite the death of her pupil, Nelly Weeton was kept on as companion to Mrs Pedder, but being in the remote Lake District it was difficult to keep up-to-date, as she admitted to a friend in August 1810: 'I am almost out of the world here, so far as regards fashion, seeing and hearing less than I used to do at Holland [Upholland]; for Mrs. P. and I have no female acquaintance except a village surgeon's wife, and an acquaintance of hers, both of them as plain in their dress, and knowing as little about fashion as can be.'[33]

Jane Austen displayed considerable interest in fashion. On Christmas Day 1798 she wrote to Cassandra: 'I cannot determine what to do about my new gown; I wish such things were to be bought ready-made.'[34] Many women had their clothes such as gowns and jackets made to measure by professional dressmakers, commonly called mantua makers (from the French *manteau*, a 'coat'). When she was living near Liverpool in 1808, Nelly lamented her lack of decent clothes: 'This week I am going to be busy with the mantua maker for two or three days, that I may have something fit to appear in when I get to Mr. C's; for Miss Chorley told me the other day that she could not for shame take me to Christ-Church, I had nothing fit to go in.'[35] Jane confessed similar embarrassment at her outfits to Cassandra: '*I* am determined to buy a handsome one [muslin gown] whenever I can, and I am so tired and ashamed of half my present stock, that I even blush at the sight of the wardrobe which contains them.'[36]

Customers either went to the mantua maker's house or were visited by them at home. Woodforde recorded his niece's gowns being altered at home: 'Nancy's mantua-maker, Betty Burroughs of Mattishall-Burgh [4 miles away], came this morning early to our house, to alter some mourning for her. She appears to be a steady, clever young woman. She breakfasted, dined, supped, and slept here. She worked in the parlour and had a good fire &c.'[37] The work lasted three days: 'Betty Burroughs left our house this morning before breakfast, to go to her mother at Mattishall Burgh, having work to do at home ... Nancy paid her for her 3 days work 0.2.0 which I think very reasonable tho' boarded here.'[38] Mantua makers often refurbished old garments: 'Nancy had a brown silk gown trimmed with furr brought home by Cary from the mantua maker Miss Bell. It was a very good rich silk that I gave her that formerly belonged to my poor Aunt Parr, whose effects came to me.'[39]

Whatever their class, most girls learned crafts like needlework, embroidery and knitting, which were vital accomplishments for everyday life, because women spent much of their time mending, altering and embellishing garments and bonnets, turning something old into something new, either for themselves, for younger family members or for charitable gifts. Smaller items of clothing, such as nightwear and undergarments (including men's shirts), were commonly made at home from new fabrics or by reusing old garments and linen. Dorothy Wordsworth was frequently sewing and mending, as in August 1800: 'I sate on the wall making my shifts till I could see no longer.'[40] Jane Austen was likewise proficient at needlework. In one letter to Cassandra she mentioned her plans for a gown that was unfit to wear: 'I will not be much longer libelled by the possession of my coarse spot; I shall turn it into a petticoat very soon.'[41] Jane also sewed shirts for her brothers: 'We are very busy making Edward's shirts, and I am proud to say that I am the neatest worker of the party.'[42]

When women talked of buying new gowns, they meant lengths of cloth for their mantua maker to form into garments. Numerous shops, market stalls and salesmen travelling on foot or by cart sold everything needed for needlework. In mid-April 1782 Woodforde purchased a quantity of fabrics, ribbon and lace from one Norwich salesman:

One Mr [William] Aldridge who carries about cottons, linens, muslins, lace, holland, &c. in a cart and comes round regularly this way once in ten weeks, called at my house this morning, and I bought of him a piece of holland (alias Irish cloth) for shirts, 25 yards at 3s/od per yard, for which I pd him 3.15.0. For half of yard of cambrich for chitterlons 0.5.0. For 7 yards of lace edging for Nancy pd 0.5.0. For 4 yards of ribband for my 2 maids pd 0.2.0.[43]

Beautiful lace for embellishing garments was also sold by travelling 'lacemen' (rarely women) and in shops, but it was frequently made in deplorable conditions by women and children. A letter to the *Gentleman's Magazine* in 1785 about lacemaking in Buckinghamshire and Northamptonshire revealed that 'many of the *workers of lace* are deformed, occasioned by their uneasy posture, and many more are diseased, seemingly owing, in a great measure, to their inclined posture while working'.[44] The duty on foreign lace made it expensive to import, so it was smuggled in by ingenious methods. One seaman near Custom House Quay in London was spotted walking from his ship with a loaf of bread:

> the guardian of public revenue therefore demanded of the man what he embraced so closely; '*Only a stale loaf*,' was the answer. The Officer then took hold of the loaf, which immediately came asunder, and discovered a quantity of valuable prohibited foreign lace. After seizing the lace, the officer returned the loaf to the unfortunate smuggler, and coolly observed, 'this is indeed a very stale loaf, and you may keep it for your breakfast.'[45]

Sometimes smaller items were hawked by salesmen travelling on foot, and in March 1784 Woodforde obtained ribbon and sewing thread from one such packman who periodically called at his village: 'Of one Bagshaw a Derbyshire man and who carries a pack with divers things in it to sell, bought a whole piece of black ribbon 18 yards of it at 3¼d per yard worth 5d, pd. 0.3.3. Nancy bought some coloured ribbon at 5d worth 8d ... To a qr of a pound of 4d thread very good, pd. 0.1.4. To 2 oz: of 4d thread and 2 oz: of 3d thread pd. 0.1.0.'[46] Most sewing thread was of silk, but cotton thread was becoming available.

When in London the Woodfordes visited the better drapery stores with their greater range of goods. Jane Austen did likewise, her favourite stores being Bedford House in Covent Garden and Grafton House in New Bond Street. 'We ... must have reached Grafton House by half-past 11,' she told Cassandra on one visit, 'but when we entered the shop, the whole counter was thronged, and we waited full half an hour before we could be attended to. When we were served, however, I was very well satisfied with my purchases.'[47] Benjamin Silliman praised how the merchandise was displayed in such stores:

You will see a shop at the corner of two streets, completely glazed on both sides, that is, forming one continued window from top to bottom, and from the sides to the corner. This is filled with goods, unrolled and displayed in the most advantageous manner, and cards are usually pinned to the articles, informing the reader how good and how cheap they are. For instance;—'this beautiful piece of muslin at so much, two shillings in a yard cheaper than any other shop in London.'[48]

In northern England in the 1790s, according to Frederick Eden, most families made their own clothes, but there were 'many labourers so poor, that they cannot even afford to purchase the raw material necessary to spin thread or yarn at home'.[49] In London, he said, 'working-people seldom buy new cloaths: they content themselves with a cast-off coat, which may be usually purchased for about 5s. and second-hand waistcoats and breeches. Their wives seldom make up any article of dress, except making and mending cloaths for the children.'[50]

Unwanted garments might be sold as rags for papermaking, for making into items such as rag carpets or for the thriving second-hand clothing market (giving rise to the term 'rag trade' for the entire garment industry). In her native Lake District Dorothy Wordsworth was collecting mosses one morning near Grasmere when she noticed 'sitting in the open field upon his sack of rags the old Ragman that I know. His coat is of scarlet in a thousand patches.'[51] To Silliman, the spectacle of worn-out clothes being sold in London was surprising:

*June* 24 [1805].—As I was going to the London Dock, this evening, with some companions, we passed through a great crowd of dirty ragged people, to the number of some hundreds. They appeared to be very busy in displaying and examining old clothes which they were pulling out from bags ... This, I was informed, is *rag fair*. It is held here every evening for the sale of old clothes which are collected all over London, principally by Jews, who go about with bags on their shoulders, crying, with a peculiarly harsh guttural sound, *clothes, clothes, old clothes*. You will meet them in every street and alley in London, and at evening they repair to Wapping, where a grand display is made of every species of apparel in every stage of decay. Sometimes they are in tatters, and at other times merely soiled. Here people of the lower ranks may make a selection which is to them really useful.[52]

Old footwear was also recycled, and shortly after meeting the ragman Dorothy Wordsworth encountered 'a woman with two little girls, one in her arms, the other, about four years old, walking by her side, a pretty little thing, but half-starved. She had on a pair of slippers that had belonged to some gentleman's child, down at the heels ... it was not easy to keep them on, but, poor thing! young as she was, she walked carefully with them.'[53] Some retailers offered ready-made footwear, and one shop in London's Fleet Street advertised 'a large assortment of fashionable BOOTS and SHOES, warranted of the best materials and workmanship, equal to bespoke, where Gentlemen may be fitted as well as when measured, without the trouble of waiting'.[54] Silliman also saw much poor-quality footwear on sale in the city: 'there are hundreds of boot and shoe stores, where these articles are sold of such rude workmanship and of such inferior materials that there are few who cannot buy, at least among those articles which are second hand'.[55]

Those with money had their shoes made to measure by cobblers. Men's footwear mainly comprised conservative black leather shoes with a small heel and a large buckle. As styles changed according to fashions, they sometimes sported square toes, sometimes pointed. When dining with friends in June 1784 James Woodforde was astonished to note that 'Mr Micklethwaite had in his shoes a pair of silver buckles which cost between 7 and 8 pounds. Miles Branthwaite had a pair that cost 5 guineas.'[56] Men's shoes were not sufficiently robust to cope with poor weather, and in the Lake District in February 1802 Dorothy Wordsworth recorded: 'We stopped at Park's to get some straw in William's shoes'[57] – the age-old custom of stuffing footwear with anything that might keep feet warm and dry.

That same month, February 1802, James Woodforde wrote in his diary: 'Mrs. Custance with her two daughters called on us this morning, they came walking and very wet and dirty walk they had. Nancy let them have a change of shoes for each of them.'[58] Fashions in women's shoes changed from pointed styles and high stubby heels to lower heels and by 1800 to flat, pointed shoes made from fabric and secured by ribbons. Most were unsuitable for poor weather, as they resembled slippers rather than outdoor shoes. Laced boots provided more robust female footwear, as seen in *Emma* when Harriet is out walking with Emma, who stops 'under pretence of having some alteration to make in the lacing of her half-boot'.

Men increasingly wore leather riding boots, of calf or knee length, which were influenced by boots worn by army officers. In January 1806 William Holland commented on how he and his wife Mary walked home: 'Tho the road was wet yet as my wife had pattens and I boots we got on very well.'[59] In wet conditions boots were the usual footwear for men, while pattens were worn by women. These were a kind of overshoe resembling a wooden-soled sandal to the bottom of which was fastened an iron ring. When women slipped their shoes into pattens, they gained several inches in height and so raised their dress hems above the worst of the wet and the mud. In *Persuasion* Lady Russell enters Bath on a wet afternoon amidst 'the ceaseless clink of pattens'.

Labourers, male and female, were more likely to wear wooden clogs, and at Cumwhitton near Carlisle in April 1796 Frederick Eden noted their prices: 'The common expence of clogs, for a year, in this country (supposing no shoes to be worn), is 4s. 4d. for a man that works out of doors; and about 3s. 8d. for a man within doors; for a woman, 3s. 6d.; and for a boy, about 12 years old, 3s. &c.'[60] Almost a decade later, Charles Fothergill was fascinated to see the lead miners at Reeth in North Yorkshire:

On their feet they wear very formidable clogs, so large, loose and ponderous that they give their wearers a peculiarly ... awkward gait in walking; they must be worn large and loose because the soles, being made of thick wood and shod with iron cannot spring or be in any degree elastic: there is more iron put round the soles of these clogs than is used in the shoes or plates of race horses; indeed it is nailed on and formed in a similar manner.[61]

Heads were usually covered outdoors, and on the Isle of Wight in 1811 Louis Simond was gratified when 'Children and grown people took off their hats, or gave us a nod, as we passed along,'[62] but he felt disappointment with London: 'People do not pull off their hats when ... addressing anybody ... a slight inclination of the head, or motion of the hand, is thought sufficient.'[63] Carl Moritz found he could distinguish army and navy officers by their hats: 'Officers rarely wear their uniforms, but dress like other people, and are to be known to be officers only by a cockade in their hats.'[64] These cockades were ribbon decorations, like rosettes.[65]

For men, the most common waterproof hats were of felted beaver fur, for which many thousands of pelts were imported annually from Europe and North America. Three-cornered hats (known now as tricornes) gave way to flat-crowned, broad-brimmed hats (which later evolved into top-hats). By the early nineteenth century silk hats were fashionable, which were made from hatters' plush, a fine silk weave. Hats were the only item of clothing to be taxed (apart from gloves, for a brief period), and from 1784 hat retailers had to possess an annual licence and charge duty on each hat sold. This tax was repealed in 1811.

The less well-off wore whatever hats they could obtain or make themselves, including ones of oiled cloth, felted wool or the fur of rabbits and other animals. The town of Moretonhampstead in Devon was accustomed to constant military activity, but a month after the 2nd Surrey Militia arrived in July 1799, the townspeople were complaining, as Silvester Treleaven noted in his diary: 'Several cats stolen from different people, supposed to be [by] the soldiers for the skins to make caps. Mr Geo. Gray offered (by public cry) a reward of 5s/- to any person that would bring his cat alive, or if killed one Guinea to the person discovering the same.'[66]

For everyday use as well as special occasions, women would wear fabric caps indoors, and in January 1799 Jane Austen told Cassandra: 'I am not to wear my white satin cap to-night after all; I am to wear a mamalone [Mameluke] cap instead, which Charles Fowle sent to Mary, and which she lends me. It is all the fashion now; worn at the opera, and by Lady Mildmays at Hackwood balls. I hate describing such things, and I dare say you will be able to guess what it is like.'[67] Military and naval victories often influenced fashions, and as Nelson had won a stunning victory at the Battle of the Nile a few months earlier, these Egyptian-style Mameluke[68] turban-like caps were in vogue. Women's caps were mostly made at home, but they could be bought from milliners, who also made and sold items like bonnets, ribbons, handkerchiefs and aprons. At Canterbury in May 1804, a Mrs Jones advertised that 'she has *A large and fashionable selection of Millinery*, prepared for the summer season; a great variety of Straw Hats and Bonnets; white and coloured Chips [bonnets made from strips of shaved wood]; Muslin Pelices and Spencers; Fancy Cloaks; black and white Lace of the best quality, and at very reasonable prices'.[69]

Ladies wore hats or bonnets outdoors, and they also carried parasols for sunshades. These were similar to umbrellas but made from lighter silk fabrics, because they did not need to be waterproofed. Umbrellas were heavy to carry, with ribs of whalebone or split cane mounted on a sturdy stick and covered with a heavy oiled fabric. They were sold in all colours, though green was especially popular.[70] Walking along the streets during rainstorms was hazardous, as the drains or 'kennels' forced pedestrians to keep close to buildings, yet rain poured off roofs as few gutters or downpipes existed. In *Northanger Abbey* Catherine Morland is longing to go out with friends at Bath, but rain starts to fall. 'There are four umbrellas up already. How I hate the sight of an umbrella!' she says to Mrs Allen, who replies: 'They are disagreeable things to carry. I would much rather take a chair at any time.' Coachmen and the chairmen who operated sedan chairs objected to umbrellas, because they competed with their own businesses.

The philanthropist Jonas Hanway died in 1786, and the following year his biographer wrote: 'He was the first man to walk the streets of London with an umbrella over his head: After carrying one near thirty years, he saw them come into general use.'[71] The Scotsman John Macdonald also claimed to have set the trend for carrying umbrellas in the capital. He was a well-dressed gentleman's manservant, who had often served abroad, and in January 1778, after spending more than a year in France, Spain and Portugal, he was back in London:

> If it rained, I wore my fine silk umbrella, then the people would call after me, What, Frenchman, why do you not get a coach? In particular the hackney coachmen and hackney chairmen would call after me; but I ... went straight on, and took no notice. At this time there was no umbrellas worn in London, except in noblemen and gentlemen's houses; where, there was a large one hung in the hall, to hold over a lady or gentleman if it rained, between the door and their carriage. I was going to dine in Norfolk Street, one Sunday. It rained, my sister had hold of my arm, and I had the umbrella over our heads. In Tavistock-street, we met so many young men, calling after us *Frenchman!* take care of your umbrella. *Frenchman*, why do you not get a coach, Monsieur?' My sister was so much ashamed, that she quitted my arm, and ran on before, but I still took no notice but answered in French or Spanish that I did not understand what they said. I went on so for three months, till they took no further notice of me, only *How do you do Frenchman?* After this, the foreigners seeing me with my umbrella, one after another used theirs, then the English. Now it is become a great trade in London, and a very useful branch of business.[72]

By the 1780s umbrellas were more commonly seen, and in January 1787 a blizzard at Weston Longville forced Parson Woodforde to use one in the churchyard when officiating at a funeral: 'I buried a daughter of Harrisons, an infant aged only 5 weeks. I think I never felt the cold more severe than when I was burying the above infant. The wind blowed very strong and snow falling all the time, and the wind almost directly in my face, that it almost stopped my breath in reading the funeral service at the grave, tho' I had an umbrella held over my head during the time.'[73]

As a respectable man, Woodforde would also have worn a wig, made of human or animal hair. In order to wear wigs comfortably, gentlemen had their own hair cropped short or shaved. To display their higher status, professional men like clergy, lawyers and physicians had formerly worn voluminous, full-bottomed wigs – the big wigs of society – but by the late 1770s most gentlemen preferred smaller wigs, sometimes with pigtails or queues. Wigs were kept fresh with hair-powder made from starch, giving them a white or off-white appearance, and so wig wearers invariably had powder over their shoulders and backs. Younger men especially started to give up wigs and instead had their own hair styled and powdered to resemble a wig. In 1786 hair-powder was taxed, which precipitated the abandonment of wigs altogether, and while staying at Cole in Somerset three years later, Woodforde wrote: 'Old Mr. Dalton and son John called on me this morning, stayed half an hour with us. I did not know old Mr. Dalton at first as he now wears his hair.'[74]

Two years later John Byng was at Winchelsea in Sussex. 'I walk'd early to a barbers shop,' he said, 'bought a pound of powder, had my razor set, and did hope for some intelligence from him; but he was deaf.'[75] Barbers, also called hairdressers, 'dressed' men's hair and wigs and shaved them with cut-throat razors, which was a necessary service for those without access to a mirror. The following summer Byng was staying at the Tontine Inn at Sheffield, and as ever he preferred to shave himself: 'My first direction was to the hair-dressers room, where he dress'd my hair, and where I shaved myself; receiving many compliments (for the first time) on my adroitness: "Never did he see a gentleman shave so well!"'[76]

Woodforde often visited barbers to be shaved, at times accompanied by his niece for her hair to be styled, as in London in June 1786: 'Nancy walked with me to one Smiths in Surry Street, Strand, a Barber, and there had her hair full dressed ... I was shaved and had my wig dressed there. I gave him for shaving and dressing 0.1.6.'[77] In 1795 a tax of one guinea on hair-powder was made payable by the head of each household, and this triggered a radical change in men's hairstyles. Instead of paying the tax, the Whigs cut their hair short, in a style called *à la guillotine*, after those forced to have their hair cropped before being executed during the French Revolution. Those Tories who paid the tax were called guinea-pigs. The *Chester Chronicle* printed a short poem on the unwelcome tax:

On Mr. Pitt's Tax of a *Guinea* a-year, for wearing Hair-powder:
>By bob that's black, or brown, and greasy,
>You may distinguish very easy
>One of the common herd of *swine*—
>This is a never-failing sign;
>But by the powder'd hair, or wig,
>You recognize the *Guinea*-pig.[78]

Woodforde was conservative in his ways, even wearing an old wig while in the garden: 'Mr. Charles Townshend of Honingham [Hall] called on me this morning about 11 o'clock and walked round my gardens with me ... He caught me on the hop, being in my garden and dressed in my cotton morning gown, old wigg and hat.'[79] He therefore duly complied with the tax, which he noted in mid-April 1796: 'Paid Mr. Corbould £3. 3s. od to day to get three receipts for the powder tax from Norwich on Saturday next, as he goes to Norwich that day.'[80]

Dispensing with wigs markedly changed people's appearance, and their hair was now visible in its natural state. Grey or red hair was considered undesirable, but hair dyes were available, as one newspaper advertised:

### ATKINSON'S VEGETABLE DYE

for changing grey or red hair to an auburn or black. This article is presumed to merit the attention of all who have the misfortune to have grey hair early in life, a defect which always makes a person look old, the Vegetable Dye changes it whether red or grey, to a beautiful and permanent auburn or black by so simple a mode of application that a Lady or Gentleman may change the colour of their own hair with ease and secresy. Price 5s. 7s. 6d. 10s. 6d. and one guinea. CAUTION.–Ask for Atkinson's Fluid, or Atkinson's Dye, and observe the signature, as there are counterfeits.[81]

For women, caps were almost the equivalent of wigs, as they could hide their hair beneath them,[82] something Jane Austen described to Cassandra in December 1798: 'I have made myself two or three caps to wear of evenings since I came home, and they save me a world of torment as to hair-dressing, which at present gives me no trouble beyond washing and brushing, for my long hair is always plaited up out of sight, and my short hair curls well enough to want not papering. I have had it cut lately by Mr. Butler.'[83] Women curled their hair by twisting it in curling paper and allowing it to dry, or better still by applying heated iron tongs to the paper, taking care not to singe the hair. 'Mr. Howes made us a morning visit,' Woodforde remarked in 1781, 'and brought Nancy a Pr of tongs to pinch her hair with from Mrs. Davy, as a present to her.'[84] A decade later his niece was suffering from hair loss: 'Nancy made use of some rum, honey and oil, equal quantity of each, this evening, on her head to prevent the hair falling off, which it has done very much of late, it rather makes her uneasy.'[85]

Until the end of the eighteenth century, female hair fashions became increasingly high on the head, with added feathers and other decorations, sometimes making it difficult for women to move. From the 1790s, as a protest against the French Revolution, fashionable women cut their hair short in sympathetic imitation of victims' hair before they were guillotined. Writing from her lodgings near Liverpool in 1809, Nelly Weeton asked a friend: 'I am considering whether to continue my hair a crop, or let it grow again. What says Miss C. Scott? She hears more of fashion than I do. I like it best as it is, but if out of fashion, I must conform.'[86] Washing of hair must have been infrequent, and lice infestation was a nuisance for all classes. In the 1780s Francis Place associated with poor prostitutes in London: 'their hair among the generality was straight and "hung in rat tails" over their eyes, and was filled with lice, [or] at least was inhabited by considerable colonies of those insects'.[87]

Hair washing was not a simple task, because water was not readily available, and obtaining it for everyday household purposes was a constant chore. One of the greatest uses of water was for laundry – the arduous tasks of washing, drying and ironing of clothing and linen. Where feasible, houses collected rainwater from their roofs in wooden barrels, something that the surgeon Lionel Gillespie noticed on the bleak Isle of Sheppey in December 1787: 'I believe there is not a stream on the island and . . . most of the inhabitants supply themselves with water by spouts from their houses.'[88]

Elsewhere, water was fetched in heavy iron-bound wooden buckets from streams or communal wells and pumps, which was a time-consuming and laborious process considering that an imperial gallon of water weighs 10 pounds.[89] Particularly in towns, water was obtained from pumps in the streets, which were enclosed in protective wooden cases. Below ground was a shaft or bore with a wood or lead pipe containing a wooden plunger that was attached above ground to an iron handle. The pump handle was worked up and down to lift the water and force it through a spout protruding from the wooden case.

In rural areas fortunate households had a well in their garden, with winding gear to raise the water in a bucket, and when staying at Bath William Holland satirised his brother-in-law Arthur Dodwell roaming about their rented house as 'moving up and down stairs like a bucket in a well'.[90] Buckets in wells were not always reliable, and in September 1801 at his Norfolk parsonage Woodforde recorded: 'Our well-bucket fell into [the] well this morning as our folks were drawing water, the chain breaking in drawing it up. We tryed all the whole day to get it up, but in vain.'[91] The next day brought success: 'About noon we got up our well-bucket out of the well, by some large iron-creepers which we borrowed of Mr. Michael Andrews. We had some small creepers, but they did not do.'[92]

Even in towns and cities piped water supplies were uncommon and in any case were only for those who could afford to pay. William Darter recalled memories of piped water in his home town of Reading in 1814:

a large lead reservoir stood in the centre of Broad Street opposite the Wool Pack Inn, which was supplied with water by means of a three-action pump fixed in Mill Lane; its distribution being through wooden pipes. The only other means of obtaining water was from wells and pumps, but ... some wells were 30 to 90 feet in depth ... The wooden pipes to which I refer were simply elm trees, selected for straightness.[93]

These elm trunks were formed into pipes by boring, and then much smaller ¾-inch lead pipes distributed the water to individual properties, but not without problems, as there were constant complaints about an insufficient supply and obstructions from fish and eels. Some of London's better houses had a piped supply, but as in Reading the water was impure. In 1811 Louis Simond saw the old wooden pipes being replaced there:

> The water with which London is supplied, was . . . conveyed by means of wooden pipes or logs, perforated, lying under ground, from which small leaden pipes branched out to each house. Workmen are now employed in taking up these logs, which appear mostly decayed, and substituting cast-iron pipes. Those in the main streets, such as Oxford Street and Holborn, are enormously large; upwards of two feet diameter, branching out, down into the side streets, into pipes of the diameter of six inches.[94]

In times of drought, water supplies would run perilously low. In a letter to Mary Heber in the summer of 1785, her friend Miss Iremonger described a visit to Uppark in West Sussex: 'I suppose the dry summer has incommoded the country where you have been, as well as elsewhere. I never saw so little appearance of verdure, and almost all the wells and reservoirs in Sussex were exhausted . . . The near wells were guarded, and the poor people obliged to go to a distance for supply.'[95] Some years later, in October 1803, William Holland in Somerset showed more compassion for the poor in another drought when he noted: 'Most of the village coming to my well for water, never was such a scarcity before.'[96]

Water was heated for many household purposes. Some homes had a copper in a scullery, where crockery and cooking utensils were cleaned, or perhaps in a separate wash-house. A copper was like a large cauldron, used for heating water and for boiling linen such as sheets. It was supported within an encircling wall, so that its top was at waist height, and a fire was lit underneath to heat the water. In November 1795 Woodforde took delivery of an improved copper: 'A new substantial washing copper from my brazier, Manning, from Norwich, 26 inches and ¾ wide, 19 inches ½ deep, weight 45 lb ½.'[97]

The poor had no such facilities, but cleaned their clothes and linen as best they could. All classes changed their clothing infrequently, and the laundry was done only every few weeks. Many households hired washerwomen to assist their own servants or else sent everything to a washerwoman. The whole operation was so labour intensive and expensive that it might last a week or more in larger households, where people regularly referred to the 'washing week'. William Wilkinson worried about the costs. 'I hope you will find a cheap method of getting our things washed,' he warned his wife Sarah in August 1809, 'as otherwise it will be a great expense. You had better endeavour to iron them yourself, and get a woman to wash them at home.'[98]

Woodforde certainly hired washerwomen, as in June 1799: 'Washing week with us this week. We wash every five weeks. Our present washerwomen are Anne Downing and Anne Richmond. Washing and ironing generally take us four days. The washerwomen breakfast and dine the Monday and Tuesday, and have each one shilling on their going away in the evening of Tuesday.'[99] His washerwomen therefore worked for two days, and his own servants dried and ironed everything for two more. The Austens also employed a washerwoman, and with her customary wit Jane wrote to Cassandra about a new one: 'Dame Bushell washes for us only one week more. John Stevens' wife [then] undertakes our purification. She does not look as if anything she touched would ever be clean, but who knows?'[100]

Much was never washed at all, and Francis Place recollected his London childhood of the 1770s and 1780s being full of dirty people:

I can remember the wives and daughters of journeymen tradesmen and shopkeepers, [who] either wore leather stays or what some called full boned stays, and these latter sort were worn by women of all ranks. These were never washed although worn day by day for years. The wives and grown daughters of tradesmen and gentlemen even wore petticoats of camblet, lined with dyed linen, stuffed with wool or horse hair and quilted. These were also worn day by day until they were rotten, and never were washed.[101]

It was not just clothing that was infrequently washed, but linen such as sheets and towels. One physician, Robert Willan, commented in 1801: 'It will scarcely appear credible ... that persons of the lowest class do not put clean sheets on their beds three times a year; that ... they never wash or scour their blankets and coverlets, nor renew them till they are no longer tenable; that curtains, if unfortunately there should be any, are never cleaned, but suffered to continue in the same state till they drop to pieces.'[102]

Some landladies provided a washing service, as Nelly Weeton told her aunt when she was lodging at Beacon's Gutter in 1808:

> Since I came here I have had my cloathes washed by the woman of the house, who does them a great deal cheaper than Ellen [Oaks] did, or the other washer-woman I employed before Ellen came. They both charged me after the same rate – 8d. for a gown, 4d. for a petticoat, and 3d. for a shift, which made my bill for washing near 8 shillings a fortnight. Here I have them done at a shilling a dozen for large things, and sixpence small when I iron them myself; and 1s. 6d., and 8d., when I don't, which makes a very great difference.[103]

Placed in hot or cold water, the laundry was pounded or beaten with wooden bats or dollies, but washing machines constructed of wooden drums rotated by a handle were appearing. One was invented in 1782 by Henry Sidgier in London and is now a symbol on the shield of the Coat of Arms of the Worshipful Company of Launderers.[104] Other machines followed, such as those advertised in the *Hampshire Chronicle* in 1791: 'S. BIRD, original Maker and Inventor of WASHING MACHINES ... The Prices are as follow, with a Wringing Machine to each Size included: A Machine to wash 8 Shirts, three Guineas–ditto to wash 14 Shirts, three Guineas and a Half–ditto to wash 18 Shirts, four Guineas ... Carriage paid to any Part of England.'[105] Most households, though, preferred hired help and servants rather than strange machines.

Cleaning agents could be added to the water to loosen grease and dirt, such as wood ash and stale urine. Soap was better, but it was a highly taxed commodity and needed hot water to be most effective. The stench of manufacturing both soft and hard soap was terrible, using wood ash or vegetable ashes (potash) boiled with whale oil, tallow (animal fat) or olive oil (for finer soap).

The next stage in the laundry process was rinsing in cleaner water and then wringing out excess moisture, either by hand or mangled between wooden bats or rollers, which were sometimes incorporated into mechanical devices fitted with handles. Wet laundry was dried by being suspended from lines, spread over hedges or on the ground, or draped over wooden drying racks. Describing an attempted theft in March 1801, Woodforde revealed that his stockings were dried on flat wooden stocking stretchers: 'A pair of stockings that happened to be out just by the back door upon some wooden legs to dry were attempted to be taken off by some person or another, but being wet they could not pull them off.'[106]

Dorothy Wordsworth often mentioned doing the laundry, as on 16 October 1800 at Grasmere: 'A very fine morning—starched and hung out linen ... Ironed till six.'[107] Ironing was strenuous, using heavy one-piece cast-iron smoothing irons ('flat irons'), with iron handles, which were heated by an open fire and so were liable to get dirty. The correct temperature of the iron was gauged by spitting on the flat surface, and because the handle became so hot, a cloth pad was necessary for protection. Irons cooled down rapidly, so while one was in use, another was heating by the fire. Those with no access to irons used implements like wooden rollers, pebbles and glass linen smoothers – or did not bother.

Apart from the laundry, the rest of the house needed to be kept clean, and methods remained much the same until the advent of electricity. Sweeping was the most obvious form of cleaning, using handmade besoms or brooms. Carpets were taken outside where they were placed over a line or a hedge and then beaten. William Holland, out riding, 'was stopp'd by some young bullocks who stood across the road affrighted at a carpet which hung over the hedge into the road'.[108] Damp and mildew caused a big problem in houses, as well as vermin and all sorts of bugs.

Personal hygiene, or lack of it, would undoubtedly shock us today, with the overpowering body odours and the stink of clothing, stale with sweat and often musty from damp houses. Some people smelled rather worse than others, particularly if employed in a noisome industry. This was an era before anti-perspirants, before the widespread use of soap, before a time when people washed their bodies and changed their clothing on a regular basis, and when virtually nobody immersed themselves in baths or showers. Everyone would have smelled, even genteel women like Jane Austen, who in mid-September 1796 admitted to Cassandra: 'What dreadful hot weather we have! It keeps one in a continual state of inelegance.'[109]

Even in the Houses of Parliament the stench was unbearable, as Elizabeth Fremantle found during a visit in May 1806: 'Mr. Campbell and John Poulett breakfasted with us, and accompanied us to Westminster Hall. We had Peers' tickets and being rather late could only get bad places in a crowded high Gallery behind the Throne. We could see and hear but little, the heat and smell were insufferable, we therefore got away by two o'clock.'[110]

As with laundry, soap was a luxury when washing bodies. Some fine soaps were imported, and in London in 1789 Andrew Pears started manufacturing a fine, transparent soap. The washing of bodies, or more likely parts of bodies, was done with water poured from a jug into a basin, usually at a washstand within a bedroom. Bath-tubs and showers were rare, as were public baths. Manual workers such as miners and agricultural labourers were easily spotted from their stained, chapped hands and swarthy, suntanned or even blackened skin. Many never washed or washed only on Sundays. Rivers and streams provided one means of washing for those who could swim, but Robert Willan advocated public baths: 'all ranks of society would be greatly benefited by the establishment of cold and tepid baths, accessible at a moderate expense; for, by a strange thoughtlessness, most men resident in London, and very many ladies, though accustomed to wash their hands and face daily, neglect washing their bodies from year to year.'[111]

Cosmetics were used as much to hide blemishes such as smallpox scars as to add beauty. Similarly, perfumes were probably used more for hiding smells than creating a pleasing impression. Some body odours were overpowering and difficult to tolerate, as Jane Austen found in November 1800: 'Miss Debary, Susan and Sally all in black ... made their appearance, and I was as civil to them as their bad breath would allow me.'[112] Toothpicks were the most effective means of dental hygiene, most commonly pointed pieces of wood or quill, which the wealthy kept in ornate silver or gold cases. One housewives' manual suggested: 'For a stinking breath. GET two handfuls of cummin, stamp it to powder, and boil it in wine; and drink the sirup morning and evening, for fifteen days.'[113]

Toothpowder comprised abrasive materials such as bicarbonate of soda that whitened the teeth. 'The Amboyna Mouth Powder is prepared from a DRUG the Produce of a far foreign Country, and imported by a GENTLEMAN of FORTUNE,' one advertisement claimed, '... It fastens, whitens, and preserves the Teeth, makes the Gums and Lips of a beautiful red, instantly sweetens the breath ... It removes all foulness the Mouth is subject to from Diet or a disordered Stomach.'[114] Some toothpowders were so abrasive that another advertisement warned: 'Enamel becomes thinner and thinner, and at last, being quite eaten away, and clean gone, a once beautiful Set of teeth are changed into so many unsightly fibrous and rotten Stumps.'[115]

Mr James Rymer of Reigate in Surrey advocated the use of his own toothpowder, priced at 2s. 9d. per box, which 'is used in the common Way with a Tooth-Brush, or the Teeth may be rubbed with a little of it upon the Corner of a Towel by those who dislike a Brush'.[116] Bone and ivory toothbrushes had bored holes filled with coarse animal bristle, held in place by thin wire. Rymer called his toothpowder the Cinchona Dentifrice, and its main ingredient was Peruvian bark, which was also used in treating malaria and from which quinine is derived.

Menstruation is an aspect of women's personal hygiene about which little was written, except occasionally by medical men, who also advised Peruvian bark to treat period pain. An early form of hot-water bottle was also recommended by the physician Alexander Hamilton: 'If ... the pain become violent ... a bladder, two-thirds filled with hot water, should be kept applied to the lower part of the belly.'[117] It is uncertain whether girls and women wore any sanitary protection, especially as most of them wore no underwear. They may have fixed strips of linen between their legs, which would have been rinsed in water and reused, and some women possibly made disposable pads from absorbent material like cotton-wool or sheep's wool, though such materials were too expensive for most. It is also likely that women, especially outdoor manual workers, did nothing. Certainly Hamilton observed that 'Women in the higher ranks of life, and those of a delicate nervous constitution, are subject to sickness, headache, and pains in the back and loins, during the periodical evaccuation. Those of the lower rank, inured to exercise and labour, and strangers to those refinements which debilitate the system, and interrupt the functions essential to the preservation of health, are seldom observed to suffer at these times.'[118] How those women of 'the higher ranks of life' coped is difficult to comprehend, especially when thin gowns became fashionable.

How people relieved themselves while out and about is another area shrouded in uncertainty. When at their clubs or out to dinner, men urinated into ceramic chamberpots (also called 'jordans' or 'piss pots') that were hidden behind curtains, screens or in cupboards, though Louis Simond found that at dinners he attended, there was no attempt by men to be discreet: 'Drinking much and long leads to unavoidable consequences. Will it be credited, that, in a corner of the very dining-room, there is a certain convenient piece of furniture, to be used by any body who wants it. The operation is performed very deliberately and undisguisedly, as a matter of course, and occasions no interruption of the conversation.'[119] He could not understand why chamberpots were 'not placed out of the room, in some adjoining closet'.[120]

Outdoors, women and men were known to urinate and defecate in streets and side alleys. At his trial for theft Samuel Duck claimed: 'I had been to Knightsbridge [London]; coming home about a quarter after eleven, I had occasion to go up this alley to ease myself.'[121] In a letter published in the *Bath Chronicle* in July 1777, one citizen appealed for cleaner streets: 'By a proper attention to regulations, some plan might be, doubtless, formed for restraining, not only the nasty practice of easing nature on the pavement in almost every corner, but also the equally disagreeable one, of throwing urine and other foul water, &c. from the windows into the streets, (where it is very common for passengers to be greatly incommoded and injured).'[122]

Indoors at home, especially at night, ceramic chamberpots or wooden buckets were used, and chamberpots were sometimes built into a piece of wooden furniture known as a 'close stool' or 'commode'. Confusingly, some leading furniture designers began calling any piece of furniture fitted with drawers a commode, and so the term 'night commode' was adopted to distinguish those with chamberpots.[123] Servants were responsible for emptying the chamberpots into slop-pails for collection by the nightsoil men, or else the contents were poured into the outside cesspit, on a dunghill in the garden and sometimes even into the street.

Toilets for daytime use were generally in small outhouses in a corner of the garden or a yard, with a half-door for ventilation and light. The terminology is confusing, but usually the primitive toilet comprised one or more wooden seats over a cesspit or cesspool and was called an earth or ash closet. The outhouse building containing the toilet was the privy, necessary, necessary house, house of office or jericho. The Weston Longville parsonage garden had separate facilities for the servants, as Woodforde's diary entry for 13 July 1780 revealed: 'The old Jericho (alias servants necessary house) pulled down to day and a new one going to be built elsewhere.'[124] At Over Stowey in the terrible winter of 1814, William Holland referred obliquely to his building: 'It freezes hard ... The path made through the snow to a Certain House in the garden is as slippery as glass and I more than once had nearly fallen in passing along notwithstanding the caution I took.'[125] Houses and taverns without gardens or yards might have necessaries in their cellars, and communal necessaries with several seats for men and women were to be found at public attractions like pleasure gardens.[126]

The stench was minimised by sprinkling soil or ashes into the pit now and again, and while some cesspits might drain to a nearby watercourse, most had to be emptied when full. Accidents did occur, as in the summer of 1808: 'The body of a child, belonging to Sarah Lord, of Rochdale, which had been missing three weeks, was, on Tuesday se'nnight, found in a necessary, into which it is supposed to have accidentally fallen, and was smothered in the soil.'[127] In London in December 1814, another accident occurred when Catherine Tewner dropped her newborn baby into the cesspool of her necessary house. At her trial for murder, one man testified that 'we tore up the privy to get the child out; I gave all the assistance to find the child; we did not find the child; we sent for a nightman.'[128] The nightman was George Nicholls, and he also gave evidence: 'I immediately stripped, and went down; I dragged seven times, and the eighth time I brought a female child up ... A child that fell from its mother could not have gone down so low, without it had been poked down with a pole it could not.'[129] Despite his damning words, Catherine was acquitted.

Toilet paper was not then manufactured, and people cleaned themselves with whatever cheap or free materials were to hand, like leaves and moss. Necessaries might be provided with scrap paper, especially torn-up newspapers and letters, and in October 1814 Patrick Smith was found guilty of robbing David Weit, recently discharged from the militia, at Chelsea. 'This is the piece of paper that was dropped in the necessary,' one witness declared. 'The prisoner took part of this paper to wipe his backside with ... here is Weit, drummer, upon it; it is part of his discharge.'[130] In the Lake District Nelly Weeton was puzzled why human excrement was not utilised to improve the farmland, considering that 'The people in this house have, most of them, very great natural abilities that way, as the devastation amongst Mr. Pedder's newspapers can daily testify.'[131]

From the 1770s public health began to be taken more seriously. Streets were widened and paved, open drains covered over and new ones constructed, though drains were not intended for sewage, as flushing toilets – water-closets – were still rare. These water-closets had wooden seating placed over lead or glazed ceramic bowls, and in order to remove the waste, they were flushed with water from a piped supply or water stored in a cistern tank. Decent drainage was needed, and experiments were done with handles and plunger mechanisms to empty the waste into pipes, but as these pipes were unventilated, noxious gases filled the rooms. The first patent taken out to resolve the problem of the closet's inefficient valve was by the London watchmaker Alexander Cumming, and a patent for an improved version was taken out three years later in 1778 by Joseph Bramah. By 1797 nearly six thousand of Bramah's water-closets had been made, and it remained the standard model for decades. Even so, the old-style water-closets with their terrible smells continued to be built, while most people kept their cesspits and chamberpots.

In towns and cities, the contents of chamberpots were taken away in carts by nightsoil men (the 'nightmen'), who also cleared cesspits by climbing into the shafts and digging out the contents, which is what George Nicholls did when looking for the newborn child. There was no organised system of removing detritus, not just for nightsoil but everything from butchery waste to cinders from open fires. The unscrupulous dumped their waste in streets and streams, and at Cowley in Gloucestershire Samuel Rudder observed that 'the poor labouring people are so abandoned to nastiness, that they throw everything within a yard or two of their doors, where the filth makes a putrid stench, to the injury of their own health, and the annoyance of travellers, if any come among them'.[132]

Animal carcasses were disposed of in various ways, and thousands of worn-out horses died each year and were fed to dogs or passed to knackers' yards, where every part was used, such as for tallow, glue and horsehair. Some authorities employed scavengers to keep the streets clean, especially of horse dung, and much of the detritus including nightsoil was sold to farmers for manuring their fields. A survey of agriculture around London in 1794 showed how much farmers paid:

The price of night-soil, horse-bones raw, bones boiled, bones burnt, and coal-ashes, six shillings a load; soot eight pence a bushel; horn-shavings from six to seven shillings a sack . . . and hogs hair, if wet, fifteen shillings a cart-load . . . The barges on the river Thames, supply from the different dung-wharfs, those cultivators of land who reside near the banks of the river, at a much cheaper rate. This manure is composed of horse-dung and the sweepings of the streets mixed together.[133]

Jane Austen sometimes stayed with her brother Henry at his London apartment in Henrietta Street. This was a fashionable part of Covent Garden, but it was only a short distance from scenes of squalor. The state of one street just a few minutes' walk away was brought to the attention of a parliamentary committee in 1816:

I cannot pass by the filthy state of the street, and the alleys and yards in Short's-gardens, which is of a fair width, and requires nothing but the attendance of the scavenger, to be as clean as any other part of the town; on the 10th of September at the ends towards Drury-lane there was a quantity of human ordure floating down the kennel, apparently the emptying of many privies, and causing a stench sufficient to breed a pestilence.[134]

# SIX

———•◆•———

# SERMONS AND SUPERSTITIONS

The rector of a parish has much to do . . . he must make such an agreement for tithes as may be beneficial to himself and not offensive to his patron. He must write his own sermons; and the time that remains will not be too much for his parish duties, and the care and improvement of his dwelling.

*Pride and Prejudice*, by Jane Austen

The Anglican version of Protestant Christianity practised by the Church of England was the official religion, upheld by the law and financed by the people. Within a list of Church of England livings printed in the *Hampshire Pocket Companion* of 1787, the rectories for the deanery of Basingstoke included 'Dean—George Austin; Steventon—ditto'.[1] This was Jane Austen's father, who was rector of the parish of Deane and of nearby Steventon. When he retired to Bath in 1801, his son James took over as his curate at Steventon. Jane wrote to Cassandra about how they were let down in their attempts to find a curate for Deane: 'Mr. Peter Debary has declined Deane curacy; he wishes to be settled near London. A foolish reason! as if Deane were not near London in comparison of Exeter or York.'[2]

Lords, landowners and clergy were intertwined, both socially and financially, and the appointment of clergy was generally due to friends, family, influence and attending the right university college, something that the Frenchman Louis Simond had observed: 'You meet in the best society a number of young clergymen, brought up in the expectancy of some good living, of which their friends or family have the presentation.'³ Men might be selected who anticipated marrying into a particular family – the kind of social manoeuvring that occurs in Jane Austen's novels and also affected her own family. 'Yesterday came a letter to my mother from Edward Cooper to announce, not the birth of a child, but of a living,' she told her sister in 1799; 'for Mrs. Leigh has begged his acceptance of the Rectory of Hamstall-Ridware in Staffordshire, vacant by Mr. Johnson's death.'⁴

Entering the Church was for most clergymen not a religious calling but a traditional career choice for the middle classes, and also for the younger sons of the gentry and upper classes who were not in line to inherit the family's estates. Most were graduates of Oxford or Cambridge universities, such as George Austen (St John's College, Oxford) and William Holland (Jesus College, Oxford). A class divide therefore existed between clergymen and most of their parishioners, and that was exacerbated by resentment at paying tithes as well as fees for baptisms, burials and other services.

James Woodforde, also an Oxford graduate, became rector at Weston Longville in December 1774 when the living was presented to him by his college, as *Jackson's Oxford Journal* reported: 'A few days ago the Reverend James Woodford, Fellow of New College, was presented by the Warden and Scholars of that Society, to the Living of Weston-Longville, in the county of Norfolk, worth 300l. per annum.'⁵ Nowadays he is usually referred to as Parson Woodforde.⁶ 'Parson' is a title normally reserved for those clergy – rectors and vicars – who received tithes, but in popular usage any parish clergyman was called the parson.

Rectors and vicars were beneficed clergy who held the living of one or more parishes. If they had more than one living, a curate was employed to perform their duties. Charles Sturges was vicar at St Mary's Church in Reading and also rector at St Luke's in Chelsea. William Holland was his curate at Reading until 1779, when he became vicar for Over Stowey in Somerset. In 1786 Holland also became rector of Monkton Farleigh near Bath, but returned permanently to Over

Stowey in 1798, leaving a curate in charge at Monkton. These multiple livings (referred to as 'pluralism') were subject to criticism. In July 1790 John Byng was staying at Holbeach, Lincolnshire, in an inn opposite All Saints Church: 'The waiter . . . did not advise me to stay the service of tomorrow [Sunday], as their poor curate . . . had but a bad delivery . . . as for the rector of this rich living, he never was here but when presented to it. Think of that ye bishops: and yet this living was given to him by the Bishop of Lincoln!'[7] Byng was constantly irritated by non-resident clergy, as at Knaresborough in Yorkshire: 'I enquired of the Clerk if the preaching was good? "Aye", said he, "from our Curate". "But where is your Rector"? "He never comes but once't a year, at election of the Parish officers . . . He was put in by Ld. Loughborough".'[8]

The higher classes and the clergy were also bound together by Freemasonry. Woodforde summarised his introduction to the Order at Oxford on 21 April 1774:

> I went with Holmes to day to the Free-Masons Lodge held this day at the New Inn, was there admitted as a Member of the same and dined and spent the afternoon with them. The form and ceremony on the occasion I must beg leave to omit putting down. Paid on admission for fees etc. £3.5.0. It is a very honourable as well as charitable institution and much more than I could conceive it was. Am very glad in being a Member of it.[9]

There was nothing clandestine about the closeness of Freemasonry and the Church, and on a day of thanksgiving for the recovery of George III from his latest bout of insanity in 1789, one West Country newspaper covered the Freemasons' procession to St Andrew's Church at Stoke in Plymouth:

> Thursday morning, at ten o'clock . . . between two and three hundred of Free and Accepted Masons, of this neighbourhood, assembled at Brother Lockyer's, at the King's Arms, properly clothed, with standards flying, wearing sashes and cockades, embroidered on white sattin, with 'Long Live the King', preceded by a band of music; they marched in procession to Stoke church, attended by thousands of spectators; they were received at the church door with an Anthem suitable to the occasion.[10]

Louis Simond was 'struck with the smart appearance of the English clergy ... A well-brushed suit of black forms the essential of their establishment.'[11] By contrast, William Holland, who despised Methodists, criticised the appearance of his neighbour William Poole: 'he looked like a Methodist parson, thin, pallid, tall, dressed in black with a curled yellow wig, walking very demurely, gravely and sententiously, and with a broad rimm'd hat, and every now and then turning up his head sideways as if he defied all the owls in the neighbourhood to compare with him for solemnity and wisdom'.[12] This description of wig and clothing could equally have applied to many Anglican clergymen, who often wore black with a white cravat (there was no distinctive clerical collar), as well as a wig.

For church services clergymen put on cassocks and surplices, and for more important occasions their university gowns. In March 1805 Holland was at Chelsea in London and attended Sunday service at the old riverside parish church: 'A fine morning but cold and keen. Went to church and Mr Sturges in his gown and cassock but he did not do duty. His curate Mr Rush did the whole, a pleasing young man whose father I knew very well formerly at Heckfield near Reading. The church is old and too small for the congregation.'[13] Sturges, who was sixty-six years old, died the following month. Holland also wore a gown for services, as on Christmas Day 1806: 'I had a new gown from Oxford which I put on to day, prince's stuff [a type of fabric], and it cost me a fine sum almost eight pounds.'[14] He refused to wear it at one funeral in September 1810: 'in the afternoon we had the funeral of Molly Selleck, where there was a great concourse of well dress'd, respectable people. But as they neither sent me a hatband or gloves I did not think I had occasion to show much respect to them and did not wear my gown.'[15]

The rector (literally, 'governor') was the incumbent of a parish church, eligible to receive all tithes and responsible for the upkeep of the chancel, while the parishioners were responsible for the nave. In the medieval period monasteries had controlled numerous parish churches and took their tithe rights. In place of rectors at those churches, the monasteries appointed vicars (from *vicarius*, a 'substitute'). After the dissolution of the monasteries during Henry VIII's reign, many of these monastic tithe rights were bought by local lords and gentry, putting approximately one-third of church income in secular hands. These lay rectors had the same responsibilities as clerical rectors and installed vicars in their churches to provide the services. How vicars were financed varied, but the layman owning the tithe rights generally took the great tithes such as those on cereal crops, hay and wood, leaving the small tithes for the vicar. Rectors therefore tended to be wealthier than vicars. Originally, all tithes were collected in kind, when the produce was stored in huge tithe barns, but by the end of the eighteenth century most tithes were paid in money after negotiations between the farmers and rector or between the lay rector and his vicar.

The way church organisation and finance evolved, with lay landowners and sometimes clerical rectors appointing vicars, produced anomalies. In some cases the right to collect tithes was leased to the highest bidder, as seen in the *Sussex Advertiser* in 1795:

### TITHES.

To be Lett by private Contract, the Great and Small Tithes of the Rectory of Isfield, near Uckfield, in the county of Sussex. Proposals to be made to the Rector of the said Parish on or before the 14th February, 1795, and the lease to operate from Michaelmas preceding.[16]

Leasing of tithes was not straightforward, as demonstrated by Woodforde's comments when he was a curate in his native Somerset in 1772: 'Mr. Thos. and Seth Burge talked with Mr. Wickham about the tithe of Cary [Castle Cary in Somerset]. And Mr. Wickham agreed that if one Chaffin who has contracted for the tithe, will be of[f] from his agreement, Mr. Wickham will let it to them for 3 years for £130 per annum. N.B. If hay is proved to be a vicarial tithe to be excepted out of the agreement, the present tithe being only contracted for in the agreement.'[17]

A parson who held several livings could enjoy a good income from tithes, provided he could collect them, and Nelly Weeton described one clergyman she encountered as having 'that wolf-like keenness in his eyes, as if he knew which was the best method of taking tithe'.[18] Both clergymen and parishioners invariably saw the annual payment of tithes as a battleground. In 1803 William Jones, vicar of Broxbourne in Hertfordshire, gave his opinion: 'I am confident that I am *defrauded* by many of my parishioners of various vicarial dues and rights, to which the laws of Heaven and earth entitle me ... for the very word "tithe" has ever been as unpleasing and odious, to farmers especially, as "cuckoo" to the married ear. Those who pay them, pay them very partially, and I may add– "grudgingly and of necessity."'[19] Clergymen like him clearly felt they were owed a living by God-given right.

In Somerset William Holland was no less determined to receive everything owing to him. When trying to persuade a farmer to pay him a tithe of his apple crop, he pointed out that 'a tithe is but an acknowledgement of the providence of God over you and your affairs, a tribute offered in support of his worship to whom you owe everything'.[20] He encountered similar resistance on another occasion: 'I met old Ragged Ware [Thomas Ware] this day. "Well Ware," said I, "how is it not an apple have you brought me though you had many? Some acknowledgement I expect by way of paying respect to your Minister." "Sir, my wife talked of bringing some." "Talked – but that is not enough." "She shall sartainly come." "Only some acknowledgement, some mark of respect like touching your hat." "She shall sartainly come." And so we parted.'[21]

The parishioners remained reluctant to pay for the high standard of living many clergy enjoyed and resented losing one-tenth of their income on top of all the other taxes. Woodforde eased any discontent of the Weston Longville farmers by inviting them to what were evidently enjoyable 'frolics', as on one occasion in December 1776:

My frolic for my people to pay Tithe to me was this day and I gave them a good dinner, surloin of Beef rosted, a leg of mutton boiled and plumb puddings in plenty. Recd. to-day only for Tithe and Glebe of them 236.2.0. Mr. Browne called on me this morning and he and myself agreed and he paid me for Tithe only 55.0.0 included in the above, he could not stay to dinner. They all broke up about 10 at night. Dinner at 2. Every person well pleased, and were very happy indeed. They had to drink wine, punch, and ale as much as they pleased; they drank of wine 6 bottles, of rum 1 gallon and half, and I know not what ale. Old Harry Andrews, my clerk, Harry Dunnell and Harry Andrews at the Heart all dined etc. in kitchen. Some dined in the parlour, and some in the kitchen. 17 dined etc that paid me Tithe ... There was no supper at all provided for them. We had many droll songs from some of them.[22]

The most noticeable duty of a parson was conducting the church services on Sundays, and Woodforde frequently recorded his clerical duties. Nearly two weeks earlier he was well satisfied with the service:

I read prayers, preached, churched a woman, and christned two children by name Christopher and John this afternoon at Weston Church. A large congregation at church, Mr. and Mrs. Carr there. All people well pleased with the alterations at the church. This afternoon was the first time of my using the reading desk and pulpit, since its being removed, and also of a new Common Prayer Book in my desk. I can be heard much better than where it was, and easier.[23]

The main church service comprised prayers, singing of psalms and hymns, reading from the Bible and a sermon preached by the parson. When he was at Nettlebed in Oxfordshire in 1782, Carl Moritz attended a service at St Bartholomew's church:

I resolved to stop ... for the day, and attend divine service. For this purpose I borrowed a prayer-book ... It being called a prayer-book, rather than, like ours [in Germany], a hymn-book, arises from the nature of the English service, which is composed very little of singing; and almost entirely of praying. The Psalms of David, however, are here translated into English verse, and are generally printed at the end of English prayer-books ... At half past nine the service began. Directly opposite to the inn, the boys of the village were all drawn up ... to wait the arrival of the clergyman. At length came the parson on horseback. The boys pulled off their hats, and all made him very low bows. He appeared to be rather an elderly man, and wore his own hair, round and decently dressed.[24]

It was time to enter the church:

The bell now rung in, and so I too, with a sort of secret proud sensation, as if I also had been an Englishman, went with my prayer-book under my arm to church, along with the rest of the congregation; and when I got into the church, the clerk very civilly seated me close to the pulpit ... Under the pulpit, near the steps that led up to it, was a desk, from which the clergyman read the liturgy. The responses were all regularly made by the clerk, the whole congregation joining occasionally, though but in a low voice.[25]

Moritz endured the entire service, but considered it exhausting for the parson: 'The English service must needs be exceedingly fatiguing to the officiating minister, inasmuch as, besides a sermon, the greatest part of the liturgy falls to his share to read, besides the psalms and two lessons. The joining of the whole congregation in prayer has something exceedingly solemn and affecting in it.'[26] He was impressed by the singing, which a church band accompanied:

The clergyman now stopped, and the clerk then said in a loud voice, 'Let us sing to the praise and glory of God, the forty-seventh psalm.' I cannot well express how affecting and edifying it seemed to me, to hear this whole, orderly, and decent congregation, in this small, country church, joining together, with vocal and instrumental music, in the praise of their Maker. It was the more grateful, as having been performed, not by mercenary musicians, but by the peaceful and pious inhabitants of this sweet village ... The congregation sang and prayed alternately several times; and the tunes of the psalms were particularly lively and cheerful, though, at the same time, sufficiently grave and uncommonly interesting. I am a warm admirer of all sacred music; and I cannot but add, that that of the church of England is particularly calculated to raise the heart to devotion. I own it often affected me even to tears.[27]

The musicians and singers were usually located in the gallery or loft, and their standard of performance must have varied considerably. Like Moritz, John Byng was an admirer of good church music but also critical of bad, such as when he attended a service at Folkingham in Lincolnshire in June 1791: 'Here were a numerous, and decent congregation, with a singing loft crouded ... but the bassoons, and hautboys, were too loud and shreiking ... Much singing before the service; likewise the Magnificat, and two psalms.'[28] While visiting Knutsford in Cheshire the previous summer, he decided to stay for the Sunday service because the church was relatively new and dry – it had been consecrated in 1744. The church, he said, was 'a neat, well pew'd building; and was well fill'd with well dress'd company, many of whom came in their coaches; and there was one sedan chair.—The service open'd with a psalm, accompany'd by an organ [installed in 1773], and the Te Deum, and—were chaunted; so these with two other psalms, gave me singing enough: as for the sermon, it had the merit of being short. The bells are very tuneable, and they practise ringing.'[29]

On entering Aisholt church in Somerset, William Holland was met by the unpleasant noise of one musician: 'A disagreeable fellow was playing his fiddle in church when I came in, without tune or harmony intending I presume to accompany the psalm singers. I however ordered him to stop his noise, which he hardly would do and then he began trying his discordant hautboy. I had a good mind to order him to be turned out.'[30]

Apart from the services, the parson was required to perform any baptisms, burials and other duties, for which he charged fees. Often, the clergyman was given a gift of money as well, but in 1783 a stamp duty tax was also imposed on the registration of marriages, christenings and burials, as Woodforde noted in his diary in October: 'I rode down to Mr. Howletts this morning and christned a child of his, born last night, by name William – and it being the first child that I have christned since the Act took place concerning the duty to be raised on christnings burials and marriages, and therefore recd the duty of 0.0.3.'[31] Such a tax discouraged the poor from marrying in church or christening their children, and the law was repealed the following year on the grounds that it adversely affected public morals.

Some clergymen spent considerable time visiting the poor and sick in their parish and frequently made charitable donations.

Woodforde regularly gave a shilling to passing beggars who appeared deserving, as in February 1797: 'To a poor French emigrant woman, very short, who came to my house this morning to ask charity, being in great distress, gave 0.1.0 and also a mince pye and some beer. She told me as far as I understood her (as she talked but little English) that her husband with 2 or 3 children were killed in the late bloody commotions in France.'[32] At certain times of the year he favoured specific elements of his congregation, giving money to the poor housekeepers and single people of the parish on St Thomas's Day (21 December), and on Christmas Day he liked to invite the poor for a meal:

> This being Christmas Day, I went to Church this morn' and then read prayers and administered the Holy Sacrament. Mr. and Mrs. Custance [the squire and his wife] both at Church and both received the Sacrament from my hands. The following poor old men dined at my house to day, as usual, Js. Smith, Clerk; Richd. Bates, Richd. Buck; Thos. Cary; Thos. Dicker; Thos. Cushing; Thos. Carr – to each besides gave 1/0 – in all 0.7.0. I gave them for dinner a surloin of beef rosted and plenty of plumb-pudding. We had mince pies for the first time to-day.[33]

Of the thousands of parish churches across England, many were centuries old, built from the medieval period onwards and often orig-inally for the Catholic religion. High on the Quantocks, Holland encountered a parishioner, Jack Hunt, working in his garden and asked him why he did not cut down one hedge for a better view: 'Ah that is Mr Buller's hedge,' came the reply, 'but I can see twelve parish churches from my door.'[34] John Byng also admired seeing numerous churches in Lincolnshire:

> Within view, at short distance, are several churches ... I am of a very superstitious turn; and must think that the same Providence which urged great and pious people formerly, to build these houses of God still guards and preserves them. Who would, or could build them now? The expence would be enormous ... How beautiful does our land now look, from the spires and steeples; and what useful land and sea marks they are; numbers

are gone to ruin, and yearly suffered to fall down: how happens this? Have we no bishops, or do they not visit their dioceses?[35]

By the late eighteenth century few new churches were being constructed, even though there was a pressing need in the expanding towns. Elsewhere, churches were all too often in some state of disrepair, as well as being damp and cold (they had no heating), and their congregations were dwindling, particularly with the rise of Methodism.[36] Most churches were not intended as places of private prayer and were kept locked, so the first task of an interested visitor like Byng was to locate a key or find the clerk so as to gain entrance. Very often these buildings were in a sorry state, such as All Saints Church at Dodington in Somerset, where Holland officiated on a general fast day in February 1809:

The weather dark and full of snow at last Mr. Huggins appear'd, and so I begun the service and two or three more came, finish'd the service and made some strong observations to Mr. Huggins on the state of the church, a torrent of rain pour'd in on one side so as to make one side quite black, one window half gone, and pains of glass in abundance wanting and the roof full of holes that the sky was visible in many places. I told Huggins that I could not do duty in the church in this state.
Why sir replied he if next Sunday should be bad you need not come.
You know the wind blows on from all quarters, answered I.
Cant get a glazier and mason, return'd he not immediately.
Church work said I, shaking my head, must be done without delay.[37]

Those attending church services in winter must have felt the biting cold, as is evident by Holland's remarks the following year, yet again at Dodington:

The most foggy, frosty, dark morning I ever knew, the ground is glazed over and the twigs everywhere cover'd completely with a white hoar frost ... I could not ride. It was so slippery and so walked to Dodington and with difficulty made up a congregation. Yet three of the Miss Hugginses came and Mrs. Farthing, but the great Mr. Farthing himself was not there, the churchwarden. Neither did I see my old friend John

Mogg's red nose there which I lament the more as it might have warm'd the church on so very cold a morning.[38]

During the eighteenth century the medieval bench pews were often replaced by enclosed box pews, which provided some privacy and protection against draughts. Inside the church, differences in social class were reflected by the size and quality of a family's pew and its position in the nave. Wealthy families could rent a pew or build their own, while the poor shared the common pews provided by the church at the back, or sat in a gallery. Pews were built to whatever shape and size their owners desired, and the curate Gilbert White at Selborne wrote that 'nothing can be more irregular than the pews of this church, which are of all dimensions and heights, being patched up according to the fancy of the owners'.[39] One newspaper in 1789 advertised a desirable pew for sale: 'To be SOLD, A PEW, in the West Gallery of the Parish Church, at Leeds, well situated for both Hearing and Seeing, and containing Sittings for Five People.'[40]

Where a person sat in church was so important for social status that Woodforde was forced to cancel permission for the use of a particular chancel seat:

After breakfast this morning I sent my maid Betty to Mr. Press Custance's mistress (Miss Sherman) to desire her not to make use of my seat in the chancel any more, as some reflections had been thrown on me for giving her leave. I likewise sent Will to Mr. Kerr's on the same account ... Miss Sherman sent word back by Betty that she was much obliged to me for the use she had already made of it, and did not take it at all amiss in me, she knew from whence it came – and that she would get a new seat made. Mr. Kerr sent me word that he was not the least angry with me, and he expected it.[41]

Nelly Weeton, keenly aware of class distinction, complained in a letter about her local church at Liverpool:

Christ's Church nowadays is not what the Church of Christ was formerly. He used to say, 'to the poor the Gospel is preached,' but now the age is grown more liberal, so that they pay their teachers. Of course, it is chiefly to the rich that the Gospel is preached. 'The rich and poor' do not 'meet together'. The poor go to pray – nobody knows where, and any scrubby fellow may instruct them. To be 'clothed in rags' was once a recommendation to the Church of Christ, but now the surest way of being denied entrance into it . . . the present age are so little scrupulous, that Fashion, whatever garb she wears, is permitted; indeed, every pains taken to allure her to take her seat in Christ-Church.[42]

Even if they were not concerned about such class distinction, parishioners frequently resented their duty to attend church on Sundays. Although the labouring classes worked six days a week, they were still expected to spend part of the Sabbath – their one day off – at church. Benjamin Silliman, though, was surprised how all classes in London treated Sundays:

I attended public worship to-day in a great church where there were only a few people. This I have very often seen before in London. Indeed a very great proportion of the people consider the Sabbath as a day of mere rest, of relaxation, of amusement, or of dissipation, according to their employments, and rank in society. A person, while walking the streets on the Sabbath, will meet numbers of the gentry with their splendid equipages, going out into the country for an airing, or perhaps to join a party at some village in the vicinity. It is also a favourite day with them to begin a journey, as it is every where with sailors to begin a journey.[43]

There was even greater reluctance to attend church services on weekdays, such as official 'fast days' or on the king's birthday, when sermons were sent to the parishes to be read out. 'This is the general fast and a disagreeable day it is,' remarked Holland in February 1809, 'very cold and piercing and windy . . . I could scarce get any to church but I went in at last but had a very small congregation for a fast. However I went through the intricate service, and gave them a sermon.'[44] Later that year, on Wednesday 25 October, he recorded:

This is the King's accession into the fiftieth year of his reign and the bells are ringing and we are to have prayers. Few assembled. Farmer Morle after promising fairly last Sunday and to provide cyder, disappointed us all, a mean shabby fellow and Farmer Landsey tho as rich as a Jew contributed nothing tho he was at church but the other was not. However we had some few ... I believe I gave them as good a sermon and as well deliver'd as any they will hear this day in these parts though I say it myself ... and moreover it was my own composition which will not be the case in general I presume.[45]

On the king's birthday a few years later, in 1816, Holland remarked: 'I had prayers to day, but we could collect no congregation besides our own family. Indeed in country places it is in vain to expect the common people on week days.'[46] A few months after, attendance had not improved: 'I have resolved to go with my wife to every person or house in the parish to remonstrate with the inhabitants about their neglect of the public worship of the church, and so we went off this day and had conversation with many of them and made them sensible of their duty and they promised fairly.'[47]

Byng blamed the deteriorating church attendance and the decline of the clergy on countless good families deserting the countryside:

For whilst decent, and pious families therein resided, the minister attended to his double Sunday duties, and to the weekly prayers on Wednesdays, and Fridays, besides the keeping of holidays; to which the aged, and virtuous poor were urged to attend, by good example.—But the families being gone, no longer are these duties continued; and the divine, himself, from lack of company, pays a pitiful stipend to a hackney curate (who rides over half the country on a Sunday) and retires to London, or to Bath.[48]

Byng himself was no model churchgoer, attending services but often more interested in antiquarian matters, as at Folkingham in June 1791: 'the bells rang for church, to which I repair'd with my landlord, and landlady [of the Greyhound Inn]; (this I may call my religious tour, tho' I sadly fear that curiosity oft'ner than devotion leads me to church) ... during the sermon mine host slept, and I slumber'd.'[49]

In many areas nonconformist sects ('dissenters') such as the Baptists, Unitarians, Methodists and Quakers were gaining ground. Their ministers, largely drawn from the middle and lower classes, were more in touch with their congregations and tended to ask only for voluntary contributions. The 1689 Toleration Act had given limited concessions to nonconformists and granted some freedom of worship, allowing them to hold meetings in unlocked, licensed meeting places. Although no longer obliged to attend parish churches, they remained barred from Cambridge and Oxford universities and from holding political or municipal office.

Attacks flared up sporadically against Catholics and nonconformists, as in the Birmingham (or 'Priestley') Riots of July 1791, when rioters attacked many chapels and homes of dissenters. Byng learned about this unrest on his Lincolnshire travels: 'I read, in the newspapers, the accounts of the riots at Birmingham: one party inflames, and then accuse the other of warmth!'[50] One of the casualties was the house of sixty-seven-year-old William Hutton, a dissenter, bookseller and historian. His daughter Catherine Hutton wrote to a friend how the mob was convinced that unless they destroyed the meeting houses, the dissenters would destroy the Church: 'Such was the belief of the *best* part of the mob, and such belief must have been occasioned by the insinuations of their superiors, but the motive of the *greatest* part was plunder ... Dr. Priestley ... unintentionally, and himself the first sufferer, he was, I think, one of the primary causes of the riots in Birmingham, by rousing the spirit of bigotry and all incharitableness in others.'[51] Joseph Priestley was a dissenting minister and vigorous supporter of liberal reform of government, education and theology, making him unpopular with the establishment, who were suspected of inciting the riots.[52]

In the 1730s John Wesley and George Whitefield had embarked on preaching a different, evangelical type of Christianity that became known as Methodism. Wesley's preaching was hugely influential with the middle and working classes. Although his followers were Anglican, they also attended Methodist services and were encouraged to build chapels or preaching houses. Wesley hoped to transform the Church of England, but at the end of the eighteenth century, after his death, groups of Methodists split from the Anglican church, and Methodism became a serious rival. According to Simond, 'The sect of the Methodists, who preach hell and damnation, and place faith before works, has made astonishing progress.'[53] Charles Fothergill thought they were a force for good. When passing through Wilberfoss in Yorkshire in 1805, he 'observed a Methodist meeting in a very small thatched cottage which was crammed full almost to suffocation: they were singing psalms. These meetings are common to almost every village, and this sect, though in general confined to the lowest and consequently to the most ignorant orders of the people, has certainly been productive of great good whatever may have been urged against it.'[54]

Holland particularly disapproved of Methodists when they neglected to attend his Sunday services:

> I saw a great number of people passing by about dusk, I suppose it was from a Methodist meeting at Hodges. These men do a great deal of harm, they pretend to great sanctity but it is ostentation not reality. They draw people from the established church, infuse prejudices in them against their legal pastors and of late they are all democratic [revolutionary] and favourers of French principles, and I suspect that some of the philosophers get among them under the character of celebrated preachers and so poison their minds against the established government.[55]

A few months later he was ranting again: 'Met the Methodist William Hill. He squinted at me under his hat as he passed. How now, said I, at neither church this day? I have been elsewhere replied he. So much the worse, returned I, the proper place is your own parish church.'[56] Over a decade later, he was still unhappy: 'These Methodistical people tho they talk much of their piety yet have very little of the true principle of religion in them. Their chief religion consists in censuring others but giving themselves what latitude they please. We have some in this parish ... who esteem themselves great saints yet indulge themselves in every kind of sensuality and moral turpitude.'[57]

Frequently critical of Anglican clergymen, Byng lamented that the rise of Methodism was due solely to their negligence:

> about religion I have made some enquiry, (having been in so many churches) and find it to be lodged in the hands of the Methodists; as the greater clergy do not attend their duty, and the lesser neglect it; that where the old psalm singing is abolish'd none is establish'd in its place; as the organ is inconvenient, and not understood; at most places the curates never attend regularly, or to any effect, or comfort, so no wonder that the people are gone over to Methodism.[58]

While Holland felt threatened by Methodists, he tolerated the Quakers but disliked Catholics and Jews, even though they formed only a small part of the population. By 1800 there were around 100,000 Catholics in England and Wales, and many of these were Irish immigrants.[59] Substantial numbers of Jews had moved to England from Europe in the early eighteenth century, adding to the established Jewish community, mostly poor refugees from the ghettos of Germany and eastern Europe. Many of them became pedlars and dealers in secondhand clothes, forming settlements in towns such as Birmingham and Canterbury from where they travelled into the surrounding countryside offering their wares. Others traded with sailors in ports like Liverpool, London, Plymouth, Bristol and Portsmouth. The main community of Jews at Portsmouth was clustered near the dockyard gate, and the only two synagogues recorded for Hampshire in a 1787 directory were at Portsmouth, one at White's Rowe and the other at Daniel's Row.[60] Some of the pedlars did so well in the seaports that they were able to found prosperous businesses, while the Jewish banker Nathan Mayer Rothschild became a major financier to the Government, helping to fund the Napoleonic Wars. Rothschild had originally been a textile merchant in Manchester, but moved to London and established his banking business there in 1805.

Another threat to the authority of the Church was superstition – despite the 'enlightenment' of the eighteenth century, superstitions were rife. In 1787 the antiquary Francis Grose published what he called a *Provincial Glossary*, and his section on popular superstitions in this book began:

It will scarcely be conceived how great a number of superstitious notions and practices are still remaining and prevalent in different parts of these kingdoms, many of which are still used and alluded to even in and about the metropolis [London]; and every person, however carefully educated, will, upon examination, find that he has some how or other imbibed and stored up in his memory a much greater number of these rules and maxims than he could at first have imagined.[61]

Gilbert White was conscious of the tenacity of superstitions:

It is the hardest thing in the world to shake off superstitious prejudices: they ... become so interwoven into our very constitutions, that the strongest good sense is required to disengage ourselves from them. No wonder therefore that the lower people retain them their whole lives through, since their minds are not invigorated by a liberal education, and therefore not enabled to make any efforts adequate to the occasion.[62]

As a clergyman preoccupied with studying natural history, he was probably more rational than most.

Belief in ghosts was certainly widespread, something that Nelly Weeton noted with some amusement at Upholland in Lancashire in 1807: 'Scarcely a field, gate or stile is without its attendant spirit; and in some of the houses the noises these beings, or shadows, or sprites or whatever they are, are *said* to make, are terrible beyond anything.'[63] She estimated that more than 10 per cent of buildings around Upholland were haunted, and one ghost was especially troublesome:

the Mill-house below Mr. Dannett's, is the terror of the whole neighbourhood. I was the other evening at Mr. D's when a subject of this kind occupied two or three hours. Miss D. is superstitious in the *extreme* ... and she will repeat such a long string of the strangest apparitions, horrid yells, looking glasses falling, furniture moving, tongs, shovel and poker dancing, raps at the door or the window, windows being broken without hands or any living creature near, noises as if someone were spinning, churning, dancing, or a mill going; and many other appalling things not worth writing.[64]

Scornful of most superstitions, Nelly nevertheless admitted she was 'not entirely free from some little fears of this kind, but there are few, perhaps none, who in my situation would feel so little fear as I do'.[65]

Ghosts were feared as being the restless spirits of the dead, and in April 1810 the *Morning Post* reported on the superstitious rites behind one suicide's burial:

> The officers appointed to execute the ceremony of driving a stake through the dead body of *James Cowling*, a deserter from the London Militia, who deprived himself of existence, by cutting his throat, at a public-house in Gilbert Street, Clare Market, in consequence of which, the Coroner's Jury found a verdict of self-murder, very properly delayed the business until twelve o'clock on Wednesday night, when the deceased was buried in the cross roads at the end of Blackmoor Street, Clare Market.[66]

Suicides were routinely punished by denying their bodies a Christian burial, but the remaining ritual was to prevent the ghost haunting the living. Burial at night at the crossroads was intended to confuse the ghost if it tried to wander, and the stake was to stop it rising up to walk. Substantial stakes sometimes protruded above ground for years afterwards.

Many common beliefs concerned events that were interpreted as omens, usually bad omens. A howling dog signified a death in the family, while a coal spitting out of a fire and landing at someone's feet in the shape of a coffin foretold their imminent demise. 'Any person fasting on Midsummer eve, and sitting in the church porch,' Grose recorded, 'will at midnight see the spirits of the persons of that parish, who will die that year, come and knock at the church door, in the order and succession in which they will die.'[67] Tallow rising up the wick of a candle was sometimes called a 'winding-sheet' and foretold a death in the family. Even clergymen like Woodforde were not immune to such omens, and he noted several in his diary, including a similar one concerning a candle: 'There was a very large and long handle of a coffin in one of our candles this evening, as many people call it, and lasted a very long time indeed.'[68]

Another portent of death appeared when he was brewing beer: 'In the boiling of the beer this morn' I saw a great number of thick brownish kind of bubbles swimming on the surface of it, very much like ratafee-cakes, and they are called in Norfolk, burying-cakes, and the common people say here that is a sure sign of some of the family or their friends dying very soon. I never saw them before.'[69] Woodforde was frequently unnerved by such omens, and on another occasion he recorded: 'I dreamt very much last night of my losing my hat. It is said to be a sign of losing a very near friend.'[70]

Particularly popular were charms and rituals for assessing future marriage prospects, and Grose detailed one example: 'On St. Agnes night, 21st of January, take a row of pins, and pull out every one, one after another, saying a Pater-noster on sticking a pin in your sleeve, and you will dream of him or her you shall marry.'[71] He also mentioned superstitions relating to luck, many involving chance events: 'It is lucky to put on a stocking the wrong side outwards: changing it alters the luck. When a person goes out to transact any important business, it is lucky to throw an old shoe after him.'[72] Certain things were to be avoided: 'To kill a magpie, will certainly be punished with some terrible misfortune ... It is held unlucky to kill a cricket, a lady-bug, a swallow, martin, robin red-breast, or wren.'[73] To ward off bad luck or evil, amulets were valued, like the caul advertised at London in the *Morning Post* in August 1779, widely believed to be the most effective talisman against drowning:

To the Gentlemen of the Navy, and others going long voyages to sea. To be disposed of a CHILD's CAWL. Enquire at the Bartlet Buildings Coffee-house, in Holborn. N.B. To avoid unnecessary trouble the price is Twenty Guineas.[74]

Grose recorded other strange amulets: 'The chips or cuttings of a gibbet or gallows, on which one or more persons have been executed or exposed, if worn next the skin, or round the neck, in a bag, will cure the ague, or prevent it.'[75] Witchcraft was behind some beliefs: 'A stone with a hole in it, hung at the bed's head, will prevent the nightmare: it is therefore called a hag-stone, from that disorder which is therefore occasioned by a hag, or witch, sitting on the stomach of the party afflicted. It also prevents witches riding horses; for which purpose it is often tied to a stable key.'[76] A horseshoe nailed over a doorway was a common talisman against witches, as well against bad luck and evil.

Belief in witches was ridiculed by the more educated, but after explaining how witchcraft was nonsense, Grose did give some precautionary advice:

> Some hair, the parings of the nails, and urine, of any person bewitched – or as the term is, labouring under an evil tongue – being put into a stone bottle, with crooked nails, corked close and tied down with wire, and hung up the chimney, will cause the Witch to suffer the most acute torments imaginable, till the bottle is uncorked and the mixture dispersed; insomuch that they will even risk a detection, by coming to the house, and attempting to pull down the bottle.[77]

Such 'witch bottles' were also bricked up in walls of houses or placed under the hearth or eaves. They have occasionally been discovered while renovating old buildings, such as one dating to the late eighteenth or early nineteenth century found beneath the hearth of Clapper Farm at Staplehurst in Kent.[78] Witches were widely feared, particularly in rural areas, and when meeting a suspected witch, Grose suggested: 'it is advisable to take the wall [side] of her in a town or street, and the right hand of her in a lane or field; and, whilst passing her, to clench both hands, doubling the thumbs beneath the fingers; this will prevent her having a power to injure the person so doing at that time. It is well to salute a Witch with civil words, on meeting her, before she speaks.'[79]

The law generally regarded anyone claiming to be a witch as a charlatan, but they could be prosecuted for fraud or for any specific crime that had been committed, as was the case with Mary Bateman.

She had made a good living in Leeds as a fortune teller for over twenty years, but was found guilty of poisoning a client, Rebecca Perigo. Having been tried and found guilty at York, she was executed there in March 1809, aged forty-one. Part of the sentence was for her body to be dissected, but such was the notoriety of the case that the corpse was publicly displayed first. Afterwards, it was sent to Leeds: 'when the cart with her body approached the town, it was met by a number of people. The following day it was exhibited in the Surgeons' Room at the Infirmary, at three-pence each person, and an immense number of people were admitted, some of whom evinced predominant superstition by touching the body before they left the room, to prevent her terrific [terrifying] interference with their nocturnal dreams.'[80] The dissection of the body was a public affair, and the local newspaper reported that 'Mr. Hey [the surgeon] is now delivering a course of twelve lectures on the body, for the benefit of the institution, and has diffused much edifying information to a crowded auditory.'[81] The remains of her skeleton are now displayed at the Thackray Museum in Leeds.[82]

Although witches were popularly regarded as malign, another kind of magic practitioner, the 'cunning man' or 'wise woman', was considered benevolent. They were approached for cures for illness in people or animals, or for resolving problems such as lost or stolen property. Very often their success was achieved by being skilled herbalists or through the suggestibility of clients. James Murrell worked with a chemist in London, but moved to Hadleigh in Essex around 1810 and carried on a dual trade of shoemaker and cunning man. It was said that he 'pretended to have the power of counteracting the designs of witches, discovering thieves, and where stolen property was secreted. He was a herbalist, and administered potions and drugs.'[83] On his death in 1860 numerous letters relating to his occult business were destroyed, but it was later said that 'enough remain to prove that an amount of ignorance, credulity, and superstition exists, which appears incredible'.[84]

Other ways of making money from superstition and foretelling the future included almanacs (or 'almanacks') that carried astrological predictions. Originally, almanacs were compiled by astrologers who were often practising astrological physicians, but with the development of science, astrology had fallen out of favour. From the early eighteenth century onwards almanacs provided more information and entertainment than astrological predictions. Of those still carrying predictions, the most popular was *Old Moore's Almanack*, first produced by the astrologer Francis Moore in 1699 under the title *Vox Stellarum* ('voice of the stars'). Moore's *Vox Stellarum* for 1803 contained optimistic prophecies, such as that for April: 'It now looks as if the Genius of the British Nation would triumph over all its adverse Fortune. Some eminent and weighty Affairs are now transacted, and brought to a final Determination, for the good of the Public and Increase of Trade.'[85] Other prophecies are almost too convoluted to understand, such as one for June: 'Heavens defend the English Nation from future War, and visible Actions and Commotions, and may *London* be as insensible of Sickness, Piratical Damages, and sudden Insurrections, as she is insensible of a Lunar Eclipse happening in her Horizon this Year.'[86]

Almanacs of all kinds were popular on account of their range of information, since they focused on astronomical rather than astrological events, including dates and times of eclipses, tide tables and, crucially, dates of the phases of the moon and the times when the moon would rise and set each day. Moonlight was so important for night-time travelling that this feature alone sold countless copies, and many evolved into local pocket books or diaries. Almanacs also contained calendars marked with Christian festivals and holy days.

Although Christmas was observed, it was not the major holiday that it is today. Houses were decorated with greenery, usually holly or laurel. 'This being Christmas Eve,' noted Woodforde in 1791, 'had my windows as usual ornamented with small branches of Hulver (alias Holley) properly seeded [with berries].'[87] Christmas Day was marked by a church service and then a dinner with plum pudding and mince pies. The custom of giving servants and tradesmen small gifts of money – 'Christmas boxes' – was growing, but most other rituals that we now associate with Christmas were imported in the later nineteenth century from America and the Continent. New Year was more often the time for celebration and the exchange of gifts, and many still clung to the Old Christmas Day of 6 January (from where the calendar was changed in 1752, causing eleven days to be lost).[88] On one occasion, Holland grumbled: 'The Clerk was here today carrying out dung tho not yesterday it being old Christmas day as he calls it and therefore a holiday; that is after he had kept a week of holidays for new Christmas day.'[89]

Traditional customs associated with particular days of the year were often excuses for the poor, especially children, to go begging. On 14 February 1788 Woodforde gave away thirty-seven pennies: 'This being Valentines Day, I had a good many children of my parish called on me, to each of whom, gave (as usual) one penny, in all 0.3.1.'[90] It was customary for children to 'earn' their money by reciting a verse that started with words like 'Morrow, Morrow, Valentine' or 'Good Morrow Valentine', and Woodforde usually made his young visitors recite at least the first line.

Easter was a festival frequently associated with more traditions than Christmas, though these varied from place to place. In April 1789 the *New Exeter Journal* was struck by events further north:

> It is still the custom in the North of England, at this season of Easter, to present paste (or pasche) eggs to young women; they are covered with gold leaf, and stained. This is a relic of antient superstition, an egg being in former times considered as a type of our Saviour's resurrection. Chandler, in his account of Asia Minor says, 'They presented us with coloured eggs at Easter.' Originally women used to beat their husbands on Easter-Tuesday; and on the Wednesday following the husbands beat their wives. Of the great number of customs and ceremonies which prevailed in times of old, very few now remain.[91]

This notion of old ceremonies fast disappearing was probably overstated, though a decline in observing rituals was partly due to changes in working practices. Someone working shifts in a factory was much less able to celebrate the old customs than someone doing piecework at home.

Other more practical traditions also declined, such as the perambulation of the parish boundaries – usually called 'beating the boundaries' (or 'bounds'). The purpose of this ancient custom was to mark the boundaries each year, because few maps existed and there were few indications of the position of boundaries in the open landscapes. However, enclosures by private Act of Parliament – Enclosure (or Inclosure) Acts – increasingly divided the countryside into small units bounded by hedges, walls and fences. From 1750 such enclosures affected around a quarter of the total area of England and Wales.[92] Because some of these new field boundaries followed the parish boundaries, the practical need for beating the bounds was disappearing.

Wherever the custom continued, it usually took place in Rogation Week, and the rituals involved beating boundary stones and other markers with sticks, which were often carried by young boys to ensure that the boundaries were learned by the younger generation. At Ripon in Yorkshire, the *Gentleman's Magazine* mentioned, 'the day before Holy Thursday [Ascension Day], all the clergy, attended by the singing men and boys of the choir, perambulate the town in their canonicals, singing hymns; and the blue-coat charity boys follow, singing, with green boughs in their hands'.[93] On Wednesday 3 May 1780, which was also the day before Ascension Day, Woodforde recorded the more down-to-earth ceremonies in his Norfolk parish of Weston Longville:

> About ½ past nine o'clock this morning my Squire called on me, and I took my mare and went with him to the Hart [inn] just by the Church where most of the parish were assembled to go the bounds of the parish, and at 10 we all set of[f] for the same about 30 in number. Went towards Ringland first, then to the breaks near Mr. Townsends clumps, from thence to Attertons on France Green, where the people had some liquor, and which I paid, being usual for the Rector – o.4.6.[94]

Farmers along the route often provided sustenance, but on this occasion Woodforde was responsible.

The procession then continued: 'From France Green we went away to Mr. Dades, from thence towards Risings, from thence down to Mr. Gallands, then to the old Hall of my Squire's, thence to the old Bridge at Lenewade, then close to the River till we came near

Morton, then by Mr. Le Grisse's Clumps, then by Bakers and so back till we came to the place where we first set off.'[95] The complete circuit of the parish was quite a journey: 'Our bounds are supposed to be about 12 miles round. We were going of them full 5 hours. We set of[f] at 10 in the morning and got back a little after 3 in the afternoon ... Where there was no tree to mark, holes were made and stones cast in.'[96]

Some old customs could be seen in the church itself. When an unmarried woman died, a garland of flowers, usually called a 'maiden garland', might accompany the coffin. After the funeral it was hung up in the church above the seat she had used. This ritual was disappearing towards the close of the eighteenth century. In June 1790 John Byng, who was conscious of such fading traditions, noted it in the church of St John the Baptist at Tideswell in Derbyshire:

After dinner, I enter'd the church, which, without, is beautiful; (quite a model); and within, of excellent architecture: it has at one corner, a noble stone pulpit, now disused, and there are two fine old tombs, (one of the Meverils,) and several figures in stone; but the chancel, belonging to the deanery of Litchfield, is in disgraceful waste; and the church wants new benching, most grievously. They here continue to hang up maiden garlands, which, however laudable, as of tendency to virtue, will soon be laugh'd out of practice.'[97]

His melancholy thoughts led him to predict a dismal future: 'and as I now visit decay'd monasteries, so will my grandchildren ... view the ruins of churches, when they and religion altogether shall be o'erthrown'.[98]

# SEVEN

———•◆•———

# WEALTH AND WORK

'I am afraid,' replied Elinor, 'that the pleasantness of an employment does not always evince its propriety.'

*Sense and Sensibility*, by Jane Austen

Most people needed to work for a living – from clergymen, merchants and lawyers down to the lowliest labourers and servants. The professional classes were almost exclusively male, but amongst the working class countless women and children toiled equally long hours alongside the men. By contrast Sir John and Lady Middleton in *Sense and Sensibility* lead somewhat empty lives: 'Sir John was a sportsman, Lady Middleton a mother. He hunted and shot, and she humoured her children; and these were their only resources. Lady Middleton had the advantage of being able to spoil her children, while Sir John's independent employments were in existence only half the time.' The fictional Middletons represented the tiny minority who controlled the bulk of the wealth and disdained those in trade.

While the basic inequalities of the class system were tolerated, the necessity to finance the wars and the royal family through taxation caused resentment. The lower and middle classes struggled with increased taxes and prices, and at the same time the wages of manual workers were frequently being reduced. The tax burden fell disproportionately on the lower ranks, widening the gulf between rich and poor. The idea that the Government should be more equitable was expressed in 1795 by William Jenkin, a Quaker:

> I fear some of those great folks look more to their great salaries, Pensions and Synecures than to the real good of the state. If they wish to convince the public that the latter is their chief concern let them in these perilous times make a voluntary sacrifice of a part of their enormous income to the public good; or at least by acts of benevolence lighten the burdens of the lower orders of the people, many of whom now groan under the pressure of the high price of most of the necessaries of life.[1]

In his memoirs William Darter voiced a similar opinion: 'I have related these events, of which I have perfect recollection, to shew the straits to which the country was driven at this time. Everything almost was taxed, even light and air.'[2]

Although the Reverend James Woodforde was a loyal supporter of George III, in December 1797 his irritation surfaced:

> Great uneasiness in almost every part of the Kingdom respecting the new taxes to be raised for the next year. London very much against them and will not pay them. The times at present are ... very alarming. The King going in State next week, to St. Pauls, to return thanks to Almighty God, for the late signal victories, is much talked of, with regard to the great expence to the Nation must be put to. It is certainly a very good intention of his Majesty but he should come forward in it, by advancing money to pay the expences of the same out of his own purse, he being so exceedingly rich and at so critical a time.[3]

On top of more and more taxes, an income tax was introduced in 1799, which was particularly resented by the middle and upper classes. A few years later William Holland complained because deductions were made from the dividend on his shares for Maidenhead Bridge across the River Thames: 'We cannot have our dividends from Maidenhead Bridge this fortnight on account of the Income Tax. This is rather hard to detain 25 pound because thirty shillings are demanded by government.'[4]

The idle rich were truly idle, as epitomised by Edward Ferrars in *Sense and Sensibility*. He is in line to inherit a fortune, but Mrs Dashwood suggests adopting a profession to fill his time. 'I do assure you', he replies,

that I have long thought on this point … But unfortunately my own nicety, and the nicety of my friends, have made me what I am, an idle, helpless being. We never could agree in our choice of profession. I always preferred the church, as I still do. But that was not smart enough for my family. They recommended the army. That was a great deal too smart for me. The law was allowed to be genteel enough … But I had no inclination for the law … As for the navy, it had fashion in its side, but I was too old when the subject was first started to enter it – and, at length, as there was no necessity for my having any profession at all … I was therefore entered at Oxford and have been properly idle since then.

In his travels round England, the American scientist Benjamin Silliman, a young man who was actively immersed in research and education, was dismayed by such empty lives: 'Bath … is probably the most dissipated place in the kingdom. It is resorted to by many real invalids, but by far the greater number belong to that class who wear away life in a round of fashionable frivolities, without moral aim or intellectual dignity.'[5]

Wealth might be tied up in property, land and other investments, but cash was hoarded at home or deposited in banks. 'Very busy in settling Bathursts accounts,' Woodforde noted in mid-November 1782, 'as I intend going to Norwich on Monday next on his account.'[6] The clergyman Henry Bathurst held the livings of nearby Great and Little Witchingham, but his friend Woodforde collected the tithes for him because he was non-resident. Three days later Woodforde went to Norwich, calling at 'Kerrisons Bank and changed 100 pounds in cash for a note of the same value and sent it to Dr Bathurst and put the letter myself into the Post-Office'.[7] This local bank failed in 1808 with substantial debts, as did many others over the years – including the bank of Jane Austen's brother Henry.[8]

Banking was in a state of flux, and innumerable country banks were set up to meet local needs. Other businesses also conducted banking, such as a silversmiths at Oxford where Woodforde changed money in 1793: 'Called on my friend Locke the silversmith this morning who behaved very obligingly and knew me at first sight. I changed a ten pound note with him, he keeps a bank and does great business.'[9] Banknotes were technically redeemable only at the issuing banks – standardised banknotes that were legal tender, accepted by all banks, would not be fully established until 1833.

The monetary system was based on gold and silver. Twenty shillings (20s.) were worth one pound sterling (£1 or 1l.), and twelve pennies (12d.) equalled one shilling. There were no one-pound coins. The guinea (worth £1 and 1 shilling, or 21 shillings, abbreviated to £1 1s.) was a gold coin, and other gold coins included a five guinea (£5 5s.), half a guinea (10s. 6d.), quarter of a guinea (5s. 3d.) and one-third of a guinea (7s.). Silver coins included one crown (5s.), half-a-crown (2s. 6d.), one shilling (1s.), sixpence (6d.), fourpence (4d.), twopence (2d.) and some earlier pennies. As the coinage devalued over time, pennies were instead minted of copper alloy, as were the halfpenny (½d.) and farthing (¼d.).[10]

Most people were paid in coins, and they would buy whatever they needed with coins. Anyone contracted for a year, such as servants and agricultural workers, were usually paid just once or twice over that period, but large quantities of coins were needed for day-labourers and for factory workers who were paid weekly or monthly. When he was at Reeth in Yorkshire, Charles Fothergill learned about problems paying the lead miners: 'The wages of this class of labourer are good and are generally paid monthly ... this is occasioned by the scarcity of small change which must be obtained if the men are paid weekly. The men in consequence with their families are obliged weekly to go in debt to the shops for their necessary provisions.'[11]

The official mint could not meet the demand for lower-value coins because of obsolete machinery and methods, and so private companies began to issue farthing, halfpenny and penny tokens as small change. From 1787 the Anglesey Copper Mines Company issued copper tokens – around three hundred tons over the next three decades. Other companies followed, and as these tokens proliferated, shopkeepers and traders used sorting boxes to arrange them by the names of the different issuing companies. Businesses were quick to realise the potential of tokens for advertising and propaganda, which resulted in numerous designs and inscriptions, and sets of tokens bearing portraits of famous people, buildings and other features were aimed at collectors. Tokens from various sources were encountered every day, as the traveller John Byng found in Derbyshire: 'at the turnpike, I was surprised to receive in change the Anglesea, and Macclesfield half-pence; a better coinage, and of more beauty than that of the mint, and not so likely to be counterfeited'.[12] These tokens had been issued by the Anglesey company and by Roe and Company, which was a Macclesfield copper company. In 1817 the Government prohibited the manufacture of tokens and ordered issuing companies to redeem them, the only exceptions being tokens of the Sheffield and Birmingham workhouses.

The wars were a continual drain on England's gold reserves, threatening the stability of the economy and hindering commerce. Fears of invasion also caused the hoarding of gold and a run on banks, and by February 1797 the situation was so serious that the Bank of England stopped redeeming its promissory banknotes in coin. This worrying news reached Woodforde in Norfolk on 1 March: 'Mr. Custance with his son Willm. made us a morning visit, informed us, that a proclamation from the Privy Council had been issued, to stop paying in cash at the Bank of England for some time, fearing that if not stopped, there would not be . . . enough to transact necessary and urgent business. On that account, all country banks have done the same, and are at present shut up.'[13]

There was immediate opposition in Parliament, and the playwright and MP Richard Brinsley Sheridan derided the Bank of England as 'an elderly lady in the city'. James Gillray made use of this idea in a cartoon termed 'The Old Lady of Threadneedle Street', a nickname for the Bank that has persisted. The shortage of coins brought some industries to a standstill, and the radical writer and historian John Blackner related what happened in Nottingham where he was living: 'In 1797, the refusal of the Bank of England to pay its notes in cash [coins] in February was attended with the most serious consequences to Nottingham and its vicinity, by causing an immediate stoppage of a great number of [knitting] frames for want of cash to go on with, nor could the ordinary business of the town be carried on, until one or both of the then banking-houses had issued out a quantity of seven shilling tickets.'[14] In mid-March that year, Woodforde wrote anxiously: 'There being little or no cash stirring and the country bank notes being refused to be taken, create great uneasiness in almost all people, fearful what consequences may follow. Excise officers refuse taking country notes for the payment of the several duties. Many do not know what to do on the present occasion having but very little cash by them.'[15]

The Bank of England did have sufficient reserves and was now authorised to issue banknotes for £1 and £2, where previously it could not issue them below £5. Once the new paper currency was found to be convenient, the panic subsided. The drain on gold reserves was abated, and although banknotes were not officially legal tender, they effectively became token money.[16] Problems did recur, as William Holland discovered in July 1810: 'I walked to [Nether] Stowey to change a bank bill [banknote] for cash but no cash to be had and I would not take any country bills, there being a run on the banks at this time, and I would not part with what is good for what is doubtful.'[17] In case they proved to have no value, he had refused to accept smaller banknotes.

What did ease the coin shortage was the capture in naval battles of Spanish silver dollars, which were circulated as legal currency after being overstamped. Woodforde, who liked to collect unusual coins, commented in late March 1797: 'Went up to Betty Carys [his local shop] this evening and got of her two Spanish dollars, having our Kings Head in miniature stamped on the neck of the King of Spain, alluding to the great victory over the Spanish fleet [Battle of St Vincent], lately, by Sr. Jon. Jervis. They are made current now in England and go for 4s/9d. I gave Betty for the two 0.9.6.'[18]

It was not long before counterfeit dollars were being produced, and the increase in paper money also made banknotes a prime target for forgers. Many forgeries were the work of foreign prisoners-of-war, as one newspaper reported in 1810:

A great number of Bank of England forged notes and counterfeit seven shilling-pieces are now in circulation in Plymouth and its neighbourhood: several persons detected in uttering them were taken into custody on Saturday night. They are supposed to be the manufacture of French prisoners, whose ingenuity this way is very astonishing. Several of the one-pound notes had been sold at one shilling each.[19]

The main method of putting counterfeit coins and notes into circulation was through the retail trade, and the magistrate Patrick Colquhoun said that many criminals, gamblers, hawkers and pedlars left London in the spring, 'carrying with them considerable quantities of counterfeit silver and copper coin, by which they are enabled ... to extend the circulation by cheating and defrauding ignorant country people'.[20] London with its many shops also suffered. In 1815 James Hill appeared before a magistrate 'charged with having passed several counterfeit sixpences, knowing them to be so. It appeared that the prisoner had gone into many shops in the neighbourhood of Kentish-town, and purchased trivial articles, in payment of which he tendered the sixpences.'[21]

A popular way of sending one-guinea gold coins in the post was to hide them beneath the wax seal of a letter, while banknotes could be slipped inside. Because the mail contained cash and banknotes, robbing unarmed post-boys proved lucrative, and so in 1782 the Post Office advised sending banknotes in two separate halves. This led to serial numbers being duplicated on banknotes, one at each end, so that the two halves could be matched and presented to a bank. The practice of duplicate numbers continues today.[22] As a precaution, Holland sent his banknote halves on separate days to the surgeon who had treated his wife's leg at Bath: 'I called at [Nether] Stowey and deliver'd a letter to Mr Paddock directed to Mr Baynton with banknotes in it for the cure of my wife's leg which (by the by) is not perfectly cured, and the sum required is large, no less than thirty pound and a multiplicity of expences besides.'[23] Then a week later: 'I have been very busy in writing letters and inclosing halves of notes for Mr Baynton for the cure of my wife's leg, if it may be call'd so, for I do not think it is quite well.'[24]

Most people obtained goods and services locally and paid in cash. Living close to the busy city of Norwich, just 8 miles from Weston Longville, Woodforde had accounts with many tradesmen and merchants there. Norwich was a sizeable place, with a population of some 36,000 in 1801, and on special trips Woodforde settled outstanding bills and bought or ordered anything else that was needed, as in June 1780:

| | |
|---|---|
| To my barber Mileham gave | 0: 1: 0 |
| To his boy for bringing down my wig, gave | 0: 0: 2 |
| | |
| I went to Freemans shop and bespoke some furniture | |
| To 4 Pappa-marche [papier-mâché] decanter stands | |
| of Baker pd. | 0: 7: 6 |
| To snuffer stand of ditto paid | 0: 1: 6 |
| To a small burning glass of do pd | 0: 1: 0 |
| To 2 small combs and cases of do pd | 0: 1: 2 |
| To Miss Bell, mantua maker, for Nancy, pd. | 1: 4: 6.[25] |

Those with money could purchase goods in London, and even Jane Austen's household had tea supplied direct from the city to Chawton.[26] In 1782 Carl Moritz was amazed by London's huge range of shops:

It has a strange appearance, especially in the Strand, where there is a constant succession of shop after shop, and where, not infrequently, people of different trades inhabit the same house, to see their doors, or the tops of their windows, or boards expressly for the purpose, all written over from top to bottom, with large painted letters ... there is hardly a cobbler, whose name and profession may not be read in large golden characters by every one that passes. It is here not at all uncommon to see on doors, in one continuous succession, 'Children educated here', 'Shoes mended here', 'Foreign spiritous liquors sold here', and 'Funerals furnished here'.[27]

Outside the major towns and cities, temporary market stalls were far more common than shops, and most towns and even large villages had weekly markets for fresh produce. Woodforde was fortunate to have Betty Cary's shop nearby, but for such retailers there was no modern system of distribution and supply. 'As posterity may be ignorant what a bag-man is,' John Byng explained, 'let them learn that he is a rider, who travells, with saddle bags, to receive of shop keepers a list of what goods are wanting from manufactories, and wholesale dealers; and to collect the debts.'[28]

In London and elsewhere, pedlars sold all kinds of goods in the streets, from fruit and vegetables to cooked food, milk, shellfish and flowers. Really poor street traders might be part-time beggars, selling the lowest-value items such as matches. Woodforde found it convenient to buy from pedlars who obtained their merchandise in small quantities from manufacturers and sold door-to-door. In May 1780 he noted his recent purchases: 'To a man (whose name was Pedralio an Italian and who is the manager of the fire works at Bunns Gardens at Norwich) and who makes thermometers and barometers and carries them about the country, called at my house this morning with some of them and I bought one each for which I paid him 1.16.0.'[29] One of the most awkward household purchases was firewood and coal. William Holland in Somerset had an account with a local coal merchant: 'Hawkins brought in his bill for coal this day, which I paid,' he wrote in January 1802. 'I believe he has not charged one load, which I shall inquire into. He is a very civil, honest man.'[30] This was praise indeed from Holland, as he was normally highly critical of most people.

Households and the steam-driven industries were ever hungry for coal – literally the power behind the Industrial Revolution. The conversion from manual labour to steam-driven machines led to increased coal production, which in turn led to a demand from the coal industry for steam engines for pumps and winding gear. The improved steam engines were also used for manufacturing, which brought about the factory system of working that replaced many cottage industries. Although coal was mined elsewhere in England, the predominant source was 'sea coal', an old term for coal mined in north-east England, while 'coal' tended to mean charcoal.

The export hub for sea coal was Newcastle-upon-Tyne, a large port surrounded by countless mines and associated industries. A traditional folk song from there begins:

> As I cam thro' Sandgate, thro' Sandgate, thro' Sandgate,
> As I cam thro' Sandgate, I heard a lassie sing,
> Weel may the keel row, the keel row, the keel row,
> Weel may the keel row, that my laddie's in.[31]

The Sandgate, taking its name from the Sand Gate in the city walls, was a street in Newcastle forming the heart of the community of keelmen, and the 'lassie' was very likely to sing 'well may the keel row that my laddie's in', because their income depended on it. A 'keel' was a small boat that carried a load of around 20 tons of coal from the mines down the River Tyne and then transferred it to the seagoing ships known as 'colliers'. During a visit to Newcastle in November 1787, the surgeon Lionel Gillespie was impressed by the industry's scale:

> The coals are brought down the river in flat vessels called keels and the number of those employed is immense, each of them carries three men and a boy or old man. These vessels are sail'd, row'd, dragged or poled along the river, and sometimes two or three of these means are put in practice at one and the same time, for as the keelmen are pay'd by the trip, the incentive to industry is strong.[32]

Thousands of keelmen were employed on the Tyne river, who Frederick Eden described a few years later: 'Keelmen, (of whom 6000 or 7000 are constantly employed in navigating keels with coal, from the collieries on the Tyne to Shields,) are paid from 15s. to 20s. a week. Sailors, in time of war, are paid, from 6 to 11 guineas, for a voyage to London, which is often performed in a month, or less.'[33] As the mines were clustered close to the port, land transport costs were minimised, giving Newcastle its supremacy and resulting in the phrase 'taking coals to Newcastle', meaning a pointless exercise.

When Louis Simond was at Newcastle in 1811, he was surprised that the coal was exported: 'The continent of Europe draws from

England, notwithstanding the war, a quantity of coals ... said to amount to £500,000 or £600,000 a year. Some are exported to the West India islands, and the inhabitants of the larger seaport towns of the United States warm themselves almost entirely with English coals, cheaper than the wood of their forests.'[34]

At all stages, the transportation of coal involved gruelling manual labour, sometimes coupled with considerable danger. Frequent accidents occurred in the loading and unloading of the coal, and the sea passage down the east coast saw numerous shipwrecks. The mines themselves held the greatest risks, and newspapers carried countless depressing reports of pit disasters. Even without explosions, though, coal mining was hazardous, with many miners killed or injured in accidents and roof falls. Simond chanced going down one mine:

> The mode is rather alarming. The extremity of the rope which works up and down the shaft being formed into a loop, you pass one leg through it, so as to sit, or to be almost astride on the rope; then, hugging it with both arms, you are turned off from the platform over a dark abyss, where you would hardly venture if the depth was seen. This was 63 fathoms (378 feet). One of the workmen bestrode the loop by the side of me, and down we went with considerable rapidity. The wall of rock seemed to rush upwards, the darkness increased, the mouth above appeared a mere speck of light. I shut my eyes for fear of growing giddy, the motion soon diminished, and we touched the ground ... Each of us had a flannel dress and a candle, and thus proceeded through a long passage, rock above, rock below, and a shining black wall of coal on each side.[35]

Conditions were more brutal down the mines than those endured in most other occupations, particularly as the amount of wages depended on the amount of coal produced. Simond observed how it was cut: 'The ceiling of [the main road is] ... high enough for a man to stand upright, while the side streets are no higher than the stratum of coals (4½ feet), therefore you must walk stooping. The whole extent of the mine is worked in streets intersecting each other at right angles, 24 feet wide and 36 feet asunder, leaving solid blocks 36 feet every way.'[36] This was the 'pillar and stall' method, which extracted about half the available coal. It was so-called because the coal was mined from areas called 'stalls', leaving large rectangular pillars of coal to support the roof. The other common method of mining was the 'long wall'. First, a shaft was dug following the coal seam. Then one side of the shaft was cut away by the miners who dumped the waste rock on the other side of the shaft. This helped to support the roof as the 'long wall' of the shaft moved sideways through the coal seam.

There were frequent roof falls, as happened to young Josh Gibson, who in about 1796 started working 'in a pit at Shipley [Yorkshire] when seven years old; drove a pony until he was above nine, when he then went behind, and was hooked to the waggon with a belt. He found it hurt him much ... when about 12 years old he was crushed bad by the roof falling.'[37] For the men, women and children who worked down the mines, there was often little alternative employment. In Scotland the miners were virtually slaves until an Act of Parliament came into force in 1775.[38] South of the border, in the northern counties of England, a similar situation prevailed, with the miners commonly hired on a yearly basis. They signed a bond agreeing to work without strikes or absences, and in return were paid a premium that could be relatively high. In 1795 Frederick Eden thought that the wages of the miners around Newcastle were generous:

Pit men earn from 1s. 6d. to 3s. 6d. a day; on an average, about 16s. a week; besides which, they are allowed rye from their masters, at 4s. the bushel. Notwithstanding these high wages, they are seldom richer than their neighbours. They use a great deal of butcher's meat, during the three or four first days of the week; but, towards the close of it, as their earnings of the preceding week become nearly exhausted, they are generally obliged to live more frugally and abstemiously.[39]

Miners did break their bond from time to time, and mine owners would advertise for their capture, as in the *Newcastle Journal* in 1777:

## PITMEN ABSCONDED.

Whereas Thomas Norton, aged about 35 years or thereabouts, and Thomas Green, aged 46 years or thereabouts, colliers, lawfully bound and hired to work at Byker-hill colliery from the 9th day of October 1776, to the 9th day of October 1777, have unlawfully absented themselves from the said colliery:– Notice is hereby given, to all Coal-owners, their agents, or others, not to employ the said persons, or they will be prosecuted as the law in that case directs; and any person giving information where they may be apprehended, to Mr Joseph Hunter, at Byker-hill, shall be well rewarded.[40]

The expansion of coal production depended on cheap transport. Once the coal reached the sea ports, it was taken inland by river and canal craft via a network of waterways, though the final few miles might need to be by horse and cart or by packhorse. From the early eighteenth century canals were built to join rivers, and rivers themselves were canalised to make them navigable. Canals were increasingly regarded as the solution to the problem of transporting heavy and bulky goods, including coal, though one canal between Stourbridge and Dudley, designed to carry cheaper coal to the Stourbridge-based industries, was not universally welcome:

an act [of Parliament] was obtained for carrying the plan into execution, though not without great opposition from the coal-owners upon the Birmingham canal, and the owners of the mills upon the river Stour: the first because this canal would enable the coal-owners upon it to under-sell the others at the market, and the latter upon account of the supposed loss of water to their mills, for which they had very little reason, for nearly all the water ... must be raised out of the mines.[41]

First proposed in 1775, this canal was given parliamentary assent the following year and was operational by the end of 1779.

The success of canals saw an explosion in canal building and speculation in the 1790s – such that it became known as 'canal mania'. There were no mechanical excavators because steam engines were not easily moved about, and so canals were formed by hundreds of labourers digging with hand tools and shifting the spoil in wheelbarrows. These workmen were drawn from all over the country, some through advertisements, such as one that appeared in an Exeter newspaper in 1810:

To CANAL CUTTERS &c.

WANTED, TWO or THREE HUNDRED good WORKMEN on the WORCESTER and BIRMINGHAM CANAL, where liberal Prices will be given to Agg Masters [subcontractors]; and good Wages to Workmen that are ready and deserving encouragement, by applying to Mr. Charles Holland, at Tibberton, near Worcester.[42]

With increasing numbers of canals being cut, gangs of labourers moved from job to job, setting up camp wherever they went. They were originally called 'canal cutters' or simply 'workmen', but because canals were known as 'inland navigations' and the engineers who oversaw the projects were called 'navigators', this term was eventually extended to the labourers and then abbreviated to 'navvies'. The better-known gangs of Victorian railway navvies evolved from these bands of Georgian canal navvies.

Relentless effort and skill were needed to wield tools like picks, mattocks, shovels and loaded wheelbarrows, and not all labourers could work sufficiently fast to earn a living, because it was piece-work – a set price for digging a certain distance of canal or tunnel, such as the £7 per yard paid to the subcontractors cutting the Sapperton tunnel in Gloucestershire on the Thames and Severn Canal. When the Basingstoke Canal began to be constructed in 1788, this problem was witnessed by the Reverend Stebbing Shaw at the Greywell tunnel, some 13 miles from Steventon where Jane Austen was then living:

I ... saw above 100 men at work, preparing a wide passage for the approach to the mouth, but they had not entered the hill ... The contractor, agreeable to the request of the company of proprietors, gives the preference to all the natives who are desirous of this work, but such is the power of use over nature, that while these industrious poor are by all their efforts incapable of earning a sustenance, those who are brought from similar works, cheerfully obtain a comfortable support.[43]

The absence of safety measures was especially evident to John Byng during an uncomfortable visit to the tunnel being constructed at Sapperton:

Nothing cou'd be more gloomy than . . . being dragg'd [by sledge cart] into the bowels of the earth, rumbling and jumbling thro mud, over stones, with a small lighted candle in my hand, giving me a sight of the last horse . . . When the last peep of day light vanish'd, I was enveloped in thick smoke arising from the gunpowder of the miners, at whom, after passing by many labourers who work by small candles, I did at last arrive: they come from the Derbyshire and Cornish mines, are in eternal danger and frequently perish by the falls of earth. My cart being reladen with stone, I was hoisted thereon . . . and had a worse journey back, as I cou'd scarcely keep my seat . . . I understand that they have made an equal progress (½ mile) at the other end, and hope to meet in 3 years; when the first passage thro', in a barge, must be glorious, and horrid.[44]

When it opened in 1789, the Sapperton Tunnel was the longest in England at over 2 miles, and the canal running through it linked the Thames and Severn rivers.

Travelling near Bath over a decade later, Richard Warner commented on the growing canal network:

At a short distance from hence [South Stoke], in the bottom below, we meet with the *canal*, a recent undertaking, intended to convey the coals of the Timsbury, Paulton, Camerton, and Dunkerton pits to Bath. The course of this cut, which is not yet compleated, will embrace in its various windings, to its junction with the Radstock cut, a distance of ten miles, and pass through a country as highly picturesque as any in the kingdom.[45]

New canals provided an increasing amount of work for the many thousands who ran boats, but with real wages falling, it made sense for a boatman's family to live on board rather than pay rent for lodgings. In 1815–16 one Christian organisation undertook a survey of the Grand Junction Canal's floating population:

> It appeared upon inquiry, that the number of boats was between four and five hundred; that the number of men on the line of the Grand Junction Canal, the collateral branches, with the engine and lock houses, might be estimated at six thousand; and that, including their wives and children, the number of persons to be taken into consideration was probably not less than twenty thousand. These may be said almost to live upon the water, and, by the peculiar nature of their occupation, are precluded from all opportunity of attending public worship on the Sabbath-day.[46]

Once it became cheaper and easier to transport coal inland, there was a greater incentive to develop steam engines to power machinery of all kinds, from which the woollen and cotton textile industries in particular benefited. Since the Middle Ages textile manufacture based on wool was a major element of England's economy, organised and funded by businessmen dealing in finished cloth. Each process needed to transform raw sheep's wool into a saleable product was carried out by thousands of scattered individual workers, usually paid on a piecework basis. Middlemen bought and supplied the materials, such as spun yarn to the weavers or woven cloth to the fullers, afterwards collecting the finished work. They might even lend or lease looms and other equipment. Spinning was done by hand, mostly by the women of farming families or those who worked in the textile trade, and by the end of the seventeenth century the term 'spinster', originally meaning a female spinner, had become the term for an unmarried woman. Weaving was a task more often done by men. By the late eighteenth century none of the textile processes was particularly well paid, but being piecework with such a loose organisational basis, families could live and work together at home, taking off as much time as they wanted.

The introduction of machines made some workers redundant

and forced many more into the factories, which were considerably more efficient and yielded higher profits for their owners. However, the factory hands found that not only did they need to work more hours for the same money, but they lost the old freedom to choose when to work and when to rest. They even had to arrive punctually or lose wages. Although some factories installed a bell or whistle to signal shift changes, it was the individual's responsibility to get to work on time, and so a new job sprang up – that of the 'knocker-up', who for a small fee went round and roused workers for their shift.

Some workers owned pocket watches, and wealthier households might possess one or more clocks. William Holland had a seven-day clock, which he wound every Saturday evening, as he noted in October 1800: 'The evening by ourselves, and spent as we usually do the Saturday evenings, poring over sermons, winding the clock and to bed.'[47] The chiming of the church clock was also an important indicator of time, but most people estimated time by the level of daylight. In towns, night watchmen often called out the hour, and William Darter in Reading praised one watchman who was always helpful: 'I remember well Norcroft's features, and the sound of his voice "Past two o'clock and a cloudy morning," &c.'[48]

Another great change for the new factory workers was the necessity to travel to work, which could add significantly to the length and effort of an arduous day. Some began to view the recent past as a golden age, cruelly stolen from them, and a contemporary song lamented the changes:

So come all you cotton-weavers, you must rise up very soon,
For you must work in factories from morning until noon;
You mustn't walk in your garden for two or three hours a day,
And you must stand at their command and keep your shuttles in play.[49]

The textile industry thrived and remained the second largest employer in the country after agriculture, despite the job losses due to mechanisation. In 1800 Warner described the changing woollen cloth production in Somerset:

Frome has for many years been famous for working Spanish and English wool into broad-cloths and kerseymeres ... The quantity of wool manufactured here is since considerably increased, but the number of people employed is diminished, the introduction of machines having lessened, in a prodigious proportion, the call for manual labour. At present there are in the town of Frome twenty-seven manufacturers of cloth, who make ... about one hundred and sixty miles of cloth, in length, every year.[50]

The cotton industry was also on the rise, rapidly adopting the new ways of working, although it would not dominate British manufacturing as 'King Cotton' for many decades to come. In June 1790 at Cromford in Derbyshire, John Byng observed Arkwright's water-powered spinning mill: 'These cotton mills, seven stories high, and fill'd with inhabitants, remind me of a first rate man of war; and when they are lighted up, on a dark night, look most luminously beautiful.'[51] On a tour from Oxford to the Lake District a few years later, Johnson Grant stopped at nearby Bakewell, where he was concerned about the effects of such factories on the health of workers:

[I] passed a cotton manufactory; the people all coming out to dinner, for it was already one o'clock. From the glance I had of their appearance, the observations I made were these: They were pale, and their hats were covered with shreds of cotton. Exclusive of want of exercise, the general bane of all manufactures, the light particles of cotton must be inhaled with their breath, and occasion pulmonary affections. Owners of factories should consider this ... Let every such person, then, order his work-people to bathe every morning, and let him have a piece of playground for them, wherein some athletic and innocent exercise might be enjoyed for an hour or two, each day. In cottonworks, let them drink much water.[52]

Grant was a clergyman, traveller and prolific writer, and he was afraid that the factory workers might question the class system and therefore the established order. Wages, he argued, should not be exorbitant, though limited education was desirable: 'establish a

Sunday-school, where they might be instructed orally, without being taught to read. This I deem a necessary precaution, as they would have all the advantages of improvement of mind and morals, without their common banes – low political club-rooms, with their idleness, their liquors, and neglect of families.'[53] In his opinion, too much education might encourage the realisation that there was no natural or God-given basis to the inequalities in society, and this might be a road to revolution. He feared that factory hands already went unwillingly to work, 'discontented, and cursing all laws, human and divine, which have so arranged matters, that yon stately house [nearby Chatsworth], and the gilded coach in which its owner rides, should belong to what the Corresponding Society, the illuminati and illuminantes of this country, have deluded him ... is an individual with no better title to it than himself.'[54] This particular individual was the immensely wealthy Duke of Devonshire.

Many workers were already pushed to the brink of destitution and starvation and were increasingly aware of injustices in society. The song called 'The Hand-Loom Weavers' Lament' was written sometime between 1807 and 1815 and was about those made unemployed by the advent of the factories. Two verses in particular addressed their so-called superiors:

When we look on our poor children, it grieves our hearts full sore,
Their clothing it is worn to rags, while we can get no more,
With little in their bellies, they to their work must go,
Whilst yours do dress as manky as monkeys in a show.

You go to church on Sundays, I'm sure it's nought but pride,
There can be no religion where humanity's thrown aside;
If there be a place in heaven, as there is in the Exchange,
Our poor souls must not come near there; like lost sheep they
    must range.[55]

The 'Exchange' was the Royal Exchange in London, equivalent to the modern shorthand of 'the City', meaning the financial establishment. If these verses caused discomfort, the chorus caused alarm:

You tyrants of England, your race may soon be run,
You may be brought unto account for what you've sorely done.[56]

Popular at the time, and intermittently popular ever since, this has been labelled a Luddite song, and it certainly arose at a time and place where the Luddites were active.

'Luddite' was the name given to a shadowy group of workers who reacted to the new practices within factories by destroying the machines. Their initial target was the wide knitting frames that were introduced to cut costs. These machines produced large pieces of cloth from which stockings were cut and then sewn into shape. Previously they were knitted into shape and the woven edges joined in a seam. The new process was faster and needed less skilled labour, but the resulting stockings were inferior, tending to lose their shape and unravel where the seams were formed from the cut edges. The drop in quality gave the whole trade a bad name and affected prices.

Several stories arose that tried to account for the Luddite name, and according to John Blackner in Nottingham, the Luddites 'assumed this appellation from the circumstance of an ignorant youth, in Leicestershire, of the name of Ludlam, who, when ordered by his father, a framework-knitter, to square his needles [adjust the machine because his knitting was too loose], took a hammer and beat them into a heap.'[57] Those factory owners and middlemen who did not produce the substandard stockings tacitly approved of the machine-breaking. Blackner recorded how Luddites operated in Nottinghamshire: 'The practice of these men was to assemble in parties of from six to sixty, according as circumstance required, under a supposed leader, that was stiled *General Ludd*, who had the absolute command of them, and directed their operations; placing the guards, who were armed with swords, firelocks, &c. in their proper places, while those armed with hammers, axes, &c. were ordered to enter the house and demolish the frames.'[58] Blackner also described the Government's frantic response:

In consequence of these outrages being continued, a considerable military force was brought into the neighbourhood; two of the London police magistrates, with some other officers, came down with a view of assisting the civil power in discovering the ringleaders; a considerable sum of money was also placed at the disposal of a secret committee, for the purpose of obtaining private information; but ... these deluded men [the Luddites] continued their course of devastation for several months, and at the end of February, 1812, it was found that no less than six hundred and twenty-four frames had been destroyed.[59]

More concerned with crushing dissension than promoting justice, the Government passed an Act in March 1812 making machine-breaking a capital offence, but the Luddites then attacked machines in other areas. In July that year Nelly Weeton moved from the Pedders in the Lake District to take another post as governess in Yorkshire. Her new employer was Joseph Armitage, a wool manufacturer, and she confided in a friend about the fear of reprisals there from machine-breakers:

Mr. A is engaged in the woollen trade, has a handsome fortune of his own, and had another with his wife, though their parents are all living; at whose death, I suppose, they will have considerably more. They have no carriage, no in-door man-servant; there are four women servants. They kept a man till lately, but as Mr. Armitage's house at Lockwood was one of the first that was attacked by the Luddites a few months ago, he has not ventured to keep a man in his house, as many gentlemen have been betrayed by their servants, who have been discovered to be of the Luddite party.[60]

Very few men were arrested and tried for being Luddites. A few were hanged, more were transported, but the Government was unsuccessful in its attempts to crush the movement. It gradually faded away, having gained little more than a temporary halt to mechanisation. Rather than meaning someone who resists oppression, the word 'Luddite' nowadays refers to a person who holds back progress.

Improved machines had not yet made much impact on agricultural work, which was still labour-intensive. Over one-third of the population worked in farming, which was still England's largest employer.

The work was long and hard.[61] In a single day a ploughman might walk upwards of 11 miles behind a horse-drawn plough just to plough one acre. In October 1784 Woodforde's servant hoped to join their ranks: 'Jack [Wharton, about nineteen years old] told me this morning that he is advised to get another place, being too old for a Skip-Jack [servant boy] any longer. He wants to be a Plow Boy to some farmer to learn the farming business as he likes that best. I told him that he was very right to try to better himself, and at Lady Day next he is to leave my house for that purpose.'[62]

There was always a need for workers capable of handling horses. One enduring English folk song about ploughing, which has several titles, is most commonly known by its chorus line 'We're all jolly fellows who follow the plough'. A cheerful song, it was in circulation by at least 1794[63] and relates how the ploughmen rose around four in the morning to get the horses ready. After breakfast they each go out to plough an acre of ground, returning by two in the afternoon. The farmer then suggests that they have not finished their work:

> I stepped up to him, and I made this reply,
> 'We have all ploughed an acre, so you tell a lie,'
> Our master turned to us and laughed at the joke:
> 'It's past two o'clock boys, it's time to unyoke.'[64]

The horses then had to be cared for and settled down for the night before the men could go home after the long day's work.

Farming was not yet in any real sense mechanised, but improvements in stock breeding were resulting in healthier, hardier animals that provided more meat and milk, while the introduction of some machinery and experimentation with plants and seeds were improving crop yields. Emphasis was placed on improving the fertility of the soil, which had traditionally been maintained by rotating crops to allow fallow periods and by the penning of animals so that land could benefit from their manure. New methods of manuring included the spreading of chalk or lime, though old ways persisted, as a survey of agriculture in Dorset in 1812 noted:

*Chamber-lye.–* In the Isle of Portland, they have a practice of long standing, of preserving all the urine that is made in winter, carrying it out in
casks, and distributing it over the wheat crops, in a manner somewhat
similar to that used in watering the streets of large towns. This kind of
manure has been found to answer well, as may be believed, from the
average produce of the Isle being 18 bushels of wheat per acre.[65]

Many clergymen did some farming, either of church lands or
their own land, which supplemented their income. Jane Austen's
parents farmed land near her father's rectory at Steventon in
Hampshire, and farming activities are mentioned in her letters, as in
November 1798 when she asked Cassandra, who was staying at
Godmersham in Kent, to 'tell Edward that my father gives 25*s.* a
piece to Seward for his last lot of sheep, and, in return for this
news, my father wishes to receive some [news] of Edward's pigs'.[66]
Woodforde also farmed, generally employing a man and a boy for
much of the work and hiring extra labour when needed, particularly
for harvesting, as in September 1776: 'Very busy all day with my
barley, did not dine till near 5 in the afternoon, my harvest men
dined here to day, gave them some beef and some plumb pudding
and as much liquor as they would drink. This evening finished my
harvest and all carried into the barn – 8 acres. I had Mrs. Dunnell's
cart and horses, and 2 men, yesterday and to day. The men were her
son Thos. and Robin Buck.'[67]

Unlike today, farming activities were forced to follow the cycle of
the seasons, with the most intense work during the long days of
summer. Harvest time was the highlight, and the writer and com-
poser William Gardiner had fond memories of helping out at
Rothley near Leicester as a seven-year-old boy in 1778:

With what glee did I mount the harvest waggon for the fun of jolting
over the rugged roads, to the wheat field. From shock to shock it slowly
moved to gather the rustling sheaves. In the rear of the reapers were a
flock of gleaners – some pretty village girls ... The day's toil over, we
hastened home for the harvest supper. At the head of the board sat the
worthy host, by whose side I was placed. Then came Will, Ralph, Joe, and

Jim, with their wives and helpers. Presently a shoulder of mutton, scorching hot, as the day had been, a plum pudding, and a roasted goose were put on the table, when they soon fell to, each playing his part in good earnest ... The gingered ale went merrily round. Joe, who was a good singer, was called upon to entertain the company.[68]

Samuel Pratt gave an equally romantic picture, this time of when the work had subsided during the early winter months:

The fields are no longer populated, and labour is not so enlivened by the song, and the converse of the labourer ... Every store-house is full, and in every cottage, so benign has been the past season, there are the means of comfort and content. The alterations have increased, the beauty of the autumnal foliage has lost its last charm of variegation – and if the naked boughs remind us of the decline of nature, a few leaves only remain, and these tremble at every breath of wind, as if they were conscious of their defenceless situation.[69]

Yet he knew that after helping with the harvest, the poor could starve whenever the farmers withheld their crops to obtain better prices:

famine must enter the cottage of the peasant, whose industry has led smiling plenty into the houses of his employer – and multitudes of the most useful members of the community must cry aloud for bread, while those nefarious robbers of the public, known by the names of Forestallers and Monopolizers – which, I fear, are but other words to cover a certain class of the ENGLISH FARMERS – are permitted to hoard up the stores, which the indulgent God of nature gives to supply the wants of all his creatures.[70]

In the later eighteenth century, with grain prices rising and rents for farmland soaring, particularly for enclosed land, it became economic for large landowners to pay to have even more land enclosed. In old-fashioned open fields, small farmers in a community worked their own strips of land, an inefficient system dating back to the Middle Ages. Some claimed that enclosure was vital to improve these open fields, as well as the commons and waste land, so that more food could be produced. But others believed that enclosure was evil, because rents were forced upwards and the poor were deprived of their land, their common rights and the means to be self-sufficient.

Land was the most acceptable way for gentlemen to earn a living, and they relied on their agents and stewards to maximise the income from their estates. The largest landowners often had no legal right to all of the land they wished to enclose, but as enclosure of specific areas was by individual Act of Parliament, the rights of the poor were not considered, and the smaller landowners were squeezed out. The writer and educationalist William Fordyce Mavor commented on the pitfalls of the enclosure system: 'Various are the instances, within my own knowledge, of twelve farms, which once supported as many families in credit, having been thrown into three or four upon an inclosure.'[71]

In his lengthy poem *The Deserted Village*, published in 1770, Oliver Goldsmith expressed his sadness at the effects of enclosure. He imagines a deserted landscape, where all the old sounds of the former village have disappeared. Just one old woman remains:

> But now the sounds of population fail,
> No chearful murmurs fluctuate in the gale,
> No busy steps the grass-grown foot-way tread,
> But all the bloomy flush of life is fled.
> All but yon widowed solitary thing
> That feebly bends beside the plashy spring;
> She, wretched matron, forced, in age, for bread,
> To strip the brook with mantling cresses spread,
> To pick her wintry faggot from the thorn,
> To seek her nightly shed, and weep till morn;
> She only left of all the harmless train,
> The sad historian of the pensive plain.[72]

According to Mavor, the greed of large landowners created unemployment and hardship:

If three men monopolize the land which maintained and employed twelve before, nine of course and their families must turn day-labourers, or manufacturers [factory workers], and eventually become chargeable to the parish ... Will three farmers raise as much marketable produce as twelve would do? Was it not formerly owing to the small occupiers of land, that many of the necessaries and comforts of life were to be procured in such abundance, and sold at such a moderate rate?[73]

In many parts of England John Byng witnessed the changes caused by enclosures, which he prophesied would lead to the countryside's devastation:

How wisely did the fost'ring hand of ancestry provide for the poor, by an allotment of a cottage right of common in the open fields; the village green before their door; the orchard adjoining their house; and the long close behind it! These two latter being seiz'd by the greedy farmer, and the two former being forced from them by the hand of power (upon some inadequate infamous bargain) has driven away the poor; has levell'd the cottage; has impoverish'd the country; and must, finally, ruin it.[74]

He felt that Parliament was too focused on the problems of slavery in the British colonies and was deliberately ignoring the virtual slavery suffered by the working classes: 'I would that Mr Wilberforce, and Mr Burke were obliged to survey, and report upon Hamerton [in Lincolnshire], to a select committee of the House of Commons; and no more to think and prate of East, and West Indian miseries, and depopulations.'[75] William Wilberforce, now better known for his role in abolishing the slave trade, had a parliamentary record of enthusiastically supporting measures such as anti-trades union legislation that severely repressed the working class.

The position of black people in England was different to that in the British colonies. In a test case in 1772, brought by campaigners for the abolition of slavery, Lord Mansfield, the Lord Chief Justice, ruled that a black man purchased abroad as a slave and brought to England by his owner could not be forced to leave the country.[76] The basis of the judgment was that since slavery had no legal foundation in England, any coercion of the man was unlawful. But if he did return to America, he would revert to the status of a slave under that colony's laws. This was unacceptable to some owners, who considered these people were still their slaves in England.

Benjamin Silliman recorded that while he was at Liverpool in 1805, he descended into the hold of a slave ship 'and examined the cells where human beings are confined, under circumstances which equally disgust decency and shock humanity ... Liverpool is *deep, very deep* in the guilt of the slave-trade.'[77] Although black people formed a minority of England's population, they were present at all levels of society, mostly in urban areas. Silliman particularly noticed that many worked as servants in rich households:

> A black footman is considered as a great acquisition, and consequently negro servants are sought for and caressed. An ill dressed or starving negro is never seen in England, and in some instances even alliances are formed between them and white girls of the lower orders of society ... As there are no slaves in England, perhaps the English have not learned to regard negroes as a degraded class of men, as we do in the United States, where we have never seen them in any other condition.[78]

The plight of children forced down mines, up chimneys and into factories was perhaps the closest to the misery endured by slaves taken across the Atlantic from Africa, but other features of English society were compared with slavery, including impressment into the Royal Navy. Because press-gangs were permitted to force men and boys into the navy, seizing them from the streets or even their homes, impressment was said to be legalised slavery. One naval captain, Thomas Pasley, commented in 1780: 'Poor Sailors – you are the only class of beings in our famed Country of Liberty really *Slaves*, devoted and hardly [harshly] used, tho' the very being of the Country depends on you.'[79] The smuggler Jack Rattenbury from Beer in Devon was often targeted by the press-gangs. 'Our country is called the land of liberty', he complained; 'we possess a just and invincible aversion to slavery at home and in our foreign colonies, and it is triumphantly said that a slave cannot breathe in England. Yet how is this to be reconciled with the practice of tearing men from their weeping and afflicted families ... and chaining them to a situation which is alike repugnant to their feelings and principles?'[80]

Press-gangs caused much fear and anxiety in London and other ports and coastal settlements, as William Darter in Reading recalled:

During the protracted war [with France and America] ... no young man could safely go to London. I remember a young fellow of the name of Chandler living in Mount Pleasant, who with another ... went to town for the purpose of working at their business as carpenters and joiners. They had not been there more than a few weeks, when on their way back to their shop after dinner they stopped to look into a shop window. A Press Gang came up and forcibly took them down to the water where they were put into an armed boat and taken down to the Nore. These men fought in several battles on board His Majesty's ships, and after many years Chandler returned home, but his comrade was killed in action.[81]

Unlike the navy, the army was not allowed to seize anyone it pleased, but had to tempt young men with cash bonuses or trick them into joining. The militias also needed men to defend Britain against invasion from abroad or revolution from within. They were organised on a local basis, and eligible men were put into a lottery. Those drawn had to serve or find someone else to take their place. In September 1779 Woodforde nearly lost a servant to the militia: 'Lent my man Ben my little mare to go to Norwich this morning to try to get a substitute to serve for him in the militia as he is drawn ... Ben Legate [Leggett] returned home in the evening from Norwich having got a substitute and seen him sworn in immediately as well as accepted. He is obliged to give the substitute 9.9.0. I gave him, in part of it, this evening 1.1.0.'[82] Woodforde's contribution appears less than generous considering that Ben was his valued farming man.

Plenty of unemployed people were available to replace men lost to the armed forces, but in rural areas the unemployed were trapped, unable to travel beyond their parish to the Midlands and northern England where expanding industries had jobs. This lack of mobility also hindered mill owners, who could not find enough workers. It was actually easier for the Irish to cross the sea and find work in Lancashire or Yorkshire than for destitute people from southern counties. The only options for the unemployed were to apply for poor relief or go into the workhouse or poorhouse. Such assistance was financed at parish level by the poor rates. At Castle Carrock in Cumberland in December 1794, Frederick Eden listed those receiving parish relief, including:

> J.G. aged 30; was incapacitated from working by a kick from a horse: he is allowed 2s. a week.
> J.D. aged 70; gained his settlement here by service: old age, and poverty, threw him on the parish: his weekly allowance is 1s. 6d. ...
> A child, 8 years old, whose parents are dead, costs the parish 1s. a week.
> A male bastard, of the same age, costs the parish 1s. a week.[83]

One woman receiving aid at nearby Cumwhitton was 'A.S. 60 years of age, a farmer's widow, receives a weekly allowance of 1s: she resided in another parish, but, upon becoming burthensome, was removed hither.'[84] A parish was responsible for anyone born within their jurisdiction, though on marriage a woman came under her husband's parish. If someone did manage to settle in another parish for a year, that parish was responsible for them if they became destitute. Wealthier households paid the poor rates, and because this was an increasing and often resented burden, every effort was made to repatriate paupers to their home parish. As Louis Simond put it: 'The poor of England are under certain regulations, called poor-laws, forming one of the distinctive features of this government. Their object is half police, and half charity; but their utility very questionable ... Parishes being bound to provide each for their own poor, it becomes a matter of importance to prevent new comers from acquiring a *settlement*, by removal to a new parish.'[85] John Byng considered the welfare system terrible:

'why, in God's name, is this country to be swallowed up by poor rates? And the oppress'd, miserable inhabitants to be hunted about from village, and village; and at last to be starved to death in a work house!!!'[86]

Some paupers were maintained in parish workhouses or poor-houses, while others were privatised or 'farmed' – given to private contractors for an agreed price. The clergyman William Jones described the facilities at Broxbourne, Hertfordshire: 'The poor house, as it is called, in this parish, is a wretched hovel, considerably below the level of the adjoining road. The workhouse of [nearby] Hoddesdon is not badly situated, but its almshouses are in a miserable, confined alley.'[87] In 1795 Eden noted how paupers at St Albans, a few miles west of Broxbourne, were farmed out for £400 a year: 'The Poor of this parish have generally been farmed ... The contractor finds food, cloaths, fuel, &c.; and the parish provides the house and furniture, which the farmer is bound to leave in good condition. He has 39 poor people at present in the house, 10 of which are old women, 7 men, and the rest children.'[88]

In Norfolk, Woodforde had few illusions about the workhouses. In March 1781 he and a companion visited one: 'we took a ride to the House of Industry about 2 miles west of Dereham, a very large building at present tho' there wants another wing. About 380 poor in it now, but they don't look either healthy or cheerful, a great number die there – 27 have died since Christmas last.'[89] The situation for the destitute was no better eleven years on, and Woodforde took pity on a man who had fled from a workhouse. He was heading for London but was so poor that he could have been arrested as a vagrant at any time and returned:

To a man of Bargewell (by name Brighton whose father and mother lately kept the Bell Inn at Billingford) who escaped this morning out of Bargewell's Poor House being hardly kept alive there, the allowance so very short, the house being farmed out at 1s/6d, per week for each poor person. I gave him as he appeared to be a very civil spoken man and as one that once knew better days 0.1.0. He was going for London he said to his wife who is a housekeeper to some person in town.[90]

Illegal ways of obtaining money, such as begging and stealing, might be resorted to by those unable or unwilling to work, especially if they were not eligible to receive assistance. Louis Simond was surprised that 'at the entrance of most towns or villages, you see written a notice, "To vagrants, and other idle and disorderly persons;—that such as may be found in it will be proceeded against with the utmost rigour of the law;" that is to say, of the poor-laws.'[91] Within their own parishes, clergymen often dispensed charitable gifts both on a casual basis and to meet specific needs. In the harsh winter of 1789 Woodforde made his servant distribute money among the poor: 'Bitter cold day again with high wind, it froze in all parts of the house. Sent Ben round my parish with some money to the poor people this severe weather, chiefly those that cannot work at this time, some 1 shilling apiece – some at 1s/6d apiece. In all, Ben gave for me this day 1.14.6.'[92]

While the war dragged on, changes in agriculture and industry threw increasing numbers of people out of work, so that by 1811 John Blackner in Nottingham despaired of the situation: 'Such was the reduced state of trade of this town, that half-famished workmen, belonging to almost every branch of its principal manufacture, were constrained to sweep the streets for a paltry support. They were employed by the overseers of St. Mary's parish, because the workhouse was too full to receive their families, and other employment could not be found.'[93]

Many were drawn to London in the hopes of improving their fortune, so that the city had increasing numbers of paupers and beggars on the streets – some literally scraped a living like the 'grubbers':

[They] procure a livelihood by whatever they find in grubbing out the dirt from between the stones with a crooked bit of iron, in search of nails that fall from horse-shoes, which are allowed to be the best iron that can be made use of for gun-barrels: and though the streets are constantly looked over at the dawn of the day by a set of men in search of sticks, handkerchiefs, shawls &c. that may have been dropt during the night, yet these grubbers now and then find rings that have been drawn off with the gloves, or small money that has been washed by the showers between the stones. These men are frequently employed to clear gully-holes and common sewers, the stench of which is so great that their breath becomes pestilential.[94]

Everyone pinned their hopes on the wars ending, but, as William Darter noted, improvements did not actually materialise for everyone: 'Cheap bread we did not get, and John Bull had to pay the piper ... At this time the working classes were suffering great privations, as there was very little call for their services, and provisions of all kinds were very dear.'[95] From 1814 when Napoleon was exiled and again in 1815 after Waterloo, thousands of soldiers and sailors were laid off. Unemployment rose sharply, and attempts to drive down wages caused unrest, as *The Times* reported in August 1816:

What is denominated a strike has ... taken place amongst the wool-sorters, who at the present rate of wages can earn from 3l. to three guineas a week. The masters wished to reduce the rate of wages one-third, on account of the reduction which has taken place in their prices, and to enable them to meet the foreign market. This proposition the men refused to accede to; and the masters, not being able to give more, many of them standing still, whilst the men, in consequence of their own obstinacy, are many hundreds of them become burdensome to their respective parishes, together with their families. Would it not be well, whilst so many thousands are out of employ and starving, or burdensome to their parishes from absolute want of employment, that parish officers should make inquiry and refuse to relieve all such as might have work and refuse to do it.[96]

The hardships of the labouring classes and the destitute poor are well documented in the works of Charles Dickens and other Victorian writers. Caused by wars, industrialisation and enclosure of the countryside, these hardships were approaching their worst by the end of Jane Austen's lifetime, with people literally starving in the streets:

Saturday last, a poor fellow, about thirty years of age, was going through Stoke Newington in search of employment, and being weak through hunger and want, sat down at the gate of Mr. Hugh's house, where he was found by the porter in an expiring state. On being questioned he was unable to answer anything, but that he was dying. He was taken inside the gate and some victuals offered to him, but he was too far gone to use any; he took half a glass of water and expired.[97]

———•◆•———

# EIGHT

# LEISURE AND PLEASURE

One half of the world cannot understand the pleasures of the other.

*Emma*, by Jane Austen

Leisure was a luxury available only to those with time and money. Most working people had little opportunity for entertainment, and although his wages with a tailor were good, Thomas Carter thought the cost was high:

> I would gladly have taken three shillings per week less in wages, if thereby I could have escaped from the pressure of that incessant, and to me exhausting toil ... especially in so hot and otherwise unhealthy a place as is a tailor's workshop, in which I was confined for full twelve hours per day, the hours of working being from six o'clock in the morning until seven o'clock in the evening, one hour only being subtracted for dinner.[1]

For servants, apprentices, manual workers and many others, long hours were normal. The concept of the two-day weekend did not exist; the weekend was simply 'the end of the working week', usually just Sunday. Similarly, there were no long holidays, only 'holy days', the original meaning of the word. The poet Robert Southey, when writing in the guise of a foreign traveller, said that the English 'reproach the Catholic religion with the number of its holidays, never considering how the want of holidays breaks down and brutalizes the labouring classes'.[2]

Skilled workers, notably those on piecework, were accustomed to more generous free time. Many did only as much work as necessary, and according to the historian William Hutton in 1795, 'if a man can support his family with three days labour, he will not work six'.[3] These workers added Monday to their 'weekend' (and sometimes Tuesday and Wednesday too), a state of affairs so widespread that it was known as 'Saint Monday'. A satirical definition appeared in Francis Grose's dictionary of slang: 'SAINT MONDAY. A holiday most religiously observed by journeymen shoemakers, and other inferior mechanics. A profanation of that day, by working, is punishable by a fine, particularly among the gentle craft.'[4] Such chaotic working practices were condemned, not least by religious campaigners against alcohol consumption who believed that workers spent all this free time drinking to excess.

But not everyone considered the concept of Saint Monday harmful. Francis Spilsbury, a London chemist who wrote about illnesses such as gout and scurvy, was of the opinion that exercise and fresh air were beneficial to health, while bad air and working indoors were detrimental:

> In this view it may be doubted whether there is so much room for censure of a celebrated saint, so often idolized by the labouring mechanic . . . for through an attention to sacrifice at his shrine on his festival day, many of the workmen are enabled to hold out much longer than they otherwise would do (particularly in some manufactories which are very inimical to health) provided they could abstain from partaking so freely of the libations generally poured out at their revels on SAINT MONDAY.[5]

The 'lower orders' were expected to work inordinately long hours, and live-in servants were given minimal freedom. In September 1805 one maidservant in William Holland's household was allowed to attend the fair at nearby Nether Stowey, but failed to return on time:

Kitty did not come till nine o'clock which her mistress [his wife Mary] resented much as she had ordered her to be back from the fair by six. John came a little after nine which was very well for him, being a man. Kitty was at the Globe in very good company as she says. However her mistress did not think a Publick House so proper for her and was angry and the girl inclined to be saucy, but my wife does not mean to give way to her.[6]

In the face of ongoing changes in industry and agriculture, many fairs were losing their original function, such as the hiring fairs where the labour exchange element was disappearing. Instead, fairs concentrated much more on entertainment, though some retained their cattle and produce markets. Nelly Weeton described the anticipation before Wigan's fair in 1816:

The town is going to be in a great bustle this week; for the fair commences tomorrow [23 May], on which occasion, it is usual for everybody to clean their houses thoroughly, to white-wash, paint, &c.; the confectioners begin of baking for the fair a week beforehand; and the shop-keepers to polish, and set their wares, in the neatest order; large caravans enter the town with wild beasts, monsters, and jugglers; likewise wooden horses, whirligigs, gambling tables, barrel organs, fiddlers, and hordes of beggars.[7]

Some two decades earlier, Johnson Grant was less enthusiastic about a fair he encountered: 'We set out for Leeds, where we found a fair in the market-place; a horrible scene of tygers roaring, organs grinding, trumpets sounding, blackguards bellowing and thronging, together with the effluvia of fish from the market, and every combination of attack upon the senses.'[8] Urban fairs like Wigan and Leeds were more sophisticated than rural ones, which perpetuated simple, traditional and sometimes barbaric entertainments. The *Reading Mercury* in June 1789 carried an advertisement for the annual country fair known as the Yattendon Revel:

THIS is to give notice, that Yattendon Revel will be kept as usual, on Friday the 10th of July next, and, for the encouragement of gentlemen gamesters, and others, there will be given a good Gold-Lac'd Hat, of 27s. value, to be played for at Cudgels; the man that breaks most heads to have the prize; 2s. will be given to each man that positively breaks a head, for the first ten heads that are broke; and 1s. to the man that has his head broke; but the man is not to receive the 2s. unless he gets up and plays the ties off; the blood to run an inch or be deemed no head.[9]

The revel's second day also featured long-established pastimes:

July the 11th, Will be given, Half-a-guinea to be run for by Jack Asses; the best of three heats. No less than three will be allowed to start. Also will be given, a fine Holland Smock to be run for by women; the best of three heats. No less than three will be allowed to start. Also, a Gold-Lac'd Hat, of 27s. value, to be played at Cudgels for . . . Likewise, Tobacco to be Grinn'd for, by old women, through a horse collar, as usual.[10]

The austere times were having an effect on some celebrations, and in Oxfordshire four years earlier, in the summer of 1785, John Byng lamented the decline of familiar traditions: 'A book of antient customs says – "That at Burford was a yearly procession of great jollity on midsummer eve; when a painted dragon, and a painted giant were carried about the town in commemoration of a battle won by the Saxons near this place":– But all such exhibitions are lost in the poverty and distress of the lower people; and a fair is now no more than a larger market.'[11]

Other customs were dying out for different reasons. Royal Oak Day on 29 May, later known as Oak Apple Day, marked the restoration in 1660 of Charles II after the Civil War. Now that the Hanoverian dynasty had superseded that of the Stuarts, this day of festivity was largely confined to Jacobite sympathisers, who regarded the Hanoverians as usurpers. Byng was therefore surprised to find Derby preparing a large celebration in 1790: 'Here every house was adorn'd with oaken boughs in honor of the old 29th of May; and the boys preparing and begging for their bonfires.'[12]

Apart from regular fairs and revels, special events such as the frost fairs were an excuse for merriment. In the bitterly cold winters the

River Thames in London would freeze over so hard that it was safe to walk on, as happened in January the previous year:

> No sooner had the Thames acquired a sufficient consistency than booths, turn-abouts, &c. &c. were erected; the puppet-shews, wild beasts, &c. were transported from every adjacent village; while the watermen, that they might draw their usual resources from the water, broke the ice close to the shore, and erected bridges, with toll-bars, to make every passenger pay a halfpenny for getting to the ice. One of the suttling booths has for its sign, 'Beer, Wine, and Spiritous Liquors, *without a License.*' A man who sells hot-gingerbread has a board, on which is written, 'No Shop Tax nor Window Duty' . . . the Thames is generally crowded.[13]

The very last frost fair took place in February 1814. Never again would the Thames freeze so solidly once the old London Bridge was removed in 1831, after which the flow of the river improved.

Other celebrations were inspired by pleasing news about royal events or military victories, although sometimes the expressions of jubilation were hardly spontaneous, as William Darter saw in his home town of Reading:

> This year [1811] brought us intelligence of a victory, gained by Wellington over Soult in the Peninsula, and in consequence another illumination occurred of greater splendour than the last, as the inhabitants had by this time become accustomed to these demonstrations, and had provided themselves with appliances for lighting up, which they had not before. I may also mention that many of them had their sense of loyalty some-what quickened by having their windows broken when they were not illuminated.[14]

Darter also enjoyed the start of each new year in Reading, when the military forces joined in:

> It was customary on New Year's Eve for the ringers of St. Lawrence's parish to ring a few peals of changes and leave the bells up on their stays, and some time before midnight to return. At the same time the

Militia Band assembled at the upper part of London Street, and all was still, until the moment St. Lawrence's clock began to strike twelve, when off went the merry peal of eight bells, and at the same moment three loud strokes of the big drum led off the Berkshire Band down London Street to the Market Place, and from thence through a portion of the town.[15]

The ringing of church bells was the dominant sound in towns and countryside, with few other noises able to compete. Even in Darter's old age, the bells at new year remained a happy childhood memory: 'Seventy-one years have elapsed since I first experienced the magic effect of this music of the band and the merry peal of St. Lawrence's bells breaking out in the stillness of midnight, suggesting that the old year had passed away, and welcoming the dawn of its successor. After a short interval, the old watchman, Norcroft, went up London Street, calling out "Past twelve and a starlight mornin'".'[16]

Blood sports were regularly enjoyed by all classes. The baiting of dogs, badgers, bulls, cockerels and other animals was legal, though bear-baiting had died out because the wars with the Continent had stopped the supply of bears. Cock-fighting was often carried on at public houses throughout England, and some had purpose-built cock-pits. In March 1772, when living at Ansford in Somerset, James Woodforde noted: 'Brother John came to the Parsonage this evening merry ... He had been to Evercreech, cock-fighting and won there six or seven guineas by betting.'[17]

Bull-baiting provided a more impressive spectacle, and Darter detailed one occasion at Wokingham in Berkshire:

It was St. Thomas' Day [21 December], which was dark, damp and foggy ... Very soon a stir occurred amongst the people, and they ran in all directions out of the way of a fine young bull, which was on his way to the Market Place. When the animal arrived he was fixed to a ring which was attached to an oak post level with the ground. The bull had about five yards of chain, and at first dashed about and tried to get his liberty; this had the effect of making the people rush against each other, and many of them tumbled down in the mud.[18]

Dogs were then set upon the tethered bull, along with active participation from the crowd:

> Soon arose a cry of 'A lane, a lane'; this was for the people to form a narrow avenue leading up to the bull, which was quickly done ... and then a man holding a bull-dog between his knees would let him slip and run up the 'lane' to catch hold of the bull's nose, which, if he succeeded, would pin his head down, and this would be called 'pinning the bull'. In this case, the dog, which I heard was brought from Staines, ran at the animal who instantly caught him on his horns and threw him high in the air. The people immediately closed together to catch him, or probably his neck would have been broken.[19]

The bull continued to be tormented until it was finally taken to the slaughterhouse and killed, only to be replaced by another bull. Darter found the whole event depressing: 'Then the men, most of whom had been quarrelling, took to fighting ... Taking the affair altogether, a more brutalising scene could not well be conceived.'[20] By 1802 the baiting of animals had fallen so far from favour with the ruling classes that a bill for abolishing bull-baiting was presented to Parliament. Despite vigorous support it was defeated, largely for fear of public opposition at a time when the threat of revolution loomed. It was not until 1835 that the baiting of animals for entertainment was outlawed.

Wealthier sportsmen concentrated on hunting, shooting and fishing (with nets as well as rods). The abundant wildlife, far more prolific than today, posed a real threat to crops, so there was a practical side to these sports, and only the hunting of foxes failed to produce something edible. Jane Austen wrote of one of her brothers: 'Edward is no enthusiast in the beauties of nature. His enthusiasm is for the sports of the field only ... He and George [Knight] are out every morning either shooting or with the harriers. They are good shots.'[21] Few people were bothered about the preservation of wildlife, though occasionally some concerns were raised, like Holland's observation during deep snow in Somerset in early January 1802: 'What terrible weather this is for all kind of birds, no food to be found, any where. And man, cruel man adding to their calamity but hunting after their lives in every quarter, the whole region resound with pops and explosions.'[22]

Woodforde was an enthusiastic supporter of shooting, fishing and hare-coursing. On a visit to his native Somerset in the summer of 1789 he fished several times in the River Brue at Cole where he was staying, catching numerous trout and eels, which were eaten for dinner. On one successful day, he recorded: 'I spent most of the day a fishing, caught a brace of trout and three eels.'[23] Other days were less productive: 'Was out fishing almost the whole day but had no sport whatever – never caught a fish.'[24] Hare-coursing might be undertaken almost casually if a hare was spotted, but usually men set out deliberately to hunt for them. Woodforde frequently recorded his hare-coursing activities in Norfolk:

> After breakfast I walked out a coursing and took Ben, Briton and my boy Downing with me. I took my three greyhounds, Fly, Snip and Spring, and two spaniels, Spring and Carlo with me. We stayed out till two o'clock and coursed only one hare which we killed. We saw no people out either shooting or coursing, but heard some guns at a distance. Dinner to day, giblet-soup, fryed beef and potatoes, and a fine young hare rosted.[25]

Hares and other animals and birds killed in hunting would be given away to friends and neighbours if there were too many to use before they became inedible, and sharing and exchanging food in this way helped to bind country communities together.

Brutal sports did not just involve animals. Boxing was legal, but the newspapers routinely reported vicious prize fights (boxing for a cash prize), such as one near London in March 1812: 'A pugilist contest took place at Harford, near Hounslow, for twenty guineas a side, between William Swallow, a youth of promise, aged nineteen, from Suffolk, and a farmer of the name of Coulthard. The combatants fought fifty-seven hard rounds in one hour and forty-eight minutes, when Coulthard was declared the victor. It was what was termed a good stand up fight.'[26] These matches were fought for money and were subject to heavy gambling by the spectators. Prize fighting was in a dubious position legally, and magistrates often broke up fights or tried to prevent them, as in November 1805: 'The celebrated pugilist the *Chicken* arrived in town [London] on Saturday last from Somersetshire, where he had been several days in durance vile [prison], by order of the Magistrates of the District charged with attempting to disturb the public peace by the introduction of a prize fight intended to have been fought in the neighbourhood of Bath. Chicken was to have been second to the favourite.'[27] Generally, all the magistrates achieved was to postpone the fight for a few weeks or move it elsewhere. To avoid even this much interference, most prize-fight venues were kept secret until the last minute.

In Yorkshire in 1805, Charles Fothergill learned that the lead miners at Arkendale pursued various rough sports: 'Amusement amongst the miners: Fives, football, cricket, wrestling and leaping. Wrestling and leaping generally practised at public times, particularly at Whitsuntide and Easter when belts are wrestled for and gloves are leaped for.'[28] A few miles north, he chatted with the parish clerk at the public house at Fremington, who told him about the sports there:

Athletic exercises among the lower of the people are seldom practised now ... they have given place to pitchhalfpenny ... criket [cricket] and such like ... I am glad however to hear that wrestling is still in vogue amongst the miners on certain public occasions, festivals and merry-meetings: they have two modes of setting to; one by taking hold of each others hand and directing their efforts at the feet and legs, the other the old fashioned way round the waste [waist] where more strength is required.[29]

Fothergill was also told about a ferocious form of football that used to be played:

Football was amongst the former athletic games but it seems to have been dropped in consequence of accidents happening not unfrequently, particularly broken legs in consequence of the players wearing such terrible thick shoes armed with iron. The men of Arkendale were particularly famous at this game and they frequently challenged to play 13 of their men against 13 from any other quarter.[30]

Born in Derby, William Hutton had come across several football matches there. The best players, he said, were treated like celebrities:

I have seen this coarse sport carried to the barbarous height of an election contest; nay, I have known a foot-ball hero chaired through the streets like a successful member [of parliament], although his utmost elevation of character was no more than that of a butcher's apprentice. Black eyes, bruised arms, and broken shins, are equally the marks of victory and defeat. I need not say this is the delight of the lower ranks, and is attained at an early period; the very infant learns to *kick*, and then to walk.[31]

Although cricket was played by miners and other labourers, the major matches were the preserve of the gentry. In 1787 Thomas Lord established a cricket ground in London, which became the home of Marylebone Cricket Club. John Blackner in Nottingham acknowledged that the club had the best players:

1791, during the summer, was played, what is called, *the great cricket match*, which was thus occasioned. A Colonel Churchill happening to be quartered here with his regiment, was struck with the superior activity of the Nottingham cricketplayers; added to which, their fame was already up by having won several matches. The colonel sent a challenge to the Mary-le-bonne club to play for a considerable sum; which challenge being accepted, eleven noblemen and gentlemen, with the Earl of Winchelsea at their head, came to Nottingham to play. But, notwithstanding the Nottingham players excited the admiration and applause of their opponents, they had no chance of success.[32]

Lord's Cricket Ground moved to its present-day site in St John's Wood in 1814, and the first match played there, with the usual gambling on the outcome, was between Marylebone Cricket Club and Hertfordshire on 22 June. The *Morning Post* carried a brief account: 'CRICKET.– The grand Cricket Match at Lord's Ground, between the Marylebone Club against the County of Hertford, with HAM-MOND, was decided on Saturday . . . Marylebone won by 27 runs in one Innings.– Bets 5 to 4 at starting in favour of Marylebone.'[33]

All kinds of races – on foot, horseback and in boats – provided popular sport. Many events included races for women, and in September 1772 Woodforde watched the sports at Castle Cary in Somerset: 'There was running this morning in Cary Park between two women for half a guinea, and which was run by Peg Francis; also boys running. There was a great multitude to see it in the Park.'[34] Not all events went to plan, as revealed by Silvester Treleaven's description of the Whitsun revel at Mardon Down in Devon in May 1801:

> Being Tuesday in Whitsunweek a revel on Mardown, wrestling, skittle playing, and females racing for 2 yards of Holland [linen], three started but unfortunately for the girl who depended on getting the prize, after running a few land yards, triped [tripped] on a stone and fell with such violence that she exposed herself to vast numbers of spectators who gave such shouts at the unfortunate young woman's accident that she got off the course and was not seen on the ground afterwards.[35]

For ladies especially, the horse races were a fashionable place at which to be seen, and in October 1809 the writer Mary Berry, a prominent literary figure, went to a race meeting at Newmarket in Suffolk:

> The inn is almost opposite what are called the rooms, where men only meet, and which have rather a handsome entrance of three arcades from the street; and in this street Tattersall was selling horses by auction, and all the young men, whose faces one knows in London, were walking about, as well as all the fathers of the turf, such as Sir Frank Standish, Sir Charles Bunbury, &c. &c. It had the oddest effect possible to see so many figures one hardly ever sees out of London, walking about in a sort of village-town, for Newmarket is no more [than that], with the exception of some good houses.[36]

They next moved to the Heath to follow the horses:

About one o'clock all these men mounted their horses, and proceeded towards the Heath, half a mile from the town. We followed them in the carriage, with many other carriages, and Lord Hardwicke[37] on horseback ... When they got upon the Heath, it is so vast that they seemed only like small groups upon it ... But the style in which all this is managed here, the rapidity with which one race follows another, though on different courses – that is, on different parts of the Heath – the scene at the betting post, one of which belongs to each course, and is the only permanent thing upon it, for the ropes are immediately moved, and the winning post (a little machine upon wheels) is moved from one to the other, – all this was new and entertaining to me.[38]

As with so many sports, gambling was the prime attraction, and Mary observed that 'between each race all the men and all the carriages are collected at the betting-posts'.[39] The winning horses that day were Hymen, Yellow-hammer, Vexation and Morel, all somewhat conservative names, but there was a huge variety of names, from the patriotic Heart of Oak or Briton Strike Home to the whimsical – such as Blue Ruin, Shake My Rags and Bumtrap – and the down-to-earth Sod. Racecourses were to be found all over England, and in 1795, on another trip to his Somerset relatives, Woodforde joined a party heading for the local races:

About four o'clock this afternoon, my sister Pounsett and daughter, Mrs. Clarke, my brothers wife, and Mrs. Willm. Woodforde, and myself, all got into the coach, and drove to Bruton Races, to a field called Burrow-field where the races are kept, about half a mile from Bruton, and there we stayed till after 7 o'clock, and then returned home to Cole. The races were very indifferent, but a vast concourse of people attended, both gentle and simple ... We stayed in the coach all the time and very hot we were.[40]

Races also took place on the water, and one regatta held on Lake Windermere in July 1810 was described in the *Lancaster Gazette*:

The two fine sailing boats, the *Victory*, belonging to Mr. Bolton of Storrs, and *Endeavour*, the property of Mr. Wilson of Elleray, started a little after eleven o'clock, with a good breeze, and afforded the best entertainment to an immense crowd of spectators . . . This was the best boat-race that was ever seen on the lake [the *Victory* won a close contest]. There were many other races of inferior note, some of them well contested.[41]

Edward Pedder, Nelly Weeton's employer at nearby Dove Nest, was involved with staging this regatta, but another event in August fell below expectations. Nelly told her aunt what happened:

The second Regatta was expected to have been more splendid still, in consequence of which, Mr. Pedder invited a number of friends. We were sadly disappointed; it was one of the most blackguard things ever conducted. After a rowing match or two, which began the entertainment, there followed a footrace by four men. Two of them ran without shirts; one had breeches on, the other only drawers, very thin calico, without gallaces [braces]. Expecting they would burst or come off, the ladies durst not view the race, and turned away from the sight. And well it was they did.[42]

Nelly had no qualms in watching and gave an eyewitness description: 'during the race, and with the exertion of running, the drawers did actually burst, and the man cried out as he run – "Oh Lord! O Lord! I cannot keep my tackle in, G–d d–n it! I cannot keep my tackle in."'[43] The ladies were disgusted and left, she reported, and 'there were many of fashion and of rank; amongst other, Lady Diana Fleming, and her daughter Lady Fleming, and the Bishop of Landaff's daughters; several carriages, barouches, curricles; but all trooped off. Wrestling and leaping occupied the remainder of the day, we were told.'[44]

Seaside resorts also staged regattas, and John Byng witnessed one at Weymouth in Dorset in 1782, before the town became fashionable, but he was unimpressed:

To-day is a day of gala at Weymouth, and has been long announced for a regatta, and sailing-race, for the purpose of drawing company to the place; and of engaging seamen for the Orestes frigate, who lays in the road [safe anchorage] . . . the beach was crouded by horse, foot and phaetons, and the windows throng'd with beauties, to view this famous regatta, that consisted of a number of ill-looking luggers, sailing round the bay for two hours and an half; but of which the company understood not the skill, and so seem'd heartily tired; and of having raised their expectations to such little effect.[45]

Regattas were only one of the attractions of the seaside. Bathing in seawater (and even drinking it) became a popular health remedy that encouraged the rise of places like Brighton (then called Brighthelmstone) and Weymouth. As with inland spas such as Bath, seaside resorts became places where the higher ranks would spend their time socialising, dancing, gambling and gossiping. Jane Austen's final, unfinished novel *Sanditon* is set in the fictitious village of Sanditon, which is being remodelled into a resort, like so many on the south coast. One character, Mr Heywood, argues the case against resorts: 'Every five years, one hears of some new place or other starting up by the sea, and growing the fashion. – How they can half of them be filled, is the wonder! Where people can be found with money or time to go to them! – Bad things for a country; – sure to raise the price of provisions and make the poor good for nothing.' In fact, Jane Austen liked seaside places, and in September 1804 she was staying at Lyme Regis, where she wrote to Cassandra, who was further along the coast at Weymouth: 'I continue quite well; in proof of which I have bathed again this morning. It was absolutely necessary that I should have the little fever and indisposition which I had: it has been all the fashion this week in Lyme ... The Ball last night was pleasant, but not full for Thursday.'[46]

Dancing was enjoyed primarily by the better-off. Some balls were public occasions, but more often private entertainments held in someone's house. Jane Austen loved dancing and going to balls, and her letters gave critical comments about the latest ones attended, as in October in 1800 at Deane in Hampshire: 'It was a pleasant ball, and still more good than pleasant, for there were nearly sixty people, and sometimes we had seventeen couple ... I danced nine dances out of ten.'[47] This was a country ball that attracted nowhere near the numbers of the London events. Upper-class balls in wealthy London mansions were grand affairs, and a decade later Mary Berry arrived at one given by Lady Shaftesbury in Portland Place:

> The dancing began immediately: first, an English dance; then two quadrilles, admirably well danced; high benches round the room, upon which everybody mounted. Then another English dance; and then Miss Montgomery danced a Bolero, and Lady Barbara immediately afterwards the Tambourine dance, which was really admirable. The ball, upon the whole, both with respect to numbers, lighting, company, dress and dancing, one of the most brilliant I ever saw in London.[48]

Apart from occasional spontaneous dancing in inns, the working classes tended to dance mainly at festivals and celebrations such as those held after the harvest. For labourers and servants, such events were rare treats, and as in most households Woodforde's servants needed permission to attend: 'Our servant maid, Sally Gunton, had leave to go to Mr. Salisbury's harvest frolic this evening and to stay out all night. Our servant man, Bretingham Scurl, had also had leave to be at Mr. Bidewell's harvest frolic this evening and to stay out all night.'[49]

News of Nelson's victory at the Battle of the Nile in 1798 prompted displays of thanksgiving, and in a letter to her friend Mary Heber, Lady Banks described what they did in rural Isleworth, west of London:

> as we wish'd to have a little festivity to celebrate this famous victory, we had a treat in the evening. Besides all our own domesticks, we invited the labourers we usually employ, and their wives, and gave them some beef and plum pudding and punch in the servants' hall, and they had a dance in the barn. We went to visit them and sang God Save the King and Rule, Britannia, in which they all most heartily join'd in chorus.[50]

She explained how they deterred gatecrashers: 'by a little care in keeping our gate shut, we had no more *Company* than we chose, which is liable to happen so near London'.[51] Harriet Wynne mentioned a dance given on Lady Buckingham's birthday for the tenants on the Stowe estate: 'In the evening we all danced with the tenants ... I laughed a great deal to see the different mixture of people. We could hardly breathe it was so hot and the smell was beyond anything. We danced Sir Roger de Coverly, attended their supper &c. Delighted were we to go to bed.'[52]

Some balls were fancy-dress affairs, such as one enjoyed by Woodforde's niece:

Nancy did not return till after 9 o'clock this evening as the young folks at Weston House had something of a Masquerade-Ball this evening. Dramatis Personae, Miss Custance in the character of an old woman, Emily Custance a flower girl, Devonshire Miss Bacon a fortune-teller alias gipsy, Miss Bacon in the character of a fool, Miss Maria Bacon, a ghost – none of the young gentlemen acted at all or were dressed.[53]

Amateur theatricals were also in fashion, something reflected in Jane Austen's novels, and as a teenager she herself had taken part in family plays. For those who could afford the price of tickets, going to the theatre was also popular, and in London and larger towns and cities, several theatres offered plays and sometimes concerts. London was a special case in that only three theatres, each called the 'Theatre Royal', were licensed for 'serious drama', usually defined as 'spoken drama'. They were often referred to simply by their location – Drury Lane, Covent Garden and Haymarket. Covent Garden put on operas as well as plays and later specialised in opera – it is now the Royal Opera House.

Other theatres in London were not supposed to allow plays to be performed, but avoided this ban by providing a mixture of entertainment, often musical, which might include part of a play. When visiting relatives in the capital, Jane Austen enjoyed the theatre and in September 1813 she wrote to her brother Frank: 'Of our three evenings in town, one was spent at the Lyceum and another at Covent Garden. "The Clandestine Marriage" was the most respectable of the performances, the rest were sing-song and trumpery ... I wanted better acting. There was no actor worth naming. I believe the theatres are thought at a low ebb at present.'[54] *The Clandestine Marriage* was a comedy by George Colman the Elder and David Garrick, first performed in 1766. Nelly Weeton sometimes saw famous performers at the theatre in Liverpool, as she told her brother Tom in July 1809:

I wish you could have been here this week to have seen Mrs. Siddons . . . Henry Latham [Nelly's cousin] has been with me a fortnight, and one day last week he and I went to see her as Lady Macbeth. We got a very comfortable front seat in the gallery, and I was highly gratified. I have seen her before at Lancaster as Belvidera, but had almost forgot her, it is so long ago. Much as I expected, my expectations were exceeded; particularly in that scene where Lady Macbeth is represented as walking in her sleep. The whole audience seemed wonder struck.[55]

In Nelly's view the stage was far too bright for Shakespeare's *Macbeth*, though by modern standards theatre lighting was wretched, relying on oil lamps and chandeliers of candles. Even so, she had trouble adjusting to the pitch-black streets and had 'a dismally dark walk home. It was eleven when we left the theatre. The glare of the house, with its lights, had so affected my eyes, that it was with difficulty I could distinguish my way. Luckily Henry could see better than me, and we got home very safely. We were a full hour in walking two miles and a half.'[56]

Theatres were not places of respectful, quiet calm, as Carl Moritz discovered at the Haymarket in 1782:

For a seat in the boxes you pay five shillings, in the pit three, in the first gallery two, and in the second, or upper gallery, one shilling. And it is the tenants in this upper gallery who, for their shilling, make all that noise and uproar, for which the English playhouses are so famous. I was in the pit, which gradually rises, amphitheatre wise, from the orchestra, and is furnished with benches, one above another, from the top to the bottom. Often and often, whilst I sat here, did a rotten orange, or the peel of an orange, fly past me, or past some of my neighbours; and one of them actually hit my hat, without my daring to look round, for fear another might come plump in my face. Besides this perpetual pelting from the gallery, which renders an English playhouse so uncomfortable, there is no end to their calling out, and knocking with their sticks, till the curtain is drawn up ... In the boxes, quite in a corner, sat several servants, who were said to be placed there, to keep the seats for the families they served, till they should arrive.[57]

Outside London, travelling players went from town to town putting on performances, something that Silvester Treleaven recorded at Moretonhampstead in Devon in May 1802: 'A company of comedians came here from Crediton, and are going to act a few nights in Mr. Hancock's Barn, in Pound Street, which is fitting up for said purpose. A Mr. Smith manager.'[58] Three days later, their makeshift theatre was ready: 'Last night the comedians acted for the first time in Mr. Hancock's Barn, in Pound Street, which is fitted up for the purpose in a very decent manner. The play was "The Farm House", after which an interlude called "The Village Barber". To which was added the farce of "The Spoil'd Child".'[59]

Rather than the theatre, Woodforde was more partial to music, but even for him the tickets were expensive – the equivalent of two weeks' wages for one servant:

The tickets to the miscellaneous concert to night [at Norwich] were 7 shillings and 6 pence each. Mrs Custance being a subscriber and having a transferable ticket, was so kind as to lend my niece hers for this evening ... A great deal of company indeed at the Hall and full dressed – 911 supposed to be present. The concert was very fine indeed, and Madame Mara, the famous singer, sung delightfully. I never heard so fine a voice – her notes so high. The kettle drums from Westminster Abbey sounded charmingly, beat by a Mr. Ashbridge. Near 100 performers in the orchestra.[60]

Especially with the attraction of celebrity performers, musical concerts were increasingly attended by the wealthier classes. Composers such as Haydn, Mozart and Beethoven were writing new works and exploring new musical forms that were becoming ever more popular. Music was no longer just an accompaniment to dancing, eating or singing, but an entertainment in its own right.

Whatever anyone's class or wealth, leisure occupations were largely active rather than passive. Songs and music were mostly learned from printed sheets. More formal music was sold in shops, while street sellers sold broadside song sheets, also called broadsheets, which were printed on one side of sheets of coarse paper. Moritz noticed the ballad sellers: 'The [English people's] love of their country, and its unparalleled feats in war, are in general the subject of their ballads and popular songs, which are sung about the streets by women, who sell them for a few farthings.'[61] Over two decades later, Benjamin Silliman also heard the ballad singers and saw them selling the words on printed sheets. Crowds gathered to hear and learn the tunes, since these song sheets had the words, but no music:

> Returning home, about 10 o'clock at night, I observed one of those little circles which are very common in the streets of London; I allude to the audiences which gather around the ballad singers. They are usually poor women, or little girls, with every appearance of extreme poverty, who collect a few pence by singing ballads at the corners of the streets, under the bow-windows of shops, and the porticoes of public buildings. Although their voices are harsh from being so often exerted, and their performances, in every respect indifferent, they immediately draw a circle around and detain them a long time.[62]

Contrary to the observations of Moritz and Silliman, ballad selling was not restricted to women, and in March 1780 Woodforde paid sixpence 'to a poor old man for some ballads'.[63] Three years earlier, George Williams appeared before a justice of the peace in Somerset, accused of being a 'rogue and vagabond'. He swore on oath that he was a former soldier, aged about sixty, and had worked as a day labourer and ballad seller for the last two decades.[64]

Most people created their own entertainment at home with friends and family, and diarists like Woodforde noted such everyday events, as in August 1788: 'Mr. Walker and Betsy Davy came over on single horses this morning from Foulsham and they breakfasted, dined and spent the afternoon with us. We had a good deal of singing to day from my niece and Mr. Walker – the latter sung many new songs. We spent a very agreeable day together.'[65] They may well have been singing new ballads bought from a street seller.

An afternoon spent with guests over dinner and in various forms of entertainment was something the idle rich could enjoy. The labouring classes could relax only in the evening, after their work, when the tavern provided a welcome refuge with its candles and a fire, where customers could drink beer, smoke a pipe and perhaps play cards or join in the singing. Francis Place recalled the taverns of the late 1770s: 'It was the custom at this time as it had long been for almost every man who had the means to spend his evenings at some public house or tavern, or other place of entertainment. Almost every public house had a parlour . . . for the better sort of customers. In this room which was large and well lighted with tallow candles the company drank and smoked and spent their evenings.'[66]

Tobacco was used by all classes. It was sometimes chewed, but was more likely to be smoked in white clay pipes that were made locally and sold in shops or by the pipe makers themselves. Taverns were the biggest outlet, where pipes could be reburned in an iron rack in the fireplace. Some clay pipes were 12–15 inches long, though shorter ones were preferred by workers since pipes were easily broken – fragments of clay pipe stems are common finds on archaeological sites and in gardens of old houses. Smoking was more popular with the working classes, women and children included, and in July 1809 a woman's pipe set off an explosion at Portsmouth, killing many people. According to the local newspaper, 'The cause of this calamity is attributed to the wife of one of the soldiers, who relates, that she was washing near where the baggage lay, on the beach, when another soldier's wife, who was smoking, asked her if she would take a whiff? She did; but finding the tobacco would not burn, she struck the bowl of the pipe against the pebbles.'[67] The smouldering tobacco fell out, causing a fire that spread to several barrels of gunpowder.

Having given up smoking several years earlier, the clergyman William Jones decided to stop taking snuff as well: 'Left off snuff, & hope I shall never return to the *filthy*, worse than *beastly*, practice! Gave Mrs. Jones [his wife] my whole stock – four ½ lb canisters full of No 37, & Strasburgh – 1 lb. 37 in lead, ¾ lb. of Strasburgh in lead,

& my common box full.'[68] With a stock of around 4lb of snuff, Jones must have been a heavy user. Snuff was a fine tobacco that was inhaled, a habit largely confined to the upper classes. Woodforde noted purchases of both tobacco and snuff, as in 1790: 'at Mr. Carys shop for ½ lb. tobacco, pd. 0: 1: 4. At Ditto – for 2 oz: of Scotch snuff 0: 0: 2.'[69] After giving away his snuff, Jones said of his wife: 'O that my *deary* would give up *snuff* & *novels*!!'[70]

Woodforde also indulged in drinking a fair amount of alcohol and was particularly fond of card games and of gambling for moderate stakes with friends and family. He recorded his failures and successes in his diary and was triumphant in April 1783: 'At quadrille this evening won 0.4.0. I played the finest Sans Prendre Vole to night, that I ever had – not a loosing card in hand – it was Mattadores, 9 black trumps in spades and the King of Hearts – I was the last player; after the first card was played, I declared the Vole. I did not get home to Weston till 10 at night.'[71] Quadrille, a popular game for four players, originated in France, but its complicated rules and special vocabulary were later simplified to make it more like whist. It was eclipsed by other card games in the Victorian period. Lydia Bennet in *Pride and Prejudice* is obsessed by gambling and by card games, and 'talked incessantly of lottery tickets, of the fish she had lost and the fish she had won'. The lottery she was playing was a simple card game of chance, in which counters were amassed. Frequently in gaming, the bone or ivory counters were made in the shape of fish.[72]

A State Lottery was run by the Government to raise revenue, for which an Act of Parliament was passed each year. Licensed brokers sold tickets, which were expensive, as well as cheaper shares in tickets, frequently sixteenths, and the winning tickets were drawn by lot over several days. Prizes were substantial – half a million pounds in the years 1796 to 1798 and even more in subsequent years. For many, the lottery was their only chance of acquiring wealth, and lottery clubs sprang up, such as one at Moretonhampstead. In February 1800, Treleaven described the hysteria that gripped its members: 'Last night members of the Lottery Club met at the Red Lion. In the midst of their business a great confusion ensued, owing to many of the members being overheated with liquor, and almost in a state of insanity under an idea of gaining a 30,000 £ prize! Several battles fought ... the no. [number] of members now amount to 245, and consists of a few Christians, some Jews, and a number of heathens. Their meetings are every Monday fortnight.'[73] A few days later he wrote: 'Last night the members of the Lottery Club met at the Red Lion, and closed their books. No. of members were 241, each of which subscribed £1.5.0 (viz) £1.2.0 to the fund and 3/- spent in ale: amount to purchase lottery tickets £265.2.0, spent in ale £44.3.8.'[74]

In November 1807 William Holland went to Bridgwater to see his lawyer: 'Ruscombe Poole informed me that Mr Stone his father in law had got a prize in the Lottery of twenty thousand pound, a great thing indeed and will be chiefly for Ruscombe Poole's benefit, for Mr. Stone cannot want it and he has but two daughters and one of them is Ruscombe's wife. The Poole family are rising fast.'[75] Many poor people were ruined by such gambling, pawning their possessions in the expectation of winning. Frederick Eden described how they were addicted to gambling, especially the lottery: '[a]maidservant who has saved a guinea is sensible that if she attempts to be her own banker it will melt away piecemeal. Upon principles of prudence she purchases the sixteenth of a ticket, and concludes that her honesty and frugality will find their reward in a fortunate number.'[76]

For the wealthy, travelling abroad – particularly doing the Grand Tour of Europe – was once fashionable, but the continued wars had halted this trend. As Elizabeth Ham witnessed, 'the Continent was quite shut to the British idler, and Weymouth was all the fashion'.[77] She herself lived at this seaside resort, but such attractions were not to everyone's taste. Some travellers began to explore the more sparsely populated areas of Britain that were formerly regarded as barren and dangerous waste land. Accounts of these travels were increasingly published, many illustrated with topographical prints. What emerged from this new appreciation of the wilder parts of Britain was the Romantic Movement that developed in the arts, with poets such as Wordsworth in the Lake District who went on tours, taking inspiration from nature, and artists such as Constable and Turner painting scenes and landscapes.

Those inclined to scholarly study, but who were prevented from exploring the classical ruins of the Continent, turned their attention to the more prosaic sites and ruins at home. This happened to coincide with the adoption of the new farming methods, the improvement of roads and the digging of canals, all of which were damaging and destroying prehistoric and historic monuments and unearthing a great number of strange artefacts. Many of the well-to-do, and particularly clergymen who were classically educated and had time on their hands, became 'barrow diggers'. The architect John Repton, son of the land-scape designer Humphry Repton, was one such barrow digger, and in 1808 he 'opened' a Bronze Age barrow near Aylsham in Norfolk: 'Having ordered a hole to be opened [by workmen] in the middle, about four yards wide, and two yards deep, we came to the sand, the natural soil of the whole heath, but continued digging through the sand, about two yards deeper, without finding anything; but on shov-ing down the side to fill up the cavity . . . a curious Urn was discovered, which was cut through in the middle by the spade.'[78] After this unfor-tunate accident, all Repton could do was make a quick sketch before the rest of the urn 'was quite destroyed, it being too soft a substance to be taken up in large fragments'.[79]

From such clumsy beginnings, the modern science of archaeology was born and it ran in parallel with a growing curiosity about the history of the country, to the point where it was considered 'that without a competent fund of antiquarian learning, no one will ever make a respectable figure, either as a Divine, a Lawyer, Statesman, Soldier, or even a private Gentleman'.[80] In November 1805, Benjamin Silliman was in London: 'through the introduction of a friend, I attended a meeting of the Antiquarian Society, which holds its sit-tings in a spacious room in Somerset-House . . . Lord Leicester, a nobleman, of a grave and plain appearance, was in the chair. The antiquities are still far from being exhausted, and this society is use-fully employed in bringing them to light.'[81] This was the illustrious Society of Antiquaries of London, and Lord Leicester would be its president until his death in 1811.[82] The discovery and recording of antiquities had in fact barely started.

For those seeking an impression of places abroad, panorama dis-plays provided the solution. These were models or large paintings (or a mixture of both), depicting views of foreign cities and battles as well as topics closer to home such as the British fleet at Spithead and the state funeral of Admiral Lord Nelson. In London in July 1809 Mary Berry visited the Panorama in Leicester Square, run by Henry Barker:

> Went in the morning with Mr. Playfair to see the two panoramas of Cairo and of Dublin. That of Cairo admirable. The sandy arid look of the country so well given, and contrasting so remarkably with the green fringe of land on each side of the course of the Nile. The near buildings – many of them picturesque and well painted. The interior of the city of Dublin is an ugly subject, but extremely well done, and giving a perfect idea of a meaner dirty-looking London.[83]

The purpose-built Panorama still survives, having been converted in 1868 to the Church of Notre Dame de France. Louis Simond saw new exhibits there two years after Mary Berry:

> There are new panoramas this year at Mr Barker's ... We have just seen Malta. The gairish light of day, white and dazzling;—the strong and perpendicular shadows;—the dusty land;—the calm and glassy sea ... The inhabitants overcome, lie about in the shade of narrow streets;—a centinel alone is seen pacing his watch before the gate of the arsenal. The smallest details are characteristic ... We learned, with much regret, that the panorama of Dover, which we admired so much last year, was painted on this identical cloth. Malta is laid over Dover, and Dover covers half-a-dozen more *chefs-d'oeuvre!* ... The circumference of the panorama is about 270 feet, the height 30 feet, the surface about 900 square yards.[84]

London possessed more leisure attractions than anywhere else, and the rival pleasure gardens of Vauxhall and Ranelagh were famous. In 1782 Moritz visited Vauxhall gardens:

> Vauxhall is, properly speaking, the name of a little village, in which the garden, now almost exclusively bearing the same name, is situated. You

pay a shilling on entrance ... As you enter the garden, you immediately hear the sound of vocal and instrumental music. There are several female singers constantly hired to sing here. On each side of the orchestra are small boxes, with tables and benches, in which you sup. The walks before these, as well as to every other part of the garden, are crowded with people of all ranks ... The rotunda, a magnificent circular building, in the garden, particularly engaged my attention. By means of beautiful chandeliers and large mirrors, it was illuminated in the most superb manner; and every where decorated with delightful paintings and statues, in the contemplation of which you may spend several hours very agreeably, when you are tired of the crowd and the bustle in the walks of the garden.[85]

Despite its attractive appearance, Moritz found Vauxhall to be a haunt of prostitutes: 'what most astonished me, was the boldness of the women of the town, who often rushed in upon us by half dozens, and in the most shameless manner importuned us for wine'.[86] Criminals also frequented the place, and at one point 'there arose all at once a loud cry of, "Take care of your pockets." This informed us, but too clearly, that there were some pickpockets among the crowd, who had already made some fortunate strokes.'[87]

Moritz was more impressed with Ranelagh:

coming out of the gloom of the garden, I suddenly entered a round building, illuminated by many hundred lamps, the splendour and beauty of which surpassed every thing of the kind I had ever seen before ... above, there was a gallery divided into boxes; and in one part of it an organ with a beautiful choir, from which issued both instrumental and vocal music. All around, under this gallery, are handsome painted boxes for those who wish to take refreshments ...

I sat down in one of the boxes, in order to take some refreshment ... when a waiter very civilly asked me what refreshment I wished to have, and in a few moments returned with what I asked for. To my astonishment, he would accept no money for these refreshments; which I could not comprehend, till he told me that every thing was included in the half-crown I had paid at the door.[88]

A possible portrait of Jane Austen (though disputed), published by William and Richard A. Austen-Leigh in *Jane Austen. Her Life and Letters: A Family Record* (1913). The girl wears a muslin gown and flimsy shoes, and carries a parasol.

The cottage in Chawton, Hampshire, where Jane Austen lived from 1809 to 1817. It overlooked the main road from London to Gosport (Portsmouth) as well as another road leading to Winchester. The cottage is now a popular museum.

Parchment indenture of Richard Cureton, apprenticed in 1783 to William Wakelin (or Wakelen), girdler.

A view of London and the River Thames in 1814 from Blackfriars Bridge, with St Paul's cathedral on the left and Southwark on the far right. Before its embankment, the river was much wider than today.

A woman using water from a pump near cottages in Wenlock, Shropshire, in 1815.

A 1794 halfpenny token of John Fowler, a London whale oil merchant, depicting four men in a boat about to hurl a harpoon at a whale spouting water.

Building new terraced houses, with a bricklayer standing on wooden scaffolding while a labourer mixes mortar.

A fashion plate of 1800 called 'Afternoon dress', which was the formal 'half dress' worn by wealthier women for attending afternoon functions like dinners. The women are carrying fans and wearing simple muslin gowns and fashionable caps.

A weaver making worsted stockings on a stocking loom.

A hairdresser cutting and dressing the long hair of a male customer. Both men are wearing knee-length breeches and stockings.

St Peter and St Paul church in Over Stowey, Somerset, where William Holland was vicar from 1798 until his death in 1819. He lived in the vicarage on the opposite side of the lane.

A copper penny token issued at Bath in 1811 depicting the city arms with clasped hands above. The reverse says 'a pound note for 240 tokens given by S. Whitchurch and W. Dore'. Whitchurch was an ironmonger and Dore a hatter and draper.

Reverse of a copper 'cartwheel' twopence of George III, so-called because of its large size (41mm diameter, 5mm thickness and weighing 2 ounces). Such coins were made from 1797 at Matthew Boulton's Soho mint in Birmingham using the new steam-powered machinery.

A copper halfpenny of 1791 (obverse and reverse) issued by the copper works of Charles Roe at Macclesfield. The year before John Byng received Macclesfield halfpennies as change at a turnpike.

The obverse and reverse of a halfpenny copper token of the industrialist John Wilkinson. The reverse shows a drop hammer suspended above a piece of iron on an anvil. Around the edge the place-namess Willey, Snedshill, Bersham and Bradley showed where the tokens were redeemable.

A man viewed from the rear seated at a loom, depicted on a 1791 copper halfpenny token. It was payable at the warehouse of John Kershaw, a Rochdale mercer and draper.

By 1792 the design changed, as seen on this halfpenny token, also payable at the warehouse of John Kershaw, a Rochdale mercer and draper.

Advertisements requesting employment as a mantua maker and a cook in the *Morning Chronicle* newspaper for 29 October 1807.

A workhouse depicted on a copper penny token issued by the Overseers of the Poor at Sheffield. This workhouse was located at Workhouse Croft (now Paradise Street), West Bar. Such workhouse tokens were given as poor relief and were accepted by local retailers.

Joseph Johnson, a crippled black beggar and former merchant seaman, travelled round London and nearby villages and market towns, performing nautical songs and wearing on his head a model of the warship *Nelson*.

"POTATOES, FULL WEIGHT!"

A boy selling matches in a London street.

A child street hawker selling potatoes from a wooden wheelbarrow. This romanticised view dating to 1812 shows an unlikely well-nourished child.

The River Tyne in 1789 with shallow-draught keels for transporting coal, looking towards Newcastle-upon-Tyne, with the castle keep and cathedral on the right.

Such noisy and public entertainment contrasted sharply with the London coffee-houses he also visited:

> In these coffee-houses there generally prevails a very decorous stillness and silence. Every one speaks softly to those only who sit next to him. The greater part read the newspapers, and no one ever disturbs another. The room is commonly on the ground floor, and the seats are divided by wooden wainscot partitions. Many letters and projects are here written and planned, and many of those that are inserted in the papers are dated from some of these coffee-houses.[89]

Newspapers were taxed with a stamp duty and were relatively expensive, and so men frequented coffee-houses in order to read them there rather than buy their own. Newspapers provided the only regular source of news, but they looked very different to those of today, because they had no illustrations, were printed in black ink only, and the front page was traditionally reserved for columns of advertisements rather than big headlines and leading news items. Despite their cost, annual sales were riding high both locally and nationally. This was partly because after the Franking Act of 1764, Members of Parliament were allowed to purchase newspapers in bulk and send them through the post free-of-charge,[90] greatly increasing the circulation of London newspapers and helping to keep down their price.

Literacy levels were improving, though the numbers of people who were literate varied according to class. Statistics on the subject are little more than guesswork, but it has been estimated that two out of three working men could read to some extent, though rather fewer had writing skills, and not nearly as many working women could read. If they did not read themselves, most people knew someone who would read to them. Moritz was surprised to meet so many people who could read:

> My landlady, who was only a taylor's widow, reads her Milton; and told me, that her late husband fell first in love with her on this very account, because she read Milton with such proper emphasis. This single instance, perhaps, would prove but little; but I have conversed with several people of the lower class, who all knew their national authors, and who all have

read many, if not all of them. This elevates the lower ranks, and brings them nearer to the higher.[91]

He attributed this apparently increasing spread of education to the availability of classical authors in 'cheap and convenient editions ... At stalls, and in the streets, you every now and then meet with a sort of bibliopolists [booksellers], who sell single or odd volumes; sometimes as low as a penny; nay even sometimes for a half-penny a-piece. Of one of these I bought the two volumes of the Vicar of Wakefield for sixpence.'[92] Street sellers who offered cheap song sheets and sensational stories would also sell chapbooks, which were flimsy booklets containing stories about ghosts, mermaids, recent crimes and executions, fables or anything else thought likely to titillate a mass market. One chapbook from 1772 began on an optimistic note – a fantastic tale perhaps purchased by those desperately hoping for better times:

> Good News for England being A strange and remarkable ACCOUNT how a stranger in bright Raiment appeared to one Farmer Edwards near Lancaster, on the 12th of last Month, at night; containing the discourse that past [passed] between the said Farmer and the Stranger, who foretold what a wonderful Year of Plenty this will be, and how wheat will be sold for four shillings a bushel, and barley for two shillings this Year; all which was confirmed to the Farmer by four wonderful signs.[93]

There was an exciting boom in the publishing of books – not just novels, but an impressive range of volumes on history, travel, biography and science. The number of novels to choose from was large, and they were advertised in national and regional newspapers across the country, with many names of publishers still familiar today. On Christmas Day 1815 the front page of the *Morning Chronicle* – as usual – consisted of nothing but advertisements. Under 'Books published this day' was an extremely modest notice:

> In 3 vols. 12mo price of 1l. 1s.
> EMMA: a Novel. — By the Author of Pride and Prejudice.
> Printed for John Murray, Albemarle-street.[94]

Traditionally, novels were published in several volumes, usually three. As in the book itself, the advertisement did not reveal Jane Austen's name. The same publisher placed larger notices for two other books, *An Account of the Kingdom of Nepaul* by Colonel Kirkpatrick and *Oriental Memoirs* by James Forbes, perhaps reflecting the publisher's slender expectations for *Emma*. Today, few people have heard of those two books, while *Emma* is known and loved worldwide.

The best places in London to buy books were Ludgate Hill, Paternoster Row and St Paul's Churchyard (not the burial ground but the adjacent street lined with small shops). Booksellers and printers were often one and the same, selling the books that they published, and most bookstores were small, but James Lackington's bookshop was huge. His first shop had been in Chiswell Street, but in 1794 he opened larger premises in Finsbury Square, a celebrated bookstore that became known as the 'Temple of the Muses'. This was one of the wonders of London until it burned down in 1841. Lackington accepted only cash, not credit, and claimed to sell the cheapest books in England.

Other places in London had bookshops clustered together, as Samuel Pratt observed:

> On one side of a long narrow passage called Middle-row [in Holborn], I observed a few literary loungers inspecting the old book-shops, for which this part of the town has long been famous. Pausing a little at the different stalls, I noted several persons enquiring for odd volumes to compleat broken sets, which had been lost by the commerce of lending or borrowing; for you must know, that detention of books, is amongst the negligences, or petty larcenies in friendship ... The same spot is also frequented by authors, who are on the hunt for such of their writings, as are, what we technically call, 'out of print' – that is, not to be heard of either at the original publisher's, or amongst the regular trade.[95]

Books and newspapers tended to be a luxury because of their high price, but private subscription lending libraries existed, even if of varying quality – Jane Austen thought the library at Dawlish in

Devon 'pitiful and wretched'.[96] Most towns and many villages had a reading room or book club, something that Simond noticed:

There are almost everywhere book societies or clubs, variously constituted. They are generally composed of ten or twelve persons, contributing annually a certain sum for the purchase of books. Any of them may propose a book, which, when read by all the associates who choose, is put up for sale among them. The person who recommended the purchase is obliged to take it at half price, if no one bids higher. The annual contribution is commonly from one to four guineas.[97]

William Holland belonged to a book club, and in May 1804 he wrote in his diary: 'we went to the Globe [Inn at Nether Stowey], where we all dined, being members of the Book Society ... We spent a very agreeable evening together, had a good dinner and sold our books and entered into fresh subscriptions.'[98]

Reading was not necessarily a solitary occupation. Books and newspapers were read aloud, as part of the tradition of shared entertainment. It was too expensive for everyone to read their own book on dark winter evenings, because each person would need a candle. Throughout her life, Jane Austen read books aloud or listened to others. Such a pastime was relatively cheap and always available, and on a day in October 1805 when it rained heavily for many hours, Holland recorded: 'My wife read the novel of Camilla to us all the whole day with little intermission so that we were all much entertained with that very affecting narration.'[99] Fanny Burney's *Camilla* – her third novel, an immensely long work in five volumes – had been published nearly a decade earlier, in 1796.

Books were also a fashion item, and most wealthy households had a library, although in some cases the books were there to be admired, not read, as Nelly Weeton lamented of her employer's library at Dove Nest: 'Mr. P[edder], like many of the wealthy, possesses a library of little real use. He himself reads little, so that the shelves make a display of knowledge he possesses not; many a volume, I dare say, has never been opened. The collection is numerous, valuable, and well selected. How rich I should be in books if I had all in Mr. P's library that have never been read.'[100]

Letters also provided entertainment when read aloud among family and friends. Writing was essential for long-distance communication, and those who had the time corresponded on a daily basis with friends and family. Jane Austen was a prolific letter writer, but the greater part of her letters were destroyed by her sister Cassandra and other family members. One surviving letter to Cassandra, written in June 1808, gives a glimpse of the constant communication: 'I assure you I am as tired of writing long letters as you can be. What a pity that one should be so fond of receiving them!'[101]

The cost of sending a letter was relatively high, charged according to the distance travelled and the number of 'enclosures', such as if more than one sheet of paper was used. Most letters comprised a single sheet folded in on itself. A rectangle in the middle of the outer side of the sheet was left blank to carry the address, and the last fold was tucked in and sealed with red-coloured beeswax (black for funerary correspondence) or a piece of glued paper called a 'wafer'. Woodforde often recorded his purchases of wax, as in July 1788: 'at a bookseller's shop at Bungay for a large stick of red sealing wax, paid 0: 1: 0'.[102]

To minimise postal costs, writers needed to plan the length of a letter carefully, which did not always happen, as Nelly Weeton admitted to her brother Tom: 'I feel myself in a writing humour, and as I have entirely filled one large half sheet, I will, for once, put thee to the expence of a double letter; had I thought, when I begun, that I should have scribbled so much, I would not have cut the sheet, and then I might, with a safe conscience, have informed the Post-master that it was only a "single sheet".'[103] The cost of postage was paid by the recipient of the letter, not the sender, so a failure to economise might be unwelcome. Within London, a Penny Post pre-paid system operated, increased to twopence in 1801.[104]

One way of keeping to a single sheet of paper was by crosswriting. Once a sheet was covered with writing, it was turned 90 degrees and the writing was continued at right-angles over what was already written. This allowed double the number of lines of writing, but the resulting letter was difficult to read, as Nelly warned a friend: 'I am afraid you will scarcely be able to read this cross writing – a little more and I will have done.'[105] Envelopes only began to be manufactured and sold in large quantities when uniform (and lower) postal charges, irrespective of the number of enclosures, were introduced in 1840.

There were no mailboxes as there are today, and letters had to be posted at a Post Office to be delivered to the Post Office closest to the recipient's address. Letters were collected in person, or arrangements were made for a servant or friend to collect and pay for them. The postal service was generally reliable, but over long distances, letters might be in transit for several days. It was well known that Members of Parliament would put their frank on letters written by their family, friends and even distant acquaintances, because they had the privilege of franking their own letters, which were delivered free-of-charge. Such a frank might merely consist of a sheet of paper with a legible and authentic signature. This sheet was used as part of the letter, folded so that the signature was visible on the outside.

The upper classes frequently resorted to such franks, and Jane Austen used them whenever the opportunity arose. In April 1811 she wrote to her sister: 'I had sent off my letter yesterday before yours came, which I was sorry for; but as Eliza has been so good as to get me a frank, your questions shall be answered without much further expense to you.'[106] Simond was not impressed by the stinginess of the wealthy and the business of franking: 'Nobody thinks of writing to a friend without a frank, and letters are received with a perceivable expression of surprise, at least, when there is postage to pay. You may pay the postage of your own letters; and I had availed myself of that expedient, as infinitely preferable to that of begging a frank, but I found it was considered as a great impropriety.'[107]

Most of Jane Austen's letters were to family members, but when her books began to be published, she also had business correspondence with her publishers, and a few of these letters have survived. In 1815 she commented on one letter from her publisher: 'Mr Murray's letter is come; he is a rogue of course, but a civil one. He offers £450 but wants to have the copyright of M.P. [*Mansfield Park*] & S.&S. [*Sense and Sensibility*] included. It will end in my publishing for myself I daresay. He sends more praise however than I expected. It is an amusing letter.'[108]

# NINE

————— •◆• —————

# ON THE MOVE

Open carriages are nasty things. A clean gown is not five minutes' wear in them. You are splashed getting in and getting out; and the wind takes your hair and your bonnet in every direction. I hate an open carriage myself.

*Northanger Abbey*, by Jane Austen

Some people never saw new places, never travelled any distance in their entire lives. Elizabeth Ham remembered her Uncle Thomas of Haselbury in Somerset, who lived to the age of ninety and 'died in the house in which he was born, and from which he was never absent but once in his life, when, in his youth, he went to Bristol for a week'.[1] His journey to Bristol, 30 miles away, was the furthest he ever travelled. Others did travel a great deal to see friends and family and on business, but nothing moved faster than a galloping horse. Horses were the main source of power, and engines are still measured in 'horsepower', a unit originally based on the number of horses needed to do the same work as a steam engine.

Walking was the most common means of transport, often over considerable distances and in miserable conditions. Thick, squelching mud was the bane of all travel, exhausting to walk through and a hazard for horses and wheeled vehicles alike. At Steventon in Hampshire, Jane Austen and Cassandra would certainly walk 'when the roads were dirty',[2] wearing pattens to raise their shoes above the mud. When conditions outside were bad, most middle- and upper-class ladies avoided travelling on foot altogether, and Jane wrote in one letter: 'Anna ... is quite equal to walking to Chawton, and comes over to us when she can, but the rain and dirt divide us a good deal.'[3] In Norfolk, Parson James Woodforde constantly noted in his diary that church attendances were low because of poor weather, as in late January 1790: 'None from Weston House at church, none of my gentry [family guests] at church being wet and dirty.'[4]

Even those who owned horses often walked a great deal. In the summer of 1794 Woodforde was visiting friends in the neighbourhood with his niece, but being concerned about her painful knee, he calculated the distance they covered: 'Nancy had a good deal of walking to day, near seven miles has she walked this day and very well.'[5] Few people chose to undertake long excursions on foot, but Carl Moritz was an exception, as he deliberately spent some seven weeks in 1782 walking through England. On one occasion, when leaving Oxford, he used a stagecoach and asked a fellow passenger why Englishmen avoided travelling on foot: 'O! said he, we are too rich, too lazy, and too proud. And most true it is, that the poorest Englishman one sees, is prouder and better pleased to expose himself to the danger of having his neck broken, on the outside of a stage [coach], than to walk any considerable distance, though it might be done ever so much at his ease.'[6]

Paupers could not travel long distances at all, not even on foot, because under the poor laws anyone found outside their own parish without sufficient money and reason to be there was liable to be arrested and returned. When he arrived at inns without horses, Moritz was invariably treated with contempt, as happened at Eton: 'I entered the inn and desired to have something to eat ... the waiter soon gave me to understand, that I should there find no very friendly reception. Whatever I got, they seemed to give me with such an air, as shewed too plainly how little they thought of me; and as if they considered me but as a beggar.'[7] Even so, he added, 'they suffered me to pay like a gentleman'.[8]

Elsewhere, he found various obstacles in his path and began to realise why pedestrians kept to the well-worn routes and avoided short-cuts. One morning he set out on foot from Windsor:

I rose very early . . . in order to climb the two hills, which presented me with so inviting a prospect; and in particular that one of them, on the summit of which a high, white house, appeared among the dark green trees. I found no regular path leading to these hills; and therefore went straightforward, without minding roads; only keeping in view the object of my aim. This certainly created me some trouble: I had sometimes a hedge, and sometimes a bog to walk round; but at length I attained the foot of the so earnestly-wished-for hill, with the high, white house on its summit, when, just as I was going to ascend it . . . behold I read these words on a board: 'Take care; there are steel traps and spring guns here.' All my labour was lost, and I now went round to the other hill; but here were also 'steel traps and spring guns'.[9]

These traps were mantraps that had two strong steel jaws, often with serrated edges, which snapped shut by means of powerful springs when someone stepped on the pressure plate between the jaws. Hidden in grass and undergrowth, they were designed to trap and detain intruders, but frequently resulted in a badly cut or broken leg. Spring guns were mounted with a trip wire to the trigger, and the gun was fired when the trip wire was pulled.

Wherever traps and spring guns were laid, being on horseback was no better than walking, but riding could be hazardous on the open road as well. In late January 1773, after spending a convivial afternoon with friends at Cole in Somerset, Woodforde and his brother returned to Ansford Parsonage:

Brother John got quite merry and coming home was thrown from his horse, but blessed be God received no great hurt. His horse run away home . . . I walked with him home and led my horse in my hand. I was most miserably terrified by his fall, he riding in so disagreeable a manner as to frighten me every step till he was thrown. It was a great mercy of thine O God that he was not killed, as there was a waggon not twenty yards before him when he fell and the horse full stretch almost . . . My man Willm. also met with an accident this evening at my door in his return from Cole. Soon as the chaise stopped, the horse which he rode fell down and bruised his leg much. The horses breath was stopped by the harness.[10]

Because so many men and some women rode horses and donkeys, alighting stones (mounting blocks) were common in public places, such as by churches or in market squares, and at Moretonhampstead in Devon in 1800, Silvester Treleaven noted: 'A new alighting stone erected at the lower end of the Shambles by subscription.'[11] Gentlemen wore spurs when riding, but the Reverend William Holland was annoyed to discover his manservant using them: 'Mr Robert among his other excellencies has been in the habit of wearing my spurs. I have once or twice had a hint of his riding hard and now I have found out the method he takes to get his horse on.'[12] Servants were not always reliable riders, as Woodforde also found: 'Ben went yesterday in the afternoon with a Mr. Watson steward to Sr. John Woodhouse to Kimberly Hall, where having made too free with the Baronets strong beer, fell of[f] his horse coming home and lost her, so that he walked about all the night after her and did not find her till about noon, she was found at Kimberly in a stable of Mr. Hares, a boy happening to see and put her in there.'[13]

Like modern vehicles, horses required much maintenance, as did carts and carriages. Apart from food, water, grooming, stabling, harness and veterinary care, horses needed to be properly shod. This was not a problem near home, close to familiar blacksmiths, but a cross-country traveller might have to make 'running repairs', like John Byng soon after leaving Basingstoke:

> In a miles riding I overtook a conversable farmer, and we jogged on together being both bound for Reading; but soon, oh grief of griefs! my horse went miserably lame as if he had wrenched his foot; the farmer said it would walk off but the poor beast being unable to move, I dismounted to examine his foot, into the frog of which a great horse-nail had enter'd so deeply that with difficulty we extracted it. As soon as possible we stop'd at a blacksmith's, who burnt in some turpentine, which, secured by tow, enabled my horse to go on tolerably.[14]

Horses and other pack animals were the only option for haulage in some parts of England, because wheeled vehicles were impossible on narrow, winding and steep roads. In counties such as Devon and

Cornwall, the roads tended to be simply packhorse trackways. In the summer of 1795, John Manners travelled westwards from Devon into Cornwall: 'To-day we for the first time observed the husbandmen bringing in their barley and oats ... The manner in which they carry their harvest in Cornwall is very curious. Having no carts on account of their hills, they make use only of little ponies, and carry their loads in a kind of pannier, placed like a saddle on the horse.'[15]

Coal was carried from the north Somerset mines into Bath using donkeys, and in September 1800 Richard Warner saw one of these animals at work, delivering to the grand houses, a 'little, wasted, panting wretch, staggering under its unconscionable burthen, and labouring up the steep streets of Bath; now dropping with fatigue, and again urged to exertion by reiterated blows'.[16] The animals, he explained, were kept overnight at nearby Holloway:

> Wearied and panting with the labour of the day, here the wretched beasts are driven ... as the evening closes, into yards hired for the purpose, not so much for the sake of rewarding their services with rest, as to prevent their escape from the toil of tomorrow. As they pick a scanty pittance from the ditches and hedges during the day, the inhuman master thinks himself exempted from the necessity of giving them food at night; and what is still more barbarous, never removes from their backs the heavy and incumbering wooden saddle on which the coals are packed, but suffers it to continue girded on for weeks together, inflaming and increasing those galls which its pressure originally occasioned.[17]

Normally, goods were conveyed in carriers' carts and waggons. Long-distance carriers made cross-country trips using large waggons pulled by six or eight horses, and some operated in the same way as stagecoaches, changing horses at wayside stops and claiming to be a fast service with names like 'Flying Waggon', even though their speed was slower than walking pace. Although these waggons primarily carried freight, they could also accommodate passengers. Other than walking, this was the cheapest means of travel and gave some shelter from the weather. A household might own horses and a small cart for transporting passengers and for haulage, and on one occasion Holland noted: 'My daughter [Margaret] is to return with the two Miss Lewis's and (because they cannot procure a better conveyance) to go in my cart. Robert is to drive.'[18] At other times this cart was involved in tasks like moving dung, hay, timber and coal.

Wealthy gentry and the aristocracy would own at least one carriage that was solely for passengers, but their horses might be used for riding and farm work as well. Small carriages that were open to the elements were not suited to winter conditions, as with the donkey carriage used at Chawton by Jane Austen: 'this is not a time of year [January] for donkey-carriages, and our donkeys are necessarily having so long a run of luxurious idleness that I suppose we shall find they have forgotten much of their education when we use them again. We do not use two [donkeys] at once however; don't imagine such excesses.'[19] Only the very rich could afford the cost of keeping large, enclosed carriages, emblazoned with their coats-of-arms, along with teams of horses and liveried servants.

There was a trade in secondhand carriages, and in London in May 1806 Ralph Heathcote accompanied a friend who was looking for something suitable to buy: 'We went out to look at carriages, T. [Colonel Taylor] meaning to buy a chaise ... We went to all the principal coachmakers. The average price for a second-hand chaise still in fashion (about two years ago) and good order, newly painted, etc., is £150.'[20] Then, as now, sellers emphasised the vehicle's good condition, and the following year this 'one careful lady owner' advertisement appeared in the *Morning Chronicle*:

COACH to be DISPOSED of, late the property of a lady, deceased; has been built but a few months, in the present stile, compass sides and projecting elbows, the lining and every part in the nicest condition, and scarce inferior to new, painted yellow and black, built by Hatchett and Co. at a considerable expence, and to be disposed of for about one-third of the original cost, at Turner's, coach-maker, opposite Shoreditch Church.[21]

With no restrictions on who could drive a vehicle, carriage drivers varied enormously in their abilities. Young aristocratic men had a reputation for driving fast and often irresponsibly, but elderly drivers could equally pose a hazard, as Woodforde observed:

Mr. Du Quesne returned to his own home to dinner, though we asked him to dine with us ... He complained much of being terribly shook about in his chaise by the badness of the roads ... Mr. Du Quesne is very far advanced in years but he will not own it. He is by no means fit to drive a single horse chaise. His servant man that came on horseback with him, was afraid that he would overturn coming along, he cannot see the ruts distinctly, he will not however wear spectacles at all. He cannot bear to appear old.[22]

This was the Reverend Thomas Roger du Quesne, who died four months later at the age of seventy-five.

For long journeys across England, people resorted to public transport, of which the stagecoach was the most popular. These were roofed four-wheeled vehicles, driven by coachmen at speeds of 6–7 miles per hour and running to a schedule on established routes. The term 'stage' referred to each stage of the journey between the points where the horses were changed. To Moritz, stagecoaches seemed strange: 'Persons, to whom it is not convenient to pay a full price, instead of the inside, sit on the top of the coach, without any seats, or even a rail. By what means passengers thus fasten themselves securely on the roof of these vehicles, I know not; but you constantly see numbers seated there, apparently at their ease.'[23]

When he first arrived at Liverpool from America in May 1805, stagecoaches were also a novelty to Benjamin Silliman: 'people ride on the roofs of the English stage coaches. This situation affords fine views of the country, and is often a convenient refuge when the inside places are all taken. I mounted the roof, and although the situation was so giddy, that at first I grasped the iron railing with great care, I soon learned to hold my arms in security, trusting to the balance of position.'[24]

The horses slowed or stopped these vehicles – there were no brakes. In hilly areas Silliman noted that wheels would be chained: 'They took the wise precaution of chaining a wheel at the top of every steep hill, a practice which is common in England, and which is rendered doubly necessary by the great weight of people and luggage which an English stage coach carries on its roof. I have been one of a party of eighteen, twelve of whom were on the top.'[25] Unsurprisingly, the stagecoach was not always a safe means of transport, especially when coachmen drove their overloaded vehicles recklessly over potholed and rutted roads. In 1816 the *European Magazine* reported attempts at improvements:

> The country magistrates are exerting themselves to bring to punishment all drivers of stage coaches within their jurisdiction, who shall be found furiously driving, or shall carry more passengers than allowed by law. The following are among the various penalties to which the offending parties are liable:– Coachmen driving furiously, or permitting others to drive, forfeit 10l [£10].
>
> TEN passengers allowed on the outside of a carriage, drawn by *four* horses, besides the coachman: ONE only to sit on the BOX, THREE on the FRONT of the roof, and SIX BEHIND; a penalty of 10l. for each passenger beyond that number and DOUBLE that sum if the coachman is owner or part owner.
>
> LUGGAGE not to EXCEED TWO FEET in HEIGHT ON THE ROOF; penalty 5l/ [£5] for every inch above two feet. No passenger to SIT on the LUGGAGE; penalty 50s. to be paid by the passenger.[26]

Travelling inside a stagecoach was more costly, but it was safer and gave shelter from the weather. The lurching motion could cause nausea, and being inside also meant suffering other passengers. In 1802 Henry Hole was on his way to India, and he wrote to his father about the stagecoach journey from Exeter to Plymouth:

> We had scarcely got through the City when the coach suddenly stopp'd, the door opened and an overgrown female of the Wapping breed made her appearance, puffing and panting as if she had not half an hour to live. A considerable difficulty then arose how she was to get in. I look'd at her and the door alternately, and really conceived it impossible; however, by a little squeezing and a great deal of shoving in the rear by the coachman

[the driver] and guard assisted by half a dozen by-standers she contrived to effect her purpose in something less than a quarter of an hour. We screw'd ourselves up in each corner and allowed her to take the middle, when she sat or rather fell down with the grunt of a rhinoceros and remained a complete fixture for the whole journey. Not so her tongue; for the moment she recovered a sufficiency of breath, she attack'd me in a most barbarous dialect.[27]

In addition to the driver, there was also a guard, as Silliman explained: 'Most of the English stage coaches travel with a guard. He is armed with a blunderbuss, or more commonly with pistols ... To the duty of defending the coach he is rarely called for; for ... the stage coaches are seldom attacked. Besides guarding the coach, he is expected to open and shut the door, and aid in case of accident, so that the coachman is never called upon to leave his seat.'[28]

In the event of a stagecoach overturning, the outside passengers were flung off and would undoubtedly suffer injuries, while those inside could be trapped, crushed or even drowned. Newspapers were full of coaching incidents, as in *The Times* in December 1807:

As the Salisbury coach was coming to town [London], on Tuesday night, it met with a shocking accident. The fog was so thick that the coachman could not see his way, and at the entrance of Belfont [now Bedfont, near Hounslow], the horses went off the road into a pond called the King's Water, dragging the coach along with them. A young man of the name of Williams was killed on the spot. He belonged to a regiment of dragoons ... In the inside of the coach were four females: the wife of the deceased, her maid, a Swiss governess who lived in the family of a gentleman in Davies Street, Berkeley Square, and another female. They all narrowly escaped drowning.[29]

Given such disaster stories, it is no wonder that Woodforde wrote in his diary on 6 July 1778: 'My poor dear sister shook like an aspin leave [aspen leaf] going away, she never went in a stage coach before in her life.'[30]

For faster journeys or ones not on stagecoach routes, post-chaises could be hired at post-houses, which were usually inns. 'Post' was equivalent to 'stage'. These chaises (literally, 'chairs') were roofed four-wheeled vehicles, yellow in colour. Their speed was maintained by frequent changes of horses, and like stagecoaches, they had no brake. The drivers rode on the horses, not on the chaises, and were called postillions or post-boys, even though they were usually men. In early June 1782, Moritz took a chaise from Dartford to London:

> these carriages are very neat, and lightly built, so that you hardly perceive their motion, as they roll along these firm, smooth roads; they have windows in front, and on both sides. The horses are generally good, and the postillions particularly smart and active, and always ride on a full trot. A thousand charming spots and beautiful landscapes, on which my eye would long have dwelt with rapture, ere now rapidly passed with the speed of an arrow.[31]

He may not have noticed some of the faults that the experienced horseman and carriage driver John Byng railed against two years later:

> My nerves are either so weak or my fears so overpowering, that I never (but from necessity) ride in an hackney post-chaise; jolted, winded; harness that don't fit, horses that won't draw; and left at the mercy of an ignorant, drunken post-boy, who cannot drive, and is everlastingly brutal to the poor beasts under his lash. Young gentlemen are ever in violent haste to hurry to nothing; and laugh when I desire a post-boy not to gallop; not to hurry down hill; or to abstain from cutting at the horses eyes![32]

In Somerset William Holland occasionally hired a chaise for local journeys as in January 1807 when he and his wife were driven home from Enmore to Over Stowey along narrow lanes:

> We ... got on very well till we came past Radlet Common when we met a loaded waggon in a narrow part of the road. The waggoner did all he could to close the waggon up to the hedge but when we drove on a little

the chaise driver began to doubt our being able to pass, especially as there was an ugly ditch on our side. I call'd and told him it would be best to get out. You cannot, returned he, get out in this dirty place. Oh cannot we, answered I, I'll warrant you, for I deemed it far better to dirty our shoes and get wet than to be overturned and get our limbs broke, so out we got, but it was with some trouble and danger that they were able to pass afterwards. After this we got to Overstowey safe without further obstructions.[33]

From the 1790s onwards horse-drawn omnibuses were operating in London, from which modern buses developed, but the most common form of public transport in towns was the hackney coach, the forerunner of the hackney cab or taxi. The word 'hackney' meant a horse, or a horse for hire.[34] Hackney coaches tended not to be purpose-built vehicles until around 1814, when the 'chariot' was introduced, which carried two passengers inside and one outside. Before that, hackney coaches were usually old or worn-out private carriages, and their comfort varied considerably, as did the fares charged, which led to constant disputes. A succession of regulations tried – in vain – to control the exploitation of passengers by cabmen.

Particularly for elderly or invalid passengers, sedan chairs (also called hackney chairs if they were for hire) were an option. The sedan chair had a seat for a single passenger set inside a structure resembling a small sentry-box. A stout pole on either side provided the carrying handles for two chairmen, one in front and one behind. Chairmen waited at stands to catch passing trade, and a 1790 manual of advice for those staying in London said that the fares were a shilling for the first mile and sixpence for every subsequent mile. In cases of grievance, the customer should 'take the number of the chair, which is fixed just under the top, near the hinge, and complain at the hackney-coach office'.[35]

John Byng was not impressed by this form of transport at Cheltenham: 'their fare is very exorbitant; and as the master of ceremonies [at the spa pump rooms] dares not, and the company care not to make alterations, many such exactions and abuses continue here unrectified.'[36] Even this sedate method of travel carried risks, as revealed in a letter from William Jenkin to a friend: 'Thy mother met with an accident this week – as two men were carrying her in her chair, she slid out of it and fell to the ground, by which she received some hurt, one of her legs is bruised and she is likely to be confined to her room for some time.'[37]

For those who could afford the fare, sedan chairs were invaluable in towns in bad weather to avoid having to walk through filthy streets. Urban authorities were making some effort to install paved walkways or pavements for pedestrians, at least in the main thoroughfares, and London was sometimes hailed as the best paved city in Europe. Certainly Moritz was impressed by the capital's streets:

The footway, paved with large stones, on both sides of the street, appears to a foreigner exceedingly convenient and pleasant; as one may there walk in perfect safety from the prodigious crowd of carts and coaches that fill the centre. However, politeness requires you to let a lady, or any one to whom you wish to show respect, pass, not as we do [in Germany], always to the right, but on the side next the houses or the wall, whether that happens to be on the right or on the left. People seldom walk in the middle of the streets in London, excepting when they cross over; which at Charing-Cross, and other places, where several streets meet, is sometimes really dangerous.[38]

The surfaces of the actual streets might be laid with cobbles, though they would still become filthy, while minor streets and lanes were more likely to remain unsurfaced, dusty in dry weather and a quagmire when wet. Paupers who could get hold of a broom appointed themselves crossing-sweepers, clearing a path for anyone wanting to cross the street, in the hope of a tip. This method of begging continued long into the Victorian era. With so many horses, huge quantities of manure filled the streets, made worse by the herds of animals that were driven to market, and so houses had boot scrapers outside for scraping footwear clean of detritus. In April 1809 Sarah Wilkinson was living in Church Street, Kensington, awaiting the return of her husband William from the navy: 'This morning while at breakfast, hearing the bell ring and somebody scrape their shoes as you used to do, I told Fanny it was you, and I ran down like a wild thing. Then think what I felt on seeing the washer woman stand at the door.'[39]

In towns and cities, the numerous wheeled vehicles led to congested streets and accidents, and there was endless noise from the iron tyres and the hooves of the horses, added to which was the sound of horns, animals being herded, the hubbub arising from traffic jams and the cries of pedlars and hawkers trying to sell their wares. In May 1805 Silliman arrived for the first time in London: 'We drove [on top of the stagecoach] through Piccadilly, and were instantly involved in the noise and tumult of London. We were obliged to hold fast as we were driven furiously over rough pavements [the street surfaces], while the clattering of wheels, the sounding of the coachman's horn, and the sharp reverberations of his whip, had there been no other noises, would have drowned conversation.'[40]

Only heavy snowfall could silence the city, as Gilbert White experienced in January 1776: 'the metropolis itself exhibited a still more singular appearance than the country; for being bedded deep in snow, the pavement of the streets could not be touched by the wheels or the horses' feet, so that the carriages ran about without the least noise. Such an exemption from din and clatter was strange, but not pleasant; it seemed to convey an uncomfortable idea of desolation.'[41]

In the countryside, the condition of roads varied greatly. The problem was that there was no central fund or taxation to pay for their upkeep. Instead, everyone was supposed to spend several days each year repairing the roads near where they lived, but the organisation of such labour was inefficient and haphazard. 'Mrs Poole's cart busy in doing statute labour,' William Holland noted with pleasure in June 1800. 'I hope we shall have the road a little better. A great many stones I see have been carried and laid down in the middle of the road. The Somersetshire Boobies have strangely mended the road.'[42] It was not feasible to bring in good-quality materials to those areas that had no stone, and so many roads in England remained pitted and rutted in dry conditions and deep in mud once it rained.

Such was the bad state of roads that John Byng preferred travelling on horseback during his annual summer excursions: 'Whoever speaks of touring in chaises or phaetons, (as many ignorants will,) let him attempt to travel thro' these ... rough roads; and then he will recant, and say with me, – there is no touring, but on horseback.'[43] He deplored the short-cut practices of the roadmenders in obtaining materials: 'how barbarous to pull down old ruins, as is commonly done; to fill up cart-ruts!'[44] Charles Fothergill in Yorkshire likewise opposed the destruction of ancient monuments for repairing roads: 'What will the lovers of antiquity and all wise and good men say to this when they are told ... that this is a co[u]ntry abounding with stones and every necessary material for the making and mending of roads.'[45]

On main cross-country routes, the solution to poor roads was privatisation, and from the mid-eighteenth century turnpike trusts had been established on a piecemeal basis, each one authorised by Act of Parliament. These private companies were licensed to maintain and operate turnpike roads as toll roads, and in return for collecting tolls, they took responsibility for their maintenance. Turnpike roads were so-called because of their barriers, often gates, that were set across the road where tolls were collected. The term 'turnpike' had been used from at least the early fifteenth century for a spiked barrier of pikes (a long-handled spear) that was rapidly placed as a makeshift obstacle, especially against attackers on horseback. By the mid-eighteenth century 'turnpike' was used generally for barriers, even for the locks and barriers on navigable waterways.

Turnpike trusts usually gained their initial capital by publishing a prospectus and inviting investors to lend them money, offering interest in the region of 4 or 5 per cent. This money covered initial repairs to the road, the establishment of gates and tollhouses at regular intervals and the wages of the toll collectors who were paid to live in the tollhouses and collect tolls at all hours, every day of the year. Once established, the trusts often farmed out the collection of tolls and repairs of the road to a contractor, in return for a guaranteed fixed sum, leaving the contractor to squeeze as much profit from travellers as possible. Understandably, toll collectors were unpopular, and 'turnpike man' became a derogatory term for a clergyman, on the grounds that his fees for baptisms and burials were tolls on passing in and out of the world of the living.

Many travellers tried to avoid the toll gates, but some trusts forced people to use them by blocking up alternative routes. Gangs occasionally broke down the gates, destroyed tollhouses and assaulted toll collectors. Turnpike roads did greatly improve many cross-country routes and opened up the country by making it easier to travel long distances, but not all were of high quality, as Byng found near Gloucester: 'No turnpike road is so bad as the last six miles to Gloster, narrow, wet, and stoney; and only mended with black iron ore, dangerous to man, and horse.'[46] Less than 20 per cent of the road network was run by the trusts; the majority of minor routes and side roads remained as bad as ever.

Along turnpike roads travellers had relatively little trouble finding their way, because there were milestones or mileposts at every mile, which appealed to Moritz: 'The English mile-stones gave me much pleasure, and they certainly are a great convenience to travellers. For, besides the distance from London, every mile-stone informs you, that to the next place is so many miles; and where there are cross-roads, there are direction-posts, so that it is hardly possible to lose one's self in walking.'[47] Each turnpike had an individual style of milestone, and a guidebook to Norfolk published in 1803 was impressed by the local design: 'The mile stones from Thetford to Norwich are well adapted for travelling in carriages, having two sides towards the road, not square, but slanted so that the number may be seen at a great distance.'[48] The turnpike trusts erected these milestones and mileposts, and they are still shown on modern Ordnance Survey maps, marked as MS or MP, revealing the old arterial roads.

Away from the turnpikes, following the correct route was not so easy, with no road names and little to guide the traveller. In August 1781, William Dyott was travelling by night in a post-chaise to Chester: 'I was awakened by the chaise stopping, when the post-boy did me the satisfaction of telling me he was lost, for which I made him a low bow and then kicked him. It was in the middle of an immense forest, and not near light.'[49] Even close to home it was easy to go astray, as Woodforde discovered: 'I went to Brand this morning for Mr. Bodham and there read prayers and administered the H.

Sacrament for him, as he served Mr. Hall's church at Garveston. Brand is about 7 mile from my house and very difficult road to find.'[50]

Most people had scant geographical knowledge beyond their own locality, something Byng noticed at Buxton in Derbyshire in June 1790: 'I travell by map, for none can inform you [of the way]; the only people who become acquainted with counties, are tourists, or a canvasser at a general election.'[51] Three weeks later he was exasperated with one hostler: 'enquiring the road to Grantchester, only 3 miles distant, he answer'd, (after a long stammer) "Were you ever there, sir?" "No, or I wou'd not have ask'd you the way".'[52] Maps were little better than sketches, which experienced travellers like him found wholly inadequate:

I have often thought that maps, merely for tourists might be made. And have wish'd that some intelligent traveller (for instance Mr [Francis] Grose) wou'd mark on such touring maps, all the castles, Roman stations, views, canals, parks, &c &c. which accompanied by other common maps, wou'd lead the researching tourist to every proper point & object; and not subject him (as at present) to ask questions of ignorant innkeepers, or to hunt in books, for what is not to be found; for till lately we had no inquisitive travellers and but few views of remarkable places.[53]

The threat of invasion during the wars with France made an accurate survey of England essential. It was begun in 1790, and its primary purpose was to enable the best positions to be chosen for defensive gun (ordnance) emplacements. They were therefore called Ordnance Survey maps, the name by which they are still known. Surveying started in the southern counties, where invasion was most likely, and the first map, of Kent, was produced in 1801. These maps were not available to the public until years later.

Long-distance travel was so slow that overnight stops were unavoidable. While Moritz was shunned at inns whenever he was on foot, Silliman noticed the difference between the treatment shown towards those passengers arriving by post-chaise and those by stage-coach: 'the strangers in the post-chaise were expected to pay well . . . while the men on top of the coach might possibly have money, but, in all probability, rode there to save it. Thus it is, that . . . the attentions which a traveller receives at the inns are proportioned very exactly to the style in which he arrives.'[54] He also found that everyone expected to be tipped: 'The guard and coachman as well as the servants at hotels expect their regular douceur . . . This tax is inevitable, and Americans, from ignorance of the country, and fear of being thought mean, usually pay more liberally than the natives.'[55]

When Silliman first arrived in London, 'We were driven through the Strand, Temple Row . . . and Fleet-street. The coach stopped at the Belle Savage on Ludgate Hill. The coachman, by a short turn, drove us, with astonishing swiftness, through a narrow opening, where the least deviation would have overturned the coach, and we were set down in a large back yard, full of coaches, horses, servants, and baggage.'[56] Surviving inns of this period usually retain the tell-tale arched entranceway for horse-drawn vehicles, and some still have the yard at the rear as well.

Whenever he travelled to London, Woodforde always stayed at the same historic coaching inn as Silliman, the Belle Sauvage, despite its bedbugs. In June 1786 he wrote: 'I was bit so terribly with buggs again this night, that I got up at 4 o'clock this morning and took a long walk by myself about the City till breakfast time.'[57] The next night he tried a different tactic: 'I did not pull off my cloaths last night but sat up in a great chair all night with my feet on the bed and slept very well considering and not pestered with buggs.'[58]

In *Emma* Mrs Elton says of Selina, her sister, that if staying at an inn, 'She always travels with her own sheets; an excellent precaution.' Byng regularly took his own sheets, but failed to do so when he was at the Black Bear Inn at Rugby in July 1789: 'My sheets were so damp, and the blankets so dirty and stinking, and the room so smelling of putridity, that I slept very little; tho' I took off the sheets, and employed all the brandy, near a pint, in purifying the room, and sprinkling the quilt, and blankets.'[59] The following year, the Black Bull Inn in Trumpington Street in Cambridge provoked his anger even more:

I never was in a worse or a dirtier inn; for ALL Cambridge is in comparison of Oxford . . . about 100 years behind hand: the best Cambridge inn wou'd form but a bad Oxford alehouse! – Dirty glasses; bad wine; vile cookery; but I answer to any question of hope, 'Oh, it is excellent'; and why should I not? . . . I, resolv'd never to come again, don't like to vex myself; and so I say 'It is all very good'. Tho here it went much against the grain . . . This wretched inn, with most of this wretched town, ought to be burnt down![60]

Cambridge was not burnt down, but the inn was rebuilt in 1828 and renamed 'The Bull'.

Rather than stay at inns, some people travelled all night, and Byng complained that inns wanted to do business only in horses, not hospitality: 'Most inns, now, are kept by, and for, a change of post horses, as fine gentleman never step out of their chaises in the longest journies; and all others travell in the mail, or post coaches: so that the tourist who wants only a supper and a bed, is consider'd as a troublesome unprofitable intruder.'[61] This kind of non-stop travel, with the horses being changed at intervals, was relatively fast but bitterly cold in winter. In November 1805 Silliman had left London and was journeying from Newark to York by stagecoach: 'The night had been one of the coldest that I have experienced in England; we were obliged to close the windows of the coach entirely; but still my feet suffered considerably . . . The coachman and guard, who had been all night in the open air, were completely encrusted [with frost].'[62]

Night journeys were hazardous because of the absence of lighting. It was much easier if a full moon lit the way, which Woodforde and his niece Nancy found when travelling from Bath to London in 1795: 'I thank God we had fine weather and a good moon all last night, and about 10 o'clock this morning we got safe and well to London . . . We were not much fatigued with our journey or otherwise indisposed, tho' travelling all night.'[63] In Weston Longville on another occasion Woodforde had an unpleasant night-time walk from a neighbouring house: 'As there was no moon to come home by, it was very disagreeable to come home thro' the wood that I did, but I thank God I got safe and well back tho' very dark. When there is no moon for the future will get back before it is dark.'[64] Moonlight was desirable for going to evening entertainments, and in

*Sense and Sensibility* Sir John Middleton is hoping to organise a small social gathering at the last minute, 'but it was moonlight and every body was full of engagements'.

Only in the main urban streets was there any street lighting, and London's was praised by Moritz in 1782: 'I was astonished at the admirable manner in which the streets are lighted up; compared to which our streets in Berlin make a most miserable show. The lamps are lighted whilst it is still day-light; and are so near each other, that even on the most ordinary and common nights, the city has the appearance of a festive illumination.'[65] An improved type of lighting was tried in May 1803, which *The Times* reported:

> A satisfactory experiment was first made on Friday evening last, at the Upper end of New Bond Street, to dissipate the great darkness that has long prevailed in the streets of this metropolis. It consisted in the adaption of twelve newly invented lamps with reflectors, in place of more than double that number of common ones; and notwithstanding the wetness of the evening ... that part of the street [was] illuminated with at least twice the quantity of light usually seen.[66]

Although this experimental lighting still comprised oil lamps, they were so effective that 'the faces of persons walking, the carriages passing &c. could be clearly seen',[67] an indication that the old lamps were very inadequate. Shops began to be lit by gas in 1805, and gas street lighting was demonstrated in Pall Mall in 1807, which gradually replaced oil lamps from 1812, making a significant improvement.

Lamps were useless during the dense fogs caused by adverse weather conditions and coal smoke, and Lady Bessborough described one terrifying journey she made in London on the night of 5 November 1805:

> The fog, which was bad when I set out, grew thicker and thicker, but when I got into the park was so complete it was impossible to find the way out. My footman got down to *feel* for the road, and the holloing of the drivers and screams of people on foot were dreadful. I was one hour driving thro' the park; Queen St it was impossible to find, and as ... it was

as dangerous to try to go home, I set out with two men walking before the horses with flambeaux [flaming torches], of which we could with difficulty perceive the flame – the men not at all. Every ten or twenty yards they *felt* for the door of a house to ask where we were – it was frightful beyond measure; in three hours' time I reached Chelsea.[68]

That very night Lieutenant Laponetiere was groping his way towards the Admiralty through the same fog, bringing news of the naval victory at Trafalgar and the death of Nelson.[69]

Bad weather regularly disrupted travel, particularly as winters in England were more severe than today. Heavy snowfall at times persisted into spring when the thaw would lead to severe floods. In Norfolk in early February 1799, during one bitter winter, Woodforde described the roads still blocked with snow:

Most of the poor people employed in clearing the public road from the late great fall of snow. Never known such a depth of snow for the last 40 yrs. People obliged to walk over hedges &c. In almost every place the roads impassable. The snow near our great gate in the yard almost as high as the gate, above the pales in some places. Dreadful weather indeed for the poor people now ... All travelling is almost at a stand, the drifting of the snow making almost every place impassable.[70]

Two weeks later, conditions had not changed:

Very dismal accounts on the papers respecting the last severe weather – many, many people having lost their lives thro' the inclemency of the same. Mail coaches &c unable to travel. The roads in very, very many places impassable. The long continuance of so severe cold weather having scarce been ever known for the last century. It has lasted now (with scarce any intermission) from the 17th of December last past and [more] still likely.[71]

In November 1800 an early winter snowstorm hit Exmoor, followed two days later by a violent rainstorm, which caused unprecedented flooding in St Thomas, a low-lying suburb of Exeter:

The inundation became violent on Sunday about noon, at which time the water began to flow over the streets of St. Thomas, and continued to increase with great rapidity until about five o'clock in the afternoon, when it had arisen in every street of that parish, and in the Exe Island, to the height of about six feet. At this period the appearance was dreadful, all the inhabitants were obliged to betake themselves to their upper rooms, whilst some, whose houses were built with mud (cobb) walls, were under the most serious alarm that they should be buried in the ruins. The current of the river [Exe] was then astonishingly strong, hurrying ... large pieces of wood, hayricks, and other matters which had been swept by its force from the neighbouring grounds, insomuch that serious apprehensions were entertained for the safety even of the New Exe Bridge.[72]

That same day two post-chaises set off from Okehampton to make their return journey to London, and on coming down the hill into St Thomas they suddenly encountered the floodwater:

here the water was so high, that it flowed over the backs of the horses, and reached nearly to the windows of the [first] carriage. One horse having dropped dead, it was necessary immediately to cut the traces, so as to extricate the others from the carriage, and prevent, if possible, the whole from being carried off by the violence of the current. As the waves continued rising it was judged impossible to preserve the lives of the persons in the carriage, unless a boat could be procured from the quay.[73]

In a dangerous operation, a boat was brought up close, 'just in time, for the persons were still sitting in the carriage, immersed above their middles, and so rapid did the water rise, that they had scarcely been extricated ... and the carriage lashed to prevent its being washed away, when the stream flowed over the roof'.[74] The travellers were the architect Henry Holland, his family and servants, who were all saved, along with the remaining horses.

Attempts at scientific weather forecasting were not published in newspapers until later in the nineteenth century, although most newspapers and magazines gave some weather details for preceding weeks or months. Many country gentlemen used barometers and thermometers to compile records, but forecasting relied heavily on observation and experience. Woodforde keenly observed the weather and had great faith in folklore. On 30 January 1794, after an intensely cold period, he wrote:

A frost again but not so sharp as yesterday. It did not freeze within doors last night ... It froze ... in the afternoon, and the barometer still rising, but in the evening it thawed and some rain fell. I was saying before dinner that there would be alteration of weather soon as I a long time observed one of our cats wash over both her ears – an old observation and now I must believe it to be a pretty true one.[75]

Faced with poor weather and poor roads, it was cheaper and easier in coastal areas for freight and even passengers to be conveyed by sea. Small ships did not need proper ports, but could be loaded and unloaded by boat while anchored offshore. Alternatively, ships were beached, as on the north Norfolk coast at Cromer where in 1798 Samuel Pratt witnessed coal being offloaded from ships into carts: 'There is now no harbour at Cromer, yet corn is exported, and coals, deals, &c. received in return ... at high water they [the ships] are laid upon the beach, and, as soon as the water is sufficiently ebbed, carts are drawn to the side of the ship, and the coals shot into them, as they are into lighters in other places.'[76] The carts, he said, only carried a small load because of the steep road up the cliff: 'In this manner the carts continue working, till the water flows so high as to wash the sides of the horses, and just to float the carts ... When the vessel is empty it floats on a high tide, and continues at a little distance from the shore, and is then loaded with corn by boats.'[77]

With canals making substantial improvements in the carriage of goods by water to inland areas, the condition of roads consequently benefited, because heavy waggons were no longer using them. William Hutton who lived in Birmingham said that before the canal was constructed from there to the Wednesbury coalfields, 'It was common to see a train of carriages for miles, to the great destruction of the road, and the annoyance of travellers.'[78] Canals were also used for passenger transport, and as early as 1774 a letter to the *Annual Register* reported:

> The Duke of Bridgewater has just built two packet-boats, which are every day towed [by horses] from Manchester to Warrington; one carries six score passengers, the other eighty: each boat has a coffee-room at the head, from whence wines, &c. are sold out by the captain's wife. Next to this is the first cabin, which is 2s. 6d., the second cabin is 1s. 6d. and the third cabin 1s. for the passage or voyage upon the canal.[79]

A few years later Nelly Weeton travelled from Wigan to Liverpool in a similar packet-boat, on a branch of the same canal network, and because of the canal's winding route and the stops to pick up passengers, the journey took most of the day:

> I arrived again at my lodgings after a very pleasant sail down the canal, perfectly safe and sound both in body and mind, with a little less fat perhaps in the evening than I had set out with in the morning; for, whether inside or outside, I was almost half baked. The cook generally begins her operations by ten o'clock in the morning, frying bacon, eggs, beef steaks, potatoes, and mutton chops; roasting meat, warming meat pies, &c., and seldom finishes before 3 or 4 o'clock in the afternoon; for most people who go in the tail end of the packet seem to think that eating and drinking is the most delightful amusement of travelling.[80]

It was also convenient to transport troops by canal boats, as *The Times* showed in 1806:

> The first division of the troops that are to proceed by the Paddington canal [London end of the Grand Junction Canal] for Liverpool, and thence by transports for Dublin, will leave Paddington today, and will be followed by others tomorrow and Sunday. By this mode of conveyance the men will be only seven days in reaching Liverpool, and with comparatively little fatigue, as it would take them above fourteen days to march that distance. Relays of fresh horses for the canal boats have been ordered to be in readiness at all stages.[81]

Canal boats did not yet have engines, but were pulled by horses, and Hutton was appalled by the cruelty he witnessed on the Birmingham to Wednesbury canal: 'The boats are nearly alike, constructed to fit the locks ... and are each drawn by something like the skeleton of a horse, covered with skin; whether he subsists upon the scent of the water, is a doubt; but whether his life is a scene of affliction is not; for the unfeeling driver has no employment but to whip him from one end of the canal to the other.'[82]

Steam engines, already transforming manufacturing industries, would soon do the same for transport. The Cornish engineer Richard Trevithick began working on models and prototypes of a portable steam engine, and in London in 1808 he demonstrated a self-propelled engine running on a rail track. Other engineers were making similar experiments, and although steam engines began to be used for the haulage of coal on rail tracks from mines, it would not be until 1825 that the Stockton and Darlington railway provided the first steam train for passengers.

Steamboats were also making an appearance, and a passenger service between Yarmouth and Norwich was started in 1813, but it was balloons that caught people's imagination. Balloon flights had already taken place on the Continent, and the first man to ascend in a balloon in England was an Italian, Vincenzo Lunardi. After some problems with the hydrogen balloon, Lunardi successfully took off from the grounds of the Honourable Artillery Company in City Road, London, on 15 September 1784. Once the mooring ropes were cast off, 'For a moment, the globe hung suspended, as if inclined to fall, but Mr. Lunardi instantly kicking out a considerable portion of his ... ballast, ascended triumphantly, standing erect in the gallery, and waving his flag as a return to the incessant acclamations that were paid him at his departure.'[83]

The crowd watching the balloon flight numbered over a hundred thousand and included the Prince of Wales. They had never seen anything like it, as the newspapers reported: 'The fine spectacle presented to the public, produced curious effects upon John Bull – while Lunardi ascended, some held up their hands in admiration, while others burst into tears, very expressive of sensibility and pleasure ...

Old persons ... declared they had lived till now to see the greatest Wonder of their Age.'[84] It was reported that 'Mr Sheldon, who followed Mr. Lunardi from London, on a fine hunter, changed his horse three times, and kept so well up with him, as to be enabled to dine in his company at Ware [in Hertfordshire]'.[85] For now the horse could still keep pace, but its days as the fastest form of travel were drawing to an end.

———— •◆• ————

# TEN

# DARK DEEDS

Let other pens dwell on guilt and misery.

*Mansfield Park*, by Jane Austen

The novels and surviving letters of Jane Austen give an impression of a world barely touched by crime or warfare. Yet for much of her life Britain was at war and threatened by invasion, there was widespread fear of crime, and criminals were treated harshly. By the early Victorian era, the laws of England in the late eighteenth and early nineteenth centuries were being referred to as the 'Bloody Code', because of the number of offences that carried the death penalty. Indeed, the phrase 'You might as well be hung for a sheep as a lamb'[1] arose when stealing a sheep was added to that list. There was more meat on a sheep, but stealing either a lamb or a sheep could mean execution.

A major part of the Bloody Code was the Black Act, an Act of Parliament that came into law in 1723 in response to two gangs of poachers in Hampshire and Berkshire who were known as 'blacks' because they blackened their faces. This Act made many offences punishable by death, including activities not previously treated as crimes, such as entering a forest in disguise or with a blackened face. The modern equivalent might be a mandatory death sentence for wearing a mask or hooded jacket. This draconian law was deliberately designed to protect the interests of the elite, particularly those with large estates, and it remained the backbone of the Bloody Code for a century.

It was the lower ranks who felt the brunt of the Bloody Code. The rich and powerful could, and did, bribe their way out of almost anything. Most laws were designed to protect people's possessions, and as the gap between rich and poor widened, more and more property-related offences were made punishable by hanging. In reality, though, the death penalty was only routinely carried out for murder, violent crimes or those involving valuable property. Before the 1770s nearly 150 crimes were capital offences, increasing to over 220 during Jane Austen's lifetime. Many capital crimes were by modern standards no more than misdemeanours.[2] John Byng expressed his dismay at the justice system: 'Go on my poor deluded country . . . Transport felons by thousands: fill the globe with your convicts. Hang by hundreds: and when reason is almost lost, and laws multiplied beyond comprehension, may some surviving few of the nation who do not thrive by politics and stratagem, endeavour at a reform.'[3]

Depending on the nature of the crime, including the type of goods stolen and where the offence took place, such as inside a shop or in the street, criminals could be executed for stealing goods valued at more than a shilling. This was a period when the lowliest labourers earned less than £25 a year and often as little as £12, while the upper classes enjoyed incomes of £10,000 or more, sometimes as much as £50,000,[4] and the annual Civil List payment – from taxes – to support the royal family exceeded £1,000,000.[5] With such great disparities of wealth and living conditions, when one person's pocket watch cost as much as another's yearly wage, the temptation to steal was strong. The number of crimes against property rose and fell in line with bad and good harvests, and famine could drive normally law-abiding but desperate people to steal rather than starve.

Such vicious penalties were intended as a deterrent, but proved woefully ineffective. A better deterrent would have been effective policing, but this was resisted because of fears of a repressive police state as witnessed in France before the Revolution and under Napoleon. Even county police forces would not be introduced for decades to come because of the dread of introducing networks of informers and secret police. While London had its Bow Street Runners, outside the capital reliance was placed on parish constables.

There were rarely more than one or two constables in any parish, but these officers could swear in temporary constables to help when needed, as William Darter explained for his home town of Reading: 'We had no police, but a head constable was chosen from the ratepayers on the election of Mayor, and he selected a number of others to serve under him, the names being submitted to the Chief Magistrate before being sworn.'[6]

Towns also paid night watchmen, literally to watch out for wrongdoers, but the provision of watchmen could be poor, and John Blackner outlined how Nottingham's citizens made their system work:

> about 35,000 inhabitants are scattered through upwards of 400 streets, lanes &c. and ... nine or ten men, four of whom watch the marketplace, are employed to walk *almost* twenty streets. In 1815, in consequence of the numerous depredations committed in several streets, *where no watch was kept*, the housekeepers therein obtained permission to be sworn in the capacity of special constables, and by taking their turns as watchmen of the night, have preserved the neighbourhood in security.[7]

If a public disturbance could not be contained by the constables, magistrates could call for troops, but they might take some time to arrive. Magistrates, also known as Justices of the Peace, were the mainstay of the law. Appointed from among the large landowners of an area, they were unpaid and performed relatively mundane duties such as the regulation of markets, fairs and alehouses, as well as judging and punishing minor offenders, without a jury, in petty sessions (later known as 'magistrates' courts'). Those accused of more serious offences were tried at the Quarter Sessions, held in towns and cities four times a year, where the Justices of the Peace presided in courts with a jury. The main criminal courts were the Assizes (literally, 'sittings'), and judges moved from town to town within their circuit to hear serious cases like murder and counterfeiting. The Assizes were usually held two or three times a year, so that prisoners could wait months for their trial. In London serious crimes were tried at the Old Bailey.

The Assizes were also an excuse for social gatherings, and in March 1811 Louis Simond saw the ceremonial first day at York: 'On Sunday the judges, just arrived for the assizes, came to church *en grand costume*, with their huge powdered wigs, and black robes ... The mayor and corporation swelled the train, and in the rear footmen and white liveries, and large nosegays at the button-hole; the whole town was in motion. The assizes in a country town are an event.'[8] The following day provided an even better spectacle:

> we met the judges going to open the sessions, with the same wigs and the same train as yesterday. The whole town was in motion,—the streets full of misses in white muslin,—citizens in dark-blue coats, carefully brushed, glossy hats, and shining boots,—and military people in red. It seemed a day of rejoicing; and, in fact, the whole of the sessions is a period of amusement; yet we learn that the prisons here are unusually full. There are eight cases of murder, and among them a young couple for beating their own child, an infant, to death.[9]

The Assizes covered their surrounding area and on this occasion at York cases were about to be heard from as far away as Halifax and Hunslet near Leeds.[10]

Crime rates were lower outside the main towns and cities, as Byng observed: 'When I was at Knutsford [Cheshire], I remark'd the purity of the country, at seeing young women riding alone: why, within 50 miles of the devilish metropolis, they would have been all robb'd, and r—.'[11] Crime was indeed an urban plague, and London as the capital city was also the capital of crime. To try to reduce its high levels of crime, the Bow Street Runners had been established by the novelist and magistrate Henry Fielding in 1749.[12] In 1792 seven more 'police stations', besides the magistrates' office in Bow Street, were set up, and the runners were even called on to tackle crimes outside the capital.[13] William Darter spotted them at the horse races at Ascot in Berkshire in 1814: 'I arrived at Ascot some time before the races were to commence ... where I saw [John] Townsend, at the time a well-known Bow Street officer, giving instructions to his men, who were usually called Bow Street Runners.'[14]

Large gatherings, as at racecourses, were the haunt of pickpockets, the cream of criminals according to Carl Moritz: 'The highest order of thieves are the pick-pockets or cutpurses, whom you find every where; and sometimes even in the best companies. They are generally well and handsomely dressed, so that you take them to be persons of condition.'[15] Benjamin Silliman gave useful tips on how to elude pickpockets:

If you are going, by night, into crowds, or any where on foot, leave your money at home, except what you want for immediate use; either leave your watch, or drop the chain into the fob [small pocket]; if you have valuable papers or a pocket book, carry it in a pocket in the breast of your coat; button your coat; if in a crowd and danger be apprehended, fold your arms, and let one hand rest on the pocket book. The pocket handkerchief may be in danger, but the loss of this is not serious, and even this may be prevented by wearing it in a pocket opening within the skirt of the coat ... By observing these precautions, I have never lost any thing in London.[16]

In the streets, pickpocketing was often committed by young boys in gangs, and if one was caught, he might be beaten and released, rather than handed to the law, as happened on one occasion in London during the summer of 1784:

A gentleman gazing at a print-shop in the Strand, had his pocket picked of his purse, in which were bank notes to the amount of 700l. A poor woman that stood by observed the transaction, gave notice, and the fellow was pursued and taken, and the purse recovered. The fellow, after being rolled in the kennel [drain], and had undergone the discipline of the mob, was permitted to escape, and the woman who had discovered the theft rewarded with five guineas.[17]

This pickpocket may not have realised what he was stealing, but had he been prosecuted, such a substantial theft would have warranted the death sentence.

For lesser amounts, the judge might reduce the sentence to

transportation, as in the case of thirty-five-year-old Sarah Smith. At her trial for 'pocketpicking' in April 1793, John Harrison testified:

> I am a breeches maker in Fleet-street, and I keep the Crown, Clement's Inn-passage. I was coming from that house to my house in Fleet-street, this woman accosted me with, my dear, will you go home with me? I said, good woman is that your home, pointing to the Hole in the Wall [a tavern], the next door but one to mine, she said it was, and ran after me down to my own door; I said, good woman I am at home, you had better go home yourself and I rung the bell to go into my own house; she hung about me, my breeches pocket being open, and she took the money out of my breeches, and I never perceived it.[18]

On being asked 'Where did she rob you?' Harrison replied, 'In the street; it was at my own door ... I pushed her from me, and she went away easy enough, I did not miss the money till after I had rung the bell ... and I put my hand into my breeches pocket as I was standing by the door, and I found my money gone.'[19] Harrison said that he immediately cried out for the night watchman, before pursuing the woman, who was arrested and his money recovered.

Sarah Smith was accused of stealing nine guineas and three half-crowns, a total of 196s. 6d. (£9 16s. 6d.). Before the law was changed in 1808, the theft of property worth more than forty shillings by picking a pocket would incur a death sentence, but the jury found her guilty of a lesser charge, valuing the guineas and half-crowns well below the amount she had actually taken. This legal fiction was regularly used by juries to allow a judge to avoid a mandatory death penalty. Sarah Smith was sentenced to seven years' transportation, and she sailed on board the *Surprise* in February 1794, landing in New South Wales in October after a voyage of 176 days.[20]

Next to pickpockets in the hierarchy of criminals, according to Moritz,

> come the highwaymen, who rob on horseback; and often, they say, even with unloaded pistols, they terrify travellers, in order to put themselves in possession of their purses. Among these persons, however, there are

instances of true greatness of soul; there are numberless instances of their returning a part of their booty, where the party robbed has appeared to be particularly distressed; and they are seldom guilty of murder.[21]

Highwaymen haunted roads (highways) on the outskirts of towns and cities, preying on travellers. Many were ex-soldiers – officers and cavalry-men – who were excellent horsemen and could make a rapid escape. They had some reputation for gallantry, even chivalry, and a few tried to portray themselves as latter-day Robin Hoods. Most were not particularly violent or brutal and might even be deferential towards their victims.

Dick Turpin, the highwayman best known today, belonged to an earlier era. He was executed in 1739, but his legend lived on, and Francis Place noted that 'Oh Rare Turpin Hero' was a popular ballad sung in the streets.[22] It was first published as a broadside ballad around the time of Turpin's execution under the title 'Turpin's Rant: A New Song',[23] but over the years the song changed and expanded as it circulated by word-of-mouth.[24] Only the central theme remained constant, that of Turpin fooling the better-off, which three verses common to most versions related:

On Hounslow Heath, as I rid o'er,
I spy'd a Lawyer just before,
I asked him if he was not afraid,
Of TURPIN, that mischievous blade?
Sing, O rare Turpin, O rare Turpin, O.

Says Turpin, I have been most cute,
For my Money is hid within my Boot,
Says the Lawyer, there is none can find
For mine lies in my Cape behind.

They rid till they came to the Powder Mill,
When Turpin bid the Lawyer to stand still,
Stand, Sir, your Cape I must cut off,
For my Horse does want a saddle cloth.
Sing, &c.[25]

Whether the victim was a lawyer, exciseman, judge or wealthy farmer, what made the song popular was the notion of an establishment figure being brought low. Turpin may not have been a true Robin Hood, as he did not bestow money on the poor, but widespread satisfaction was felt from his robbing the rich.

Highwaymen could be violent, and a common tactic of theirs was to shatter the glass windows of vehicles and then fire at passengers, though some resisted, as in one incident reported by the *Oxford Journal* in January 1797:

> Tuesday night, as the Earl of Strathmore was returning to town [London] from Wimbledon, he was attacked by a highwayman, who, without ceremony, broke the glass, and fired into the carriage, but luckily missed his aim; on which the Earl, who had a loaded blunderbuss between his knees, fired, and immediately killed the assailant on the spot, who appears to be one Lancaster, liberated out of prison for want of evidence only a few days since. He had an accomplice, who escaped.[26]

The dead highwayman was the notorious criminal William Lancaster, who had until recently been detained on a charge of robbing Lord Boringdon.[27] The death penalty seemed little deterrent to highwaymen, and the unpredictability of their behaviour and the number of robberies made travellers nervous. In 1805 a Horse Patrol of mainly ex-cavalrymen was established as an offshoot of the Bow Street Runners, which led to a decline in the number of highwaymen.

Footpads (highway robbers on foot) were another source of anxiety for travellers, and Moritz considered them worst of all because they 'often murder in the most inhuman manner, for the sake of only a few shillings, any unfortunate people who happen to fall in their way. Of this several mournful instances may be occasionally read in the English papers. Probably they murder, because they cannot, like the highwaymen, aided by their horses, make a rapid flight.'[28] Footpads often operated in gangs, and they would even ambush coaches at bridges and other constricted places where horses were reined in: 'On Wednesday [13 June 1792] night as JAMES FRY, Esq. of Wimpole-street, in company with five young Ladies, were returning home from the Richmond Theatre, they were stopped in a coach by six footpads, who robbed Mr. FRY of four guineas and some silver. Previous to the robbery the villains fired a pistol at the window, the bullet of which shot away one of the young Ladies earrings.'[29]

In 1796 the magistrate Patrick Colquhoun published a treatise on crime in London,[30] demonstrating that it went far beyond the obvious street offences and burglary. In his view, there were worse crimes, such as counterfeiting, metal theft and the vast amount of pilfering from warehouses and ships along the Thames. As a result, the Marine Police Force was set up in 1798 at Wapping, and when William Holland was in London in 1805, he visited the Wapping police office as a guest of his friend William Kinnaird, one of the justices there. Holland was impressed by the office and amazed at the river traffic it policed: 'We padded through many dirty narrow streets and got at last to the water side. There we took boat, and pass'd through groves of shipping. There seem'd to be no end of 'em; it was a gloriously awful [awesome] sight and gave a lively idea of the greatness of this nation. Boats were passing and repassing continuously.'[31]

Most people were understandably terrified of being robbed at home, and stories were constantly circulating about all manner of thefts from houses. In the summer of 1775 the *Bath Chronicle* reported: 'Monday morning [31 July], at two o'clock, three fellows got into Copt-hall [Copped Hall], the seat of John Conyers, Esq., near Epping, and bound the butler neck and heels and took away [silver] plate to the value of near 2000l. They carried it off in a post-chaise which waited for them at the Park-gate.'[32] This weekly newspaper was published far from the scene of the robbery, but such unsettling crimes were newsworthy right across England.

The *Bath Chronicle*'s account had actually been overtaken by events, because the ringleader was already in custody – Lambert Reading, a former coachman at Copped Hall. In the ensuing one-day trial, the butler testified as to how he had been threatened: 'three men entered his chamber [around 3.00 a.m.], one of whom, with a drawn sword and dark lanthorn, came to his bedside, and swore in a most violent manner, that, if he spoke or made any resistance, he would cut his throat; after which he threw the bed-cloaths over his head, and stood as a guard over him, whilst the others collected a large quantity of plate'.[33] This was an ambitious robbery: 'from the conversation that passed between them, he apprehended they filled four sacks with the house-plate'.[34] Their downfall was locking the butler in his room rather than killing him, and while the rest of the gang was not apprehended for some weeks, Lambert Reading was executed just five days afterwards.

Such a deliberately planned theft from a large country house was exceptional. It was easier to attack less wealthy establishments, which generated a universal dread of burglary, and in January 1808 Fanny Platt wrote from Kensington to her sister Sarah Wilkinson: 'The robbing trade is so brisk here you cannot think, scarce a night but one or more houses are broken into and robbed. James has hitherto escaped but I believe he quakes thinking he shall not much longer, as they last night were robbing on each side of him.'[35]

Thefts were often little more than opportunistic crimes, but the penalties could still be severe. In August 1814 the *Morning Chronicle* reported:

> an old man, who makes a living by picking up bones in the street, was yes-terday charged by Mrs. Hill, of Tottenham-court-road, with stealing a silver spoon, her property, which she gave a child at the door to play with, who having dropped it, the prisoner picked it up and went off with it . . . he denied any knowledge of it, but being searched by a constable the spoon was found in his possession. He was committed to Newgate for trial.[36]

The accused man was Thomas Norman, a street scavenger. The charge was grand larceny, stealing property with a value of more than one shilling with no aggravating circumstances. Because the spoon was valued at fifteen pence (1s. 3d.), he was facing a possible death sentence if found guilty. As was customary, the victim or any inter-ested party was the prosecutor, not the state. The husband William Hill actually owned the spoon, but he failed to attend the court case three weeks later, and so the old man was acquitted.[37]

Servants were often accused of stealing from their employers, and one such theft at a London public house was featured by the *Morning Chronicle* in August 1806 in its regular 'Police' column:

> On Sunday se'night a female servant of Mr. Jaggers, of the Hand and Racket, in Whitcomb-street, very unexpectedly left her place. In a short time after she was gone, Mrs. Jaggers discovered that she had been robbed of cash, several articles of plate, and wearing apparel.– Application was made to Donaldson, a constable, to apprehend her; the officer learnt, from her connection in St. Giles's, that she was gone to Bristol, whither he pursued her.[38]

St Giles was the overcrowded warren of narrow streets, courts and alleys centred around Seven Dials, a refuge for beggars, poor street traders and criminals, with a substantial Irish population. For George Donaldson, a Bow Street Runner, it was the obvious place to start pursuing the servant Eleanor Russel, because it was not many streets away from the Hand and Racquet public house. He finally caught up with her in Bristol, just before she sailed to Ireland, as he testified at her trial for 'theft from a specified place': 'GEORGE DONALD-SON sworn. I am an officer; I went to Bristol after this woman, I . . . took [arrested] her there; I found the gown, the shirt, the pinafore, and the gold pin, in her box, and two guineas and a half in gold, and three shillings and six pence in silver.'[39]

Despite the value of the recovered items exceeding seventy shillings, the jury merely found her guilty of 'stealing to the value of thirty-nine shillings',[40] a shilling short of a capital punishment for this crime. She was sentenced to seven years' transportation and sailed for New South Wales on board the *Sydney Cove* in January 1807. The transportation register describes her as 'Eleanor ux [*uxor* – Latin for 'spouse'] William Russell',[41] though soon after arriving in Australia she married another convict, Simon McGuigin.[42]

It was rare for any member of the gentry and upper classes to be tried for theft. They were much more likely to buy off the prosecutor before their case came to trial, and if that failed, they had a much greater chance of being acquitted since they could afford to pay for lawyers or resort to bribery. When Mrs Jane Leigh-Perrot was arrested in August 1799 for stealing lace worth twenty shillings from Elizabeth Gregory's shop in Bath, she was refused bail, but instead of being held in the County Gaol at Ilchester, she was allowed to live with her husband in the adjacent prison-keeper's house. For people of their rank, even this situation was intolerable, as a letter written a few months later to Mrs Leigh-Perrot from a cousin reveals: 'You tell me that your good sister Austen has offered you one, or both, of her daughters to continue with you during your stay at that vile place, but you decline the kind offer, as you canot procure them accommodation in the house with you, and you cannot let these elegant young women be your inmates in a prison nor be subject to the inconveniences which you are obliged to put up with.'[43] The two elegant young women were Jane Austen and her sister Cassandra, and Mrs Leigh-Perrot was their aunt.

The trial took place at the next Assizes at Taunton Castle, at the end of March 1800, when Mrs Leigh-Perrot was accused of grand larceny. Whether or not she was guilty of shoplifting (and many believed the shopkeeper had deliberately set out to extort money), the stakes were high because such a high-value theft from a shop was a capital offence. On 22 March, a few days before her trial, William Holland was in Nether Stowey, some 10 miles from Taunton, and he was told about rumours that the prosecutor (the shopkeeper Elizabeth Gregory) had been bribed:

> Met Mr Symes the lawyer at Stowey. He told me that Mrs Parrot [Perrot] had bought off her prosecutor. Alas, Alas! that money should be able to screen a person from justice in this kingdom so remarkable for good laws and uncorrupted judges. She was accused of stealing lace out of a shop in Bath, is a person of considerable fortune and has a poor Jerry Sneak of a husband, who adheres to her through all difficulties.[44]

Mrs Leigh-Perrot was acquitted by the jury, but her expenses were considerable. The case was still being gossiped about a month later when Holland was in Bath and went to a different shop from the one that had accused her of theft: 'Went to Brookman's the milliner, a clever woman, sensible and well behaved ... Miss Brookman was present at a detection of Mrs Lee Perrot [in another crime] many years ago, confirmed the fact, everything clear against her.'[45]

Penelope Hind, the long-time friend of Holland, learned in November 1804 that she was once again being accused of theft in Bath, this time of a plant, but no prosecution followed.[46] Five months later, the extremely wealthy Mrs Leigh-Perrot appeared in one of Jane Austen's letters, none too favourably: 'My aunt is in a great hurry to pay me for my cap, but cannot find it in her heart to give me good money.'[47] Instead, Jane was invited to accompany her to 'the Grand Sydney-Garden Breakfast'. Polite society in Bath was already avoiding her aunt, and possibly for this reason Jane declared: 'such an offer I shall of course decline'.[48] Two days later, she added to her letter: 'My Uncle and Aunt drank tea with us last night, and in spite of my resolution to the contrary, I could not help putting forward to invite them again this Evening. I thought it was of the first consequence to avoid anything that might seem a slight to them. I shall be glad when it is over.'[49]

Other prisoners on trial at the same Assizes at Taunton in March 1800 were not so lucky as Mrs Leigh-Perrot. Those found guilty included 'John Branch, aged 14, for burglary . . . Robert Phillips, for sheep-stealing; Thomas Coles, and William Hartland, for burglary at Langport'.[50] They were all sentenced to death – a real demonstration of the Bloody Code in action – while three more were sentenced to seven years' transportation: 'Wm. Spratt, for stealing wheat from an out-house; Thomas Broadhurst for stealing sundry pieces of muslin from his master, Mr. Slack, of this city [Bath]; and Joseph Jones, for stealing a trunk'.[51]

While it was very rare for any of the elite to be sentenced to death or transportation, even for killing someone, most convicted murderers faced execution. Sensational crimes generated lengthy accounts far beyond their locality, and murders were avidly covered by the newspapers. In Somerset on 25 October 1807, Holland wrote in his diary: 'No material news in the paper but a shocking account of a murder committed in Hertfordshire.'[52] The murder scene was a house in the High Street of Hoddesdon village, in the parish of the Reverend William Jones, who wrote in his diary:

Poor, wretched mortals! what horrible consequences follow their being given up into the power of Satan, & their own mad, unbridled passions, for ever so short a season! I know not how even to glance at two most horrid murders, which were last night committed in my parish [Hoddesdon], at old Mr. Borham, the farmer's house. Mrs. Warner, B—m's daughter, who was within 5 or 6 weeks of her delivery, & Mrs. Hummerstone, Batty's housekeeper, were the poor sufferers. The villain's name is Simmons, not more than 20 years of age! To describe the shocking circumstances would be too painful![53]

The newspapers were not so sensitive, and the *Hampshire Chronicle* revelled in the gory detail:

Elizabeth Harris, on seeing his approach, retired within the scullery, and shut the door against him. He demanded admittance, which she refused: high words accordingly arose and he plunged his hand, armed with a knife, through a window-lattice at her, but missed his aim. The noise alarmed the company in the parlour ... Mrs Hummerstone was the first to come forth, in hope of being able to intimidate and send away the disturber, but just as she had reached the back-door, leading from the parlour to the stone-yard, Simmons, who was proceeding to enter the house that way, met her.[54]

Thomas Simmons was a former servant of the house and had been courting Elizabeth, but he had an uncontrollable temper and was judged unstable. She was persuaded to break off the relationship, and Simmons was dismissed. Now he was seeking revenge and attacking anyone in his path:

with his knife he stabbed her [Mrs. Hummerstone] in the jugular artery, and pulling the knife forward, laid open her throat on the left side. She ran forward ... but fell, and rose no more. The murderer pursued his sanguinary purpose, and rushing into the parlour, raised and brandished his bloody knife, swearing a dreadful oath, that 'he would give it to them all'. Mrs. Warner was the person next to him, and without giving her time to rise from the chair, he gave her so many stabs about her neck and

276

breast that she fell from her chair, covered with streams of blood, and expired.[55]

Several others were injured in the confusion, and Elizabeth was again targeted: 'she struggled with him, caught at the knife, and was severely wounded in the hand and arm. The knife fell in the struggle. She, however, got out at the back door, and made her way into the street, where, by her screams of murder, she alarmed the neighbourhood.'[56] Simmons fled and tried to hide, but was arrested, covered in blood.

When the trial took place at Hertford Assizes, the counsel for the prosecution 'intreated them [the jury] to dismiss from their minds all they had heard elsewhere, and attend only to the evidence'.[57] The jury found Simmons guilty, and the young man was hanged three days later, on Monday 7 March 1808. It was suggested that he suffered from hallucinations.

In this instance, murder had definitely been committed, but the circumstances of death were not always so clear, as little forensic investigation of sudden deaths was carried out. Some murders certainly went undetected, and in April 1808 Nelly Weeton told a friend about a suicide case at Upholland in Lancashire that seemed more like murder:

an old woman . . . quite a cripple, was found hung in about two hours after her husband (who was a good deal younger) had left her to go to his work. She was suspended from the tester [canopy over a bed] at the foot of the bed. From her being such a cripple, the neighbours say she could not possibly have done it herself, and her husband, who has been known to have used her ill, is strongly suspected to have done it. But no proof can be brought.[58]

Suicide or 'self-murder' was a crime because it was considered blasphemy by the Church and it robbed the king of a subject. The archaic legal term was *felo de se* (Latin for 'felon of oneself'). Although insanity was technically no defence, coroners' juries often found that a suicide was 'not of a sound mind', because if a suicide was judged sane, his property was forfeited. Anyone assisting a suicide was tried for murder, but one problem for the law was how to punish the corpse for the crime. All that could be done was to deny burial in consecrated ground. In 1790, the year before his own death, the Methodist preacher John Wesley expressed his thoughts:

> there is no country in Europe, or perhaps in the habitable world, where the horrid crime of self-murder is so common as it is in England! ... we have laws against it, and officers with juries are appointed to inquire into every fact of the kind. And these are to give their verdict upon oath, whether the self-murderer was sane or insane. If he is brought in insane, he is excused, and the law does not affect him. By this means it is totally eluded, for the juries constantly bring him in insane ... let a law be made and rigorously executed, that the body of every self-murderer, lord or peasant, shall be hanged in chains, and the English fury [the high suicide rate] will cease at once.[59]

Few agreed with Wesley, and some thought that eradicating the gloomy preaching of the Methodists would be more effective in decreasing the number of suicides.

Spending money on criminals was unpopular, which ruled out imprisonment as the main method of punishment. Prisons were largely for those awaiting trial, transportation or execution, but debt could lead to people ending up in prison (gaol) for a long time, because usually the only way a creditor had of recovering money was to have the debtor imprisoned until he paid up. Since many individuals had no money to pay debts, they might be confined for lengthy periods, and being held in a debtors' prison was itself costly.

The stupidity of such punishment was obvious to Benjamin Silliman: 'There is a great number of debtors confined in Newgate and the adjoining prisons, and most of them are immured for small sums, and have little hope of escaping, because they are miserably poor.'[60] Such was the case with the Devon County debtors' prison, called Sheriff's Ward, in the St Thomas suburb of Exeter, which the penal reformer John Howard visited: 'In 1779 one debtor, on attachment from the court of chancery, had continued here from May

1758 ... but at my last visit he was dead. Here is still an older prisoner, *Grace Hooper*, whose warrant of commitment is dated 30th of November 1741.'[61] Grace had been a prisoner there for over forty years. Howard noted Exeter's table of charges:

A TABLE of the RATES and FEES allowed to be taken
by the Keeper of the Sheriff's Ward for the County of *Devon*. £. s. d.

| | | | |
|---|---|---|---|
| For the commitment fee of every prisoner for debt, damages, and contempts though it be on several actions or processes only | 0 | 13 | 4 |
| To the turnkey | 0 | 1 | 0 |
| For every *liberate* | 0 | 2 | 0 |
| For the use of a bed in a single room for one person by the week | 0 | 3 | 0 |
| The use of a room where there are two or more beds and two lodge in a bed each person | 0 | 1 | 3 |
| The use of the common room if the keeper finds bedding each person by the week | 0 | 1 | 0 |
| If the prisoner finds bedding | | nothing[62] | |

A debtor could usually pay for extras by arrangement with the prison-keeper. Charges varied between prisons, but there were always some compulsory fees, such as for beds, because many prisons were privately run businesses.

Houses of correction, or 'bridewells', were for punishing minor offenders who had been given short sentences of imprisonment by Justices of the Peace. Most were put to hard labour during their sentence. The original Bridewell was a combined prison and poor-house converted from one of Henry VIII's London palaces. By the eighteenth century the term was used loosely for a local prison for minor offenders, for a workhouse or for a combination of both. During his penal reform work, Howard inspected England's county gaols, but was unimpressed by the County Bridewell at Winchester in Hampshire:

The four rooms are too close, and the court (which is not paved, 37 feet 5 inches, by 13 feet 10) is too small for the prisoners, who are commonly numerous; especially at quarter sessions, when they are brought hither from the other bridewells. There is only *one* day-room (26 feet by 20 feet 4 inches) for *men* and *women* . . . At my visit in 1779, there were four *young women*, and in 1782 five, among the prisoners . . . This prison has been fatal to vast numbers.[63]

Many houses of correction kept inmates crammed together, provided poor food and dire sanitation and often had no source of water within the building. Disease always threatened, and typhus, often called 'gaol fever', was a frequent killer. It was probably the cause of so many deaths at Winchester.

In this period when England was often at war, another Winchester prison housed foreign prisoners-of-war, one of many such prisons for those men (mainly ordinary soldiers and sailors) who were considered unlikely to honour their word not to escape.[64] From time to time Jane Austen must have witnessed them being marched from ports to their place of imprisonment, especially as prisoners-of-war were at Southampton where she lived from 1806 to 1809. William Darter described some he saw in Reading: 'One day, about the year 1813, I saw a long line of French prisoners escorted down London Street to the "Saracen's Head" stables, where they were put with clean straw to lie down upon; they were formed three or four deep, and presented a very miserable appearance, their clothes being in rags, and shoes nearly worn out.'[65]

In numerous 'parole towns', captured officers who gave their word of honour (*parole d'honneur*) not to try to escape were allowed freedom within the limits of the town. One parole town was Odiham in Hampshire, 10 miles north of Chawton where Jane Austen later lived, and another was Alresford, about 12 miles to the south. She almost certainly saw and may even have met foreign officers on parole in such places. They tried to live as normal lives as possible, were often accepted by the gentry and sometimes married and settled in England.

Hundreds of prisoners-of-war of lower rank were confined aboard prison hulks – redundant naval ships with their masts removed, which were converted into floating prisons and moored in rivers and creeks. These hulks had initially been sanctioned for housing convicted criminals ('convicts') by a law passed in 1776 when the American War of Independence stopped the transportation of convicts to the former colonies. When convicts began being sent to Australia, the hulks were also used to hold prisoners-of-war.

Transportation to America had begun in the seventeenth century. This was the punishment given to Alice Walker when she was tried at the Old Bailey on 9 September 1772 for stealing from Thomas Atkins two days earlier. She was accused of taking a canvas bag and some money, worth more than £24 in all. 'I did not rob him at all;' she said in her defence, 'he took me to Bartholomew fair, and asked me to drink; he asked me to go to the Inn, I went with him; then he asked me to go down into the country with him, and gave me the money to buy some wearing apparel. I did not confess I took the money, he gave it me.'[66] The jury found Alice guilty of theft (grand larceny). She was sentenced to transportation and sailed for America in the *Justitia*, landing at Rappahannock, Virginia, in March 1773.[67] Like her fellow convicts, she was sold as an indentured servant – effectively a slave – to plantation owners looking for labour. The local newspaper, the *Virginia Gazette*, carried advertisements of such sales:

JUST ARRIVED *in RAPPAHANNOCK*, *The* GOOD INTENT, *Captain* CLODD, With FORTY HEALTHY INDENTED SERVANTS, among whom are many TRADESMEN, particularly shoemakers, a cooper, a tailor, a carpenter and joiner, a blacksmith and farrier, some good clerks, a surgeon, several country labourers, some fine boys, many good sempstresses, mantuamakers, house women &c. &c. The sale will commence at Leedstown on Tuesday the 3rd of August; and, if required, a reasonable credit will be allowed, on giving bond and approved security.[68]

Alice was purchased by two prominent members of the colony, Sampson and George Matthews, but after only a few weeks she made a bid for freedom. The same newspaper carried a notice of the reward offered for her recapture:

TEN POUNDS REWARD. RUN away, last night [May 1773] ...
English convict servants, viz. JOHN EATON, by trade a shipcarpenter,
about 23 years of age, and 5 feet 3 or 4 inches high; had on, and took with
him, a blue broadcloth coat and breeches, a Damascus waistcoat, a pair of
ticken trousers, worsted stockings, three striped cotton shirts, one
oznabrig [coarse linen] over shirt, a felt hat, and a pair of old shoes.
ALICE EATON, alias WALKER (who goes for the said John Eaton's
wife) a low, well set woman, about 20 years of age, and has sandy coloured
hair; had on a brown stuff gown, a red stuff petticoat, and four red silk
handkerchiefs ... Whoever secures the above servants in any gaol, so
that we may get them, shall receive FIVE POUNDS, and if brought to
Mr. Sampson Matthews, in Richmond, the above reward. SAMPSON &
GEORGE MATTHEWS. All masters of vessels are hereby forwarned
from carrying either of the said servants out of the colony.[69]

Despite this warning, Alice did manage to sail back to England, but
was then recognised and rearrested. This time the offence was returning from transportation before the end of her sentence. She was found
guilty and sentenced to death, but the jury recommended mercy. In July
1774 her sentence was changed to fourteen years' transportation.[70]

People could be punished with transportation for extremely minor
crimes, such as Robert Jones, a pickpocket who was sentenced in
May 1774 to seven years' transportation for stealing a linen handkerchief.[71] The following January, Elizabeth Smith received the same
sentence, this time for stealing twelve pounds of sugar valued at four
shillings.[72] After the American War of Independence started, over ten
years elapsed before convicts began to be transported to Australia,
and the first fleet of ships sailed for Botany Bay on 13 May 1787.
Between then and 1810 over twelve thousand convicts were sent to
Australia. Several ships, often carrying over a thousand convicts
between them, sailed every year until 1868.[73] Transportation was considered a deterrent to crime and usefully removed many criminals
from England, but it was not without expense. To reduce costs the
Government passed the responsibility for transportation to private
contractors, and it was their cost-cutting that caused many of the
hardships suffered by the convicts during their voyage to Australia.

Because of the reluctance to use imprisonment as punishment, anyone convicted of crimes not sufficiently serious to warrant the death sentence or transportation might well receive corporal punishment such as the pillory or whipping. The pillory was intended to expose offenders to public shame and ridicule. It had a wooden frame, usually on a raised platform or scaffolding, and the culprit stood with head and hands placed through openings in a tightly secured, two-part hinged wooden board. If offenders were lucky, they were pelted with soft missiles such as eggs, something Darter witnessed:

> About the year 1811 or 1812 I was standing with my father near the *Mercury* Office [in Reading], when a man was placed in the pillory, which stood in a central part of the Market Place, for some offence; and the people threw eggs at him, many missing. I saw Mr. Moody, the coach proprietor, bring two baskets of eggs ... and he threw so well that the poor fellow, whose head and arms were fixed, was literally covered with yolks of eggs and other matter, and to complete the affair he was bespattered with refuse from Hiscock's slaughter house. I don't know what his offence was.[74]

If the crowd was particularly hostile, they would throw all manner of missiles, including stones, causing serious injury or even death. It was this unpredictable nature of the pillory as a form of punishment that led to it being used only for minor offences or as an additional penalty for a serious crime.

For other crimes culprits might be publicly whipped, sometimes from where the crime had been committed to where they lived, or over some other specified distance. They were tied to the back of a cart and made to walk, as Darter described:

> A man of the labouring class, living on the west side of Silver Street [in Reading], in one of those old houses which have overhanging eaves ... had been out of work for some time and in want of food. In passing up Castle Street he stole a loaf of bread from the shop of a baker of the name of Turner. He was apprehended, tried and sentenced ... to be publicly

whipped at the cart's tail from the Grey Friars Prison to his cottage in Silver Street. He was stripped to his waist, and he had to walk behind a horse and cart with his hands so tied that he could not alter his position.[75]

Darter was so appalled that the memory of the scene never faded:

When the crowd arrived opposite our house, I ran to see the cause of it. I then witnessed a shocking sight ... There was not a portion of this poor fellow's back that was not literally cut into shreds; his sufferings were dreadful, and with the blood running down, it presented a dreadful and sickening sight. I merely followed at a distance to see where they took him ... In point of fact, the poor fellow, for merely stealing a loaf, was whipped to death, for he never left his room alive; therefore, for this trifling offence, this man was punished to a greater extent than would have happened had he committed murder.[76]

Desperation drove many to crime, anything from stealing a loaf of bread to murder. In December 1775, the same month Jane Austen was born, her local newspaper reported the execution of an unmarried mother who had killed her newborn son in London:

Sarah Reynolds was executed at Tyburn ... for the murder of her bastard child. The unhappy convict wept bitterly, and was very intent on her devotions. The fate of this unhappy woman naturally gives rise to the following reflections: What a false pride is that which can induce a woman to murder her own infant, rather than submit to a temporary disgrace? What punishment is due to a man who willfully debauches a poor girl, and then refuses to make her the only reparation in his power by marriage?[77]

Sarah had given birth to a healthy boy, strangled him with a handkerchief and dumped his body in 'a ditch or gully-hole by Broad Street, Mary-le-bon',[78] a watercourse probably located north of Oxford Street.[79] She was tried for infanticide, found guilty and ordered 'to be executed ... and her body to be afterwards dissected and anatomized'.[80] With the death penalty intended as a deterrent, executions were performed in public, usually by hanging. A noose was put around the condemned person's neck, and the rope was either hauled up or, more often, the cart or other support was removed to leave the victim hanging. Strangulation was usually the cause of death, but some fell so violently that they broke their necks.

Sarah was hanged at Tyburn, which was London's public place of execution, but because the final journey of prisoners from Newgate prison to Tyburn became such a carnival, not the sober warning the authorities desired, executions were later moved to Newgate. The first ones took place there on 9 December 1783, when nine men and one woman were executed on a temporary scaffold.[81] A different method of execution was introduced as well – a noose was placed round the neck of each prisoner, and they were then dropped through a trapdoor. One Oxford newspaper, in a lengthy account of the new location, commented:

> The unhappy Criminals themselves acknowledged the Propriety of the Change, and professed themselves happy in not being, as usual, dragged through the Streets from Newgate to Tyburn. A Bell tolled all the Time of the Ceremony, and produced a wonderful Effect upon the Prisoners [in Newgate] who survived their more unfortunate Fellows. The Spectators who attended appeared much impressed by the solemnity of the Ceremony.[82]

Nearly all urban centres had their own gallows, usually erected for a particular execution and dismantled afterwards, and occasionally criminals were hanged at the scene of their crime. Following execution, the body might be 'hung in chains' in a public place as a warning to others – this involved the corpse being bound by iron chains or fitted into a cage of iron bands to hold it together while it rotted. Sometimes the corpse was coated with tar to delay putrefaction. In March 1785 Woodforde remarked on the trials at Thetford in Norfolk:

> At the Assizes at Thetford in this county 8 Prisoners were condemned, three of the above were reprieved. The other five left for execution. One Jˢ Cliffen a most daring fellow was hanged ... on Thursday last at Norwich on Castle-Hill and behaved most daringly audacious. His crime

was robbing 2 old men, brothers, by names Seaman on the Yaxham Road, knocked them both down first of which blows one of them died soon after; the other recovered. Cliffen's body was this day carried to Badley Moor and there hung in chains at one corner of the said moor.[83]

Over a week later Woodforde and a manservant 'took a ride ... thro' Hockering, North-Tuddenham to Baddeley Moor where Cliffen stands in chains, most shocking road all around where he stands ... thought we should have been mired'.[84]

Gibbets with corpses suspended from them were such features of the landscape that they were landmarks for travellers, and Johnson Grant described the Sheffield neighbourhood '*adorned* with men hanging in chains'.[85] Gibbets were commonly set up on waste ground within sight of thoroughfares, but one anonymous author of the poem 'On The New Gibbet On Hounslow Heath' considered some were too close to the highway, causing a foul stench:

> In former times, whene'er in chains
> Judges hung rogues up, like Jack Hains,
> Whose Gibbets, Hounslow-heath adorning,
> To their old fellow-rogues gave warning,
> 'Twas thought the Gibbets did their duty
> If they stood near enough to shew t'ye
> Their tenants in a distant ken,
> Far from the highway path of men.
> So distant stood they, no offence
> Was giv'n to any other sense.
> But K_ _, or some Judge as wise,
> Not satisfied to strike our eyes,
> Now sets his gibbet at our noses;
> And, forasmuch as he supposes
> That folks may turn their head or wink,
> He makes examples by the stink.[86]

Whatever remained of the corpse was eventually taken down and buried in unconsecrated ground. In Reading in the early 1800s Darter saw one that was discovered 'in sinking a grave at the north-west corner of the church-yard (as you enter to the Butts); it seemed perfect, but it had on the legs and wrists, rings with a chain which were attached to a ring in the centre; on inquiry I was informed that this man must have been hung in chains, as the ground where the body lay was for many years appropriated to the burial of those who were executed at Gallows Tree Common.'[87]

In the eyes of the law, criminals found guilty of treason deserved the harshest penalties of all. Women were burned at the stake, while men were hung, drawn and quartered. In 1782 David Tyrie was put on trial at Winchester Assizes for

> falsely, wickedly, and traitorously, (being a subject of Great Britain) compassing, imagining and intending, the king of and from the royal state, crown, title, power, and government of Great Britain, to depose and wholly deprive; and the king to kill, and bring and put to death, and to fulfil, perfect, and bring to effect, his treason, compassings and imaginations, as such a false traitor, falsely, wickedly and traitorously composing and writing, and causing to be composed and wrote, divers letters.[88]

The indictment goes on at length in this overblown legal language, but basically Tyrie had been caught sending letters to the French giving sensitive strategic information about the Royal Navy. As a clerk in a naval office at Portsmouth, he was well placed to obtain such information.

There was little doubt that Tyrie was guilty of spying, and he was sentenced to be hung, drawn and quartered at Portsmouth on 24 August 1782:

> The Crowd of People of all Ranks assembled by Four o'Clock this Morning at the Gates of the Gaol to see Tyrie set off for the Place of Execution, was very great. About Five o'Clock he was put into a Coach with six Horses, attended by the Ordinary, Under Sheriff, Gaoler, &c. and conveyed to Portsmouth, where being delivered up to the Mayor and Police of the Town, he was drawn on a Sledge to the Place of Execution. After praying a little Time he was turned off, and hanged till

almost dead; was then cut down, his head severed from his Body, his Bowels taken out, and his Heart shewed to the surrounding Multitude, and then thrown into a Fire made for that Purpose; the Body was then quartered, and put into a Coffin. The Concourse of People was immense, and such was the singular Avarice of many who were near the Body, that happy was he who could procure a Finger, or some Vestige of the Criminal.[89]

Tyrie was the last man to be executed in this way. Although men in later trials were given the same sentence, they were simply hanged or else hanged and their corpse beheaded.

Other treasonable offences included counterfeiting, and in 1789 husband and wife 'Hugh and Christian Bowman were convicted of counterfeiting divers pieces of base metal so as to resemble shillings and sixpences.'[90] Christian was taken from Newgate and 'chained to the stake, placed a few yards nearer Newgate-street than the scaffold, and a stool being taken from beneath her feet, she was suspended by the neck for near half an hour, when the faggots surrounding her were set on fire, and her body was consumed to ashes'.[91] Because this kind of execution was unusual, her story was quickly written and printed as a chapbook, described as 'The Life and Death of Christian Bowman, Alias Murphy; Who was burnt at a Stake, in the Old Bailey, on Wednesday the 18th of March 1789 for High Treason in feloniously and traitorously counterfeiting the Silver Coin of the Realm. Containing her Birth and Parentage, youthful Adventures, Love Amours, fatal Marriage, unhappy Connections, and untimely Death.'[92]

The law changed the following year, 1790, and the sentence for such crimes for both men and women was reduced to hanging or transportation. Those convicted of capital crimes were being increasingly sentenced to transportation, and many people condemned to death were reprieved and transported. It was not until the 1820s–30s that the death penalty was abolished for numerous lesser offences – the last person hanged for stealing a sheep was executed in 1831.[93]

Surprisingly, riots were not generally punished by death or transportation, unless the rioters were guilty of other crimes, and people were certainly not deterred from protesting against personal hardships like lack of work and food. Some riots were more sinister, verging on revolution, and summoning the troops was often the only way of quelling them. On 29 October 1795 Woodforde and his niece Nancy witnessed an assassination attempt on George III during a riot in London:

As we heard when we got to London that the Sessions of Parliament was to be opened this day, at one o'clock I walked with Nancy to St. James's Park about half a mile, where at two o'clock or rather after we saw the King go in his State Coach drawn with eight fine cream-coloured horses in red morrocco-leather harness, to the House of Lords. The Park was uncommonly crouded indeed, never was known a greater concourse of people before, and I am very [sorry] to insert that his Majesty was very grossly insulted by some of the Mob, and had a very narrow escape of being killed going to the House, a ball [bullet] passing thro' the windows as he went thro' old Palace-Yard, supposed to be discharged from an air gun, but very fortunately did not strike the King or Lords.[94]

The jeers of the crowd that day were mingled with shouts of 'Give us peace and bread!', 'No war!', and 'No King!'[95] – as ever, the king and his government were blamed for prices having risen to famine levels, causing widespread hardship. It was with some difficulty that a strong force of Guards enabled the royal coach to reach Parliament.

The crowd did not disperse, and Woodforde watched as the king departed:

On his return from the House to James's Palace he was very much hissed and hooted at, and on his going from St. James's to the Queen's Palace in his private coach, he had another very lucky escape, as the mob surrounded his coach and one of them was going to open the door but the Horse Guards coming up very providentially at the time, prevented any further danger. The state-coach windows going from St. James's to the Mews were broke all to pieces by the Mob, but no other damage done to the coach ... The Mob was composed of the most violent and lowest Democrats. Thank God the King received no injury whatever, neither did we as it happened ... It was said that there were near two hundred thousand people in St. James Park about 3 o'clock. I never was in such a croud in all my Life.[96]

This was by no means the largest riot of the era. Serious disturbances had taken place four years earlier in Birmingham against dissenters, and before that anti-Catholic riots had terrified London in early June 1780, incited by Lord George Gordon. For several days, the mob effectively had a free hand, despite being confronted by troops.[97] Many buildings were set ablaze and several prisons destroyed, including Newgate and the Fleet. It was the worst riot in London's history and was brought under control only when large numbers of troops were ordered into the capital with instructions to shoot to kill.

Riots on a smaller scale were endemic, and Woodforde's diaries are littered with incidents. At the beginning of 1801, another year of shortages, successive entries show the growing unrest, as in early April: 'A great many mobs or risings of the poor in many parts of the country, said to be owing to the enormous price that wheat is at, risings in Somersetshire particularly named. Pray God! preserve our friends we have there.'[98] Only five days later he noted: 'Mobs in the West of England, Plymouth, Wellington and other places on account of the dearness of corn and other provisions – some lives lost.'[99] Many disturbances were not true riots but the actions of desperate crowds, often of angry women, whose purpose was to force a farmer, miller or baker to sell at the old uninflated prices. Although such actions were illegal, many sympathetic magistrates ignored them, particularly if no violence was used.

People were trying to survive in difficult circumstances, and one way was through the crimes of smuggling and buying goods from smugglers, something that people of all classes did. Because taxes on imported goods were particularly resented, there was no stigma in purchasing smuggled goods. Even clergymen happily bought from smugglers, though people with status were fearful of informers. In October 1792 Woodforde recorded: 'John Buck, the blacksmith, who was lately informed against for having a tub of gin found in his house that was smuggled, by two excise officers, was pretty easy fined'[100] –

something of an understatement, since Buck was a key smuggler in that part of Norfolk. Smugglers were shielded because few people would testify against them, and even magistrates were their customers. Some of the elite actually financed smuggling ventures and were powerful enough to influence or bribe the authorities to protect their associates.

So many people were involved in smuggling that it was only a partially covert trade. Smugglers were often surprisingly open about their activities, and it was not unusual to come across caravans of smuggled goods comprising more than a hundred packhorses or a long string of carts. One day in September 1790 John Byng stopped at an inn at Aylesford in Kent and gazed enviously at some fine horses: 'We saw, whilst at dinner, a gang of well-mounted smugglers pass by. How often have I wish'd to be able to purchase a horse from their excellent stables.'[101]

Such gangs often outnumbered the excisemen, who dared not tackle them or were easily bribed to stay away. Occasionally, excisemen were keen to publicise significant captures, as in June 1792 when *The Times* reported: 'A gang of near 100 smugglers, a few nights since, were overtaken by the Supervisor of Yarmouth, and three other officers, near Helmsley Beech, and, with very little resistance, had seven carts and eight horses taken from them, containing 1012 gallons of gin, and 200 wt. [2 cwt] of tobacco, the largest seizure ever remembered by so small a number of persons.'[102]

The biggest single market was London, where smuggled merchandise was openly peddled in the streets, something that Benjamin Silliman noticed:

as I was returning home from the strand, a short fat man, in a scarlet waistcoat, addressed me in this style; 'young gentleman—sir—your honour!' So many titles, in such rapid succession, made me stop short, when he put his mouth to my ear, and said in a low voice; 'I have got some nice French cambric, will you buy?' ... To-day, while I was passing rapidly along Holborn, a fellow singled me out with his eye, and after following me a few paces through the crowd, said with a low, cautious voice, 'sir, sir, will you buy a little French cambric? I have some very fine' ... They were undoubtedly smugglers of that article, and had either evaded or defied the laws of the country.[103]

With London expanding at a rapid rate, there was a growing market for both legal and illicit goods, and all kinds of criminals besides smugglers were attracted to the city. It was effectively a boom town, seen as a place of boundless opportunities. In the popular comedy *The Heir-at-Law* by George Colman the Younger, first performed in 1797, one character sings a few lines conveying that message:

> Oh, London is a fine town,
> A very famous city,
> Where all the streets are paved with gold,
> And all the maidens pretty.[104]

Not everyone took such a rose-tinted view, and visitors from the countryside rightly saw the city as the crime capital of England. William Jones in 1803 summed up the views of many: 'Returned from Town last night, where I had been since Wedny., & I never came home with more pleasure. Nothing, I think, could tempt me to live in London; indeed, its bustle, & dissipation, (without taking its fog & variety of stench into account), would soon destroy me.'[105]

———◆———

# ELEVEN

# MEDICINE MEN

Nobody is healthy in London, nobody can be.

*Emma*, by Jane Austen

Illness or accident could happen to anyone, irrespective of their rank in society, but how they were treated depended on what they could afford to pay. In October 1815 Jane Austen's brother Henry was seriously ill in London. 'Henry is an excellent patient, lies quietly in bed and is ready to swallow anything,' she told Cassandra. 'He lives upon medicine, tea and barley water.'[1] It is unlikely that his medicine was proving beneficial, because so little was understood of the nature of illnesses, infection and treatment. Even minor medical complaints generated fear, and unexplained deaths were especially unnerving.

Letters and diaries of the time are littered with obsessive details of daily evacuations and putrid discharges, all trying to make sense of the body's behaviour. 'I have had an attack of my old complaint,' Nelly Weeton confided in a letter to her brother Tom in 1809,

a pain at my stomach, brought on by eating sallad with a little vinegar, and drinking milk to it. The milk turned sour, and came up again as black as ink; and from that time till within these two days I have scarcely been able to crawl. My appetite was quite gone. Last Saturday I ventured to get an emetic at a Druggist's. I took it that afternoon, and got up an amazing quantity of yellow stuff, since which time I have recovered rapidly.[2]

While medical knowledge advanced slowly, deep ignorance prevailed. The world of superstition merged imperceptibly into that of folk wisdom, and much was blamed on the weather or the moon. Before going to the expense of calling on a professional medical man, it was customary to try remedies known to the family or possibly a local healer. Alternatively, information was obtained from the growing number of medical books or herbalist manuals such as *Culpeper's Complete Herbal*. James Woodforde habitually tried such cures. In his diary for 23 March 1779 he described a method of first aid: 'in shaving my face this morning I happened to cut one of my moles which bled much, and happening also to kill a small moth that was flying about, I applied it to my mole and it instantaneously stopped the bleeding'.[3] On another occasion he had a painful sty:

The stiony on my right eye-lid still swelled and inflamed very much. As it is commonly said that the eye-lid being rubbed by the tail of a black cat would do it much good if not entirely cure it, and having a black cat, a little before dinner I made a trial of it, and very soon after dinner I found my eye-lid much abated of the swelling and almost free from pain. I cannot therefore but conclude it to be of the greatest service to a stiony on the eye-lid. Any other cats tail may have the above effect in all probability – but I did my eye-lid with my own black tom cat's tail.[4]

After putting his faith in a feline cure, his eye worsened: 'My right eye again, that is, its eye-lid much inflamed again and rather painful. I put on a plaistor to it this morning, but in the aft[ernoon] took it of[f] again, as I perceived no good from it.'[5] The following day brought mixed results: 'My eye-lid is I think rather better than it was, I bathed it with warm milk and water last night. I took a little rhubarb going to bed to night. My eye-lid about noon rather worse owing perhaps to the warm milk and water, therefore just before dinner I washed it well with cold water and in the evening appeared much better for it.'[6]

The root of rhubarb, dried and powdered for medicinal purposes, was a popular cure-all, and in February 1807 William Holland wrote down a description of how it was used:

[I] mounted my horse and rode to farmer Morle. He seemed poorly and feverish and had a bad cough. I told him he should take something. He answer'd that he did not like doctor's stuff. I asked him whether he had got any rhubarb. He believ'd there was some so they brought sad stuff. However I called for a grater, put my hand in my pocket and took out a lump of rhubarb and grated it and then some ginger and mixed all together and then had some brandy and water and made him presently a draught and off it went and they all seemed wonderfully pleased.[7]

A few days later, he was convinced that his remedy had worked: 'He is got pure and well since I gave him a dose of rhubarb.'[8]

Woodforde also habitually used rhubarb for all manner of ailments: 'I was taken very ill this afternoon with a violent pain in my right ear and it continued so till I went to bed. I took a good dose of rhubarb.'[9] The next day he felt unwell:

I got up very ill this morning about 8 o'clock, having had very little sleep all the night, owing to the pain in my ear which was much worse in the night and broke and a good deal of blood only came away. The pain continued still very bad all the morning, tho' not quite so bad as before. It made me very uneasy abt it. A throbbing pain in my ear continued till I went to bed. I put a rosted onion in my ear going to bed to night.[10]

An onion roasted in embers was an old herbal remedy, one recommended by *Culpeper's Complete Herbal*: 'The juice of Onions ... takes away all blemishes, spots and marks in the skin: and dropped in the ears eases the pains and noise of them.'[11] Woodforde also tested various cures on his niece Nancy and on his servants. One servant was probably suffering from malaria, which was then common in England: 'My boy Jack [Wharton] had another touch of the ague about noon. I gave him a dram of gin at the beginning of the fit and pushed him headlong into one of my ponds and ordered him to bed immediately and he was better after it – and had nothing of the cold fit after, but was very hot.'[12]

If all else failed, an apothecary, a surgeon or a physician might be consulted. Apothecaries (druggists) were allowed to prescribe, prepare and sell substances for medicinal purposes, but many of these were little better than the strange concoctions sold by itinerant quacks. Such professional treatment often cost a great deal and may even have caused more harm than the folklore remedies. Many in the medical profession were not highly regarded, and as he set out on an excursion from London in 1781, John Byng was hoping to remain healthy so that he could avoid the country doctors: 'We are tolerably well accompany'd with touring, road books, maps &c., and I am also stock'd with James's powder; so shou'd a fever overtake me, I will hope that by taking some of his doses and being well wrap't up in blankets I shall chase away sickness, without consulting the medical country blockheads, who kill, or cure, by chance.'[13] In a diary entry in January 1800, Holland was of a similar opinion, saying of his local surgeon from Nether Stowey: 'met Mr. Forbes on foot going to kill a few patients'.[14]

Most surgeons were reasonably educated, and in their early to mid-teens they were apprenticed from three to seven years to surgeons or surgeon-apothecaries. At the end of their apprenticeship some continued practising without formal qualifications, while others were examined in London so that they could become members of the Company of Surgeons, a professional body formed when surgeons broke away from barber-surgeons in 1745.[15] Many surgeons had medical degrees from universities such as Edinburgh, Glasgow and Leiden. London had no university, but it was an important medical centre where students were taught in private anatomy schools and by walking the wards at the leading charitable hospitals, practising their art on the poor.

Holland's acquaintance Penelope Benwell (later Hind) was distressed by the situation of the poor: 'In sickness they must labour on till they sink into their beds; when there they have often neither medicine or food to assist them.'[16] Catherine Hutton was equally concerned about the plight of the poor, and when staying at Blackpool in August 1788, she heard about the 'Whitworth Doctors', James and John Taylor, from the village of Whitworth near Rochdale: 'Surgery is practised in a curious manner by some individuals [two brothers] of the name of Taylor ... They were originally farriers [treating horse ailments], and, by a transition easy in the country, they became bonesetters and surgeons.'[17]

Although untrained, the Taylors were highly successful and widely consulted by poor and royalty alike, and their business was passed down through the family.[18] 'No patient is visited at his lodgings,' Catherine learned, 'if he is able to attend at the house of his doctors; and there, no attention is paid to rank or circumstances, the first comer being first served.'[19] The most famous of the two brothers was John Taylor, and Catherine related that the eminent Manchester physician Charles White 'said to Dr. John ... "Well, how many patients have you killed this year?" "It matters not how many," replied John; "I kill them cheaper than you."'[20] Catherine added: 'Cheap, indeed, does this doctor kill or cure; his terms to those who attend at his house being only two shillings a week, including operations, applications, and medicines.'[21]

Even though surgery was developing into a skilled profession, physicians were higher in status because they did not undertake manual work. Instead, they examined patients and prescribed appropriate treatments and medication, largely for internal ailments. In order to become a fellow of the Royal College of Physicians, it was necessary to belong to the Church of England and to be a graduate of Cambridge or Oxford university (where practical training was of no consequence). Graduates of other universities were admitted only as licentiates. For medical training, physicians went to universities like Leiden or Edinburgh or into hospitals and the private anatomy schools.

The Royal Navy employed surgeons, not physicians, on board their warships, because they needed medical men with practical skills. These surgeons were also expected to act as apothecaries and physicians. The medical men employed in the army varied, with some highly trained and experienced surgeons and physicians, while others had a limited education. There was no government regulation of medicine, and especially outside London, a medical man would often practise as a combined apothecary, surgeon and physician, rather like the Whitworth Doctors. The Apothecaries Act of 1815 introduced some regulation, after which such general practitioners were obliged to be qualified apothecaries.[22]

Some effective medical treatments were beginning to be developed, the most notable of which was a method of preventing smallpox – a frightening, virulent disease that affected all classes. It had a high mortality rate (up to 60 per cent) and left survivors with disfiguring scars and sometimes even blindness. Inoculation (or variolation) had begun in Britain from 1721, using the technique of cutting a patient's arm or leg and introducing infected pus from someone already ill with smallpox. Around 2 per cent of those inoculated died. Parson Woodforde made several references to smallpox and inoculation in his diary, as in November 1776:

Dr. Thorne of Mattishall came to my house and inoculated my servants, Ben Legate and little Jack Warton ... Ben is about 25 years old, Jack about 9. The Dr. took out of his pocket a small [container] where the matter was ... They then each stripped, and the Dr. taking a small bit of the cotton thread saturated with matter between his left hand finger and thumb, with the launcet in his other hand, he then dipt the point of the launcet in the cotton thread, and with the point of the launcet made two dotts ... about two inches apart in each of their arms, dipping now and then his launcet in water and then with the cotton thread, scarce to be felt or to draw blood, they then stood with their arms exposed to the cold air for about 3 minutes, till almost dried up. The matter took effect almost instantaneously ... No plaister or any thing else whatever to be put to their arms afterwards.[23]

Inoculation was too expensive for the poor, but Woodforde paid for these servants because smallpox was ravaging the parish at the time. Five days later, he settled Dr Thorne's bill:

My inoculating folks brave [well]. Ben complained of a pain under his arms to day. Jack complained of nothing at all ... Dr. Thorne who inoculated my servants dined and spent the afternoon with us ... I paid the Dr. for inoculating our people o.10.6. I gave him also towards inoculating a poor family o.10.6 ... The Doctor's price for inoculating a single person is only o.5.3 ... Ben's arms look much inflamed, much forwarder than the boy's, Jack complained of a pain under his arms to night.[24]

Smallpox remained a killer despite inoculation, but the situation was transformed when Edward Jenner developed vaccination. After serving an apprenticeship to a surgeon in Gloucestershire, Jenner had studied at St George's Hospital in London and then returned home in 1772, where he made the first scientific investigation into cowpox (vaccinia). He experimented by inoculating patients with cowpox to offer some protection against smallpox, calling this procedure vaccination. By 1800 vaccination was increasingly employed, making smallpox the first infectious disease to be curbed in this manner. Even so, medical men could be backward, and in 1809 Holland was unhappy that Jenner's vaccination was not being used:

I went to Dodington in the morning very few at church as there is an innoculation for the small pox which shuts up Mr. Farthing and one or two families more. But now the cow pox [vaccination] is so much approved of and so much safer I do not think it right in Mr. Bennet recommending innoculation for the small pox, which is infectious and if one family begins it obliges others to adopt the same measure whether they approve of it or not.[25]

Despite new medical discoveries, there was much to dread from other viral and bacterial diseases and assorted afflictions, including consumption (tuberculosis), gonorrhoea, syphilis, malaria, cholera, typhus, scarlet fever, measles, rabies from dog bites, cancer and influenza. 'Very sickly in London in the influenza. Very few escape,' Woodforde remarked during a visit to the capital in June 1782.[26] Luckily, he kept healthy, since an influenza pandemic had recently spread across Europe from Asia, and deaths in London reached a peak during his visit.[27] In November 1807 Nelly Weeton expressed concern in a letter to her brother about another killer, whooping cough (also then called 'chincough'): 'How are your little ones? Do they escape the hooping cough? Great numbers have it here, and it is very fatal. Many die of it; several children have gone blind with it, and some thrown into fits. My cousin Latham's two youngest boys have it; the youngest is very ill.'[28]

In an age of poor food, scant hygiene and no refrigeration, other commonplace disorders included intestinal worms and food poisoning. Gout was a problem that often afflicted the better-off who consumed too much alcohol and meat, causing a crippling inflammation of the joints of the extremities, especially the big toe. Holland wryly recorded that 'Old Weymouth our neighbour I called upon to see his foot which is much swelled. I think it is the gout. I congratulated him on becoming a gentleman, as the gout never attacked any but gentlemen. He shook his head and said that he could not be a gentleman without money.'[29]

Woodforde was first aware that he himself had gout in April 1790: 'When I got up this morning, perceived a violent pain in my right great toe on my foot about the middle joint and swelled a great deal indeed, could scarce get on my slipper, and then could not keep him on long, but get into a pair of shoes. I should think it must be the gout. This is the first attack I ever met with before now.'[30] Gout becomes a recurring topic of his subsequent diary entries, as in mid-January 1795: 'Got up this morning very bad indeed in the gout in my right foot, could scarce bare to put him on the ground, and so it continued the whole day and night, not free one minute from violent pain . . . I had my bed warmed to night and a fire in my bed-room. I never was attacked so severe before in my life. Obliged to put on my great shoe, lined with flannel.'[31] Like many at the time, he thought gout floated around the body: 'The gout, tho' not very painful, but continually flying about my constitution makes me very weak both in body and mind &c.'[32] His constant dosing with rhubarb would actually have exacerbated his condition.

For those with money, it was fashionable to take the waters at spas, to maintain good health or to cure disease, sometimes as a last resort. Spas were situated where a good supply of mineral water could be exploited, such as at Bath, Cheltenham, Leamington, Hotwells in Bristol, Buxton and Harrogate. The water was not simply drunk. Communal baths, filled with warm or hot water from the springs, were considered especially effective for those with skin diseases and running sores. Such collective bathing was a novelty for most people, who otherwise never bathed in their lives, in the same way that sea bathing became popular for reasons of health.

It was still widely believed that health problems were caused by an imbalance of the four humours of the body – blood, phlegm, black bile (melancholy) and yellow bile (choler). Dr Radcliffe's Elixir claimed to cure this problem: 'FOR a general alterative Medicine this Elixir has stood unrivalled for more than Eighty Years, and the Public cannot have recourse to a more efficacious Remedy, as a Purifier of the Blood from all Humours, whether contracted by too free Living, or from Surfeits, Jaundice, Scurvy, or Humours after the Measles, or Small-Pox, &c.'[33] For good measure, the advertisement added: 'For all Obstructions in the Bowels and for the Cure of Worms in Children or Adults, it will be found equally serviceable.'[34]

Medical treatments to ensure the proper balance of these humours concentrated on purging and bleeding, and such treatments mainly comprised bloodletting, cupping (blistering), the application of leeches, emetics to cause vomiting and clysters (enemas). When his maid Nanny was ill, Woodforde 'gave her a vomit [emetic] about noon and it kept down near an hour and then it operated very briskly indeed, brought off a great quantity of nasty green thick stuff from her stomach. She was soon after better ... in the evening gave her a small dose of rhubarb with a little ginger.'[35]

Bloodletting was the staple work of surgeons, though it was more likely to weaken sick patients and give them blood poisoning. Cupping involved applying a warmed glass to the skin, which created a vacuum as it cooled and caused a blister, or else it could be used to extract pus from a boil. The skin might be incised or scarified before-hand so that blood was drawn. Woodforde certainly believed in blistering: 'This morning taken very ill, could scarce get down stairs. Sent for Mr. Thorne, who ordered me immediately to bed ... In the night had a blister put between my shoulders which discharged very much indeed in the night and which made me soon better.'[36]

Cupping was a treatment to which Jane Austen's father at Bath was subjected, as she described in a letter to her brother Francis: 'Our dear Father ... was taken ill on Saturday morning, exactly in the same way as heretofore, an oppression in the head, with fever, violent tremu-lousness, and the greatest degree of feebleness. The same remedy of cupping, which had before been so successful, was immediately applied to, but without such happy effects. The attack was more violent, and at first he seemed scarcely at all relieved by the operation. Towards the evening however he got better.'[37] Two days later, on 21 January 1805, he died.

The most common method of taking blood was to cut the vein of an arm with a lancet or fleam, and Catherine Hutton was told that the Whitworth Doctors undertook bloodletting in a workshop which patients visited: 'on Sundays, the days they bleed gratuitously, the patients are arranged around the room; one operator opens the veins, another holds the basins, and a third follows and binds the arms'.[38] Applying live bloodsucking leeches, obtained from ponds and streams, did a similar job. When walking in the Lake District in October 1800, Dorothy Wordsworth and her brother William encountered an elderly man, bent almost double. 'His trade was to gather leeches,' she remarked, 'but now leeches were scarce, and he had not strength for it. He lived by begging, and was making his way to Carlisle ... He said leeches were very scarce ... He supposed it owing to their being much sought after, that they did not breed fast, and were of slow growth. Leeches were formerly 2s 6d per 100; they are now 30s.'[39] Based on this chance meeting, William wrote a poem, 'The Leech-Gatherer', with the lines:

> He with a smile did then his words repeat;
> And said that, gathering leeches, far and wide
> He travelled; stirring thus about his feet
> The waters of the pools where they abide.
> 'Once I could meet with them on every side;
> But they have dwindled long by slow decay;
> Yet still I persevere, and find them where I may.'[40]

When Holland was at the hamlet of Rose Ash in Devon in September 1803, he suffered such severe pain in his face that he requested Mr Bryan from nearby South Molton to call: 'He soon perceived what was the matter with me, a perfectly nervous case he said ... Said that he would send over Mr Ling [his assistant] with leeches and give me Dover's powders.'[41] Mr Ling called later that evening, but Holland found the treatment with leeches distasteful: 'He did come at last, we dined and after dinner I had leeches put to my cheek, or rather lip under the nose. It is a tedious, unpleasant operation and I hope it will do me good. It is over after two or three hours.'[42]

Similar notions of medicine were applied to animals, and blood-letting was commonly carried out with the aim of curing and preventing illness. In mid-May 1779, Woodforde noted: 'Bled my three horses this morning – 2 quarts each.'[43] Treatises were published to help farmers and others keep animals healthy, but Woodforde's methods were contrary to the advice of a manual published five years earlier: 'It is safer to take a gallon at five or six bleedings, than two quarts at once, for it robs him of two [too] much animal spirits. Always bleed a horse in a pint or quart pot, for when you bleed at random upon the ground, you never can know what quantity you take, nor what quality his blood is. From such violent methods used with ignorance, proceed the death of a great number of horses.'[44]

On a post-chaise trip in Sussex in July 1811, Louis Simond encountered similar ignorance:

we perceived that one of the horses was streaming with blood about the neck; he had been put in harness too soon after a bleeding. The post-boy stopped on the road, and wept through the operation of fresh twisting the skin, tying, and pinning,—very clumsy and painful,—but unavoidable: he agreed with me that it was very wrong to work the horses too soon after bleeding, *for*, said he, this is the third time we have had in this situation, and the others died of a mortification, and *they cost L.37 [£37] a-piece!*[45]

Although animals were so often treated cruelly, there were instances of kindness: 'Mr. Willm Custance also called here but did not come in,' Woodforde recorded in November 1799, 'a favourite spaniel of his by name, Dash, having his leg broke by another dog in pursuit of a hare near us. My nephew assisted him in binding up the leg, with a bandage and splices of wood, and bathing it with vinegar.'[46] When all else failed, injured animals were killed. Like most country people, Woodforde allowed his dogs to wander: 'In the afternoon my dog Pompey came home shot terribly so bad that I had her hanged directly out of her misery. My greyhound Minx who was with her did not come and we suppose she has met with the same fate.'[47] The next day Minx returned, 'very much shot in one side, but I hope not mortally. They were both shot by black Jack [a gamekeeper].'[48] Stray dogs were a common sight and could pose a real hazard as rabies was prevalent. John Byng also loathed their constant barking, as on one occasion in Lincolnshire: 'This morning I was awaken'd by the barkings and fightings of dogs, upon the market place; such nuisance, and noise is intolerable: one dog can disturb a whole town.'[49]

For dog bites and other serious injuries to people, a surgeon might need to be called in. The Whitworth Doctors boiled up salves in their workshop for treating wounds: 'In the shop stand two jars containing four gallons each; the one filled with a green digestive ointment, the other with a white cerate; and from one of these every patient, who is able, spreads his own plaister, on paper, if he has not brought his own lint or rag. On an average, the doctors dress one hundred and forty persons daily.'[50] What they were dispensing was a form of healing sticking plaster, and recipes abounded for making such plaster at home. For superficial wounds court-plaister wrapped in paper was sold, made from silk or cotton coated with adhesive isinglass (a form of gelatine) – 'ladies' court-plaister' cost sixpence, and other types of plaister sold by apothecaries included 'corn plaister' for feet and 'family plaister'.[51] Woodforde kept this sort at home: 'My servant Will has a bad leg owing to its being scalded two days ago ... I put to it some family plaister and a poultice over it.'[52]

Broken bones could heal if there were no complications, and farriers were usually willing to help. The Whitworth Doctors were renowned as bonesetters, but in hospitals the incidence of infection meant that amputation was often the best solution. Any complicated breaks that could not be set or dealt with by amputation were effectively untreatable. In February 1796 Woodforde heard news of the death of a relative: 'Nancy had a letter this evening from Miss Pounsett brought from Norwich ... The death of my Uncle Thos. Woodfordes wife occasioned by a late fall she met with, wch. broke one of her thigh bones, and being at an advanced age, above 84, could not be set.'[53]

Because manual labour was so physically demanding, working-class people often suffered from hernias, usually referred to as ruptures. Hernias occurred where an organ protruded into another part of the body, generally part of the intestine through the abdominal wall. The army and navy, although constantly short of men, refused to accept new recruits with hernias. Little could be done for this distressing condition except to wear a supporting truss. Different models were devised, and in 1805 George Barwick, a gunmaker at Norwich, advertised: 'Elastic Steel Trusses and Bandages, OF EVERY DESCRIPTION, For Ruptures in Men, Women, & Children ... Hundreds have been made by him, and many entirely cured ... These Trusses, Bandages, &c. for Groin, Navel, and other Ruptures, are made on a superior plan, and worn without any inconvenience whatever.'[54]

That same year saw the founding of the New Rupture Society, whose aim was to provide the poor with effective trusses. One report stated: 'at least one person in fifteen is ruptured: but among those classes of the community which are much exposed to laborious employment, the average may be fixed at one in eight or nine [and] ... in some particular parishes, the proportion may be computed at even a *fourth of the labouring population!*'[55] At least a quarter of a million people (perhaps many more) suffered from a rupture at any one time.

The Whitworth Doctors, Catherine Hutton said, also helped patients with constipation, for which 'Glauber salts were bought by the hogshead'[56] – naturally occurring salts that were used as a laxative. This was an age when many people's diet was poor, not helped by the state of their teeth. There were no trained dentists, but from the 1770s dentistry was becoming a respectable profession, and surgeons such as John Hunter were undertaking research and publishing their results on the subject. Cavities in teeth could be filled with lead, silver or gold, but most sufferers had their painful teeth extracted. In London and large towns surgeons were available to pull out teeth, but elsewhere apothecaries, quack tooth-drawers and even blacksmiths might oblige. At Weston Longville in June 1776 Woodforde had a tooth removed by the farrier:

My tooth pained me all night, got up a little after 5 this morning and sent for one Reeves, a man who draws teeth in this parish, and about 7 he came and drew my tooth but shockingly bad indeed, he broke away a great piece of my gum and broke one of the fangs of the tooth, it gave me exquisite pain all the day after and my face was swelled prodigiously in the evening and much pain. Very bad and in much pain the whole day long. Gave the old man that drew it however 0.2.6. He is too old, I think, to draw teeth, can't see very well.[57]

Years later Jane Austen accompanied three of her nieces to a more reputable dentist in London, as she related to Cassandra:

The poor Girls and their Teeth! ... we were a whole hour at Spence's, and Lizzy's were filed and lamented over again and poor Marianne had two taken out after all, the two just beyond the eye teeth, to make room for those in front. When her doom was fixed, Fanny, Lizzy and I walked into the next room, where we heard each of the two sharp hasty screams. Fanny's teeth were cleaned too – and pretty as they are, Spence found something to do to them, putting in gold and talking gravely ... I would not have had him look at mine for a shilling a tooth and double it.[58]

When living near Liverpool in 1808, Nelly Weeton had four teeth removed, as she told a friend:

I might have been Boreas [god of the north wind] himself, with one cheek, it was so puffed, and had you met me, you would have seen that cheek almost half a mile before you saw the other ... However, as I am a great advocate of equality, I sent for Mr. Aranson, who extracted four teeth, and the operation soon reduced the great cheek to the level of its neighbour. Since that time, I have been in perfect good health, equally good spirits, and, (if you will believe me) in a good humour.[59]

Mr Pascoe Aranson was a surgeon-dentist who practised at Liverpool but also offered his services elsewhere for short periods. Two weeks after Nelly's extractions, he was advertising in the *Leeds Mercury* that 'he Purposes spending a few Weeks in Leeds, and any Lady or Gentleman who may favour him with their Commands, will please to address him at his Lodgings, at Mr. Hodgson's, Tea-Dealer, No. 2 Boar-Lane.'[60] Aranson claimed to provide a range of services 'without the least pain or Injury to the enamel ... Mr. A. is also noted for Drawing Teeth, with the greatest Ease, and extracts stumps, even if covered with the Gum.'[61]

When most people smiled, they displayed rotten teeth and gaps where teeth were missing. Holland complained that one man, by the name of Briffet, had 'a mouth as wide as a barn door and lips as thick and projecting they look like two rollers of raw beef bolstered up to guard as it were the approach to his nasty rotten ragged teeth. However he is a good pig killer.'[62] For many afflicted with toothache, it must have been a blessing when they lost all their teeth. Dorothy Wordsworth noted in May 1802: 'My tooth broke today. They will soon be gone.'[63] Already at the age of thirty, she was facing the prospect of no teeth.

Some chose to have a rogue tooth rammed back into place, and Colonel Peter Hawker in March 1812 wrote of this brutal experience: 'After being tortured for three days and three nights with the toothache, I had a tooth drawn and driven in again, by which severe operation you effectually remove all pain (by destroying the nerve), and at the same time restore the tooth for mastication.'[64] An alternative solution for front teeth was to insert a dead person's tooth. 'I would recommend to every dentist to have some dead teeth at hand,' wrote the surgeon John Hunter, 'that he may have a chance to fit the socket. I have known these sometimes last for years, especially when well supported by the neighbouring teeth.'[65]

Another possibility was a live tooth transplant, which was fashionable for a few decades from the 1770s. As a desperate way of earning money, a pauper might allow a sound front tooth to be extracted, which was then implanted in a wealthy patient. Transplanted teeth could transmit diseases like syphilis, but Hunter did not understand this risk: 'the new teeth should always be perfectly sound, and taken from a mouth which has the appearance of that of a person sound and healthy; not that I believe it possible to transplant an infection'.[66] In order to avoid filing the tooth to the correct shape, he said, the 'best remedy is to have several people ready, whose teeth in appearance are fit; for if the first will not answer, the second may'.[67]

A few women practised medicine, usually alongside their husband as apothecaries, surgeons, oculists, opticians or dentists, or perhaps continuing a business on his death. In the 1770s and 1780s Mrs de St Raymond was a dentist in York and London, and on occasions she went to Winchester for short periods, as in January 1782:

MRS. DE ST. RAYMOND, DENTIST, at Mr. SHEPPARD's, fronting the White Lion, High-street ... She takes judiciously away from the teeth all *Tartarous Concretions*, destructive to them and the gums: draws and transplants teeth, and extracts stumps, be they ever so difficult, even when the skills of others proves ineffectual. She fills up and fastens teeth ... fits in either *human* or *artificial Teeth*, from one to an entire set; and executes her newly invented *Obturators* for the loss of the *Palate*.[68]

Artificial teeth or dentures were crafted from a single piece of bone, ivory or porcelain, but none was satisfactory, as bone and ivory had no enamel coating and so became discoloured and decayed rapidly, and porcelain was noisy, lost its glaze and tended to shatter. The best dentures were constructed from human teeth taken from corpses and set on an ivory or animal-bone base, but these were expensive to manufacture. Lower dentures were more commonly made than upper ones because they could be securely fitted.

The battles of the Napoleonic Wars provided many opportunities for obtaining human teeth and satisfying a great demand amongst the wealthy for dentures. In 1814, during the Peninsular Wars, the London surgeon Astley Cooper sent a man by the name of Butler to his nephew Bransby Cooper in Spain in order to obtain teeth. When Bransby asked him how this was to be achieved, Butler replied: 'Oh, Sir, only let there be a battle, and there'll be no want of teeth. I'll draw them as fast as the men are knocked down.'[69] Bransby noted that some of the legitimate sutlers were also bodysnatchers who followed the army to strip teeth and other valuables from the dead:

> They generally obtained the teeth on the night succeeding the battle, only drawing them from those soldiers whose youth and health rendered them peculiarly fitted for the purposes to which they were to be employed. Nothing but the large sums of money derived from the depradations could have prompted them to encounter the risk ... for I do not believe a soldier in the whole army would have hesitated one moment to blow out the brains of a person whom he found robbing the corpse of a comrade in this manner.[70]

At the Battle of Waterloo in June 1815, over eighteen thousand men died on the battlefield itself,[71] and they were ruthlessly plundered. Clients back in England were happy to wear dentures made from the teeth of fit young men killed in battle, which became known as 'Waterloo teeth' or, more coyly, 'Waterloo ivory'. They would have been less happy to learn that many dentures were actually made from teeth plundered from English graveyards.

Bodysnatchers mainly sold bodies to anatomists for dissection, but they also sold teeth to dentists or surgeon-dentists. Even if a body was putrefying and no good for the anatomists, its teeth could still be taken. Joseph Naples, a former able seaman in the Royal Navy, recorded in a diary his gang's activities in London, which included sales of 'canines' (sets of teeth). After obtaining some corpses in November 1812, Naples noted that Jack, one of his gang, 'sold the canines to Mr. Thomson for 5 Guineas'.[72] According to Bransby Cooper, 'Every dentist in London would at that time purchase teeth from these men and the public can have but little idea of the immense sums of money which persons thus occupied could earn.'[73]

False teeth and trusses were not the only aids and accessories available. With amputations being the remedy for some injuries, wooden legs used with wooden crutches provided some mobility. Invalids, particularly at Bath, were carried about in sedan chairs, as well as in three- or four-wheeled 'Bath chairs' with folding hoods. Constructed by coachmakers, they could be manoeuvred by one person, rather than the two chairmen needed for sedan chairs. Benjamin Silliman noticed these chairs in Bath and described how 'infirm people are drawn about by servants, in little hand carriages, with three wheels; a pair of wheels is placed behind, in the usual manner, and the third beneath the middle of the carriage before [in front]; connected with this last there is a lever, passing to the hand of the invalid, who is thus enabled to steer the vehicle.'[74]

For those who were partially deaf, hearing trumpets could offer an effective solution, consisting of a flaring end and a long narrow tube that channelled sound when inserted into the ear. Problems with vision such as myopia could be corrected with spectacles, which had convex or concave glass lenses that were round in shape, though by the early 1800s an oval shape was preferred. The lenses were set in frames that were lodged on the nose or held in front of the eyes by means of a short handle (which might fold up and serve as a protective case). Other frames resembled the form of modern spectacles, with sides or arms that gripped the head. These were made from materials such as steel, silver, brass, whalebone, leather, horn and tortoiseshell.

Opticians stocked a range of lenses with different focal lengths, and clients picked the most suitable, at times choosing split lenses or 'double spectacles', an early form of bifocals.[75] A quizzing glass (or 'quizzer') was a single lens in a frame that was held in the hand by a handle. Magnifying glasses that folded into a case were similar, but were for close work such as reading. Opticians also made mirrors and anything else that needed glass, from tooth mirrors for dentists to linen smoothers for laundry. Some even offered framing services for prints. Like dentists, a few opticians moved between towns, such as G. Lyons who advertised in the *Hampshire Chronicle* in 1802:

### G. LYONS, OPTICIAN

RESPECTFULLY informs his numerous Friends he is arrived in Winchester with a large Assortment of SPECTACLES, to suit any Age or Sight; READING and OPERA GLASSES, TELESCOPES, MICROSCOPES, &c. &c. and being regularly Bred to the Science of

Optics, will, he trusts, be enabled to give entire Satisfaction. N.B.– G.L. will stay about a Fortnight, and will attend any Lady or Gentleman, being applied to at the Three Tuns Inn, Gaol-Street.[76]

The poor would not have been able to afford spectacles and so had to live with eye defects, while somebody like William Holland owned more than one pair. On New Year's Day 1809 he had to conduct an afternoon church service at Over Stowey, but found it too dark and gloomy to see clearly: 'I begun the service so late and the evenings now so short and the fogg so thick and dark, that I knew not how to make out my sermon. I had two spectacles with me and one magnified more than the other, so I very deliberately put up one and took out the other and then went on, and by that means got through.'[77]

People of all classes wore hats and therefore had some protection against the sun, but sunglasses with green or blue tinted lenses were available. Chronic contagious conjunctivitis of the eyes known as 'Egyptian ophthalmia' afflicted soldiers fighting the French in Egypt after Napoleon's invasion of 1798. It was brought back to England and transmitted to the civilian population, and William Darter recalled that in Reading and elsewhere in Berkshire 'we had many ... who were partially or wholly blind from opthalmia caught in the earlier war in Egypt. Some of these invalids from the East could be easily distinguished from others on account of their wearing green shades or coloured glasses.'[78] If left untreated, cataracts in the eye could also cause blindness, but some surgeons (oculists) carried out procedures to dislodge ('couch') or extract the affected lens.

With an inadequate understanding of the body, all surgery was risky. There were also no modern aids like blood transfusions and anaesthetics, although in the late 1790s the physician Thomas Beddoes and his assistant Humphry Davy tried out various gases on tuberculosis patients at the Pneumatic Institution in Hotwells, Bristol.[79] Nitrous oxide ('laughing gas') was found to relieve pain and cause sedation. 'As nitrous oxide in its extensive operation appears capable of destroying physical pain,' Davy wrote in 1800, 'it may probably be used with advantage during surgical operations in which no great effusion of blood takes place.'[80] Despite these findings, more than four decades would elapse before nitrous oxide was used in anaesthetics for surgery and dentistry.[81] Instead, patients were given alcohol or laudanum, their hands were tied together, and they were held down while the surgery was carried out. One of the keys to a successful operation was speed, otherwise the patient might die of shock or bleed to death.

Most types of surgery undertaken today were simply not attempted then, because infection could not be prevented, and survival rates were appallingly low. Surgery was limited mainly to the amputation of limbs, along with operations that were not too invasive, such as on cysts, some cancers, cataracts, strangulated hernias and bladder stones (by lithotomy). Although surgeons might strive after cleanliness, they did not realise that they were transmitting lethal bacteria from sources such as their instruments and dissected corpses. Surgery on private patients was done in their homes, a far safer environment than any hospital – wealthy people did not attend hospitals for any treatment whatsoever.

As well as seeing private patients, some surgeons held positions in hospitals. Many of these had been established as charities in towns and cities from the early eighteenth century and were funded through public subscriptions to provide free medical care for the deserving poor with injuries and ailments.[82] However, any hospital patient too ill to be cured was released, as were those with infectious diseases. When John Byng was in Northampton in 1793, he saw the town's brand-new hospital for the poor: 'Their new County Infirmary looks magnificently, let a foreigner travell England, and he must suppose it the land of disease and roguery; "What great building is that? That is an infirmary. What magnificent house is this? This is the county jail." Every poor man must wish himself in one, or the other.'[83]

Surgical operations in hospitals were undertaken either on the wards alongside other patients or in theatres, which were literally places of spectacle for students and visitors.[84] In 1771 the surgeon John Aikin wrote about the perils of hospitals and recommended amputation for complicated fractures: 'Every Surgeon attending a large and crowded hospital, knows the very great difficulty of curing a compound fracture in them. This is so universally acknowledged, that the most humane and judicious of them have been obliged to comply with that dreadful rule of practice, immediate amputation in every compound fracture.'[85] Because he had no idea of infection, Aikin thought that the 'malignancy of hospital air' was to blame, because he knew that such fractures could heal successfully at home and in rural hospitals.

Dr John Percival of Manchester gave some advice to Aikin on how to control 'the noxious effluvia which arise from so many distempered bodies, afflicted perhaps with mortifications, carious bones, malignant ulcers, or putrid fevers'.[86] His suggestions included washing hospital wards with vinegar and tar water, fumigating with the steam from boiling vinegar and tar, ventilating the bedclothes of patients who could sit up or walk about, and 'obliging the sick to conform strictly to the rules of nicety and cleanliness'.[87] He also recommended that patients should smoke tobacco:

> If any of them have been accustomed to smoaking, they should be allowed pipes and tobacco, when such an indulgence will not be injurious to them. The patients should have their linen very frequently renewed, and their shirts and sheets should be fumigated with frankincense, before they are used. The dressings of foul ulcers, &c. as soon as they are removed, should be thrown into vessels of vinegar, and carried out of the wards with all convenient expedition.[88]

For the poor, there were also charitable hospitals that provided specialist care, such as the lying-in hospitals for pregnant women and a few lock hospitals for venereal disease.[89] Eye hospitals were established as a direct result of the contagious ophthalmia brought back from Egypt, and the first one opened in 1805 in London (which is now the Moorfields Eye Hospital). Other specialist institutions included the lunatic asylum and madhouse, which imprisoned those regarded as insane, including sufferers from conditions like epilepsy, post-natal depression and dementia. Whatever their illness, they were often locked away as nobody knew what else to do. As Aikin said in 1771, 'besides their own sufferings, they are rendered a nuisance and terror to others; and are not only themselves lost to society, but take up the whole time and attention of others'.[90]

Private madhouses, some very small, were intended for patients whose families could afford to pay. Pauper lunatics might also be put in these private madhouses if their fees were paid by the parish, but more likely they were confined in poorhouses or workhouses, as described by Holland in Over Stowey:

> The man in the workhouse is chained and lies upon straw, shocking situation – Alas! poor human nature. How many afflictions art thou liable to ... Went to the messrs Riches this evening about the madman in the workhouse, both determined to join in sending him to the madhouse in Bristol, be the expense what it will. Eh, says James [Rich], Master Holland I reckon it be a bad business. He is a very bad fellow there is something in it more than madness I count. In short, James thinks ... that he is possessed by the Devil or bewitched.[91]

It was commonly believed that lunacy was due to evil or to an imbalance in the body's humours, for which William Ricketts, a surgeon who had run a madhouse at Droitwich in Worcestershire for twenty years, undertook purging:

> When a patient is brought ... I generally found depletion necessary, if the Lunatic is violent; I afterwards have him cupped; and the first thing I do is to empty the stomach and bowels by small doses of emetic tartar, or to purge them briskly with calomel ... I believe the disease to proceed most frequently from a derangement of the digestive organs ... In the majority of females between the ages of fourteen and forty, I think, it arises from a sexual cause.[92]

He was also convinced that too much hair was harmful: 'I conceive in all cases of excessive mania, there is too great a determination of blood to the head, and that the head ought to be kept as cool as possible, the head being loaded with hair, that must increase the heat.'[93]

Conditions in madhouses and asylums were often no better than those of prisons, though humane treatment and good intentions were evident, with a gradual shift from confinement towards cure and care. Even so, lunatics were commonly shackled or kept in straitjackets. Some charitable asylums existed, and the most famous institution was Bethlem ('Bedlam') Hospital at Moorfields, which accepted lunatics from the entire country. At Newcastle-upon-Tyne a charitable hospital for pauper lunatics was opened in 1767, but the 'chains, iron bars, and dungeon-like cells, presented to the unhappy inmates all the irritating and melancholy characteristics of a prison ... Many of the cells were close, dark, cold holes (less comfortable than cow-houses)'.[94] Its physician was Dr John Hall, and he also ran a private madhouse that claimed to offer humane treatment. One advertisement appeared in the *Newcastle Courant* in May 1774:

Dr Hall's Private House for Lunatics, Known by the Name of St LUKE's HOUSE. DIET, WASHING, and LODGING, for lunatics, at 20l. a year, or 8s. per week, or less where the circumstances of the patient require the expence to be made still more moderate. This house has been universally admired for its healthy, pleasant situation; as also its conveniences for the accommodation of boarders ... The greatest care will be taken of all Patients intrusted to him.[95]

In 1774 an Act for regulating private madhouses was passed, requiring them to hold a licence and for two doctors to sign a certificate, so as to stop wrongful confinement. In 1808 the County Asylum Act also allowed Justices of the Peace to levy a rate for the establishment of publicly funded asylums for pauper and criminal lunatics, in order to remove them from the workhouses.[96] After the General Lunatic Asylum opened in Nottingham in 1812, John Blackner congratulated those responsible, who 'very early saw the necessity of an asylum for the wandering, half lost, and sometimes wholly neglected maniacs ... These humane and praise-worthy gentlemen could not see their fellow creatures, clothed in rags, or half naked, when deprived of their reason, parading the streets, the sport of coxcombs and thoughtless boys, without being painfully struck with the sight.'[97] However, few new county lunatic asylums were built over the following decades.

A House of Commons Select Committee in 1816 revealed the dreadful conditions in licensed madhouses in England. William Ricketts of the Droitwich madhouse gave evidence of the gulf that existed between the rich and the poor, even in lunacy:

I think about one half [of about eighty-five inmates] are paupers ... I have accommodations according to the different classes; according to their pay; patients of a superior class pay, some four guineas a week, some three, some two and a half, some two, some a guinea, and fourteen shillings a week pauper Lunatics, except the town of Birmingham, they pay only ten shillings, and the major part of the pauper Lunatics are from the town of Birmingham ... we have different sitting rooms for the different classes ... the pauper Lunatics are taken out by my men-servants and work in the garden ... Patients of the superior orders amuse themselves at cards; some of them are musical; they have a piano-forte; one lady plays and sings most admirably.[98]

The previous year, 1815, a new Bethlem Hospital (now home to the Imperial War Museum) had opened at St George's Fields. Conditions were not ideal at this new building, and because Ricketts had seen this new hospital only the month before, the Select Committee cross-examined him: 'Do you remember that in the old gallery in Bethlem [at Moorfields] many of the patients were chained round a table on the left-hand side, almost in a state of nudity?—Yes, I do. There is nothing of that kind now?—No, they are better covered now. There are several patients in what is called the dirty room.'[99] Mrs Elizabeth Forbes, the matron in charge of female patients, was also questioned by the committee:

Do you consider the patients in the basement story to have suffered from the damp?—They have had bad colds, and have been rather unhealthy this winter.

Have you lost any patients in that story this winter?—Yes, Four ...

What were the circumstances of the four deaths which have taken place?—It was from cold.

What were their ages?—None of them were under forty; one was eighty years of age, the other three between forty and fifty.[100]

Many elderly people who were treated as lunatics probably had dementia, but most old people were obliged to work for as long as they could, rather than being rewarded with retirement: 'I met old John French on the road hard at work, tho' 83,' William Holland noted in his diary in April 1813.[101] State aid for the elderly consisted of relief given by the parish, which all too often meant going to live in the workhouse. In 1795 at Petersfield in Hampshire, Frederick Eden reported: '22 persons, (mostly old women and children,) are at present in the work-house: they are, principally, employed in cleansing the streets.'[102] Apart from the Chelsea Hospital, which supported some old soldiers ('Chelsea Pensioners'), and a similar Greenwich Hospital for old naval seamen, the workhouses and some charitable almshouses were the only institutions providing for the elderly.

Most workhouses were inadequate and badly run, and the poet George Crabbe bitterly condemned them in 'The Parish Workhouse' (part of his long poem *The Village*, published in 1783). He pointed out that people who were comfortably off had no idea of the deprivation and loss of pride, dignity and hope suffered by workhouse inmates. John Byng set down his own compassionate vision of an ideal place for the elderly to live:

As for the very aged, and helpless, I should revert to that good, old (now neglected,) Custom of Alms Houses ... therein I should place 12 of the most pitiable and deserving aged poor, with each their several slips of garden ground; where such as were able might employ themselves: before their doors, a shady walk of trees fronting the south, with some benches, would tempt forth the, not unhappy, lodgers, to bask in a summer's sun, or to endeavour at a winter's walk. Is not this a reasonable, a cheap, an heartfelt satisfaction?[103]

For elderly paupers, Crabbe wrote, their only escape from the work-house was death:

Up yonder hill, behold how sadly slow
The bier moves winding from the vale below;
There lie the happy dead, from trouble free,
And the glad parish pays the frugal [burial] fee.[104]

Whatever the cause of death – perhaps illness, childbirth, accident, old age or execution – it was not necessarily a case of resting in peace, particularly for the poor. In some parts of the country, especially those within convenient distance of a medical school, bodies were in danger of being stolen immediately after burial. Anatomists (who were usually surgeons) in the private medical schools and teaching hospitals were always desperate for corpses to dissect in front of students and for their own research. Not enough corpses could be acquired through legitimate means (only a few bodies of executed criminals), and the Government was reluctant to draw up a Bill for the proper provision of bodies, as happened on the Continent. Cadavers were therefore bought from bodysnatchers, and surgeons knew exactly what was happening. It was an abhorrent trade, but one without which medical advances would not have happened.

Some corpses were stolen from their coffins before burial, but most were robbed from graveyards soon after a funeral when the soil was loose and the body relatively fresh. Graverobbers, or bodysnatchers, chose dark nights, without the light of the moon, and their work was so skilled that graves would look undisturbed. Even where thefts were noticed, records of such crimes seldom survive. Pauper bodies were preferred, as their graves were more shallow. Because of decomposition and the overpowering stench, corpses were useless for the anatomists after a few days.

Bodies were sometimes shipped in casks to the capital from elsewhere in the country or else were sold to anatomists in places like Bristol and Manchester, but the heart of the trade was London – from October to May, when the private anatomy school classes were running. A satirical piece, published in the *Morning Post* newspaper at the start of the classes in October 1811, claimed to be the minutes of a general meeting of the guild of bodysnatchers who were worried about their profession:

At a general meeting of the Gentlemen in the *resurrection* line, vulgarly called *'body snatchers,'* *'dead carcase stealers,'* &c. held at their hall the *Bonehouse, Rotten-row*, in the parish of *St. Sepulchre, Gravesend*.

*Dick Drybones* in the chair,—it was resolved unanimously

1. That as anatomy is the end of *physic*, all those who contribute to the study and improvement of that noble science, are entitled to public support and the most liberal remuneration.

2. That of late certain persons not regularly brought up to the profession, have tried to introduce the practice of seizing dead bodies previous to their interment, to the great injury of the industrious members of this right worshipful fraternity.

3. That this assembly can view such conduct in no other light than as being illegal, and as a scandalous outrage of the rights and privileges of this community.

4. That persons concerned in such practices be forthwith scouted [scorned], unless they chuse to become regular members, paying the usual introductory gallon of gin, as also a forfeit of five shillings, to be spent in bread, cheese, and porter.

5. That in consequence of the effect of the Comet on the weather, they have been unable to commence their season in the present year, till the close of October.

6. That through the circumstances above stated, they are in such distress, they scarcely know how to keep *soul* and *body* together, and consequently feel it incumbent upon them to charge an extra guinea for every subject.[105]

The imaginary meeting also urged physicians not to increase the price of physic, or medicines. The logic of this statement was that knowing the harm caused by most medicines, if the amount taken by patients decreased, then the number of deaths would be fewer and the graverobbing business would suffer. These so-called minutes concluded: '(Signed) DICK DRYBONES, PAUL PUTRID, MAT MARROWLESS, KIT COFFIN, TOM TOMBSTONE,

VALENTINE VAULT, KICKUP RESURGAM, Secretary to the Meeting.'[106]

The graverobbing business was actually thriving. In his diary for the years 1811 and 1812, Joseph Naples recorded details of his gang's activities – taking orders from surgeons, raiding graveyards, delivering corpses and collecting payment. On 7 December 1811, a few weeks after the satirical piece in the *Morning Post*, Naples noted: 'At night went out & got 3 at Bunhill Row. 1 S$^t$ Thomas's, 2 Brookes'[107] – this meant that he had stolen three bodies from the dissenters' burial ground at Bunhill Fields or possibly the nearby Quaker burial ground, one of which was taken to St Thomas's Hospital for dissection, and two were sold to Joshua Brookes.

A month later, Naples wrote: 'At 2 A.M. got up, the Party went to Harps, got 4 adults and 1 small [child], took 4 to S$^t$ Thomas's. Came home, went to Mr. Wilson & Brookes. Dan$^l$ [Daniel] got paid £8 8 0 from Mr. Wilson, I recd. 9 9 0 from Mr. Brookes. Came over to the borough [Southwark], sold small for £1 10 0, Rec$^d$ £4 4 0 for adult. At home all night.'[108] James Wilson taught anatomy at the Great Windmill Street Anatomy School, which he had founded, and Joshua Brookes ran another anatomy school on Great Marlborough Street, which he advertised in newspapers across England, as in the *Leicester Journal* in January 1812:

THEATRE OF ANATOMY.
BLENHEIM-STREET, GREAT MARLBOROUGH-STREET.

The Spring course of Lectures on Anatomy,
Physiology, and Surgery, will be commenced on
Monday, the 20th of January, at 2 o'clock,

By Mr. BROOKES ... Spacious apartments thoroughly ventilated, and replete with every convenience, are open all the morning, for the purposes of dissecting and injecting, where Mr. Brookes attends to direct the students, and demonstrates the various parts as they appear on dissection ... Gentlemen established in practice desirous of renewing their anatomical knowledge, may be accommodated with an apartment to dissect in privately.[109]

Some of the London corpses were even packed up and sent to Edinburgh for dissection in the medical schools there, and on 5 December that same year Naples recorded: 'packing up for Edinboro, sent 12 to the wharf for the above place, at home all night'.[110] This was more than a decade before the infamous Burke and Hare murders would supply the anatomists in Edinburgh with bodies. It was only in 1832 that the Anatomy Act was passed to provide an adequate, legal source of cadavers for dissection.

# TWELVE

———— ·◆· ————

# LAST WORDS

Everybody had a degree of gravity and sorrow; tenderness towards the departed, solicitude for the surviving friends; and, in a reasonable time, curiosity to know where she would be buried.

*Emma*, by Jane Austen

The service for the burial of the dead in the Church of England prayer book contains the line 'In the midst of life we are in death',[1] and this was the everyday experience of Jane Austen's contemporaries, especially when sudden, unexplained deaths occurred. In May 1793 Parson Woodforde was shocked to hear bad news from a friend:

Recd. a note this morning from Mr. Wright of Mattishall informing us of the death of his wife and requesting my attendance at her funeral ... It much surprised us as we did not hear that she had been ill at all – it was indeed very suddenly on Monday night last after eating a very hearty supper and apparently very well – but going to bed about 10. o'clock, after she got into her chamber and sitting down on a chair, her maid Judith perceived her mistress suddenly to change in her countenance and immediately fall into a fit ... in less than half an hour after she was dead, and great was the uneasiness and distress of the family on the occasion and at such a time of night. Mr. and Mrs. Bodham immediately on notice went thither – but found their sister dead. It shocked them much.[2]

Most deaths that did not result from a recognisable illness were assumed to be the natural close of 'old age'. For those who survived childhood and for women who survived childbirth, there was every chance of living to beyond seventy years of age, and William Holland was perplexed by the distraught behaviour of one of his parishioners: 'Old Kibby who was buried this day was 83 and yet his sister cried and seem'd half distracted. I could not forbear observing that she could not expect him to live for ever and therefore she might moderate her grief.'[3] The question of life expectancy interested John Byng, and at Towcester in Northamptonshire in 1789 he was pleased to learn about one elderly man from a nearby village:

In all my walks and of all the clerks, who have shewn me churches, (and I have seen some few) I have allways asked, from hope and curiosity, 'Have you any person of remarkable old age in your town?' The answer being, for ever, no, has terrify'd me: but tonight, reading this in the county paper, had rather comforted me:–
 'April 27th, 1789, Mr James French, of Fritwell, 90 years of age, walked from thence through Aynho to Banbury before breakfast, being about nine miles. He appears remarkably healthy for his age, has a fine bloom on his countenance, enjoys a good appetite, and seems likely to live many years. He ... was for a good part of his life a servant in the Mr Child's family ... by whom his faithful service is rewarded with an annuity of 20£ during life. Not long since he walked to London in three days, and there, amidst the multitude observed, that he could not find an old man. He eats but two meals a day, and never drinks any strong liquors, nor very often ale, but generally mixed beer.'[4]

Byng was an impoverished aristocrat who well understood that life expectancy depended on a person's wealth and way of life. At Sibsey in Lincolnshire two years later, he commented: 'walking about the churchyard, and reading the grave stone epitaphs, made me to remark that poor people died early, for they must work when ill; ... it is the rich man who lives longest, who has every comfort, a nice bed, and physicians at hand: look into the mausoleums of the great, and you'll find that they outlive the parish.'[5]

This was of course a generalisation, because although Jane Austen was moderately well-off, like so many others she succumbed to an illness that could not be cured or even accurately identified.[6] She was only forty-one years old when she died in the arms of her sister Cassandra – at Winchester on 18 July 1817. A few days later Cassandra was able to write to friends and relatives about Jane's final moments:

> She felt herself to be dying about half-an-hour before she became tranquil and apparently unconscious. During that half-hour was her struggle, poor soul! She said she could not tell us what she suffered, though she complained of little fixed pain. When I asked her if there was anything she wanted, her answer was she wanted nothing but death, and some of her words were: 'God grant me patience, pray for me, oh pray for me!' Her voice was affected, but as long as she spoke she was intelligible.[7]

Most people, like Jane Austen, firmly believed in an afterlife, but the quality of that afterlife was thought to depend on how well someone had adhered to religion and how moral they had been during their lifetime. The duties of Church of England clergymen included trying to convert those who had no religion, as well as visiting the sick. A few weeks before Jane's death, William Holland visited one of his poor Somerset parishioners:

> under the Quantock hill I found old ... [Thomas] Ware and his wife. He dying, he is past four score and has been a hard working man, this is his second wife, they formerly lived in the poor house. He scarce knows what religion means yet I have brought him to church at times. He lead in his younger days a reprobate kind of life, a mixture of immorality, irreligion and oddity there. He lay in his bed in a most miserable cottage or hut near the fire with pieces of linen wrapt round his head and much flushed in the face as if in a fever.[8]

Ware asked, 'Have you seen my flowers?', and Holland promised to look at them, later commenting: 'He was always fond of gardening and what he pursued all his life time continued till death for he died the next day. A few polyanthus he had but not worth much anxiety of mind during his last moments.'[9]

Parson Woodforde frequently recorded deaths in his own diary and added wishes for their afterlife, such as 'I hope he is happy' for a boy who had drowned in a clay pit.[10] Holland shared this attitude, as shown by his description of one funeral: 'After the service I walked up to the grave to view the coffin and saw his age [on the coffin plate] 72. Poor Ben said I, and turning round to the people, This man has been a good and pious man. Let us endeavour to imitate him, for he is now in a state of happiness. Yes answered someone, I hope he is now happy. No doubt of it returned I, for he was a pious inoffensive man.'[11]

This was the professional stance of the clergyman, but clerics could be just as much affected by deaths within their own family. William Holland had suffered his own terrible tragedy, with four of his five young children dying of scarlet fever in the space of two weeks in 1795.[12] Only his daughter Margaret was spared, and another son, William, was born later on, in 1797.

The lives of the lower classes were generally so wretched that cler-gymen felt a person's death was to be welcomed as a gateway to a better afterlife, although sometimes their own faith was shaken. The prolonged suffering of a young girl with tuberculosis led Holland to observe: 'we do not in general (whatever their wickedness may have been) find always that the misery and sufferings of this world bears a proportion to the magnitude of man's sins ... On the whole there is so much suffering in this world that I trust the next will be a world of happiness.'[13] He clearly recognised society's evils, yet was firmly against change and often railed against 'democrats' who wanted to improve society.[14] To him, justice would only come in the afterlife.

When someone died, the burial took place shortly afterwards, usually within three or four days, because it was difficult to slow down the decomposition of a corpse, particularly in warm summer months, though not everybody appreciated this necessity. In the summer of 1810, seven years before Thomas Ware died, he and his wife lost a child, and Holland had noted: 'Mrs Ware ... came here about burying her child on Sunday next. She has kept the child already above a week, this very sultry weather. I told her that I insisted on bringing the child immediately. She answered she would bring it tomorrow. I told her she had no right to keep the child so long, to keep the dead to destroy the living.'[15]

For this reason, and because of the expense of transporting a corpse, most people were buried in the parish in which they died. If they died far from where they lived, the possibility of being buried in their own parish was not even considered, though when Woodforde was in Somerset in 1772, he recorded the unusual circumstance of a funeral for a boy who died outside the parish: 'I . . . buried a child of Giles Francis by the name J. Francis – aged 5 years. The child died at Bath owing to a kick in the groin by another lad. Giles works at Bath and he and his son brought the child in a coffin upon their heads from Bath, they set out from Bath last night at 12.'[16]

The very wealthy proved the exception, because they could afford to transport their dead relatives to be buried in the family vault or burial plot, even if they had died abroad. In November 1810 Holland recorded that the body of one of the Acland family had come back to England: 'He is brought I understand in a pipe of Madeira [wine] to preserve him through the voyage, the usual mode they tell me there being no lead coffin to be obtained.'[17] This was a son of John Acland, the main landowner in the area, of whom Holland was not overly fond. 'Mr. Acland has now lost six children,' he commented, 'and one only remains to preserve the family name if God preserve his life too. Their wealth is immense but what is wealth alone, it cannot keep them from the grave.'[18]

People were informed about a death as fast as possible in case they wanted to attend the funeral, and letters were sent to distant relatives. The etiquette was to use black wax instead of the usual red for the seal, so that people were warned of bad news before even opening the letter. On Christmas Eve 1792 Woodforde received two letters: 'One letter was for me from my niece Pounsett sealed with black, which at first alarmed me but on my opening the letter found it was owing to the late death of Mrs. Donne of Bath, who had left a legacy of 100 pound to her.'[19]

### KING's THEATRE.

TO-MORROW will be performed the favourite Comic Opera, called, IL FORBO CONTRO IL FORBO. In which Madame Catalani will perform the principal Character. End of the Opera (2d time), a new grand Indian Ballet, called CONSTANCE ET ALMOZOR, composed by Mr. D'Egville, with entire new Scenery, Dresses and Decorations; the Music by F. Venua.

On Tuesday, May 31, will be produced a New Comic Opera, called, Le Virtuose in Pugtiglio; in which Signior Miartini will make his first appearance on this stage, and in which Madame Catalani will perform the principal character.

---

### Mr. JOHNSTONE's NIGHT.
### THEATRE-ROYAL, DRURY-LANE.

THIS EVENING, FALSE ALARMS; in which will be introduced the following Songs: ' Should e'er I brave the foaming Seas.' ' A Smile and a Tear;' and ' Smiling Kate.' End of the Play, the favourite Comic Interlude of SYLVESTER DAGGERWOOD; Sylvester Daggerwood, Mr. Bannister, with a new Comic Song, called ' The Tragedy of Othello, or fine Fleecy Hosiery.' To which will be added (first time), compressed into two Acts, a Musical Comedy, which will open with a Grand Masquerade, in which will be introduced a Shawl Dance, by Miss Gayton; and a new Allemande and Waltz, by Mr. D'Egville's pupils, called the IRISH MAN IN ITALY. O'Rafarty, by Mr. Johnstone; who will introduce the following Songs: ' O'Rafarty's Christening,' ' A Chapter on Pockets, ' The Bold Dragoon,' and ' Paddy Shannon's Courtship, or the Cruel Widow Wilkins.'

Performances at theatres in London advertised in *The Times* newspaper for 23 May 1808.

A state lottery ticket sold in 1808, a one-sixteenth share. The lottery was drawn from 20 October 1809.

The latest catalogue of Lackington's bookseller in London being advertised in the *St James Chronicle* newspaper on 19 June 1817.

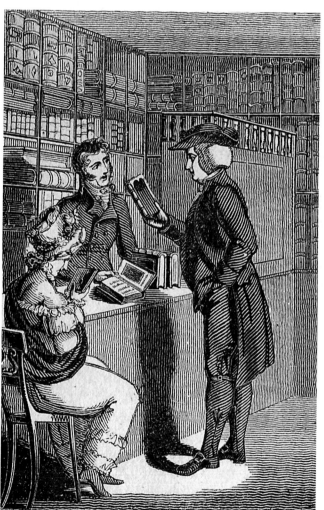

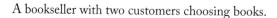

A bookseller with two customers choosing books.

Obverse and reverse of a halfpenny token issued in 1795 by Lackington's bookseller in Finsbury Square, London. The obverse had a portrait of James Lackington while the reverse claimed to be the 'Cheapest Booksellers in the World'. Lackington's issued vast quantities of tokens (about 700,000) in 1794–5, during the first two years of moving to their larger premises.

A view of Hotwells spa, near Bristol, in 1801. The spa was at the foot of the cliffs overlooking the River Avon, where hot springs were located.

Front page of the *Morning Chronicle* newspaper for 24 October 1807, with numerous advertisements, typical of newspapers at that time.

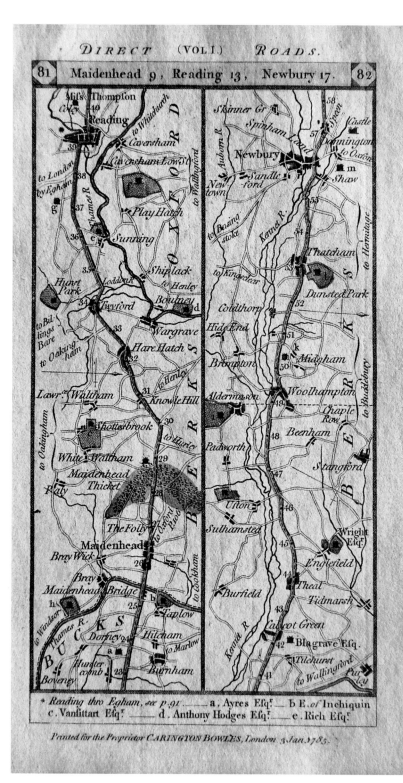

A road map of January 1785 showing the route from Newbury eastwards to Woolhampton, Theale, Reading, Hare Hatch (where the Leigh-Perrots lived) and Maidenhead, along the Bath road from London,

William Tomlins, a crossing sweeper and beggar. His stand was on Piccadilly in London, between Albemarle and St James's Streets.

A coachmaker constructing a post-chaise.

A woman being burned at the stake, used to illustrate the chapbook recounting the execution of Christian Bowman in March 1789 for counterfeiting coins.

An apothecary (or druggist) making his own medicines.

## CHING'S WORM LOZENGES.

WORMS are allowed to be the most frequent sources of Children's Diseases; their symptoms every Parent should be acquainted with. They occasion Loss of Appetite, a Paleness of the Face, Emaciation, and an irregular state of Bowels, attended with violent Pains; they bring on Convulsions, affect the growth of the Body, and often prove fatal by ending in a Consumption or Decay. Both as a Preventative and Cure for these alarming Complaints, the above excellent Medicine is allowed, on the testimony of some of the highest Characters in this Country, to have no equal; and their Public Approbation, given to the Proprietor, from a personal knowledge of its Efficacy in their own Families, stamps its merit beyond competition, and gives a sanction to it which no other Medicine of the kind can boast.

Sold in packets, at 1s. 1½d.; and boxes, at 2s. 9d. and 5s. 6d.; (by appointment) by R. Butler and Sons, Chemists, No. 4, Cheapside, corner of St. Paul's Church-yard; and by the principal Booksellers and Druggists in the Kingdom.

Ching's Worm Lozenges advertised in the *St James Chronicle* newspaper for 19 June 1817, claiming to cure and prevent intestinal worms.

A beggar with a wooden leg and crutches, then a common sight in England, especially with injured soldiers and sailors returning from the wars.

Newcastle's charitable infirmary depicted in 1789. It was constructed in 1751 on Forth Banks and was extended in 1803. The building was demolished in the 1950s.

No. 8 College Street in Winchester, Hampshire, where Jane Austen died on 18 July 1817.

The memorial tablet to the Reverend ('Parson') James Woodforde inside All Saints church, Weston Longville, Norfolk. It was erected by his nephew Bill and niece Nancy.

The cathedral at Winchester in 1809, where Jane Austen was buried in 1817 beneath the floor of the north aisle of the nave.

The usual reason for delaying a burial was that there were suspicions about the cause of death. Such cases were referred to the coroner, who might decide to hold an inquest, with a jury. 'A burial this morning, but the Coroner first is to have sight of the corpse,' Holland noted in December 1799. 'How this comes about or what suspicions there are I cannot tell.'[20] A few months earlier, Silvester Treleaven in Devon had noted: 'A young woman of Bridford [a village 8 miles south-west of Exeter] called Potter apprehended on suspicion of her having had child and destroyed it.'[21] She revealed where the baby boy was buried, in a wood 3 miles away, and the next day a coroner's inquest was held at Bridford: 'Coroner – Hugo Gent. Mr Ponsford Surgeon attended and dissected the body, from whose deposition, and from a chain of circumstances, it evidently appeared that the child was strangled. The jury returned a verdict of murder by the hand of the mother.'[22]

Woodforde also encountered suspicious or sudden deaths, recording one instance in September 1790:

The young woman Spincks (who lately had a bastard child by one Garthon of Norwich) called on me this morning to acquaint me that her child is dead, died last night, owing it is supposed to her [having] given him a sleeping pill which she had of her neighbour Nobbs whose husband is very ill and had some composing pills ... one of which Nobbs wife advised her to give her child to put him to sleep whilst she was out. The child slept for about 5 hours, then he waked and fell into convulsion fits which continued for 4 hours and half and then died in great agonies.[23]

Two days later he wrote: 'few farmers at Church this afternoon on account of an inquest being taken by a Coroner from Norwich on the body of Eliz. Spincks boy. They were from 1 till near 5 on the above business. The jury brought in their verdict – not intentionally given by the mother to her child. This evening between 6 and 7, I buried the child (by name Garthon Spincks) in the churchyard.'[24]

If the coroner was a physician, he might conduct the post-mortem examination himself, but otherwise a medical practitioner could be called in to examine or even dissect the body. When the Prime

Minister, the Marquis of Rockingham, died suddenly in 1782, his body was dissected by the eminent surgeon John Hunter, not because murder was suspected, but through a desire to know the cause of death. Subsequently, thorough post-mortem examinations were gradually accepted by the upper classes, but not yet by the masses.

Usually, the corpse was kept at home in an open coffin until the funeral, so that relatives could say farewell to the deceased, and in October 1808 when Jane Austen was informed of the sudden death of Elizabeth, wife of her brother Edward, she wrote to Cassandra: 'I suppose you see the corpse? How does it appear?'[25] When Neast Grevile Prideaux, an articled law clerk at Ilchester in Somerset, learned that his aunt had died, he hurriedly travelled to Bristol, but was too late: 'I had pleased myself, with the hope that, ere my departed relative was conveyed to the tomb, I should have had a last look at her in her coffin. But this melancholy pleasure I could not enjoy for in such a putrid state was the body, that ... it was closed up before my arrival a day or two.'[26]

It was customary for someone to sit with the corpse day and night, something that was not just a spiritual vigil, but might be of practical benefit, as Nelly Weeton discovered at Dove Nest when the body of her pupil, who had died in a fire, was awaiting burial: 'The house is so remarkably infested with rats, that whilst the body remained in it, people were obliged to sit constantly in the room, night and day, lest the body should be injured by them.'[27] The preservation of bodies by embalming started to become popular during the eighteenth century, something that was brought to wider public attention when ancient Egyptian mummies began to be shipped to western Europe, but the expense of the process ruled it out for most people.

Nonconformists such as Quakers and Baptists might choose to be buried in one of the growing number of dissenters' burial grounds, but most people were buried in churchyards. *Everyone* was buried – there was no cremation in England at this time. The only bodies that might not be buried were those of executed criminals, which could be dissected by anatomists or hung on a gibbet as a warning. Sometimes they were buried in unconsecrated ground, but unlike the bodies of suicides, there was rarely any ritual to stop their ghosts from haunting the living.

While the wealthy had ostentatious funerals and elaborate tomb monuments, paupers were buried in unmarked graves, and the parish authorities paid the cost of burial – and sometimes the cost of a priest to lead a service over the corpse. In the Lake District a pauper burial was witnessed by Dorothy Wordsworth in September 1800:

> About 10 men and 4 women. Bread, cheese and ale [for the mourners]. They talked sensibly and cheerfully about common things. The dead person, 56 years of age, buried by the parish. The coffin was neatly lettered and painted black and covered with a decent cloth. They set the corpse down at the door and, while we stood within the threshold, the men with their hats off, sang, with decent and solemn countenances a verse of a funeral psalm. The corpse was then born down the hill, and they sang till they had passed the Town-End. I was affected to tears while we stood in the house, the coffin lying before me. There were no near kindred, no children ... When we came to the bridge they began to sing again and stopped ... before they entered the churchyard.[28]

Holland reflected on one pauper's funeral that was paid for by a relative: 'They brought a corps from Spaxton a pauper and yet it is astonishing what a number of people attended, the brother ... was at the expence, which indeed was generous, the coffin was very handsome indeed.'[29] For working-class people who could afford regular contributions, many places had burial clubs that operated as friendly societies. Contributions to the club were used to fund the funeral costs of any members who died, and the club provided a group of similarly minded people who could support each other in difficult times. Poor people were starting to imitate the more costly and ostentatious funerals of the upper classes, and Frederick Eden commented on Anne Hurst of Witley in Surrey, a poor farm labourer's wife, who wanted to give her husband a respectable burial:

> people in affluence thought her haughty; and the Paupers of the parish, seeing, as they could not help seeing, that her life was a reproach to

theirs, aggravated [exaggerated] all her little failings. Yet, the worst thing they had to say of her was, that she was proud; which, they said, was manifested by the manner in which she buried her husband. Resolute, as she owned she was, to have the funeral, and everything that related to it, what she called decent, nothing could dissuade her from having handles to his coffin, and a plate on it, mentioning his age.[30]

Even for poor people funerals in rural communities were solemn, respectful ceremonies, but they might be more rushed in towns and cities, especially London, as Carl Moritz observed in 1782:

A few dirty-looking men, who bear the coffin, endeavour to make their way through the crowd as well as they can, and some mourners follow. The people seem to pay as little serious attention to such a procession as if a hay cart were driving past. The funerals of people of distinction are, however, differently regarded. These funerals always appear to me the more indecent in a populous city, from the total indifference of the beholders, and the perfect unconcern with which they are beheld. The body of a fellow-creature is carried to his long home, as though it had been utterly unconnected with the rest of mankind. Whereas, in a small town or village, every one knows every one, and no one can be so insignificant as not to be missed when he is taken away.[31]

Particularly in the countryside, local funeral customs might seem strange to outsiders. In parts of northern England, according to William Wordsworth, 'a bason full of Sprigs of Box-wood is placed at the door of the house from which the Coffin is taken up, and each person who attends the funeral ordinarily takes a Sprig of this Box-wood, and throws it into the grave of the deceased'.[32] At Porlock in Somerset, the traveller and writer Richard Ayton witnessed a quite different custom:

Before the procession moved to the church all the mourners met before the house of the deceased, and there chanted a hymn, assisted by a most incongruous accompaniment from the belfry, in which a merry and vigorous peal was ringing the whole time. The sobs and cries and singing of the people, heard only at intervals, and indistinctly, through the deafening clangor of the bells, had a strange and most mournful effect.[33]

Ayton initially assumed this was a special kind of funeral, but was informed that it 'was and had always been considered as a simple part of the ceremony'.[34]

For the middle classes funerals could be quite elaborate events, already showing signs of being the displays of status and wealth that would be common in the later nineteenth century. When Catherine Howes (wife of the Reverend George Howes) died in February 1782, Parson Woodforde was impressed by her funeral at Hockering in Norfolk: 'Before we went to Church there was chocolate and toast and cake with red wine and white. At half past 11 o'clock we went to Church with the corpse in the following procession – The corpse first in an hearse and pair of horses, then followed the chaises'.[35] There were six chaises in all, carrying family, fellow clergymen, the undertaker and 'Mrs Howes two servant maid[s] in deep mourning'.[36] At the rear, on foot, 'servants all in hatbands black closed the procession and a handsome appearance the whole procession made'.[37] Woodforde had himself conducted many funerals, and in his view this 'was as decent, neat, handsome funeral as I ever saw and every thing conducted in the best manner … After our return from Church we had cake and wine and chocolate and dried toast carried round.'[38]

Whatever the status of the dead person, funerals largely conformed to a basic pattern. The coffin was carried from the deceased's home to the churchyard – in a carriage, on the shoulders of pall bearers or on a special wooden frame called a bier, sometimes supported on wheels. Moritz noticed that the coffins were different from those in his native Germany: 'The English coffins are made very economically, according to the exact form of the body; they are flat and broad at top, tapering gradually from the middle, and drawing to a point at the feet, not very unlike the case of a violin.'[39]

Funerals were usually heralded by tolling a bell, which was often regarded as an integral part of the ceremony. When asked if a bell could be sounded for the burial of an unbaptised child, Woodforde refused, saying that 'as the funeral service could not be read over it, the tolling of the bell at any time [was] to be inadmissible'.[40] Being unbaptised, the baby was denied a Christian funeral, and its burial could not even be marked by a funeral bell. Before lightning conductors were properly understood, bell ringing, a seemingly mundane occupation, could actually be dangerous. One particular stormy day in June 1782, Woodforde was shocked to hear that 'there were 3 men struck down in Pilton Church [in Somerset] by the lightning this morning – one of them killed instantly, but the others like to recover. The man that was struck dead was tolling a bell for a person lately dead, the other two were near him.'[41]

When the coffin arrived at the churchyard, it was customary for the priest to meet the funeral procession at the entrance. Many churchyards had a lich-gate where mourners could wait until the clergyman arrived. These lich-gates (or lych-gates, literally 'corpse-gates' from 'lych' or 'lich', an Old English word for 'corpse') often had some means of resting the coffin and sometimes seats for the pall bearers and a roof to shelter them from the weather. After a service inside the church, the burial service was carried out at the side of the grave, which had been dug earlier, but the ceremony did not always proceed smoothly. On one occasion Woodforde was irritated by the carelessness of his clerk: 'I buried poor Miss Rose this evening at Weston aged 20 years. It was a very pretty, decent funeral. But Js. Smith the Clerk made me wait in performing the office at the grave near a qr of an hour, the grave not being long enough a good deal. It was a very great interruption. I gave it to Js. afterwards.'[42] At another funeral, this time of a young man, a different problem occurred: 'as they were about to let the corpse into the grave one of the leathern straps gave way by the thread with which it was joined being quite decayed, but luckily it slipped before the corpse was moved far from the ground. A rope was then sent for to a neighbouring House with which it was safely deposited in the ground.'[43]

After the funeral, one widely observed custom was the distribution of mourning mementos, or 'favours', to the main people involved. When Woodforde attended the funeral of an old friend, 'We each of us had a rich black silk scarf [usually tied on as an armband] and hatband, and a pr. of beaver gloves.'[44] The servant accompanying him was also given a silk hatband and a pair of gloves – servants were expected to observe the same mourning as their employers.

These favours were a diplomatic part of the etiquette, and when a friend who died was buried in a neighbouring parish, the Reverend William Holland was initially offended. But the next day the family of the deceased made amends by sending him 'a very handsome sattin hatband and scarf, white and two pair of white gloves, one for my wife as well as one for myself. I expected a hatband, but not a scarf, and it is not the value of it either I regard so much as the intimation of respect it conveys.'[45] The following Sunday Holland conducted a service at a distant church and then officiated at his own church in Over Stowey, 'which was tolerably full and a great appearance there was of hatbands, and all white, and my own sattin scarf white also ... looked quite conspicuous'.[46] He particularly mentioned that the funeral favours were white, because this was unusual. Black was always the traditional mourning colour, but white could be used for people thought to be innocent in the sight of God, usually children and young unmarried women. In this instance it was a young man who had been buried, and Holland stressed that 'He was a well disposed young man ... of great moral integrity, and uprightness and sincerity of heart.'[47]

The actual place of burial depended on social status, and the most sought-after place was inside the church, either in the ground under the floor or sometimes in a family vault. If it was not possible to have a vault inside the church, a wealthy family might have one built close by in the churchyard. Doors or hatchways provided access to some vaults, and at his aunt's funeral in Bristol, Neast Prideaux remarked: 'When the coffin was put into the vault, I looked in, and saw my late sister's coffin, which was perfectly entire.'[48]

In Woodforde's parish of Weston Longville, the privilege of burial inside the church was assumed by the local squire Mr Custance and his family, and in November 1780 Woodforde buried their infant Edward Custance, just fifty-two days old: 'Neither Mr. nor Mrs. Custance there. The coffin was lead with a copper breast plate on it and on that was engraved the age and name of the child. The breastplate was plain and made thus ◊. The child was buried in the chancel in the north aile.'[49]

These gradations of status were satirised on a gravestone set by the door to the chancel of St Edmund's Church at Kingsbridge in Devon, which carries the inscription:

UNDERNEATH
Lieth the Body of ROBERT
Comonly called BONE PHILLIP,
who died July 27th, 1793,
Aged 63 years,
At whose request the following lines are here inserted.
Here lie I at the Chancel door;
Here lie I because I'm poor;
The forther in the more you'll pay;
Here lie I as warm as they.[50]

It was not just a simple matter of being buried inside or outside the church, since different parts of the churchyard were more desirable than others. On a gravestone dated 1807 at the Church of St Andrews at Epworth in Lincolnshire, the inscription included the lines:

And that I might longer undisturbed abide,
I choosed to be laid on this Northern side.[51]

There was a reluctance to be buried on the north side of the church, which many people considered was for strangers, unbaptised infants, the poor and those suspected of suicide. In some places, there was also a superstitious dread of being buried on the north side, probably made worse by the fact that such graves were in the shadow of the church and away from the main paths leading to the west and south doors. At the Church of St Mary in Selborne, Hampshire, the curate Gilbert White expressed his concern:

all wish to be buried on the south side, which is becoming such a mass of mortality that no person can be interred there without disturbing or displacing the bones of his ancestors ... At the east end are a few graves; yet none till very lately on the north-side but, as two or three families of best repute have begun to bury in that quarter, prejudice may wear out by degrees, and their example be followed by the rest of the neighbour-hood.[52]

White himself was buried in 1793 on the north side of the church at Selborne, with a simple headstone giving his initials and date of death.

In large cities and towns with growing populations, and particularly in London, entire churchyards were becoming crammed full with burials. However, the situation had not yet reached the level of dire overcrowding that would lead to large new cemeteries being established in the mid-nineteenth century.

Burials were recorded in parish registers, and often the entry simply consisted of the name of the deceased, some indication of where they were living when they died and the burial date (not the date of death). Ever since the Burial in Woollen Acts of 1666–80, registers were also supposed to record whether a sworn affidavit had confirmed that the dead person was buried in a woollen shroud. In November 1783 Parson Woodforde recorded that he had received a shilling fee for providing 'a Certificate of Persons being buried in Woolen at Hockering according to the Act'.[53] Such a certificate ensured that the person responsible for the burial was not liable to pay the £5 fine for not burying a person in wool. The law had been designed to promote the English woollen industry, but by Woodforde's time it was already widely ignored, and the law was repealed in 1814.

After a funeral, the period of mourning continued, but the social code was not so rigid as it would become in the Victorian era. As in later decades, the time that women, particularly widows, spent in mourning was longer than for men, and their mourning dress was more conspicuous. Although there were variations between different places, between social classes and even within families, it was common for widows and close female relatives to stay in mourning for at least a year. If someone died suddenly, people might be unprepared and have no suitable clothes. Some black clothes might be quickly obtained for the funeral, but the weeks and months of mourning afterwards required a full wardrobe.

Having had to go into mourning with the family employing her at Dove Nest, Nelly Weeton asked a friend to forward her some clothes: 'Little expecting to wear black so soon after I left you, I brought nothing of the kind with me; and there are several things which might be worn to save better [ones]. What I have now is too good for every day.'[54] She asked for a parcel of her old clothes to be sent, including 'a black Chambray gown, a silk petticoat, a cambric muslin petticoat ... some black lace net, wrapped in a piece of black mode, and a black silk work bag with some crape'.[55]

When Cassandra Austen was with her brother Edward in October 1808, she found herself in a similar predicament on the sudden death of his wife Elizabeth. Jane therefore wrote to her:

> Your parcel shall set off on Monday, and I hope the shoes will fit; Martha and I both tried them on. I shall send you such of your mourning as I think most likely to be useful, reserving for myself your stockings and half the velvet, in which selfish arrangement I know I am doing what you wish. *I* am to be in bombazeen and crape, according to what we are told is universal *here*, and which agrees with Martha's previous observation. My mourning, however, will not impoverish me, for by having my velvet pelisse fresh lined and made up, I am sure I shall have no occasion *this winter* for anything new of that sort.[56]

The fact that Jane and Martha had discussed the correct mourning dress demonstrates how variable social etiquette was at this time. After being in full black mourning for a year or more, a woman might go into half-mourning, with less sombre clothes or a mixture of white and black. Men seldom went to such extremes. They generally wore dark-coloured clothes anyway, to which a black hatband and armband could be added. They also wore their mourning for shorter periods and were less likely to be censured for flouting such social conventions. In any case, mourning etiquette was largely for those who could afford to follow fashion – and fashion was set by the wealthy. The middle classes tried to follow their example, while the working classes made do with armbands, hatbands and whatever else they could afford. Servants might have mourning clothes provided for a bereavement in their employer's family, but not for a death in their own family.

When members of the royal family died, a time of national mourning was announced and the whole nation (being subjects of the monarch, rather than citizens of a state) was expected to respond. Because of the sudden overwhelming demand for black fabrics and the corresponding slump in the sale of most other colours, periods of national mourning frequently disrupted the textile industry. Sometimes, though, the response was less than zealous, and when the Duke of Gloucester died in 1805, Jane Austen wrote to Cassandra: 'I suppose everybody will be black for the D. of G. Must we buy lace, or will ribbon do?'[57] Yet when the popular Princess Charlotte died in childbirth in November 1817, a few months after Jane's death, genuine public grief was evident as William Darter recalled:

> the lamented death of the Princess Charlotte occurred at the age of 22, leaving a husband (Prince Leopold) and the whole nation in deep sorrow. No public event in my time ever produced such a universal union of spontaneous sympathy. All business was suspended and shops closed; blinds were drawn down to the windows of private houses, and even the poorest of the poor wore some humble token of sympathy.[58]

Before the period of mourning was well under way, but usually after the funeral, the will of the dead person was read, proven and executed. For anyone with any wealth to bequeath, however small, a will was essential. Jane Austen left a simple will, bequeathing to her sister most of her estate:

> I JANE AUSTEN of the Parish of Chawton do by this my last Will and testament give and bequeath to my dearest sister Cassandra Eliz'th every thing of which I may die possessed or which may hereafter be due to me subject to the payment of my funeral expenses and to a legacy of £50 to my brother Henry and £50 to Mde Bijion which I request may be paid as soon as convenient and I appoint my said dear sister EXECUTRIX of this my last Will and testament JANE AUSTEN April 27; 1817.[59]

As executrix, Cassandra distributed a few personal items among relatives and close friends, including some of her sister's hair. It was common to cut hair from a dead person as a memento, which was often put into a locket or incorporated into mourning jewellery such as a ring or a brooch.

Wills were crucial in ensuring that wealth was kept within the family and that the estate passed intact to the eldest son or another male relative. This situation is a frequent feature of Jane Austen's novels and drives the plot in *Pride and Prejudice* – although Mr Bennet owns a modest estate and has enough to keep his family comfortably, he has five daughters and no son. The terms under which he himself inherited the estate ensure that without a male heir, it will pass to his next male relative – the unpleasant Mr Collins. Mr Bennet's family could therefore be left destitute. Mrs Bennet and her daughters would never be able to find occupations to support themselves and so would be dependent on charity from relatives.

All this unspoken anxiety, resulting from middle-class attempts to maintain their position in society, is behind Mrs Bennet's hysterical outbursts. On hearing that Mr Collins is engaged to Charlotte Lucas, Mrs Bennet is immediately convinced that they will be uncharitable towards her family: 'Indeed, Mr Bennet, it is very hard to think that Charlotte Lucas should ever be mistress of this house, that *I* should be forced to make way for *her*, and live to see her take my place in it!' This complaint brings forth a typically ironic reply from her husband: 'My dear, do not give way to such gloomy thoughts. Let us hope for better things. Let us flatter ourselves that *I* may be the survivor.' The humour masks the gravity of the underlying situation, but as Jane Austen's contemporaries might have personally known people in similar situations, or be in such a position themselves, the humour was obviously pointed.

While the relatives argued over the will, the body of the dead person was left to rest in peace – except where bodysnatchers were at work. People visiting graveyards today to discover where their ancestors lie may be unaware that the body occupied the grave for only a few hours. Various measures were taken to stop bodysnatchers where they were particularly active, the simplest being to bury the coffin deeper in the ground, making it more difficult to reach. Strong, well-made coffins, especially those lined with lead, provided some deterrent, and special coffins to foil bodysnatchers were advertised in newspapers such as the *Morning Post*:

INFORMATION to the PUBLIC.—The FRAUD of ROBBING GRAVES and VAULTS, in and near London, is constantly practised, and the bodies missing bearing a small proportion to the numbers dissected, it is presumed a security for the dead from such depredations, must prove a great consolation to the living. This security is the PATENT COFFIN, which not only protects the body, but prevents the lead being stolen; nor is lead necessary where the Patent Coffin is used, but in particular cases. The Patent Coffin may be had, at a few hours notice, of Jarvis, Son, and Co. Undertakers, 15, Piccadilly.[60]

More bodies were dissected than were reported stolen, and so the advertisement was playing on the fear of readers that they might be weeping over an empty grave. Jarvis's Patent Coffins were supposedly impossible to open, but ordinary coffin lids could also be reinforced and various obstructions, such as branches and stones, placed on top, while the grave itself could be covered with heavy stone slabs. Unfortunately, most of these precautions were circumvented by bodysnatchers digging alongside the coffin rather than directly over it and breaking into the grave from the side. In some churchyards traps were set with spring guns fired by tripwires, but they could be disarmed in advance by an accomplice. Watchmen were hired to guard churchyards at night, but they could be bribed, and the only way to be certain that a corpse remained undisturbed was for trusted family and friends to keep a vigil until the body was no longer fresh enough to be a valuable commodity.

For poor people, the possibility of mustering enough friends and family to guard the grave was severely limited by their own need to keep working to survive. Nor could working-class people afford patent coffins, or indeed anything but the cheapest coffins, so it is hardly surprising that bodysnatchers preyed mainly on the graves of the poor – and there were so many more of them. In death, as in life, the wealthy enjoyed distinct advantages. This situation was summarised in a verse that is found, with minor variations, on many gravestones of the eighteenth and nineteenth centuries:

This world's a City full of Crooked streets,
And death the Market place where all men Meets,
If life was Merchandise that men could buy,
The rich would live and none but poor would die.[61]

Quite often poorer people could not afford gravemarkers, while many simply put up wooden markers, such as a cross. Alternatively, a wooden post might be placed at each end of the grave, supporting a plank on which an inscription was carved or painted. Commemorative monuments inside the church were a mark of privilege, and so those with money but insufficient influence opted for monuments in the churchyard. This fashion was gradually copied by the middle and lower classes, so that it became desirable to set up a headstone, however humble, to mark a relative's grave. More elaborate gravemarkers evolved, and from the end of the eighteenth century those churchyards with large numbers of burials had a variety of shapes, sizes and designs of tombstone.

The expansion of the canal system helped to reduce the cost of gravestones, since suitable blocks of stone were transported more cheaply by barge than by road. Although many areas had local quarries that supplied stone at a reasonable price, not all stone was well suited to gravestones, as John Byng sadly noted at Leicester in 1789: 'Much black slate, cut thick, is used here for hearths, chimney pieces, &c, looking very black and shining; but the coarser sort, used for tombstones, is very bad for us travellers, as the letters thereon are soon unintelligible.'[62]

It was already becoming popular with travellers like him to read and record the gravestones. After the service one Sunday morning in 1782, at Nettlebed in Oxfordshire, Carl Moritz wandered round the churchyard and wrote down the inscription on the gravestone of blacksmith William Strange, who had died on 6 June 1746:

I . . . went out of the church with the congregation, and amused myself with reading the inscriptions on the tomb-stones, in the church yard; which in general, are simpler, more pathetic, and better written than ours [in Germany]. There are some of them which, to be sure, were ludicrous and laughable enough. Among these is one on the tomb of a smith, which, on account of its singularity, I copied.

> My sledge and anvil lie declined,
> My bellows too have lost their wind;
> My fire's extinct, my forge decay'd,
> And in the dust my vice is laid;
> My coals are spent, my iron's gone,
> My nails are drove, my work is done.[63]

Another foreign visitor, Louis Simond from the United States, was impressed by the way the living remembered the dead, marking the graves with

an urn, an iron railing, a stone, a simple board, all bearing inscriptions, where something more than mere name and date is recorded. Rank and titles stand first, and require nothing else; these wanting, virtues are told of, and some ambitious quotation from the poets is made to vouch for them; the deceased was either great or good. I have noticed, however, inscriptions boasting of obscurity, as if it had been a matter of choice.[64]

Even sailors on shore leave would occasionally shun the dockside taverns and explore further afield, like Robert Hay in 1809. When his ship was moored at Plymouth, he and a companion travelled across Dartmoor to the village of Sourton, near Okehampton:

After washing down a comfortable supper with a glass of first-rate cyder, we strolled out for an hour to examine the village. I had lately been reading in Pope[65] an account of the partiality of the English peasantry for poetical epitaphs. This complete master of the art of rhyming quotes the following lines which he says are to be found in almost every country church yard in England:

'Afflictions sore, long time I bore
Physicians tried in vain,
Till God it pleased that death me seized
To terminate my pain.'

As an antique church and burrying ground adjoined the village, we
repaired thither to see whither the above motto could be found, and to
indulge in the perusal of other memento moris, which always reminds us
of our favourite amusement – a half hour's lounge in a bookseller's shop.
The first poetical epitaph that met our eye consisted of these identical
lines.[66]

Reading memorials in churchyards and browsing in bookshops are
still – of course – popular pastimes.

The trend towards stone gravemarkers and the desire for a permanent memorial have provided a huge resource for investigating the
lives and deaths of our ancestors from two centuries ago. The epitaphs and other inscriptions often go beyond the plain record of who
is buried to tell us something of their lives and characters. Memorial
stones, records, buildings and artefacts from Jane Austen's time
ensure that the dead – the ancestors – are not forgotten. The memorial stone to Jane herself is inside Winchester Cathedral. She was
probably buried there because it was the nearest burial place to the
house in College Street where she died, and some of her family, particularly her brother Henry, had influence with the Dean of the
Cathedral. Her grave slab in the floor of the north aisle carries the
inscription:

In Memory of
JANE AUSTEN,
youngest daughter of the late
Revd GEORGE AUSTEN,
formerly Rector of Steventon in this County,
she departed this Life on the 18th of July 1817,
aged 41, after a long illness supported with
the patience and the hopes of a Christian.
The benevolence of her heart,

the sweetness of her temper, and
the extraordinary endowments of her mind
obtained the regard of all who knew her and
the warmest love of her intimate connections.
Their grief is in proportion to their affection,
they know their loss to be irreparable,
but in their deepest affliction they are consoled
by a firm though humble hope that her charity,
devotion, faith and purity have rendered
her soul acceptable in the sight of her
REDEEMER.

The mention of the 'extraordinary endowments of her mind' is the only hint of her career as a novelist, because this was essentially a family epitaph. Only later were other memorials set up in the cathedral to acknowledge her literary achievement. But in reality Jane Austen needs no such memorial. Her books live on as classics of the art of the novelist and as a constant reminder of herself, her contemporaries and an England that has passed.

# WEIGHTS AND MEASURES

Some units of measurement that are used today had different values two centuries ago, and there were also many local variations, even between neighbouring counties and towns. Attempts to make weights and measures consistent were not entirely successful, and people still talked of a 'country mile', meaning a distance much longer than a 'standard' mile. An Act of Parliament standardising weights and measures came into force in 1826, but it was not very effective, and further changes of the law were necessary in 1834 and 1835 before any real uniformity was achieved.

In Jane Austen's time even common measures such as the stone and the bushel varied from place to place – a serious hindrance to merchants trading across the country. After the French Revolution metric measurements were adopted in France, but in England these were used only by a few, largely for scientific purposes.

Nominal weights and measures in Jane Austen's time are given below, taken from contemporary sources (Branch 1801 and Mortimer 1810).

**Length**

| | |
|---|---|
| 3 barley-corns | 1 inch (in.) |
| 4 inches | 1 hand |
| 12 inches | 1 foot (ft) |
| 3 feet | 1 yard (yd) |
| 6 feet | 1 fathom |
| 5½ yards | 1 rod, pole or perch |
| 40 rods | 1 furlong |
| 8 furlongs (1760 yards) | 1 mile |

## Area

| | |
|---|---|
| 144 square inches | 1 square foot |
| 9 square feet | 1 square yard |
| 4 roods (4840 square yards) | 10 square chains or 1 acre |

## Volume

| | |
|---|---|
| 2 pints | 1 quart |
| 4 quarts | 1 gallon |
| 2 gallons | 1 peck |
| 4 pecks | 1 bushel |
| 3 bushels | 1 sack |

## Weight

| | |
|---|---|
| 16 ounces (oz) | 1 pound (lb.) |
| 14 pounds | 1 stone |
| 28 pounds | 1 quarter |
| 8 stone or 4 quarters | 1 hundredweight (cwt) |
| 20 hundredweight | 1 ton |

## Metric equivalents

| | |
|---|---|
| 1 centimetre | 0.3937 inches |
| 1 metre | 1.09364 yards |
| 1 square metre | 1.1960 square yards |
| 1 litre | 1.7313 ale pints or 2.1135 wine pints |
| 1 kilogram | 2 pounds, 3 ounces and 5 drams (avoirdupois) |
| | |
| 1 inch | 2.54 centimetres |
| 1 foot | 30.48 centimetres |
| 1 yard | 0.9144 metres |
| 1 mile | 1609.344 metres (1.609 kilometres) |

# CHRONOLOGICAL OVERVIEW

Some key events relating to Jane Austen's life and episodes in Britain's history are given below. For a detailed Jane Austen chronology, see Le Faye 2006.

| 1760 | 25 October | George III became king. |
|------|------------|-------------------------|
| 1770 | 7 April | William Wordsworth, poet, was born. |
| 1771 | March | Nelson joined the Royal Navy. |
| | 15 August | Walter Scott, novelist, was born. |
| 1772 | 22 June | British case law established that a slave landing in England was a free person. |
| | 21 October | Samuel Taylor Coleridge, poet, was born. |
| 1773 | 16 December | Boston Tea Party, when American colonists protested against the unjust taxation of tea imports. |
| 1774 | 10 May | Accession of Louis XVI as king of France. |
| | 12 August | Robert Southey, poet, was born. |
| 1775 | 19 April | War of American Independence (American Revolutionary War) began, with the British defeat at Lexington. |
| | 23 August | J.M.W. Turner, painter, was born. |
| | 16 December | Jane Austen was born. |
| 1776 | 11 June | John Constable, painter, was born. |
| | 4 July | American Declaration of Independence. |
| 1778 | 6 February | The French became allies of America. |
| | 17 March | Britain declared war on France. |
| | 11 May | William Pitt the Elder died. |
| | 17 December | Humphry Davy, engineer and chemist, was born. |

| 1779 | 16 June | Spain declared war on Britain. |
| 1780 | 1 January | The first iron bridge, across the River Severn at Coalbrookdale, was officially opened. |
| | 2–9 June | Gordon Riots in London. |
| | 20 November | Britain declared war on the Netherlands. |
| 1781 | 9 June | George Stephenson, engineer, was born. |
| 1782 | 24 August | David Tyrie was the last man in England to be hung, drawn and quartered. |
| 1783 | 3 September | Peace of Versailles between Britain, France, Spain and America. Britain, France and Spain each recovered some of the territories they had lost. Britain recognised American independence. |
| 1784 | 20 May | Peace treaty between Britain and Holland. |
| | 15 September | Lunardi was the first man in England to ascend in a balloon. |
| | 13 December | Samuel Johnson died. |
| 1787 | May | The first convoy of convicts ('First Fleet') sailed from Britain to begin the European colonisation of Australia. |
| 1788 | 1 January | John Walter founded *The Times* newspaper. |
| | 22 January | Lord Byron, poet, was born. |
| | 15 April | Alliance between Britain and Netherlands. |
| | 2 August | Thomas Gainsborough, painter, died. |
| | 13 August | Triple Alliance between Britain, Netherlands and Prussia. |
| 1789 | 18 March | Christian Bowman was the last woman in England to be burned at the stake. |
| | 30 April | George Washington became first President of the USA. |
| | 14 July | The storming of the Bastille in Paris, and the beginning of the French Revolution. |
| 1790 | 17 April | Benjamin Franklin died. |
| 1791 | July | Priestley riots in Birmingham. |
| 1792 | 20 April | France began the Revolutionary War by declaring war against Austria. |
| | 4 August | Percy Bysshe Shelley, poet, was born. |

| 1793 | 21 January | Execution of Louis XVI. |
|------|------------|-------------------------|
|      | 1 February | France declared war on Britain and Holland. |
|      | 26 June | Gilbert White of Selborne died. |
|      | 16 October | Execution of Marie Antoinette. |
| 1794 | 1 June | The British defeated the French at the Battle of 'Glorious First of June'. |
| 1795 | 29 October | Assassination attempt on George III in London. |
|      | 31 October | John Keats, poet, was born. |
| 1796 | 5 October | Spain declared war on Britain. |
| 1797 | 14 February | The British defeated the Spanish at the Battle of St Vincent. |
|      | May–June | Mutinies aboard British warships at Spithead and the Nore. |
|      | 11 October | The British defeated the Dutch at the Battle of Camperdown. |
| 1798 | 1 August | The French fleet was destroyed by Nelson at the Battle of the Nile. |
| 1799 | 14 December | George Washington died. |
| 1800 | 5 September | Britain captured Malta from France. |
| 1801 | 1 January | Act of Union, uniting Great Britain and Ireland. |
|      | 10 March | First census of Great Britain. |
|      | 1 October | Peace treaty (of Amiens) between France and Britain. |
| 1802 | 27 March | The Peace of Amiens between France and Britain was ratified. |
| 1803 | 1 January | Parson James Woodforde died. |
|      | 30 April | The Louisiana territories were sold by Napoleon to America. |
|      | 18 May | Start of the Napoleonic Wars between Britain and France. |
| 1804 | 2 December | Napoleon was crowned Napoleon I. |
|      | 12 December | Spain declared war on Britain. |
| 1805 | 21 January | George Austen died at Bath. |
|      | 21 October | Battle of Trafalgar, when the French and Spanish were defeated by the British and Nelson was killed. |

| 1806 | 9 January | Funeral of Nelson. |
| | 23 January | Death of Prime Minister William Pitt (the Younger). |
| 1807 | 28 January | Gas street lighting was demonstrated in Pall Mall. |
| | 25 March | The British slave trade (but not slavery) was abolished. |
| 1811 | 5 February | George III was declared insane and the Prince of Wales became Prince Regent. |
| | 27 May | Census in Great Britain. |
| | 30 October | Jane Austen's first novel, *Sense and Sensibility*, was published. |
| 1812 | 7 February | Charles Dickens was born. |
| | 19 June | United States declared war on Britain (the so-called '1812 war'). |
| 1813 | 28 January | *Pride and Prejudice* was published. |
| 1814 | February | Last frost fair on the River Thames. |
| | 11 April | Napoleon abdicated and went into exile on Elba. |
| | 9 May | *Mansfield Park* was published. |
| | 24 December | A peace treaty was signed at Ghent, ending the 1812 war between Britain and America. |
| 1815 | 8 January | Battle of New Orleans in America. |
| | 15 January | Emma Hamilton died. |
| | February | End of the war between Britain and America. |
| | 1 March | Napoleon escaped from Elba and landed in France. |
| | 18 June | Battle of Waterloo. |
| | 23 December | *Emma* was published. |
| 1816 | 21 April | Charlotte Brontë was born. |
| | 17 July | Richard Brinsley Sheridan died. |
| 1817 | 18 July | Jane Austen died at Winchester. |
| | 20 December | *Northanger Abbey* was published. |
| | 20 December | *Persuasion* was published. |

| 1871 | June | Jane Austen's novel *Lady Susan* and the unfinished fragment of *The Watsons* were published. |
| 1925 | | The unfinished fragment of Jane Austen's novel *Sanditon* was published. |

# NOTES

## INTRODUCTION: KNOW YOUR PLACE

1   In 1806 the Austen family journeyed north to visit relatives, and in August they stayed at Stoneleigh Abbey. On 13 August Mrs Austen wrote to Mary, wife of her son James, that they would travel to Hamstall Ridware the next day (Austen-Leigh 1942, p. 247). It is not certain if they actually made this journey, or even if they travelled further north. Letters destroyed after Jane Austen's death may have revealed other places she visited.

2   See the Chronological Overview on p. 347.

3   October 1800. Somerset Archives and Local Studies, A\BTL/2/10.

4   13 October 1800. Somerset Archives and Local Studies, A\BTL/2/10.

5   *The Annual Register or a View of the History, Politics, and Literature for the Year 1816* (1817), p. 67.

6   George Austen's library contained some 500 volumes, which were sold off when he retired to Bath.

7   28 September 1814. Austen-Leigh and Austen-Leigh 1913, pp. 359–60. Her niece was Anna Austen, who became Anna Lefroy on her marriage to Ben Lefroy in November 1814. Anna's novel was never published.

8   *Edinburgh Magazine or Literary Miscellany* January 1799, 'On the Cause of the Popularity of Novels', pp. 33–6. First published in the *Universal Magazine* of 1798.

9   Austen-Leigh and Austen-Leigh 1913, p. 356.

10  August 1814. Austen-Leigh and Austen-Leigh 1913, p. 355.

11  Austen-Leigh and Austen-Leigh 1913, p. 356.

12  *A Review of the State of the British Nation* 25 June 1709 (vol. 6, p. 26).

13  4 December 1800. Somerset Archives and Local Studies, A\BTL/2/12.

14  29 January 1810. Somerset Archives and Local Studies, A\BTL/2/31. Andrew Guy lived at Barford near Bridgwater in Somerset.

15  Diary entry for 10 February 1795; Jupp 1991, p. 204.

16  Eden 1797b, pp. 30, 223, 528. Sir Frederick Morton Eden was born in 1766, became a baronet in 1784 and died in 1809. The three volumes of *The State of the Poor* were published under his name Frederic, but elsewhere he is spelled as Frederick. Many thanks to Professor Donald Winch for discussing this problem with us. Eden founded the Globe Insurance Company.

17  From Blake's untitled poem, written around 1804, in his Preface to *Milton, a Poem*.

18  25 January 1801. Somerset Archives and Local Studies, A\BTL/2/13. Born in 1746, Holland is known to have kept a diary from 1799 until 1818, the year before he died.

19  Ayres 1984. The diaries are now in the Somerset Archives and Local Studies, A\BTL/2.

1: WEDDING BELLS

1  The Reverend James Woodforde is traditionally referred to as Parson Woodforde, because abridged diary extracts were first published in 1923 using this title, decades before the Parson Woodforde Society embarked on full publication (Winstanley 1996).
2  The marriage took place on 25 January 1787. Winstanley and Jameson 1999, p. 205. The absent vicar of St Peter's was the Reverend Carter.
3  *Newcastle Courant* 10 February 1787.
4  Winstanley and Jameson 1999, p. 205.
5  The wedding was on 23 September 1794. Jameson 2004, p. 73. Anne's surname was actually Dunnell.
6  Brayne 1998, pp. 13–14.
7  *The Mysteries of Udolpho* was first published in 1794.
8  25 February 1810. Hall 1936, p. 239. She is referred to as Ellen in her biography, but was actually called Nelly after her father's merchant ship. Bessy Winkley did later marry, becoming Bessy Price.
9  Hall 1936, pp. 310–11. Letter to Miss Bessy Winkley dated 18 October 1810.
10  27 January 1791. Original copy of the diary for this date is missing. Jameson 2003, p. 4.
11  31 January 1791. Original copy of the diary for this date is missing. Jameson 2003, p. 4.
12  Jameson 2001, p. 66.
13  Apprenticeship indenture in authors' collection. See Chapter 3 for further details.
14  *Drewry's Derby Mercury* 29 September 1775.
15  Andrews 1891, p. 187, quoting *Harrop's Manchester Mercury* 12 March 1771.
16  *Derby Mercury* 28 December 1797. The wedding took place before 23 December.
17  28 August 1788. Jameson 2001, p. 66; Beresford 1927, p. 45. Many thanks to Martin Brayne and Peter Jameson for clarifying this quote.
18  Rowe 1796, p. 113.
19  12 November 1810. Somerset Archives and Local Studies A\BTL/2/34.
20  19 October 1800. Somerset Archives and Local Studies A\BTL/2/11.
21  Brand 1813, p. 33. John Brand lived from 1744 to 1806.
22  Brand 1813, p. 33.
23  Brand 1813, p. 35.
24  Brand 1813, p. 67.
25  Nicholson and Burn 1776, p. 620. In 1816 this bell cracked, and when it was recast, the inscription was reinstated on the new bell, with minor changes.
26  Brabourne 1884b, p. 16.
27  Rowe 1796, p. 112.
28  *Derby Mercury* 10 June 1802.
29  *Western Luminary* 21 February 1815.
30  28 December 1809. Hall 1936, p. 218.
31  Elliott 1842, p. 2.
32  Elliott 1842, pp. 18–19.

33  19 October 1800. Somerset Archives and Local Studies A\BTL/2/11.

34  The *Oxford English Dictionary* dates the first use of 'old maid' ('oulde mayde') to 1530.

35  Hayley 1786, p. 7.

36  Brabourne 1884b, p. 296.

37  17 July 1809. Hall 1936, p. 178.

38  Hall 1936, p. 178.

39  Information from Ruth A. Symes in *Oxford Dictionary of National Biography* online. Her daughter Mary was removed from her care at the separation.

40  See Vickery 2003, pp. 72–83; Moore 2009, pp. 297–303.

41  Jeffery 1907, p. 314.

42  Jeffery 1907, p. xxii.

43  *Hampshire Chronicle and Portsmouth and Chichester Journal* 9 April 1796.

44  Brand 1813, p. 37.

45  *Northampton Mercury* 7 January 1790.

46  *Morning Post* 13 January 1815. The sale took place ten days earlier.

47  27 December 1808. Brabourne 1884b, pp. 46–7.

48  Christie 1929, p. 179. William Jones had been vicar from 1801 and a curate before then.

49  Christie 1929, pp. 179–80. This was June 1805.

50  13 March 1817. Chapman 1932b, p. 483.

## 2: BREEDING

1  Austen-Leigh 1942, p. 29. Letter of 6 June 1773 to Mrs Walter, wife of the half-brother of George Austen (Jane Austen's father).

2  For example, *Derby Mercury* 8 February 1798.

3  Brabourne 1884a, p. 166. Letter written on Saturday 17 November 1798.

4  Brabourne 1884a, p. 167. The boy grew up to become the Reverend James Edward Austen-Leigh (1798–1874).

5  Chapman 1932b, p. 76. Letter to Cassandra of 29 January 1813.

6  Winstanley Hall is a Grade II* listed building but has become derelict in a planning dispute. Winstanley Park and the buildings are bordered today by the M6 motorway.

7  Hall 1936, pp. 166–7. Letter to Miss Whitehead, 23 May 1809. Despite their preparations, Mrs Bankes died in childbirth and the infant soon after. Nelly Weeton used the spelling 'Banks' in her letters.

8  Smith 1785, pp. 19–20.

9  Smith 1785, p. 20.

10  Brabourne 1884a, p. 253. Letter written at Steventon on 3 January 1801. Coulson Wallop MP died as a prisoner-of-war in France in 1807.

11  Brand 1813, pp. 6–7.

12  Later lying-in hospitals included Liverpool in 1841 and Sheffield in 1863. Most were for married women, but the New Westminster Lying-in Hospital (later the General Lying-in Hospital) admitted unmarried women. The first lying-in wards (within hospitals) were opened in London in 1747, and several lying-in hospitals were established there during the next five years.

13  Letter written at Beacon's Gutter, near Liverpool, on 23 May 1809. Hall 1936, p. 167.

14  2 November 1794. Jameson 2004, p. 91.

15  3 November 1794. Jameson 2004, p. 92.

16  Brabourne 1884a, p. 159. Letter written on 27 October 1798.

17  25 June 1783. Winstanley 1998, pp. 146–7.

18  26 June 1783. Winstanley 1998, p. 147. Frances Anne married Robert Marsham around 1804 and died in January 1874.

19  13 July 1785. Winstanley and Jameson 1999, pp. 53–4.

20  British Library Add MS 35143, fol. 71.

21  See Vickery 2003, pp. 97–8.

22  Cooper 1776, p. 231.

23  Cooper 1776, p. 221.

24  Cooper 1776, p. 222.

25  Cooper 1776, p. 231.

26  Cooper 1776, p. 227.

27  She was buried on 16 August 1774, two days after the caesarean. The churchyard was later sold to construct the Holborn Viaduct, and some bodies were placed in the church crypt (since reinterred in the City of London Cemetery).

28  She had been travelling on top of a loaded cart, had fallen off and been crushed beneath one of the cartwheels.

29  Barlow 1834, p. 569.

30  The operation was performed on 27 November 1793. Jane Foster died about 1826; her age at death is given as sixty-eight or seventy-two.

31  White 1773, p. 157.

32  White 1773, p. 115.

33  White 1773, p. 6.

34  White 1773, p. 130.

35  White 1773, pp. 283–5.

36  23 May 1809. Hall 1936, pp. 166–7.

37  *Cheltenham Chronicle and Gloucestershire Advertiser* 28 August 1817. They were John, Charles, Robert and Caroline.

38  *Norfolk Chronicle* 8 November 1817. She died on 5 November 1817.

39  White 1789, p. 13.

40  *New Exeter Journal* 22 January 1789.

41  *Hull Packet* 27 October 1801. The Constable family of Everingham Park in East Yorkshire were gentry, a branch of the large Constable-Maxwell family.

42  Upton-Wilkinson archive (071109fpwwo1).

43  Upton-Wilkinson archive (071109fpwwo1).

44  Upton-Wilkinson archive (080105wwsp).

45  This provided the perfect setting for stories about changelings.

46  Upton-Wilkinson archive (071109wwwspo1). A wet-nurse is far more likely than a nursemaid, because the family was so short of money for such a luxury.

47  Foreman 1998, pp. 122–3.

48  Downman 1803, p. 19. *Infancy* was later published as a single volume.

49  White 1773, pp. 58–9.

50  White 1773, p. 63.

51  Moss 1781, p. 60.

52  Austen-Leigh 1942, p. 28. Letter of 8 November 1772, written at Steventon.

53  Austen-Leigh 1942, p. 29. Letter to Mrs Walter of 6 June 1773, written at Steventon.

54  Austen Leigh 1871, p. 41.

55  Leviticus 12.2–8.

56  6 December 1800. Somerset Archives and Local Studies A\BTL/2/12.

57  Andrews 1935, p. 370.

58  11 March 1787. Winstanley and Jameson 1999, p. 222.

59  18 March 1787. Winstanley and Jameson 1999, p. 224.

60  More detailed pre-printed forms were required from 1812 as part of the Rose's Act of 1812.

61  10 September 1783. Winstanley 1998, p. 170.

62  11 December 1786. Winstanley and Jameson 1999, p. 192.

63  17 February 1810. Somerset Archives and Local Studies A\BTL/2/31.

64  18 February 1810. Somerset Archives and Local Studies A\BTL/2/31.

65  Sunday 25 February 1810.

66  Chapman 1932a, p. 97.

67  30 June 1783. Winstanley 1998, p. 148.

68  September 1814. Chapman 1932b, p. 400.

69  Brabourne 1884a, p. 315. Written at Southampton on 7 January 1807. Captain Edward James Foote divorced his first wife by Act of Parliament in July 1803, and one of the children of that earlier marriage was called Caroline. He married Mary Patton in August 1803 and had four daughters, including Elizabeth.

70  Moss 1781, p. 41.

71  Moss 1781, p. 44.

72  Austen-Leigh 1942, p. 29. Letter to Mrs Walter 6 June 1773, written at Steventon.

73  Moss 1781, pp. 43–4.

74  Moss 1781, pp. 159–60.

75  *Derby Mercury* 24 March 1775.

76  Moss 1781, pp. 164–6.

77  16 September 1808. Upton-Wilkinson archive (080916spww).

78  18 September 1808. Upton-Wilkinson archive (080918spww). He was either Mr Thomson or Thompson, possibly Frederick Thompson who had been a Royal Navy surgeon and was resident in Kensington from at least 1790.

79  Upton-Wilkinson archive (080925jbww).

80  Buckle commonplace book, courtesy of Trustees of the National Museum of the Royal Navy NMRN, P2002 73, f.23.

81  Moritz 1809, p. 10. Carl is also spelled Karl and at times written as Charles in English translations. Born in Hameln in 1756, Carl Moritz struggled with poverty for much of his life. He died in 1793, barely a decade after his visit to England (Winstanley 2012).

82  Price 1783, p. 253.

83  Price 1783, p. 281.

84  'Abstract of the Answers and Returns made pursuant to an act, passed in the forty-first year of His Majesty King George III, Parish Registers, ordered to be printed 21st December 1801. Abstract of the answers and returns to the population act, 42 Geo III, 1800 County of Cornwall'.

85  Perhaps as many as 8,658,265, allowing for uncounted children and those in the armed forces (Wrigley and Schofield 1989, p. 595).

86 Percival 1774, p. 55.

87 In 1811 England had a population of 9,476,700, including 1,009,546 living in London (Wrigley and Schofield 1989, p. 66).

88 Simond 1817, pp. 259–60.

89 17 October 1808. Moretonhampstead History Society manuscript of Treleaven's diary (box 2 of the Society's archives). Silvester Treleaven seems to have been the son of the first postmaster of Moretonhampstead, John Treleaven (information from the Moretonhampstead History Society website).

90 25 January 1805. Somerset Archives and Local Studies A\BTL/2/20.

91 See Chater 2009, p. 238.

92 29 October 1799. Somerset Archives and Local Studies A\BTL/2/1.

93 9 October 1800. Somerset Archives and Local Studies A\BTL/2/10. See Penhallurick 1991, p. 290.

94 White 2012, pp. 156–7.

95 *Report from Select Committee on the Education of the Lower Orders in the Metropolis* (London, 1816), p. 1.

96 Colquhoun 1796, pp. 167–8. The overall Jewish population in England certainly exceeded twenty thousand. London did have the largest Jewish community, but Colquhoun probably overestimated the numbers.

97 British Library Add MS 27827, fols 145–6. Place was writing especially of the 1770s.

98 *Morning Post and Gazetteer* 7 June 1802.

99 *Morning Post and Gazetteer* 14 June 1802.

100 *Morning Post and Gazetteer* 14 June 1802.

101 Hall 1936, p. 60. This was mid-December 1807.

102 *Western Flying Post* 7 November 1803.

103 Chapman 1932b, p. 480. Sophia Deedes was the sister-in-law of Edward, Jane Austen's brother.

104 Grose 1811. Such handbills were distributed in the streets to likely customers. Mrs Phillips had long since died by 1776, but her name continued to be used.

105 15 May 1777. Winstanley 1981, p. 130.

106 18 May 1775. Winstanley 1989, p. 141.

107 Rubenhold 2005.

108 Cyprus was home to the ancient Greek goddess of love and prostitutes, Aphrodite, hence the use of 'Cyprian' relating to prostitutes. *Harris's List of Covent-Garden Ladies: or, Man of Pleasure's Kalendar, for the year 1789* (London), p. 39.

109 Hall 1936, p. 167.

110 Watson 1827, pp. 22–3.

111 12 August 1779. Winstanley 1983, p. 164.

112 8 October 1786. Winstanley and Jameson 1999, p. 173.

113 *Harris's List of Covent-Garden Ladies: or, Man of Pleasure's Kalendar, for the year 1789* (London), p. iii.

114 *Harris's List of Covent-Garden Ladies: or, Man of Pleasure's Kalendar, for the year 1789* (London), p. viii. The 'toyman' dealt in small metal goods, of which children's toys formed only a small part. The hub of the toy trade was Birmingham.

115 British Library Add MS 35143, fol. 143.

116 Romney 1984, pp. 94–5. The White Swan is still a hotel. Fothergill went to

Canada in 1816 and became involved in politics. He died in 1840. His life was marked by profligacy and failure.

117 Romney 1984, p. 94.
118 Romney 1984, p. 171.
119 3 July 1810. Somerset Archives and Local Studies A\BTL/2/33.
120 9 July 1810. Somerset Archives and Local Studies A\BTL/2/33.

## 3: TODDLER TO TEENAGER

1 Struve 1802, p. 328.
2 Gillett 1945, p. 27. Elizabeth Ham was born on 30 November 1783 at North Perrott, Somerset.
3 Hay 1953, p. 44. This was August 1803.
4 Andrews 1934, p. 83.
5 Andrews 1935, p. 72.
6 15 May 1805. Silliman 1810, p. 86.
7 Silliman 1820b, p. 132. This was in November 1805.
8 Silliman 1820b, p. 133.
9 Silliman 1820b, p. 132.
10 Walker 1792, p. 84. He was largely self-taught and was especially accomplished in mechanics. Describing dialects as far south as Worcestershire, he commented: 'Dialects more south and east have run too much into one another to admit of definition; and ere long that will be the case with the whole kingdom.' (1792, p. 84).
11 Millard 1895, p. 44.
12 Walker 1792, p. 83. Adam Walker was no relation of John Walker.
13 *Walker's Critical Pronouncing Dictionary, and Expositor of the English Language* (1819).
14 Belsham 1795, p. 1. Briton is often misquoted as Britain. George III was deliberately identifying himself with his subjects and distancing himself from his forebears, who were often despised as German interlopers. This realignment of the monarchy mirrored a fashion for elocution. Thomas Sheridan, father of the politician-playwright Richard Brinsley Sheridan, ran extremely popular and lucrative courses of elocution lessons and published in 1762 *A Course of Lectures on Elocution*, followed by a pronunciation dictionary that ran to several editions, the precursor of Walker's dictionary.
15 24 October 1808. Brabourne 1884b, p. 26.
16 *The Mother's Remarks on a Set of Three Hundred and Thirty Six Cuts for Children* 1802 (London), p. 22, quoted in *Journal of the British Archaeological Association* 30 (1874), p. 40.
17 17 July 1802. Somerset Archives and Local Studies A\BTL/2/15.
18 10 January 1806. Somerset Archives and Local Studies A\BTL/2/25.
19 *Northampton Mercury* 27 April 1772.
20 Gillett 1945, p. 24.
21 Gillett 1945, p. 19.
22 Old Bailey Proceedings online, December 1811 (t18111204-3). This trial was of a woman wrongly acused of stealing the boy's clothes, before his real abductor had been found.

359

23  Old Bailey Proceedings online, December 1811 (t18111204-3). The two children were Thomas Dillone and his sister Rebecca. Thomas's abduction is described later in this chapter (pp. 58–9).

24  Gillett 1945, p. 27.

25  10 May 1803. Somerset Archives and Local Studies A\BTL/2/16.

26  10 September 1803. Somerset Archives and Local Studies A\BTL/2/17.

27  *Bell's Weekly Messenger* 6 November 1814.

28  *The Times* 1 May 1799.

29  This was probably a confusion with Edward Wortley Montagu, son of Lady Mary Wortley Montagu, who periodically ran away from home, and in 1726 became a climbing boy for a short while (Cullingford 2000).

30  *The Times* 12 June 1789.

31  *The Times* 12 June 1789.

32  *The Times* 12 June 1789.

33  *The Times* 12 June 1789.

34  *The Times* 12 June 1789.

35  Old Bailey Proceedings online, December 1811 (t18111204-3).

36  *Hampshire Telegraph and Sussex Chronicle* 6 January 1812. Mr Richard Magnes was a gunner on board HMS *Lightning*. The surname of Thomas was stated variously as Dillone, Deloe and Dellow in the newspapers.

37  13 June 1800. Somerset Archives and Local Studies A\BTL/2/7.

38  13 June 1800. Somerset Archives and Local Studies A\BTL/2/7.

39  19 June 1800. Somerset Archives and Local Studies A\BTL/2/7.

40  26 September 1803. Somerset Archives and Local Studies A\BTL/2/17.

41  Christie 1929, p. 128.

42  4 December 1800. Somerset Archives and Local Studies A\BTL/2/12. A pencil factory was later established at Worsley in Lancashire. In a pocket diary of 1799, fifteen-year-old Mary Filliter of Wareham in Dorset recorded purchases of a pencil costing sixpence and a slate pencil costing twopence (Dorset History Centre D/FIL/F53).

43  6 April 1807. Upton-Wilkinson archive (070406wwsp).

44  The traveller was Thomas Pennant in 1769. Pennant 1776, pp. 10–11.

45  Jenkin 1951, p. 120.

46  27 September 1775. Winstanley 1989, p. 172.

47  2 April 1789. Jameson 2001, p. 132.

48  Moritz 1809, pp. 37–9.

49  Leach 1911, p. 413. The purpose of the original medieval grammar schools, which were attached to cathedrals and monasteries, was to teach Latin to future priests and monks. Some like Winchester and Eton were independent of the Church. From 1944 the term 'grammar school' was applied to state-funded schools that required pupils to pass the 11-plus examination.

50  Moritz 1809, p. 59. The term 'public school' was officially used in England from 1860 for Eton and others. They took in pupils from all over the country.

51  11 January 1808. Somerset Archives and Local Studies A\BTL/2/28. Charterhouse was founded in London in 1611, but the school is now situated near Godalming in Surrey.

52  4 September 1813. Somerset Archives and Local Studies A\BTL/2/39. Mrs

Cecilia Windham had been widowed in 1810 on the death of her husband William (1750–1810).

53  Hall 1939, p. 62. Letter to Mrs Dodson written on 18 August 1812.

54  14 June 1809. Hall 1936, p. 173.

55  19 October 1812. Somerset Archives and Local Studies A\BTL/2/37.

56  19 and 20 October 1812. Somerset Archives and Local Studies A\BTL/2/37. Elizabeth Poole (1798–1853) was also gifted at music and algebra. Tom Poole was a patron of Coleridge.

57  Information from David Worthy and from Sandford 1888.

58  Hall 1936, p. 197. Letter written at Liverpool, 15 November 1809.

59  Corley 2005, p. 14.

60  The school was in the Abbey gatehouse at Reading in Berkshire.

61  Joseph Lancaster established his first free school around 1801 in Southwark, in which older boys, called monitors, taught the younger children.

62  Andrews 1935, p. 178.

63  18 July 1802. Somerset Archives and Local Studies A\BTL/2/15.

64  *The Parliamentary Debates* vol. 9 for 1807 (London, 1812), p. 798. Such attempts were made in 1796, 1797, 1807, 1820 and 1833, finally succeeding in 1870. Giddy later changed his surname to Gilbert so that he could inherit substantial estates from his wife's uncle (*Oxford Dictionary of National Biography* online).

65  Jenkin 1951, p. 161. Letter of 17 September 1811 to George Wilbraham of Delamere House near Northwich in Cheshire.

66  Carter 1845.

67  *Report from Select Committee on the Education of the Lower Orders in the Metropolis: with the minutes of evidence taken before the committee* (London, 1816), p. 54.

68  *Report from Select Committee on the Education of the Lower Orders in the Metropolis: with the minutes of evidence taken before the committee* (London, 1816), p. 10.

69  Manuscript in authors' possession.

70  This was Coventry's Charity, established by Thomas Coventry and Hugh Dashfield in 1636. Farm rents were paid into the charity.

71  Manuscript in authors' possession.

72  *Derby Mercury* 16 May 1793.

73  Evidence of Robert Blincoe, sworn and examined by Dr Hawkins at Manchester on 18 May 1833, in *Factories Inquiry Commission* 1833, section D3, p. 17.

74  Evidence of Robert Blincoe, sworn and examined by Dr Hawkins at Manchester on 18 May 1833, in *Factories Inquiry Commission* 1833, section D3, p. 18.

75  Evidence of Robert Blincoe, sworn and examined by Dr Hawkins at Manchester on 18 May 1833, in *Factories Inquiry Commission* 1833, section D3, p. 18.

76  Warner 1801, pp. 90–1.

77  *Parliamentary Debates from the year 1803 to the present time* vol. 33 (London, 1816), p. 884.

78  *Reports of special assistant poor law commissioners on the employment of women and children in agriculture* (London, 1843), pp. 112–13.

79  Ayton 1815, pp. 155–6.

80  Ayton 1815, p. 155.

81  *Children's Employment Commission. Appendix to First Report of Commissioners. Mines. Part II. Reports and Evidence from Sub-Commissioners. Presented to both Houses of Parliament by Command of Her Majesty* (London, 1842), p. 122.

82  *Journal of the House of Commons* 43 (1788), pp. 436–7.

83  *Journal of the House of Commons* 43 (1788), evidence of James Dunn, p. 436.

84  Pratt 1803, p. 434.

85  Pratt 1803, pp. 428, 431–2.

86  Pratt 1803, pp. 432–3.

87  Pratt 1803, pp. 433–4.

88  *Journal of the House of Commons* 43 (1788), p. 436.

89  *Christian Observer* 9 (1811), p. 614. The same evidence was later given to the parliamentary committee *Report from the Committee on Employment of Boys in Sweeping Chimnies: together with the minutes of the evidence taken before the committee and an appendix* (London, 1817), p. 35.

90  *Christian Observer* 9 (1811), p. 614.

91  Brabourne 1884b, p. 241. The house has since been largely rebuilt, but a blue plaque records Jane Austen's residence there.

92  *Christian Observer* 9 (1811), p. 182.

93  *Christian Observer* 9 (1811), p. 182. The inquest was 24 November 1810.

94  *Christian Observer* 9 (1811), p. 182.

95  Jameson 2005, p. 169.

## 4: HOME AND HEARTH

1  Brougham 1840, pp. 41–2 (speech to Parliament).

2  The situation has not improved since then. With increased landholding by institutions such as the Forestry Commission and the National Trust and also by commercial companies, the percentage of land owned by lower- and middle-class individuals has dwindled even further. See Cahill 2001.

3  Henry 2002, p. 313; Mingay 2002, p. 143.

4  11 July 1785. Andrews 1934, pp. 236–7. The Grade I listed castle is currently empty and visitors barred, so history repeats itself here. Born in 1743, John Byng was nephew of Admiral John Byng who was executed.

5  In the poem, 'The Homes of England', written in 1827. Usually known simply as 'Mrs Hemans', she was born in Liverpool in 1793, a brilliant linguist and scholar who was an extremely popular poet in Victorian times.

6  Silliman 1820a, p. 12.

7  Silliman 1820b, p. 145 footnote.

8  Andrews 1935, p. 275.

9  Trusler 1790, p. 2.

10  Simond 1817, p. 337.

11  Cunningham 1859, p. 324. Walpole (1717–97) was the 4th Earl of Orford, author, politician, antiquarian and patron of the arts.

12  6 July 1790. Bamford 1936, p. 71. Letter from Arabella Pennant. Weston Hall became the home of Sir Sacheverell Sitwell. Little is known of Mary Heber (1758–1809).

13  Mackenzie 1916, p. 179. George MacAulay (1750–1803) was originally from the Outer Hebrides but had come to London at the age of fifteen, in 1774. He

became an alderman in 1786. The construction of Finsbury Square began in 1777. The square was severely damaged in the Second World War.

14  Simond 1817, p. 259.
15  Simond 1817, p. 260.
16  Simond 1815, pp. 50–1.
17  Andrews 1935, pp. 9–10.
18  19 April 1802. Christie 1929, pp. 138–9.
19  *Report from Select Committee on the Education of the Lower Orders in the Metropolis* (1816, London), p. 40.
20  Simond 1817, pp. 338–9. He puts this in his diary as 1811.
21  Letter dated 'Good Friday 1808'. Hall 1936, p. 82.
22  Hall 1936, p. 82.
23  7 May 1817. Somerset Archives and Local Studies A\BTL/2/43.
24  See Vickery 2009, chapter 6. The first known English patterned wallpaper dates to around 1509. By the late eighteenth century London was the centre of the wallpaper industry.
25  *Ipswich Journal* 18 April 1789.
26  30 June 1785. Winstanley and Jameson 1999, p. 50.
27  Hall 1936, p. 140.
28  1 September 1809. Christie 1929, p. 230.
29  13 April 1810. Hall 1936, p. 251 (with an image of Dove Nest opp. p. 225). Nelly Weeton called the house Dove's Nest, but Dove Nest is the more usual form (Green 1819, p. 165).
30  Chorley 1836, p. 118. Mrs Hemans paid visits to Wordsworth from Dove Nest. It is today a luxury hotel, much altered.
31  10 June 1798. Christie 1929, pp. 105–6.
32  21 August 1809. Upton-Wilkinson archive (091082ıspww).
33  13 November 1809. National Maritime Museum WIL/1/38.
34  13 November 1789. Jameson 2001, p. 206.
35  8 February 1807. Brabourne 1884a, p. 324.
36  Simond 1815, pp. 12–13.
37  1 September 1784. Winstanley 1998, p. 273. Buildings still exist with such bricked-up windows.
38  15 May 1788. Jameson 2001, p. 36 (where the horse tax is omitted, though it is in Beresford 1927, p. 24).
39  27 October 1798. Brabourne 1884a, pp. 160–1.
40  Brabourne 1884a, p. 161.
41  28 December 1809. Hall 1936, p. 217.
42  18 January 1810. Hall 1936, p. 221.
43  For the problems of finding and keeping servants in northern England, see Vickery 2003, chapter 4 and appendix 5.
44  15 January 1798. Jameson 2006, p. 3.
45  On her uncle's death, Nancy Woodforde returned in 1805 to Castle Cary, which is adjacent to Ansford, in Somerset, and remained there until her death in 1830. She never married.
46  5 July 1784. Winstanley 1998, p. 256.
47  8 December 1801. Jameson 2007, pp. 90–1.

48  9 November 1799. Somerset Archives and Local Studies A\BTL/2/1.

49  Hall 1936, p. 126. Nelly was writing at Beacon's Gutter, near Liverpool, 14 November 1808.

50  Moritz 1809, pp. 12–13.

51  26 August 1782. Andrews 1934, p. 85. Byng stayed in many inns during his excursions and was very critical of poor ones.

52  26 January 1784. Winstanley 1998, p. 209.

53  30 June 1808. Brabourne 1884a, p. 367 (who cites the wrong date). Jane Austen was staying at Godmersham in Kent.

54  4 January 1789. Jameson 2001, p. 108.

55  14 January 1792. Jameson 2003, p. 103.

56  28 January 1794. Jameson 2004, p. 7.

57  25 January 1795. Jameson 2004, p. 118.

58  3 February 1799. Jameson 2006, p. 86.

59  A report from 1795. Eden 1797b, p. 397.

60  Writing in April 1795. Eden 1797c, pp. 776–7.

61  Eden 1797c, p. 797.

62  24 March 1800. Somerset Archives and Local Studies A\BTL/2/4. The 'sticks' were from where the hedge had been laid.

63  23 October 1799, Somerset Archives and Local Studies A\BTL/2/1.

64  February 1798. Knight 1904, p. 7.

65  31 July 1802. Knight 1904, p. 144.

66  Simond 1815, pp. 37–8.

67  At Alfoxton in Somerset on 2 February 1798. Knight 1904, p. 7.

68  17 December 1797. Jameson 2005, p. 198.

69  28 December 1781. Winstanley 1984, p. 192.

70  25 February 1810. Hall 1936, p. 232. Mary Gertrude Pedder died on 17 February 1810. Her mother, of the same name, had died on 18 December 1807 at the age of thirty-two.

71  31 March 1793. Jameson 2003, pp. 231–2.

72  Fire marks are still seen on some houses today.

73  25 August 1778. Winstanley 1983, p. 66.

74  Matches had to be set alight with a flame from a tinderbox, candle or fire. They could not be ignited by 'striking' them on a rough surface like modern matches. They could only be used for transferring, not originating, a flame.

75  Beeswax candles were taxed at eight pence a pound, which was reduced to threepence in 1784, the same as spermaceti candles. Tallow was taxed at one penny a pound, increased by a halfpenny in 1784 but reduced back to a penny in 1792 (Dowell 1888, pp. 306–10).

76  Beeswax candles could not be made in a mould because they contracted on cooling and stuck to the mould. Instead, the hot beeswax was ladled over the wick, layer by layer, and the soft, warm candles were rolled to shape on a moistened surface, which was an expensive process (Eveleigh 2003).

77  Simond 1817, p. 150.

78  *Morning Chronicle* 24 October 1807.

79  White 1789, p. 198.

80  A rushlight holder was a simple clamp, commonly of wood or metal, that was set

on a base that stood upright or was made to be fixed to a wall. All that was needed was a stable form of clamp to hold the rushlight at a 45-degree angle while it burned.

81  Williams 1933, p. 173.
82  Simond 1815, pp. 3–4.
83  The term 'range' was used from the seventeenth century for kitchen grates for cooking, while for fireplaces in rooms such as the parlour and bedroom, the word 'grate' was retained (Eveleigh 1983).
84  *Morning Chronicle* 24 October 1807. Spits were horizontal, but when the open fireplaces of the ranges became more narrow, with the inclusion of ovens and boilers either side, vertical spits were developed.
85  23 October 1782. Winstanley 1998, p. 71.
86  Glasse 1774, p. i.
87  Glasse 1774, pp. 3, 10, 101, 329.
88  Glasse 1774, p. 330.
89  Eden 1797c, p. 753.
90  Silliman 1810, p. 50.
91  6 November 1795. Jameson 2004, p. 220.
92  Eden 1797b, p. 267.
93  Published by Hannah Humphrey on 6 July 1795. Wright 1867, p. 496. Twelvepence was one shilling, and a crown was five shillings.
94  Carter 1845, p. 42. He was born on 5 July 1792.
95  *Morning Chronicle* 28 October 1807.
96  Middleton 1807, p. 419. This survey, done in 1806, updated a 1793 survey for the Board of Agriculture.
97  Middleton 1807, p. 423.
98  Middleton 1807, p. 424.
99  Middleton 1807, p. 422.
100  Middleton 1807, p. 424.
101  Letter written at Upholland 9 June 1808. Hall 1936, p. 91.
102  Andrews 1934, p. 359.
103  Montague 1785, p. 112.
104  28 January 1780. Winstanley 1984, p. 12.
105  From the contents list of Montague 1785, pp. 1–7.
106  13 March 1800. Somerset Archives and Local Studies A\BTL/2/4.
107  17 March 1800. Somerset Archives and Local Studies A\BTL/2/4.
108  19 March 1800. Somerset Archives and Local Studies A\BTL/2/4.
109  21 March 1800. Somerset Archives and Local Studies A\BTL/2/4.
110  18 June 1800. Somerset Archives and Local Studies A\BTL/2/4.
111  Simond 1815, pp. 154–5. Lawnmowers were not yet invented. Rollers were also used on paths and yards.
112  11 June 1794. Jameson 2004, p. 42.
113  Montague 1785, p. 139. Sack was then 'a kind of sweet wine, now brought chiefly from the Canaries'.
114  White 1789, p. 298.
115  Diary entries for 2 and 4 April 1799. Jameson 2006, pp. 105–6.
116  White 1789, pp. 301–2. This was a freak heatwave caused by volcanic activity.

117   *Leeds Intelligencer* 20 October 1789.

118   Chapman 1932a, pp. 138–9. Letter of 14 September 1804.

119   David 1994, pp. 325–7.

120   *Morning Post* 7 October 1811.

121   *Morning Post* 7 September 1802.

122   *Morning Post* 7 September 1802. The houses no longer exist.

123   Gillett 1945, pp. 39–40.

124   20 October 1794. Jameson 2004, p. 86.

125   4 January 1798. Jameson 2006, p. 1.

126   Christie 1929, pp. 208–9.

127   25 August 1782. Andrews 1934, p. 82.

128   29 October 1781. Winstanley 1984, p. 175.

129   29 March 1777. Winstanley 1981, p. 119.

130   17 May 1780. Winstanley 1984, p. 42.

131   5 January 1781. Winstanley 1984, p. 102.

132   4 September 1809. Upton-Wilkinson archive (090904wwsp).

133   Moritz 1809, p. 12.

134   11 February 1800. Somerset Archives and Local Studies A\BTL/2/3.

135   29 May 1800. Somerset Archives and Local Studies A\BTL/2/6.

136   7 February 1806. Somerset Archives and Local Studies A\BTL/2/25.

137   1 December 1790. Jameson 2001, p. 271.

138   8 June 1781. Winstanley 1984, p. 140.

139   28 May 1792. Jameson 2003, p. 141.

140   25 June 1792. Jameson 2003, p. 149.

141   Trusler 1784, p. 83. This was an updated, effectively plagiarised, version of the advice given in letters to his son by Lord Chesterfield.

142   23 December 1778. Winstanley 1983, p. 98.

143   Winstanley 1983, p. 98. Woodforde was a very sociable man, and such gatherings were undoubtedly enjoyable occasions.

## 5: FASHIONS AND FILTH

1   Raw cotton-wool was imported from many places, including South and North America, the West Indies, the Mediterranean, the Levant and India.

2   Pantaloons were based on the full-length version worn by the military, with instep stirrups, which Beau Brummell (1778–1840) made fashionable. See Kelly 2005.

3   28 December 1809. Upton-Wilkinson archive (091223wwsp).

4   14 January 1808. Hall 1936, p. 664.

5   *Northampton Mercury* 20 April 1778. The theft was on 11 April. A surviving pair of Admiral Lord Nelson's stockings are marked with II, N and a coronet.

6   Letter written at Upholland, Lancashire, 14 January 1808. Hall 1936, p. 64.

7   Some men wore a coloured cravat over a white one, which later evolved into a white collar and bowtie.

8   9 June 1810. Somerset Archives and Local Studies A\BTL/2/33.

9   Grose 1811 no pagination.

10   Written at Beacon's Gutter, near Liverpool, 17 March 1809. Hall 1936, p. 159.

11   They persist today in dress or formal shirts for evening events.

12 George Spencer, 2nd Earl Spencer, allegedly burnt his tails in an accident before the fire and ordered his tailor to cut them off.

13 Pratt 1803, pp. 632–3.

14 We might today call this a full-length petticoat or slip.

15 21 May 1780.Winstanley 1984, p. 43.

16 Smith 1785, p. 54.

17 Smith 1785, p. 55.

18 Smith 1785, p. 55.

19 The term coat, skirt and petticoat were interchangeable.

20 *The Universal Magazine* 60, 1777, p. 379.

21 4 June 1805. Silliman 1810, p. 173.

22 *Report of the Select Committee of the Court of Directors of the East India Company, upon the subject of the cotton manufacture of this country*, 1793, quoted in Baines 1835, p. 334.

23 *The Times* 11 December 1799. These coats were named after the Frenchman Jean de Bry and had padded shoulders and narrow waists.

24 21 September 1803. Somerset Archives and Local Studies A\BTL/2/17.

25 15 September 1813. Brabourne 1884b, p. 150.

26 *Morning Chronicle* 30 October 1807.

27 19 June 1799. Jameson 2006, p. 128. The term 'bosom-friend' was already in use for an intimate friend.

28 The term 'ridicule' was from the French and 'reticule' from the Latin meaning 'net' (as many of these bags were made by knotting).

29 9 January 1799. Brabourne 1884a, p. 195. Letter written at Steventon.

30 Eden 1797a, p. 558.

31 Eden 1797b, p. 639. This was the House of Industry at Shrewsbury.

32 Moritz 1809, p. 85.

33 13 August 1810. Letter written to Miss Bessy Winkley at Dove Nest. Hall 1936, p. 285.

34 Brabourne 1884a, p. 187.

35 7 November 1808. She was living at Beacon's Gutter, near Liverpool. Hall 1936, p. 122.

36 Brabourne 1884a, p. 186. Letter written at Steventon on Christmas Day 1798.

37 27 March 1799. Jameson 2006, p. 102.

38 30 March 1799. Jameson 2006, p. 104.

39 30 November 1782. Winstanley 1998, p. 82.

40 5 August 1800. Darbishire 1958, p. 46.

41 Brabourne 1884a, p. 186. Letter of Christmas Day 1798, written at Steventon.

42 Brabourne 1884a, p. 138. Letter of 1 September 1796, written at Rowling in Kent.

43 16 April 1782.This was William Aldridge of Norwich. Winstanley 1998, p. 31.

44 *Gentleman's Magazine* 55, December 1785, p. 938.

45 *Lancaster Gazette* 20 August 1808.

46 31 March 1784. Winstanley 1998, p. 226.

47 18 April 1811. Brabourne 1884b, pp. 84–5.

48 Silliman 1810, p. 283. This was in London in 1805.

49 Eden 1797a, p. 555.

50 Eden 1797a, p. 554.

51  5 March 1802. Darbishire 1958, p. 127.
52  Silliman 1810, p. 215.
53  4 May 1802, about 2 miles north of Grasmere. Darbishire 1958, p. 156.
54  *Morning Post* 8 December 1804.
55  Silliman 1810, pp. 215–16.
56  10 June 1784. Winstanley 1998, p. 249.
57  8 February 1802, in the Lake District. Darbishire 1958, p. 112.
58  10 February 1802. Jameson 2007, p. 107.
59  9 January 1806. Somerset Archives and Local Studies A\BTL/2/25. In a pocket diary for 1799, fifteen-year-old Mary Filliter recorded the purchase of 'pattens 1s 10d' (Dorset History Centre D/FIL/F53).
60  Eden 1797b, p. 76.
61  9 November 1805. Romney 1984, p. 219.
62  This was in 1811. Simond 1817, p. 307.
63  This was in 1810. Simond 1815, p. 21.
64  Moritz 1809, p. 41.
65  Military cockades with colours other than black signified rebels or enemy troops. A plume of a different colour might be worn above a black cockade. Political cockades, worn mostly at election times, were of various colours.
66  6 August 1799. Moretonhampstead History Society manuscript of Treleaven's diary.
67  Brabourne 1884a, p. 192.
68  The Mamelukes were Egyptian cavalry who had fought Napoleon's troops in Egypt.
69  *Kentish Gazette* 15 May 1804.
70  It is often said that umbrellas were usually black in colour to disguise the filthy rain, which was heavily polluted with soot from coal fires, but there is no evidence that black umbrellas were popular at this date.
71  Pugh 1787, p. 221.
72  Macdonald 1790, pp. 382–3.
73  28 January 1787. Winstanley and Jameson 1999, p. 207.
74  29 June 1789. Jameson 2001, p. 160.
75  18 August 1788. Andrews 1934, p. 355.
76  This was June 1789. Andrews 1935, p. 24. The Tontine Inn was the main coaching inn at Sheffield, near today's Dixon Lane. It was demolished in 1850.
77  28 June 1786. Winstanley and Jameson 1999, p. 145.
78  *Chester Chronicle* 20 March 1795.
79  5 October 1781. Winstanley 1984, p. 168.
80  14 April 1796. Jameson 2005, p. 28.
81  *Sussex Advertiser* 30 May 1814.
82  Women did not wear wigs, but at times their hair was styled and powdered to resemble wigs.
83  Brabourne 1884a, p. 174. Letter of 1 December 1798 written at Steventon.
84  17 February 1781. Winstanley 1984, p. 112.
85  15 October 1792. Jameson 2003, p. 182.
86  Nelly Weeton was writing from Beacon's Gutter, near Liverpool, on 6 February 1809. Hall 1936, p. 149.
87  British Library Add MS 27828 fol. 119.
88  The National Archives ADM 101/102/3.

89  A US gallon is just over 8 pounds.

90  25 April 1800. Somerset Archives and Local Studies A\BTL/2/5.

91  3 September 1801. Jameson 2007, p. 65.

92  4 September 1801. Jameson 2007, p. 65.

93  Darter 1888, pp. 58–9.

94  Simond 1817, pp. 363–4.

95  Bamford 1936, p. 18.

96  24 October 1804. Somerset Archives and Local Studies A\BTL/2/17.

97  21 November 1795. Jameson 2004, p. 224.

98  27 August 1809. Upton-Wilkinson archive (090827wwsp).

99  10 June 1799. Jameson 2006, p. 125.

100  27 October 1798. Brabourne 1884a, pp. 160–1.

101  British Library Add MS 27827, fols 50–1. Francis Place was born in 1771.

102  Willan 1801, p 255.

103  15 October 1808. Hall 1936, pp. 115–16.

104  The Worshipful Company of Launderers website is www.launderers.co.uk.

105  *Hampshire Chronicle* 12 December 1791.

106  11 March 1801. Jameson 2007, p. 19.

107  The Wordsworths were then living at Dove Cottage. Darbishire 1958, p. 61.

108  25 March 1814. Somerset Archives and Local Studies A\BTL/2/40.

109  Brabourne 1884a, p. 147. This was 18 September 1796, when staying at Rowling in Kent.

110  3 May 1806. Fremantle 1940, p. 258. This was during the trial of Henry Dundas (Lord Melville, 1742–1811). He had been impeached in Parliament on grounds of corruption in 1805. He had served as Treasurer of the Navy and First Lord of the Admiralty. This was of interest to Elizabeth Fremantle, who was married to a naval captain. She is also known by her maiden name Elizabeth (Betsey) Wynne, author of one of the Wynne diaries.

111  Willan 1801, p. 304.

112  20 November 1800. Chapman 1932a, p. 92. Letter to Cassandra, written at Steventon.

113  Montague 1785, p. 187.

114  *Northampton Mercury* 5 March 1803.

115  *Northampton Mercury* 10 June 1809.

116  *Northampton Mercury* 10 June 1809.

117  Hamilton 1813, p. 29.

118  Hamilton 1813, p. 24.

119  Simond 1815, p. 49. He was writing about London in 1810.

120  Simond 1815, p. 49.

121  Trial of Catherine Mason and Samuel Duck, April 1770, Old Bailey Proceedings online (t17700425-1).

122  *Bath Chronicle* 17 July 1777.

123  Wright 1960, p. 118.

124  Winstanley 1984, p. 57.

125  21 January 1814. Somerset Archives and Local Studies A\BTL/2/40.

126  See the satirical print of the ladies' communal facilities at Vauxhall Gardens in Gatrell 2006, p. 377.

127  *Lancaster Gazette* 20 August 1808.

128  Trial of Catherine Tewner, Old Bailey Proceedings Online, January 1815, t18150111-44. The incident occurred at Robinson's Buildings, London.

129  Trial of Catherine Tewner, Old Bailey Proceedings Online, January 1815, t18150111-44.

130  Trial of Patrick Smith, Old Bailey Proceedings Online, October 1814, t18141026-3.

131  13 April 1810. Hall 1936, p. 252.

132  Rudder 1779, p. 395.

133  Foot 1794, p. 26.

134  *Report from Select Committee on the Education of the Lower Orders in the Metropolis* (London, 1816), p. 40. The evidence was given by Edward Wakefield, a philanthropist.

## 6: SERMONS AND SUPERSTITIONS

1  Note the incorrect spelling of the Austen surname. Somerset Archives and Local Studies DD/HY 7/2/5.

2  9 January 1801. Brabourne 1884a p. 256.

3  This was 1811. Simond 1817, p. 175.

4  Letter to Cassandra Austen dated 21 January 1799. Brabourne 1884a p. 200. Cooper did take the living.

5  *Jackson's Oxford Journal* 31 December 1774.

6  Woodforde is called 'Parson' because the publication of abridged diaries in the 1920s used that term. For an explanation of the different publications of his diaries, see Winstanley 1996, pp. 3–8.

7  Andrews 1935, p. 228. Byng was staying at the Chequers Inn, which is still in the High Street. The vicar was Jacob Mountain, who also held the living of St Andrew in Norwich and in 1793 became the first Anglican bishop of Quebec.

8  6 June 1792. Andrews 1936, p. 43.

9  21 April 1774. Winstanley 1989, pp. 37–8.

10  *New Exeter Journal or General Advertiser for Devon, Cornwall, Dorset and Somerset* 30 April 1789. Stoke was also known as Stoke Damerel. The church was enlarged in 1751 to cater for the dockland population.

11  Simond 1815, pp. 174–5.

12  23 October 1804. Somerset Archives and Local Studies A\BTL/2/19.

13  March 1805. Somerset Archives and Local Studies A\BTL/2/21. When Sturges died, the new rector was a brother of the Duke of Wellington. A new St Luke's Church was consecrated in 1824, and the old one became a chapel of ease, now known as the Old Church Chelsea. Sturges had been vicar of St Mary's Church in Reading for over four decades.

14  25 December 1806. Somerset Archives and Local Studies A\BTL/2/26. Holland refers to payment for the gown in mid-January 1807, calling it a Master of Arts gown.

15  15 September 1810. Somerset Archives and Local Studies A\BTL/2/33.

16  *Sussex Advertiser* 19 January 1795.

17  31 March 1772. Winstanley 1988, p. 25.

18  Hall 1936, pp. 165–6. Written at Beacon's Gutter, near Liverpool, 19 May 1809.

19  Christie 1929, p. 147.

20  2 December 1799. Somerset Archives and Local Studies A\BTL/2/3.

21  November 1799. Somerset Archives and Local Studies A\BTL/2/1.

22  3 December 1776. Winstanley 1981, p. 94.

23  Sunday 10 November 1776. Winstanley 1981, p. 87.

24  Moritz 1809, p. 70.

25  Moritz 1809, p. 71. The church was largely rebuilt in 1846.

26  Moritz 1809, p. 71.

27  Moritz 1809, pp. 71–2.

28  26 June 1791. Andrews 1935, p. 338.

29  13 June 1790. Andrews 1935, p. 175.

30  15 April 1804. Somerset Archives and Local Studies A\BTL/2/18.

31  6 October 1783. Winstanley 1998, p. 176.

32  3 February 1797. Jameson 2005, p. 118. For all his years of learning Classical languages, Woodforde was unable to converse in French.

33  25 December 1782. Winstanley 1998, p. 91.

34  21 February 1816. Somerset Archives and Local Studies A\BTL/2/41. Jack (John) Hunt's cottage was near Over Stowey between the Crowcombe Road and Friarn Farm (information from David Worthy).

35  27 June 1791. Andrews 1935, p. 342.

36  Simon Jenkins (1999, p. xxx) says that 'There are roughly 8,000 extant pre-Reformation churches in England and about the same number of Anglican churches.'

37  8 February 1809. Somerset Archives and Local Studies A\BTL/2/29. The church was restored some decades later.

38  28 January 1810. Somerset Archives and Local Studies A\BTL/2/31.

39  White 1789, p. 316.

40  *Leeds Intelligencer* 20 October 1789. This was the church of St Peter, demolished in 1838 and replaced by a huge Victorian structure.

41  23 June 1780. Winstanley 1984, p. 53.

42  7 November 1808. Nelly Weeton was living at Beacon's Gutter, near Liverpool. Hall 1936, pp. 122–3.

43  Silliman 1810, p. 315.

44  8 February 1809. Somerset Archives and Local Studies A\BTL/2/29.

45  25 October 1809. Somerset Archives and Local Studies A\BTL/2/30.

46  3 June 1816. Somerset Archives and Local Studies A\BTL/2/42. The king's birthday was usually celebrated on 4 June.

47  24 March 1817. Somerset Archives and Local Studies A\BTL/2/43.

48  Andrews 1935, p. 238.

49  26 June 1791. Andrews 1935, pp. 337–8.

50  Andrews 1935, p. 411.

51  Beale 1891, pp. 87–9. A letter to Mrs André in August 1791. William Hutton (1723–1815) was born in Derby, worked in the textile trade and was later a bookseller and printer, being largely self-educated.

52  Joseph Priestley (1733–1804) is better known today for his scientific achievements.

53  Simond 1817, p. 178.

54  Romney 1984, p. 24.

55  11 May 1800. Somerset Archives and Local Studies A\BTL/2/5.

56  13 July 1800. Somerset Archives and Local Studies A\BTL/2/8.

57  3 June 1816. Somerset Archives and Local Studies A\BTL/2/42.

58  Andrews 1935, p. 130. Byng expressed his views while touring the Midlands in 1789.

59  Haydon 2002.

60  *Hampshire Pocket Companion* 1787, Somerset Archives and Local Studies DD/HY 7/2/5.

61  Grose 1787, p. 1 of 'Superstitions' (the pagination is duplicated within this volume for different sections). Grose was born in London and lived from 1731 to 1790.

62  White 1789, p. 202.

63  Hall 1936, p. 46.

64  Hall 1936, p. 46.

65  Hall 1936, pp. 45–6.

66  *Morning Post* 27 April 1810, quoted in Ashton 1906, p. 452. This took place close to the London School of Economics which stands on the site of Clare Market.

67  Grose 1787, p. 52 of 'Superstitions'.

68  18 November 1793. Jameson 2003, p. 309.

69  5 January 1796. Jameson 2005, p. 2.

70  24 February 1795. Jameson 2004, p. 127.

71  Grose 1787, p. 53 of 'Superstitions'.

72  Grose 1787, p. 62 of 'Superstitions'.

73  Grose 1787, pp. 62, 64 of 'Superstitions'.

74  *Morning Post* 21 August 1779. A caul is a membrane found over the head of some babies at birth.

75  Grose 1787, p. 57 of 'Superstitions'.

76  Grose 1787, pp. 57–8 of 'Superstitions'.

77  Grose 1787, p. 29 of 'Superstitions'.

78  *Archaeologia Cantiana* 80, 1965, p. 255.

79  Grose 1787, pp. 29–30.

80  *Leeds Intelligencer* 27 March 1809.

81  *Leeds Intelligencer* 27 March 1809.

82  In the second-floor gallery. Personal communication, Liz Egan of the Thackray Museum.

83  Benton 1867, p. 254.

84  He was born around 1780. Benton 1867, p. 254.

85  F. Moore 1803 *Vox Stellarum: or, A Loyal Almanack For the Year of Human Redemption* 1803, p. 9.

86  F. Moore 1803 *Vox Stellarum: or, A Loyal Almanack For the Year of Human Redemption* 1803, p. 13.

87  Jameson 2003, p. 94.

88  Traditionally, Old Christmas Day fell on 6 January and was observed widely on this date, but there are several instances in William Holland's diary of servants asking for time off to celebrate Old Christmas Day on 5 January, and at other times 6 January, so it seems that in this part of Somerset the actual date was imprecise.

89  6 January 1807. Somerset Heritage Centre A\BTL/2/26.

90  Jameson 2001, p. 12.

91 *The New Exeter Journal or General Advertiser for Devon, Cornwall, Dorset and Somerset* 23 April 1789.

92 Mingay 2002.

93 *Gentleman's Magazine* 68 (1790), p. 719.

94 Winstanley 1984, p. 38.

95 Winstanley 1984, p. 38.

96 Winstanley 1984, pp. 38–9.

97 11 June 1790. Andrews 1935, pp. 168–70.

98 Andrews 1935, p. 170.

7: WEALTH AND WORK

1 Letter to George Hunt of 24 January 1795. Jenkin 1951, p. 30.

2 Darter 1888, p. 35.

3 13 December 1797. Jameson 2005, p. 196.

4 28 March 1804. Somerset Archives and Local Studies A\BTL/2/18. The road bridge was built in the 1770s.

5 28 August 1805. Silliman 1820a, p. 142.

6 15 November 1782. Winstanley 1998, p. 77.

7 18 November 1782. Winstanley 1998, p. 77. Like Woodforde, Bathurst held the livings through New College, Oxford.

8 In 1801 Henry Austen had gone into partnership with two other men as an army agent and banker in London, which turned into a banking business (Austen and Co.) with country branches at Alton and Petersfield in Hampshire and at Hythe in Kent. The end of the war in Europe in 1815 brought a sharp deflation, and his bank crashed with huge debts in 1816 because it did not keep sufficient reserves to cover its loans. See Caplan 2004 and Ellis 2011.

9 17 October 1793. Jameson 2003, p. 299.

10 The approximate equivalents of money in Jane Austen's time to UK decimal coinage are one guinea = £1.05; one pound = £1; one crown = 25p; and one shilling = 5p. In terms of purchasing power, a shilling at that time would be about £1.60 today and a guinea about £34 (using The National Archives currency converter which translates prices in 1800 to values in 2005). However, wages were low. Woodforde paid his housemaid 3½d (47p) per day plus board and lodging and gave occasional presents such as a length of cloth to make a garment.

11 9 November 1805. Romney 1984, p. 219.

12 Andrews 1935, p. 167.

13 1 March 1797. Jameson 2005, p. 125.

14 Blackner 1815, p. 392. John Blackner (about 1770 to 1816) was originally apprenticed to a stocking maker in Derbyshire.

15 16 March 1797. Jameson 2005, p. 130.

16 This continued until 1821, and in 1833 they became legal tender for amounts over £5.

17 21 July 1810. Somerset Archives and Local Studies A\BTL/2/33. People usually preferred local banknotes, as the people running the bank would be known and trusted. Outside London, Bank of England notes were likely to be discounted (Ellis 2011).

18 24 March 1797. Jameson 2005, p. 132.

19 *Alfred and Westminster Evening Gazette* 26 April 1810.

20 Colquhoun 1796, p. 124. He was a founder of the Thames Police.

21 *The Times* 13 February 1815.

22 Campbell-Smith 2011, pp. 87–8.

23 19 June 1811. Somerset Archives and Local Studies A\BTL/2/35.

24 26 June 1811. Somerset Archives and Local Studies A\BTL/2/35.

25 21 June 1780. Winstanley 1984, p. 53.

26 The Austens lived at Chawton in Hampshire from 1809, in a cottage on the extensive estate of Jane's brother Edward.

27 In London in 1782. Moritz 1809, p. 10.

28 Andrews 1935, p. 372.

29 9 May 1780. Winstanley 1984, p. 40.

30 8 January 1802. Somerset Archives and Local Studies A\BTL/2/14.

31 Bell 1812, p. 5.

32 18 November 1787. Surgeon Lionel Gillespie's journal, The National Archives ADM 101/102/3.

33 May 1795. Eden 1797b, p. 551.

34 Simond 1817, p. 79.

35 March 1811. Simond 1817, p. 76. He does not specify the precise coal pit.

36 Simond 1817, p. 77.

37 *Children's Employment Commission. Appendix to First Report of Commissioners. Mines. Part II. Reports and Evidence from Sub-Commissioners. Presented to both Houses of Parliament by Command of Her Majesty* (London, 1842), p. 288.

38 This only became properly effective with an amendment in 1799.

39 Eden 1797b, p. 552.

40 *Newcastle Journal* 24 June 1777.

41 'An Account of the Navigable Canal now making from the several Coal-Mines in the Neighbourhood of *Stourbridge* and *Dudley*, to communicate with the Great Canal from the *Trent to the Severn*, near *Stourton*, in the County of *Stafford*', *Gentleman's Magazine*, 1777, p. 313.

42 *Trewman's Exeter Flying Post* 30 August 1810.

43 Shaw 1808, p. 318. The tunnel is east of Basingstoke, while Steventon lies to the west. Many of the investors in the Basingstoke Canal Navigation Company were known to Jane Austen and her family (Horsfall 2005).

44 Andrews 1934, pp. 259–60.

45 Warner 1801, p. 16. September 1800. This same canal may have been visited by Jane Austen a few months later, in May 1801 (Le Faye 2011, pp. 592–3).

46 'Grand Junction Canal Association' in *The Christian Observer* 17, 1818, pp. 556–7. This canal extended from Braunston in Northamptonshire to the River Thames at Brentford.

47 11 October 1800. Somerset Archives and Local Studies A\BTL/2/10.

48 Darter 1888, p. 33.

49 Known to have been sung and probably written by 'Common' John Grimshaw of Gorton near Manchester within this period. Harland 1865, p. 253.

50 Warner 1801, pp. 39–40

51 18 June 1790. Andrews 1935, p. 196. The mill was built in 1771.

52 This was in 1797. Grant 1809, p. 243.

53 Grant 1809, pp. 243–4.

54  Grant 1809, p. 244.

55  Harland 1865, pp. 259–60.

56  Harland 1865, p. 259.

57  Blackner 1815, p. 402.

58  Blackner 1815, pp. 402–3. Many proclamations and anonymous threatening letters referred to or were signed by a 'General Ludd' or 'Ned Ludd'.

59  Blackner 1815, p. 403.

60  Hall 1939, p. 57.

61  Mingay 2002, p. 141.

62  7 October 1784. Winstanley 1998, p. 282.

63  The earliest known published version was printed in London in 1794 (Roud and Bishop 2012, p. 456).

64  From the version sung by Mr Alfred Lockey, of Bedwyn, Wiltshire, published in *The Wiltshire Magazine* 50, no. 179, December 1943, pp. 283–4.

65  Stevenson 1812, p. 350.

66  Brabourne 1884a, p. 170.

67  14 September 1776. Winstanley 1981, p. 72.

68  Gardiner 1853, pp. 46–7 .

69  Pratt 1803, pp. 316–17.

70  Pratt 1801, pp. 276–7.

71  Pratt 1801, p. 287. Mavor lived from 1758 to 1837. These were Enclosure (or Inclosure) Acts.

72  Goldsmith 1770, p. 8.

73  Pratt 1801, pp. 287–8.

74  Andrews 1935, p. 324.

75  Andrews 1935, pp. 322–4.

76  This case effectively abolished slavery in England, although the slave trade was not abolished until 1807.

77  Silliman 1810, p. 47.

78  24 June 1805. Silliman 1810, pp. 216–17.

79  12 February 1780. Pasley 1931, p. 61.

80  Rattenbury 1837, pp. 15–16.

81  Darter 1888, p. 35. The Nore was the naval anchorage in the Thames estuary near Sheerness.

82  30 September 1779. Winstanley 1983, pp. 180–1.

83  Eden 1797b, p. 66.

84  April 1796. Eden 1797b, p. 73.

85  Simond 1815, pp. 222, 225.

86  Andrews 1935, p. 10.

87  Christie 1929, p. 139.

88  Eden 1797b, pp. 272–3.

89  20 March 1781. Winstanley 1984, p. 120.

90  27 October 1792. Jameson 2003, p. 186. 'Bargewell' was the nearby village of Bawdeswell.

91  Simond 1817, p. 94. Written in March 1811.

92  6 January 1789. Jameson 2001, p. 109.

93  Blackner 1815, p. 401.

94  Smith 1874, p. 30.
95  Darter 1888, p. 68.
96  *The Times* 28 August 1816.
97  *St. James's Chronicle and London Evening Post* 19 June 1817.

## 8: LEISURE AND PLEASURE

1   Carter 1845, p. 124. He was working in London in 1810.
2   Southey 1814, p. 190.
3   Hutton 1795, p. 97. He had originally worked in the textile trade.
4   Grose 1811, no pagination.
5   Spilsbury 1791, p. 64.
6   18 September 1805. Somerset Archives and Local Studies A\BTL/2/23.
7   Hall 1939, p. 145.
8   Grant 1809, p. 252.
9   *Reading Mercury* 29 June 1789.
10  *Reading Mercury* 29 June 1789.
11  Andrews 1934, p. 217.
12  Andrews 1935, p. 163. Byng was in Derby on 9 June – the inhabitants were celebrating Oak Apple Day according to the old calendar. After the reform of the calendar in 1752, eleven days had been lost, so that the old 29 May became 9 June.
13  *Oxford Journal* 17 January 1789.
14  Darter 1888, p. 31.
15  Darter 1888, pp. 82–3.
16  Darter 1888, p. 83.
17  16 March 1772. Winstanley 1988, p. 21.
18  Darter 1888, pp. 36–7.
19  Darter 1888, p. 37.
20  Darter 1888, p. 37.
21  25 September 1813. Hubback and Hubback 1906, pp. 246–7.
22  6 January 1802. Somerset Archives and Local Studies A\BTL/2/14.
23  6 July 1789. Jameson 2001, p. 162.
24  1 July 1789. Jameson 2001, p. 161.
25  13 September 1791. Jameson 2003, p. 62.
26  *Morning Chronicle* 27 March 1812.
27  *Morning Post* 5 November 1805.
28  14 November 1805. Romney 1984, p. 224.
29  4 October 1805. Romney 1984, p. 161.
30  4 October 1805. Romney 1984, p. 163.
31  Hutton 1791, pp. 218–19.
32  Blackner 1815, p. 385.
33  *Morning Post* 27 June 1814.
34  18 September 1772. Winstanley 1988, p. 73.
35  Moretonhampstead History Society manuscript of Treleaven's diary.
36  Lewis 1866, p. 398.
37  3rd Earl of Hardwicke, grandson of the Lord Hardwicke who gave his name to the 1753 Marriage Act.
38  Lewis 1866, pp. 398–9.

39  Lewis 1866, p. 399.

40  23 September 1795. Jameson 2004, pp. 201–2.

41  *Lancaster Gazette* 11 August 1810.

42  5 September 1810. Hall 1936, p. 294.

43  Hall 1936, p. 294.

44  Hall 1936, p. 294.

45  Andrews 1934, p. 100.

46  Austen Leigh 1871, p. 69.

47  Brabourne 1884a, p. 238. The ball took place on 30 October 1800.

48  Lewis 1866, p. 418. The ball was on 17 May 1810.

49  27 August 1801. Jameson 2007, p. 63.

50  Bamford 1936, pp. 183–4. Letter of 4 October 1798 to Miss Heber. Lady Banks was wife of Sir Joseph Banks.

51  Bamford 1936, p. 186.

52  19 December 1804. Fremantle 1940, p. 147. The stately home of Stowe is now the independent Stowe School, just north of Buckingham.

53  24 March 1800. Jameson 2006, p. 196.

54  Hubback and Hubback 1906, p. 246. The Lyceum was unlicensed except for the period when the Drury Lane theatre moved there while being rebuilt after a devastating fire.

55  17 July 1809. Hall 1936, p. 175. Sarah Siddons (1755–1831) was a famous actor known for playing in tragedies.

56  Hall 1936, pp. 175–6.

57  Moritz 1809, pp. 33–4.

58  25 May 1802. Moretonhampstead History Society manuscript of Treleaven's diary.

59  Moretonhampstead History Society manuscript of Treleaven's diary.

60  25 September 1788. Jameson 2001, p. 73.

61  Moritz 1809, p. 31.

62  This was June 1805. Silliman 1810, p. 171.

63  22 March 1780 at Weston Longville. Winstanley 1984, p. 26.

64  6 January 1777. Somerset Archives and Local Studies Q/SR/345/1, quarter session rolls. Williams could presumably read, even though he was unable to write.

65  11 August 1788. Jameson 2001, p. 62.

66  British Library Add MS 35142, fols 57–8.

67  *Hampshire Chronicle* 3 July 1809. Many thanks to Dr David Higgins for information about how clay pipes were sold.

68  Christie 1929, pp. 130–1.

69  5 March 1790. Jameson 2001, p. 246.

70  Christie 1929, p. 131.

71  30 April 1783. Winstanley 1998, pp. 128–9.

72  Bone fish counters are on display at Castle Cary Museum in Somerset, along with contemporary playing cards that were found during the renovation of Ansford Parsonage and were very likely used by the Woodforde family there.

73  Moretonhampstead History Society manuscript of Treleaven's diary.

74  Moretonhampstead History Society manuscript of Treleaven's diary.

75  6 November 1807. Somerset Archives and Local Studies A\BTL/2/58. Joseph Ruscombe Poole was a lawyer and his wife was Elizabeth Stone.

76  George 1930, p. 317, quoting F. Eden 1801 *Observations on Friendly Societies* p. 29.

77  Gillett 1945, p. 44.

78  Repton 1812.

79  Repton 1812. An illustration of the urn shows it to be Bronze Age.

80  Grose et al 1780, p. iii.

81  7 November 1805. Silliman 1820b, p. 75.

82  Evans 2009, pp. 350–3. The Society is now based at Burlington House, London.

83  10 July 1809. Lewis 1866, p. 385.

84  16 May 1811. Simond 1817, pp. 252–3.

85  Moritz 1809, pp. 15–17.

86  Moritz 1809, p. 16.

87  Moritz 1809, pp. 15.

88  Moritz 1809, pp. 19–22.

89  Moritz 1809, p. 10.

90  Campbell-Smith 2011, p. 82.

91  Moritz 1809, p. 18.

92  Moritz 1809, p. 18. This was Oliver Goldsmith's *The Vicar of Wakefield*, published in 1766.

93  Ashton 1882, p. 458.

94  *Morning Chronicle* 25 December 1815.

95  Pratt 1803, pp. 444–5.

96  Brabourne 1884b, p. 306 (writing in August 1814 that Dawlish was wretched twelve years previously).

97  This is June 1810. Simond 1815, p. 187.

98  9 May 1804. Somerset Archives and Local Studies A\BTL\2\18.

99  28 October 1805. Somerset Archives and Local Studies A\BTL\2\24. This was the same storm that hit the fleet at Trafalgar.

100  18 April 1810. Hall 1936, p. 255.

101  Brabourne 1884a, p. 369.

102  31 July 1788. Jameson 2001, p. 59.

103  Letter written 11–15 November 1810. Hall 1936, p. 315.

104  The Penny Post was originally set up in 1680 by William Dockwra, but was taken over by the General Post Office (Campbell-Smith 2011, pp. 59–61).

105  25 May 1810. Hall 1936, p. 264.

106  30 April 1811. Brabourne 1884b, p. 97.

107  7 May 1811. Simond 1817, p. 200.

108  Chapman 1932b, p. 425.

## 9: ON THE MOVE

1  Gillett 1945, p. 16.

2  Austen Leigh 1871, p. 38.

3  Chapman 1932b, p. 475. Letter of 24 January 1817 to Alethea Bigg.

4  31 January 1790. Jameson 2001, p. 233.

5  1 August 1794. Jameson 2004, p. 57.

6  Moritz 1809, p. 87.

7  Moritz 1809, pp. 59–60.

8  Moritz 1809, p. 60.

9 Moritz 1809, p. 64.

10 21 January 1773. Winstanley 1988, p. 103.

11 14 March 1800. Moretonhampstead History Society manuscript of Treleaven's diary. The Shambles was where the butchers plied their trade.

12 9 November 1799. Somerset Archives and Local Studies A\BTL/2/1.

13 13 December 1790. Jameson 2001, p. 272.

14 8 September 1782. Andrews 1934, p. 108.

15 14 August 1795. Manners 1805, pp. 137–8. John Henry Manners was the Fifth Duke of Rutland.

16 September 1800. Warner 1801, p. 10.

17 Warner 1801, pp. 9–10.

18 26 November 1799. Somerset Archives and Local Studies A\BTL/2/3.

19 Austen Leigh 1871, p. 159. Letter of January 1817 to Alethea Bigg.

20 Gröben 1907, p. 87. Colonel Taylor was the brother of Sir Brook Taylor, and Ralph Heathcote was a diplomat in Germany (born in 1782).

21 *Morning Chronicle* 26 October 1807.

22 2 May 1793. Jameson 2003, p. 242.

23 Moritz 1809, p. 52.

24 11 May 1805. Silliman 1810, p. 67.

25 18 May 1805, while travelling in Warwickshire. Silliman 1810, p. 123.

26 *European Magazine* February 1816, p. 129.

27 May 1802. Courtesy of Trustees of the National Museum of the Royal Navy (NMRN), P 1985/323.

28 15 May 1805. Silliman 1810, p. 82.

29 *The Times* 25 December 1807.

30 6 July 1778. Winstanley 1983, p. 55.

31 Moritz 1809, p. 3.

32 August 1790. Andrews 1935, p. 275.

33 31 January 1807. Somerset Archives and Local Studies A\BTL/2/26.

34 'Hackney' derives from an Old French word meaning a horse and had passed into Middle English by the fourteenth century. Because many hackneys were hired out, this gave rise to the word 'hack' for an ordinary horse (or for poor writers who hire out their services).

35 Trusler 1790, p. 97.

36 Andrews 1934, p. 32.

37 Jenkin 1951, p. 18. Letter of 15 September 1792. As a Quaker, Jenkin is using the archaic form 'thy' rather than 'your'.

38 Moritz 1809, pp. 9–10.

39 26 April 1809. Upton-Wilkinson archive (090426spww01).

40 20 May 1805. Silliman 1810, p. 122.

41 22 January 1776. White 1837, pp. 389–90.

42 27 June 1800. Somerset Archives and Local Studies A\BTL/2/7. William Holland had a low opinion of Somerset workmen, which is why he referred to them as 'Somersetshire Boobies' among other things.

43 Andrews 1934, pp. 211–12. Byng made these comments in an Oxfordshire tour in 1785.

44 Andrews 1935, p. 64.

45  25 August 1805. Romney 1984, p. 93.

46  Andrews 1934, p. 261.

47  Moritz 1809, p. 66.

48  Cooke 1803, p. 102.

49  5 August 1781. Jeffery 1907, pp. 2–3. Dyott had recently joined the army and was on his way to Dublin.

50  26 March 1780. Winstanley 1984, p. 27.

51  12 June 1790. Andrews 1935, pp. 170–1.

52  6 July 1790. Andrews 1935, p. 236. This was at the Black Bull Inn in Cambridge.

53  July 1787. Andrews 1934, p. 249.

54  Silliman 1820a, p. 148. This was August 1805.

55  15 May 1805. Silliman 1810, p. 83.

56  20 May 1805. Silliman 1810, pp. 129–30.

57  26 June 1786. Winstanley and Jameson 1999, p. 144. The fifteenth-century Belle Sauvage inn was more frequently referred to as the 'Belle Savage'. It was demolished in 1873.

58  27 June 1786. Winstanley and Jameson 1999, p. 145.

59  30 June 1789. Andrews 1935, p. 116.

60  5 July 1790. Andrews 1935, p. 235. This fifteenth-century inn was rebuilt in 1828, and the replacement building, called 'The Bull' not 'The Black Bull', is grade II listed and has become part of St Catherine's College, at 68 Trumpington Street.

61  Andrews 1935, p. 151.

62  18 November 1805. Silliman 1820b, p. 145.

63  29 October 1795. Jameson 2004, p. 215.

64  13 January 1777. Winstanley 1981, pp. 103–4.

65  Moritz 1809, p. 13.

66  *The Times* 23 May 1803.

67  *The Times* 23 May 1803.

68  Granville 1916, p. 131. Lady Bessborough was sister of Georgiana, Duchess of Devonshire.

69  Adkins 2004, pp. 266–8.

70  4 February 1799. Jameson 2006, pp. 86–7.

71  17 February 1799. Jameson 2006, p. 91.

72  *Exeter Flying Post* 13 November 1800. St Thomas is on the west side of the River Exe, whereas most of Exeter is on an eminence on the east side.

73  *Exeter Flying Post* 13 November 1800. The post-chaises took the old ridgeway route into Exeter, which has since been named the Trafalgar Way. Henry Holland was a prominent architect and worked on Brighton Pavilion for the Prince Regent, as well as several notable buildings in London, including Hans Place, home of Henry Austen. He had estates at Okehampton.

74  *Exeter Flying Post* 13 November 1800.

75  30 January 1794. Jameson 2004, p. 8.

76  Pratt 1804, pp. 353–4.

77  Pratt 1804, p. 354.

78  Hutton 1795, p. 402.

79  'Extract of a Letter from Warrington, September 1' in *The Annual Register, or a View of the History, Politics, and Literature for the Year 1774* (London, 1778), p. 145.

80 Hall 1936, p. 164. Letter written at Beacon's Gutter, 19 May 1809. The direct distance was about 14 miles, but it was cheaper and more comfortable by canal than by stagecoach.

81 *The Times* 19 December 1806.

82 Hutton 1795, p. 404. This is now the Wednesbury Old Canal.

83 *Salisbury and Winchester Journal & Hampshire Chronicle* 20 September 1784.

84 *Northampton Mercury* 20 September 1784.

85 *Salisbury and Winchester Journal & Hampshire Chronicle* 27 September 1784.

## 10: DARK DEEDS

1 *Cobbetts Weekly Political Register* vol. 30, January–June 1816, col. 397.

2 McLynn 1989, pp. xi–xii.

3 June 1790. Andrews 1935, p. 209.

4 Wilson 2002, p. 161.

5 Porter 1851, p. 509.

6 Darter 1888, p. 33.

7 Blackner 1815, p. 280.

8 Sunday 10 March 1811. Simond 1817, p. 87.

9 11 March 1811. Simond 1817, pp. 94–5.

10 *York Herald* 16 March 1811.

11 Andrews 1935, p. 178.

12 McLynn 1989, p. 32.

13 McLynn 1989, p. 35.

14 Darter 1888, p. 65.

15 Moritz 1809, p. 51.

16 November 1805. Silliman 1820b, p. 101.

17 *Gentleman's Magazine* 54, 1784, p. 635. The report in its 'Historical Chronicle' was dated 14 August.

18 Trial of Sarah Smith, Old Bailey Proceedings online, April 1793, t17930410-95.

19 Trial of Sarah Smith, Old Bailey Proceedings online, April 1793, t17930410-95.

20 The National Archives manuscript HO 11/1; Bateson 1969, pp. 147–8.

21 Moritz 1809, p. 51.

22 British Library Add MS 27825 (Francis Place unpublished manuscript, vol. 1.B, p. 147).

23 An example is in the Bodleian Library, Harding B22 (304).

24 Since 1739, the song has had a number of titles, including 'The Dunghill Cock, or Turpin's Valiant Exploits', 'Turpin's Valour', 'Oh, Rare Turpin Hero' and 'Turpin Hero'. It is still performed today.

25 Broadside ballad 1739 'Turpin's Rant: A New Song', Bodleian Library, Harding B22 (304).

26 *Oxford Journal* 14 January 1797.

27 *Norfolk Chronicle or the Norwich Gazette* 4 February 1797.

28 Moritz 1809, pp. 51–2.

29 *The Times* 22 June 1792.

30 *A Treatise on the Police of the Metropolis* (1796).

31 14 March 1805. Somerset Archives and Local Studies A\BTL/2/21.

32 *Bath Chronicle and Weekly Gazette* 3 August 1775.

33 *Northampton Mercury* 7 August 1775.

34 *Northampton Mercury* 7 August 1775.

35 27 January 1808, letter to Sarah Wilkinson. Upton-Wilkinson archive (080127fpsp02).

36 *Morning Chronicle* 25 August 1814. This newspaper muddles Thomas Norman's name.

37 Trial of Thomas Norman, Old Bailey Proceedings online, September 1814, t18140914-167. The court case was 14 September.

38 *Morning Chronicle* 2 September 1806. The theft was on 24 August.

39 Trial of Eleanor Russel, Old Bailey Proceedings online, September 1806, t18060917-43. She was tried for 'theft from a specified place'.

40 Trial of Eleanor Russel, Old Bailey Proceedings online, September 1806, t18060917-43.

41 The National Archives manuscript HO 11/1.

42 The National Archives manuscript HO 10/2.

43 Austen-Leigh 1942, pp. 197–8. Letter of Mountague Cholmeley Junior to Jane Leigh-Perrot on 11 January 1800. Mrs Leigh-Perrot was Mrs Austen's sister-in-law (her husband being Mrs Austen's brother).

44 22 March 1800. Somerset Archives and Local Studies A\BTL/2/4. Mrs Leigh-Perrot's trial was on 29 March 1800. Her crime was grand larceny, a capital offence for the theft of goods worth more than one shilling.

45 30 April 1800. Somerset Archives and Local Studies A\BTL/2/5.

46 Markham 1997.

47 Chapman 1932a, pp. 154–5. Written from Bath on 21 April 1805.

48 Chapman 1932a, p. 155.

49 Chapman 1932a, p. 159. Addition to letter of 23 April 1805.

50 *Bath Chronicle* 3 April 1800.

51 *Bath Chronicle* 3 April 1800.

52 25 October 1807. Somerset Archives and Local Studies A\BTL/2/28.

53 Christie 1929, pp. 216–17. Hoddesdon was then in the parish of Broxbourne.

54 *Hampshire Chronicle* 26 October 1807.

55 *Hampshire Chronicle* 26 October 1807. The house in the High Street was later called Borham House and was close to the present Lowewood Museum. It has since been demolished.

56 *Hampshire Chronicle* 26 October 1807.

57 Anon. 1808, p. 11.

58 Hall 1936, p. 84. Letter to Miss Chorley of 15 April 1808.

59 Wesley 1831, pp. 462–3, paragraph 'Thoughts on Suicide', dated Liverpool April 8 1790.

60 13 July 1805. Silliman 1820a, p. 27.

61 Howard 1784, p. 384. Even though John Howard was a dissenter, he became high sheriff of Bedfordshire. He was appalled at the treatment of prisoners, leading to his involvement with penal reform. He died in 1790.

62 A liberate was a writ issued to a gaoler for the release of a prisoner on bail. Howard 1784, p. 385.

63 Howard 1784, p. 371.

64 For POW prisons and parole towns, see Adkins and Adkins 2006.

65  Darter 1888, p. 34.

66  Trial of Alice Walker, Old Bailey Proceedings online, 9 September 1772, t17720909-46.

67  *Virginia Gazette* (printer: Purdie and Dixon) 12 August 1773.

68  *Virginia Gazette* (printer: Rind) 12 August 1773.

69  *Virginia Gazette* (printer: Rind) 27 May 1773.

70  At this point she disappears from the records.

71  Trial of Robert Jones and Thomas Cliff, Old Bailey Proceedings online, 18 May 1774, t17740518-61.

72  Trial of Elizabeth Smith, Old Bailey Proceedings online, 11 January 1775, t17750111-33.

73  Bateson 1969.

74  Darter 1888, pp. 20-1.

75  Darter 1888, pp. 51-2.

76  Darter 1888, p. 52.

77  *Hampshire Chronicle* 18 December 1775.

78  Trial of Sarah Reynolds and Elizabeth Vale, Old Bailey Proceedings online, December 1775, t17751206-82.

79  It is difficult to tell exactly where the body was found, since the two people who searched for it got out of the coach at 'the top of Broad Street' and walked an unknown distance before they came to the ditch 'with a great current of water', where they paid a passer-by to go down the slope and retrieve the bundle.

80  Trial of Sarah Reynolds and Elizabeth Vale, Old Bailey Proceedings online, December 1775, t17751206-82.

81  They were George Morley and John Burke for highway robbery; William Munro for forgery; Samuel Wilson for counterfeiting coins; William Busby and Francis Burke for returning from transportation before their seven years had expired; and John Wallis, Richard Martin, John Lawler and the woman Frances Warren for burglary. They were all tried and convicted at the Old Bailey on 29 October 1783. Information on the individuals is in Old Bailey Proceedings online, and a full report on the execution is in *Jackson's Oxford Journal* 13 December 1783.

82  *Jackson's Oxford Journal* 13 December 1783.

83  26 March 1785.Winstanley and Jameson 1999, p. 23.

84  4 April 1785.Winstanley and Jameson 1999, p. 23.

85  Grant 1809, pp. 243-4.

86  Huddesford 1804, p. 153. 'Jack Hains' was probably the highwayman John Haines, executed in 1799, whose body was gibbeted on Hounslow Heath.

87  Darter 1888, pp. 24-5. Gallows Tree Common was on the borders of Earley and Shinfield in Berkshire, near Elm Lane. Until 1793 it was the place of execution for Reading. An elm tree was used as gallows and gibbet, but it was struck by Dutch Elm Disease in the 1970s.

88  Howell 1816, p. 816.

89  *Jackson's Oxford Journal* 31 August 1782.

90  *Ipswich Journal* 21 March 1789.

91  *Ipswich Journal* 21 March 1789.

92  Ashton 1882, p. 453.

93  Halliday 2009, p. 204.

94  29 October 1795. Jameson 2004, p. 215.

95  Wright 1867, p. 497.

96  29 October 1795. Jameson 2004, pp. 215–16.

97  The Gordon Riots took place 2 to 9 June 1780 after Lord George Gordon (1751–93), leader of the Protestant Association, had failed in his attempt to get parts of the Catholic Relief Act of 1778 repealed.

98  4 April 1801. Jameson 2007, p. 25.

99  9 April 1801. Jameson 2007, p. 26.

100  12 October 1792. Jameson 2003, p. 181.

101  Andrews 1938, p. 153.

102  *The Times* 14 June 1792.

103  Silliman 1810, p. 239.

104  *The Heir-at-Law* was first performed at the Haymarket theatre in London.

105  13 November 1803. Christie 1929, p. 161.

11: MEDICINE MEN

1  Chapman 1932b, p. 426.

2  Hall 1936, p. 172. Letter written at Beacon's Gutter, near Liverpool, 14 June 1809.

3  23 March 1779. Winstanley 1983, p. 122.

4  11 March 1791. Jameson 2003, p. 7.

5  15 March 1791. Jameson 2003, p. 8.

6  16 March 1791. Jameson 2003, p. 8.

7  16 February 1807. Somerset Archives and Local Studies A\BTL/2/26. Simon Morle of Plainsfield Court died in 1811 and his wife in 1812 (information from David Worthy).

8  18 February 1807. Somerset Archives and Local Studies A\BTL/2/26.

9  13 April 1781. Winstanley 1984, p. 125.

10  14 April 1781. Winstanley 1984, pp. 125–6.

11  *Culpeper's Complete Herbal*, enlarged edn (London), 1814, p. 130.

12  22 May 1779. Winstanley 1983, p. 139.

13  29 January 1800. Andrews 1934, p. 8.

14  Somerset Archives and Local Studies A\BTL/2/3.This was Dr Alyster Forbes of Nether Stowey (information from David Worthy).

15  In 1800 this became the Royal Company of Surgeons of London (later 'of England'). The barber-surgeons developed from barbers, who added bloodletting to their hair-cutting and shaving services.

16  Markham 1990, p. 55. Penelope Benwell would in 1808 marry the Reverend John Hind. Her diary entry is 1 January 1805.

17  Beale 1891, p. 57.

18  West 1977.

19  Beale 1891, p. 58.

20  Beale 1891, p. 58.

21  Beale 1891, p. 58.

22  In Britain physicians are nowadays referred to as 'doctors' or 'GPs' (general practitioners).

23  3 November 1776. Winstanley 1981, p. 83. He was Jack Wharton.

24  8 November 1776. Winstanley 1981, pp. 86–7.

25  8 April 1809. Somerset Archives and Local Studies A\BTL/2/32.

26  20 June 1782. Winstanley 1998, p. 52.

27  The surge in influenza deaths came in the second and third weeks of June 1782.

28  Hall 1936, p. 51. Letter of 18 November 1807 written at Upholland.

29  27 March 1800. Somerset Archives and Local Studies A\BTL/2/4. William Weymouth was the sexton (information from David Worthy).

30  6 April 1790. Jameson 2001, p. 248.

31  15 January 1795. Jameson 2004, p. 115.

32  14 December 1800. Jameson 2006, p. 261.

33  *Hereford Journal* 18 October 1815.

34  *Hereford Journal* 18 October 1815.

35  7 June 1791. Jameson 2003, p. 33.

36  13 May 1797. Jameson 2005, p. 149.

37  Chapman 1932a, p. 144. Letter dated 21 January 1805.

38  Beale 1891, p. 58. This was in August 1788.

39  Knight 1904, p. 51.

40  Johnston 1857, pp. 284–5. This poem was first published in 1807 as 'Resolution and Independence'.

41  18 September 1803. Somerset Archives and Local Studies A\BTL/2/17.

42  18 September 1803. Somerset Archives and Local Studies A\BTL/2/17. Holland's problems continued and were most likely dental in origin.

43  15 May 1779. Winstanley 1983, p. 137.

44  Ringsted 1774, pp. 11–12.

45  Simond 1817, pp. 329–30.

46  2 November 1799. Jameson 2006, p. 161.

47  21 September 1777. Winstanley 1981, 165.

48  22 September 1777. Winstanley 1981, 166.

49  7 July 1791, in Lincolnshire. Andrews 1935, p. 371.

50  Beale 1891, p. 58.

51  Some court-plaister was black, and it was so-called after the black patches formerly used by ladies at court to cover facial blemishes such as smallpox scars. It was priced at sixpence in various advertisements.

52  1 October 1777. Winstanley 1981, p. 168.

53  17 February 1796. Jameson 2005, p. 13.

54  *Norfolk Chronicle* 21 September 1805. Barwick was author of *An essay on shooting*.

55  *The Literary Panorama* 2 (1807), p. 989. A Rupture Society was founded in 1796, but was later disbanded. The New Rupture Society was founded either on 4 July 1804 or 15 May 1805 (see UCL Bloomsbury Project) and was active until 1950.

56  Beale 1891, p. 58.

57  4 June 1776. Winstanley 1981, p. 51

58  16 September 1813. Chapman 1932b, pp. 327–8. Fanny was twenty years old, Lizzy thirteen and Marianne twelve (her birthday was the previous day).

59  November 1808. Hall 1936, p. 122.

60  *Leeds Mercury* 19 November 1808.

61  *Leeds Mercury* 19 November 1808.

62  11 November 1799. Somerset Archives and Local Studies A\BTL/2/1.

63  31 May 1802. Darbishire 1958, p. 167.

64  1 March 1812. Hawker 1893, p. 36. It is unclear where the dental surgery took place, but probably in London.

65  Hunter 1778, p. 219.

66  Hunter 1778, p. 221.

67  Hunter 1778, p. 223.

68  *Hampshire Chronicle* 21 January 1782.

69  Cooper 1843, p. 401. When Butler returned to England, he set up as a dentist in Liverpool under an assumed name.

70  Cooper 1843, pp. 414–15.

71  The number of overall dead and wounded was 50,000, a figure sometimes said to be the number who died on the battlefield.

72  Bailey 1896, p. 174. Tuesday 24 November 1812. Naples served under Collingwood at the Battle of St Vincent on board the *Excellent*.

73  Cooper 1843, p. 399.

74  Silliman 1820a, p. 143.

75  Benjamin Franklin wore bifocals but probably did not invent them, as is sometimes claimed.

76  *Hampshire Chronicle* 1 February 1802.

77  1 January 1809. Somerset Archives and Local Studies A\BTL/2/29.

78  Darter 1888, p. 68.

79  Davy was not the apprentice of Beddoes, as is sometimes stated.

80  Davy 1800, p. 556. Nitrous oxide was first discovered in 1772 by Joseph Priestley.

81  The first operation under anaesthesia in England was in 1846.

82  This was a belated response to the dissolution of the monasteries in the sixteenth century, which had destroyed healthcare for the poor.

83  20 August 1793. Andrews 1936, p. 315. A hospital had been established in Northampton in 1744, but this new one was built by subscription. It still survives, in Billing Road.

84  The oldest operating theatre in England of 1822 can be visited. It was once part of St Thomas's Hospital in London but became hidden and was rediscovered in 1956.

85  Aikin 1771, p. 25. Aikin later became a physician, and as a dissenter was a bitter opponent of injustice and an early supporter of the French Revolution.

86  Letter of 1 October 1771. Aikin 1771, p. 89.

87  Letter of 1 October 1771. Aikin 1771, p. 89.

88  Letter of 1 October 1771. Aikin 1771, p. 90.

89  The name 'lock hospital' was derived from the earlier leprosy hospitals.

90  Aikin 1771, p. 65.

91  5 and 7 December 1799. Somerset Archives and Local Studies A\BTL/2/3. The small Over Stowey workhouse is also referred to as the poorhouse.

92  *First Report: Minutes of Evidence taken before the Select Committee appointed to consider of provision being made for the better regulation of madhouses in England* 1816 (London), p. 51.

93  *First Report: Minutes of Evidence taken before the Select Committee appointed to consider of provision being made for the better regulation of madhouses in England* 1816 (London), p. 53.

94  Mackenzie 1827, p. 525.

95  *Newcastle Courant* 14 May 1774.

96  The provision of county lunatic asylums was not a legal requirement until 1845.

97  Blackner 1815, p. 180.

98  *First Report: Minutes of Evidence taken before the Select Committee appointed to consider of provision being made for the better regulation of madhouses in England* 1816 (London), pp. 51–2.

99  *First Report: Minutes of Evidence taken before the Select Committee appointed to consider of provision being made for the better regulation of madhouses in England* 1816 (London), p. 53.

100  *First Report: Minutes of Evidence taken before the Select Committee appointed to consider of provision being made for the better regulation of madhouses in England* 1816 (London), p. 56.

101  15 April 1813. Somerset Archives and Local Studies A\BTL/2/38.

102  Eden 1797b, p. 223.

103  Andrews 1935, p. 10.

104  Extract published in *Annual Register* (1783), p. 186.

105  *Morning Post* 29 October 1811.

106  *Morning Post* 29 October 1811.

107  Bailey 1896, p. 141.

108  8 January 1812. Bailey 1896, p. 147. 'Harps' was probably Harper, keeper of a burial ground (Bailey 1896, p. 139). The surname of Daniel is unknown.

109  *Leicester Journal* 10 January 1812.

110  Bailey 1896, p. 176.

12: LAST WORDS

1  From 'The Order for the Burial of the Dead' in *The Book of Common Prayer, and Administration of the Sacraments, and Other Rites and Ceremonies of the Church, According to the Use of the Church of England: Together with the Psalter or Psalms of David, Pointed as they are to be Sung or Said in Churches* (Oxford, 1784).

2  1 May 1793. Jameson 2003, p. 241.

3  9 February 1806. Somerset Archives and Local Studies A\BTL/2/25.

4  1 July 1789. Andrews 1935, p. 120. Fritwell is about 16 miles from Towcester.

5  6 July 1791. Andrews 1935, pp. 368–9.

6  Jane Austen probably had Hodgkin's disease (a form of lymphoma) or possibly Addison's disease.

7  Brabourne 1884b, pp. 334–5.

8  24 March 1817. Somerset Archives and Local Studies A\BTL/2/43.

9  24 March 1817. Somerset Archives and Local Studies A\BTL/2/43.

10  6 June 1780. Winstanley 1984, p. 48.

11  5 February 1806. Somerset Archives and Local Studies A\BTL/2/26.

12  Holland was then rector at Monkton Farleigh in Somerset. The children's names were William, Thomas, John and Mary (information from David Worthy).

13  6 August 1805. Somerset Archives and Local Studies A\BTL/2/23.

14  For example, in the entry for Sunday 18 May 1800 (Somerset Archives and Local Studies A\BTL/2/5), he says 'These democrats are dreadful creatures', when he was talking about the people who attempted to assassinate the king.

15  7 June 1810. Somerset Archives and Local Studies A\BTL/2/33.

16  7 June 1772. Winstanley 1988, p. 42.

17  30 November 1810. Somerset Archives and Local Studies A\BTL/2/34.

18  30 November 1810. Somerset Archives and Local Studies A\BTL/2/34. The dead man was Hugh Acland, and he died at Madeira (information from David Worthy).

19  24 December 1792. Jameson 2003, p. 204.

20  8 December 1799. Somerset Archives and Local Studies A\BTL/2/3.

21  28 August 1799. Moretonhampstead History Society manuscript of Treleaven's diary.

22  Moretonhampstead History Society manuscript of Treleaven's diary.

23  17 September 1790. Jameson 2001, p. 263. The original manuscript of Woodforde's diary has been lost since it was published in Beresford 1927, p. 214.

24  19 September 1790. Jameson 2001, p. 264. The original manuscript of Woodforde's diary has been lost since it was published in Beresford 1927, p. 216.

25  15 October 1808. Brabourne 1884b, p. 21.

26  15 December 1802. Somerset Archives and Local Studies DD\SAS/C795/FA/185.

27  February 1810. Hall 1936, p. 236. Her pupil was Mary Gertrude Pedder.

28  Knight 1904, pp. 48–9.

29  9 June 1811. Somerset Archives and Local Studies A\BTL/2/35.

30  Eden 1797a, p. 579.

31  Moritz 1809, p. 11.

32  Wordsworth 1815, p. 163.

33  Ayton 1814, p. 55. The funeral took place in the summer of 1813, probably in July. This is the same man who went down William Pit at Whitehaven.

34  Ayton 1814, p. 55.

35  12 February 1782. Winstanley 1998, p. 14.

36  Winstanley 1998, p. 14.

37  Winstanley 1998, p. 14.

38  Winstanley 1998, p. 15.

39  Moritz 1809, p. 11. This was in 1782.

40  1 February 1788. Jameson 2001, p. 9.

41  18 June 1782. Winstanley 1998, p. 51.

42  18 August 1778. Winstanley 1983, p. 64.

43  23 March 1791. Jameson 2003, p. 10.

44  25 June 1796. Jameson 2005, p. 53.

45  14 November 1799. Somerset Archives and Local Studies A\BTL/2/1.

46  17 November 1799. Somerset Archives and Local Studies A\BTL/2/1.

47  6 November 1799. Somerset Archives and Local Studies A\BTL/2/1.

48  16 December 1802. Somerset Archives and Local Studies DD\SAS/C795/FA/185.

49  15 November 1780. Winstanley 1984, p. 87.

50  The stone is now fixed to the chancel wall. Robert Phillips was a cooper by profession and made it well known what verse he wanted on his gravestone. See Hawkins 1819, pp. 19–20, which has a slightly different inscription.

51  Andrews 1895, p. 137.

52  White 1789, p. 322.

53  5 November 1783. Winstanley 1998, p. 185.

54  11 May 1810. Hall, 1936, p. 260. Letter to Miss Bessy Winkley from Dove Nest.

55  11 May 1810. Hall, 1936, p. 261. Letter to Miss Bessy Winkley from Dove Nest. Crape was a thin, loosely woven fabric.

56  Brabourne 1884b, pp. 21–2. Letter from Southampton dated Saturday 15 October 1808. Bombazeen was a thin silken material used especially for mourning clothes.

57  Brabourne 1884a, p. 311. Letter dated Friday 30 August 1805.

58  Darter 1888, p. 97.

59  Chapman 1932b, p. 509. Madame Bijion (or Bigeon) was an old family retainer.

60  *Morning Post* 1 May 1804.

61  The full text of the inscription is: 'In MEMORY OF ANTHONY CURTIS who died April 11th 1787. Aged 77 Years. This world's a City full of Crooked streets, And death the Market Place where all men Meets, If life was Merchandise that men could buy, The rich would live and none but poor would die.' From a gravestone said to be in Basingstoke Cemetery, Hampshire, and recorded in Maiben 1870, p. 38.

62  Andrews 1935, p. 91.

63  Moritz 1809, p. 72.

64  5 September 1811. Simond 1817, pp. 358–9.

65  The account does not appear to have been by Pope, but is more likely to have come from *Essays Moral and Literary* vol. 2 by the Reverend Vicesimus Knox (London, 1779), where Pope and part of this epitaph are mentioned in the same paragraph.

66  Hay 1953, p. 174.

# BIBLIOGRAPHY

Adkins, R. 2004 *Trafalgar: The Biography of a Battle* (London)

Adkins, R. and Adkins, L. 2006 *The War for All the Oceans. From Nelson at the Nile to Napoleon at Waterloo* (London)

Adkins, R. and Adkins, L. 2008 *Jack Tar: Life in Nelson's Navy* (London)

Aikin J. 1771 *Thoughts on Hospitals* (London)

Andrews, C.B. (ed.) 1934 *The Torrington Diaries containing the tours through England and Wales of the Hon. John Byng (later fifth Viscount Torrington) between the years 1781 and 1794* vol. 1 (London)

Andrews, C.B. (ed.) 1935 *The Torrington Diaries containing the tours through England and Wales of the Hon. John Byng (later fifth Viscount Torrington) between the years 1781 and 1794* vol. 2 (London)

Andrews, C.B. (ed.) 1936 *The Torrington Diaries containing the tours through England and Wales of the Hon. John Byng (later fifth Viscount Torrington) between the years 1781 and 1794* vol. 3 (London)

Andrews, C.B. (ed.) 1938 *The Torrington Diaries containing the tours through England and Wales of the Hon. John Byng (later fifth Viscount Torrington) between the years 1781 and 1794* vol. 4 (New York)

Andrews, W. 1891 *Old Church Lore* (Hull and London)

Andrews, W. 1895 *Curious Church Customs and Cognate Subjects* (Hull and London)

Anon. 1808 *The Trial of Thomas Simmons, for the Wilful Murder of Mrs. Hummerstone and Mrs Warner, at Hoddesdon, in Hertfordshire, Who was found Guilty at the Assizes Held at Hertford, Friday, March 4, 1808* (London)

Ashton, J. 1882 *Chap-Books of the Eighteenth Century with Facsimiles, Notes, and Introduction* (London)

Ashton, J. 1906 *The Dawn of the XIXth Century in England* (London)

Austen Leigh, J.E. 1871 *A Memoir of Jane Austen* (London)

Austen-Leigh, R.A. 1942 *Austen Papers 1704–1856* (privately printed)

Austen-Leigh, W. and Austen-Leigh, R.A. 1913 *Jane Austen. Her Life and Letters. A Family Record* (New York)

Ayres, J. (ed.) 1984 *Paupers & Pig Killers. The Diary of William Holland, A Somerset Parson, 1799–1818* (Stroud)

Ayton, R. 1814 *A Voyage round Great Britain undertaken in the summer of the year 1813, and commencing from the Lands-End, Cornwall* (London)

Ayton, R. 1815 *A Voyage round Great Britain undertaken in the summer of the year 1813, and commencing from the Lands-End, Cornwall* vol. 2 (London)

Bailey, J.B. 1896 *The Diary of a Resurrectionist 1811–1812* (London)

Baines, E. 1835 *History of the Cotton Manufacture in Great Britain* (London)

Bamford, F. (ed.) 1936 *Dear Miss Heber. An Eighteenth Century Correspondence* (London)

Barlow, J. 1834 'Cases of Caesarean Operations' *London Medical and Surgical Journal* 4, pp. 564–70

Bateson, C. 1969 *The Convict Ships 1787–1868* (Glasgow)

Beale, C.H. 1891 (ed.) *Reminiscences of a Gentlewoman of the Last Century: Letters of Catherine Hutton* (Birmingham)

Bell, J. (ed.) 1812 *Rhymes of the Northern Bards: Being a curious collection of old and new songs and poems, Peculiar to the counties of Newcastle Upon Tyne, Northumberland, and Durham* (Newcastle upon Tyne)

Belsham, W. 1795 *Memoirs of the Reign of George III to the Session of Parliament Ending A.D. 1793* vol. 1 (London)

Benton, P. 1867 *The History of Rochford Hundred* (Rochford)

Beresford, J. (ed.) 1927 *The Diary of a Country Parson: The Reverend James Woodforde. Vol. III 1788–1792* (Oxford)

Blackner, J. 1815 *The History of Nottingham Embracing its Antiquities, Trade, and Manufactures, from the Earliest Authentic Records to The Present Period* (Nottingham)

Brabourne, E. (ed.) 1884a *Letters of Jane Austen* vol. 1 (London)

Brabourne, E. (ed.) 1884b *Letters of Jane Austen* vol. 2 (London)

Branch, J. 1801 *Tables Comprizing a Complete Ready Reckoner* (Manchester)

Brand, J. 1813 *Observations on Popular Antiquities: chiefly illustrating the origin of our vulgar customs, ceremonies, and superstitions* vol. 2 (rev. edn by H. Ellis) (London)

Brayne, M. 1998 'Weston weddings' *Parson Woodforde Society Quarterly Journal* 31, pp. 12–20

Brougham, H. 1840 *Historical Sketches of Statesmen who flourished in the time of George III to which is added remarks on party, and an appendix,* 1st series, vol. 1 (London)

Cahill, K. 2001 *Who Owns Britain* (Edinburgh)

Campbell-Smith, D. 2011 *Masters of the Post: The Authorized History of the Royal Mail* (London)

Caplan, C. 2004 'Henry Austen's Buxton Bank' *Jane Austen Society Report for 2004,* pp. 46–8

Carter, T. 1845 *Memoirs of a Working Man* (London)

Chapman, R.W. (ed.) 1932a *Jane Austen's Letters to her sister Cassandra and others, Volume I 1796–1809* (Oxford)

Chapman, R.W. (ed.) 1932b *Jane Austen's Letters to her sister Cassandra and others, Volume II 1811–1817* (Oxford)

Chater, K. 2009 *Untold Histories. Black people in England and Wales during the period of the British slave trade, c. 1660–1807* (Manchester)

Chorley, H.F. 1836 *Memorials of Mrs. Hemans with illustrations of her literary character from her private correspondence* vol. 2 (New York, London)

Christie, O.F. (ed.) 1929 *The Diary of the Revd. William Jones 1777–1821* (New York, London, Paris)

Colquhoun, P. 1796 *A Treatise on the Police of the Metropolis* (by a magistrate) (London)

Cooke, G.A. 1803 *Topographical and Statistical Description of the County of Norfolk* (London)

Cooper, B.B. 1843 *The Life of Sir Astley Cooper, Bart.* vol. 1 (London)

Cooper, W. 1776 'An Account of the Caesarean Operation, communicated in a letter to William Hunter, M.D. F.R.S.' *Medical Observations and Inquiries* 5, pp. 217–32

Corley, T.A.B. 2005 'Jane Austen's School Days' *Jane Austen Society Collected Reports 1996–2000*, pp. 14–24

Cullingford, B. 2000 *British Chimney Sweeps. Five Centuries of Chimney Sweeping* (London)

Cunningham, P. (ed.) 1859 *The Letters of Horace Walpole, Earl of Orford* vol. 9 (London)

Darbishire, H. (ed.) 1958 *Journals of Dorothy Wordsworth* (London)

Darter, W.S. 1888 *Reminiscences of Reading* (Reading)

David, E. 1994 (ed. J. Norman) *Harvest of the Cold Months. The Social History of Ice and Ices* (London)

Davy, H. 1800 *Researches, Chemical and Philosophical; chiefly concerning nitrous oxide or dephlogisticated nitrous air and its respiration* (London)

Dowell, S. 1888 (2nd edn) *A History of Taxation and Taxes in England. Vol. IV Taxes on Articles of Consumption* (London, New York)

Downman, H. 1803 *Infancy, or, The management of children: a didactic poem, in six books* (Exeter)

Eden, F.M. 1797a *The State of the Poor: or, an history of the labouring classes in England vol. I* (London)

Eden, F.M. 1797b *The State of the Poor: or, an history of the labouring classes in England vol. II* (London)

Eden, F.M. 1797c *The State of the Poor: or, an history of the labouring classes in England vol. III* (London)

Elliott, R. 1842 *The Gretna Green Memoirs* (London)

Ellis, M. 2011 'Jane Austen and the credit crunch of 1816' *Jane Austen Society Report for 2011*, pp. 42–53

Evans, D.M. 2009 'Banks is the Villain?' *Antiquaries Journal* 89, pp. 337–63

Eveleigh, D.J. 1983 *Firegrates and Kitchen Hearths* (Princes Risborough)

Eveleigh, D.J. 2003 *Candle Lighting* (Princes Risborough)

Factories Inquiry Commission 1833 *Second Report of the Central Board of His Majesty's Commissioners appointed to collect information in the manufacturing districts, as to the Employment of Children in Factories, and as to the Propriety and Means of Curtailing the Hours of their Labour* (London)

Foot, P. 1794 *General view of the agriculture of the county of Middlesex: with observations on the means of their improvement* (London)

Foreman, A. 1998 *Georgiana Duchess of Devonshire* (London)

Fremantle, A. (ed.) 1940 *The Wynne Diaries Volume III 1798–1820* (Oxford)

Gardiner, W. 1853 *Music and Friends; or, Pleasant Recollections of A Dilettante* vol. 3 (London)

Gatrell, V. 2006 *City of Laughter: Sex and Satire in Eighteenth-Century London* (London)

George, D. 1930 *London Life in the Eighteenth Century* (London)

Gillett, E. (ed.) 1945 *Elizabeth Ham by Herself 1783–1820* (London)

Glasse, H. 1774 *The Art of Cookery Made Plain and Easy* (actually by 'a Lady' but attributed to Glasse) (London)

Goldsmith, O. 1770 *The Deserted Village, A Poem* (London)

Grant, J. 1809 'Journal of a Three Weeks Tour in 1797, Through Derbyshire to the Lakes', pp. 219–92 in W. Mavor 1809 *The British Tourist's, or Traveller's, Pocket Companion* vol. 4 (London)

Granville, C. (ed.) 1916 *Lord Granville Leveson Gower (First Earl Granville), Private Correspondence 1781 to 1821* vol. 2 (London)

Green, W. 1819 *The Tourist's New Guide, containing a description of the lakes, mountains, and scenery* vol. 1 (Kendal)

Gröben, L. 1907 *Ralph Heathcote: Letters of a Young Diplomatist and soldier during the time of Napoleon giving an account of the dispute between the emperor and the elector of Hesse* (London)

Grose, F. et al. 1780 (2nd edn) *The Antiquarian Repertory* vol. 1 (London)

Grose, F. 1787 *A Provincial Glossary, with A Collection of Local Proverbs and Popular Superstitions* (London)

Grose, F. 1811 *Lexicon Balatronicum. A Dictionary of Buckish Slang, University Wit, and Pickpocket Eloquence* (London)

Hall, E. (ed.) 1936 *Miss Weeton: Journal of a Governess 1807–1811* (London)

Hall, E. (ed.) 1939 *Miss Weeton. Journal of a Governess 1811–1825* (London)

Halliday, S. 2009 *Newgate: London's Prototype of Hell* (Stroud)

Hamilton, A. 1813 (7th edn) *A Treatise on the Management of Female Complaints* (Edinburgh)

Harland, J. (ed.) 1865 *Ballads & Songs of Lancashire Chiefly Older than the 19th century* (London)

Hawker, P. 1893 *The Diary of Colonel Peter Hawker* vol. 1 (London)

Hawkins, A. 1819 *Kingsbridge and Salcombe with the Intermediate Estuary* (anonymous, but attributed to Abraham Hawkins) (Kingsbridge)

Hay, M.D. (ed.) 1953 *Landsman Hay: The Memoirs of Robert Hay 1789–1847* (London)

Haydon, C. 2002 'Religious Minorities in England', pp. 241–51 in H.T. Dickinson (ed.) 2002 *A Companion to Eighteenth-Century Britain* (Oxford)

Hayley, W. 1786 (2nd edn) *A Philosophical, Historical, and Moral Essay on Old Maids by a friend to the sisterhood* vol. 1 (London)

Henry, M.A. 2002 'The Making of Elite Culture', pp. 311–28 in H.T. Dickinson (ed.) 2002 *A Companion to Eighteenth-Century Britain* (Oxford)

Horsfall, P. 2005 'The Austen Family and Friends and the Construction of the Basingstoke Canal 1788–94 or, How the Austen Friends Sank Their Money' *Jane Austen Society Report for 2005*, pp. 66–9

Howard, J. 1784 (3rd edn) *The State of the Prisons in England and Wales with Preliminary Observations and an Account of Some Foreign Prisons and Hospitals* (Warrington)

Howell, T.B. (ed.) 1816 *A Complete Collection of State Trials and Proceedings for High Treason and Other Crimes and Misdemeanors from the Earliest Period to the Year 1783* vol. 21 (London)

Hubback, J.H. and Hubback, E.C. 1906 *Jane Austen's Sailor Brothers* (London, New York)

Huddesford, G. (ed.) 1804 *The Wiccamical Chaplet, A Selection of Original Poetry* (London)

Hunter, J. 1778 *The Natural History of the Human Teeth, part 2: A Practical Treatise on the Diseases of the Teeth* (London)

Hutton, W. 1791 *The History of Derby from the remote ages of antiquity to the year MDCCXCI* (London)

Hutton, W. 1795 *An History of Birmingham* (Birmingham)

Jameson, P. 2001 *The Diary of James Woodforde. Volume 12 1788–1790* (Castle Cary)

Jameson, P. 2003 *The Diary of James Woodforde. Volume 13 1791–1793* (Castle Cary)

Jameson, P. 2004 *The Diary of James Woodforde. Volume 14 1794–1795* (Castle Cary)

Jameson, P. 2005 *The Diary of James Woodforde. Volume 15 1796–1797* (Castle Cary)

Jameson, P. 2006 *The Diary of James Woodforde. Volume 16 1798–1800* (Castle Cary)

Jameson, P. 2007 *The Diary of James Woodforde. Volume 17 1801–1802* (Castle Cary)

Jeffery, R.W. (ed.) 1907 *Dyott's Diary 1781–1845. A Selection from the Journal of William Dyott, sometime general in the British Army and aide-de-camp to his Majesty King George III* vol. 1 (London)

Jenkin, A.K.H. 1951 *News from Cornwall with a memoir of William Jenkin* (London)

Jenkins, S. 1999 *England's Thousand Best Churches* (London)

Johnston, W. (ed.) 1857 *The Earlier Poems of William Wordsworth Corrected as in the Latest Editions* (London)

Jupp, P. (ed.) 1991 *The Letter-Journal of George Canning, 1793–1795* (London)

Kelly, I. 2005 *Beau Brummell: The Ultimate Dandy* (London)

Knight, W. (ed.) 1904 *Journals of Dorothy Wordsworth* vol. 1 (London)

Leach, A.F. 1911 *Educational Charters and Documents 598 to 1909* (Cambridge)

Le Faye, D. 2006 *A Chronology of Jane Austen and her Family* (Cambridge, New York)

Le Faye, D. (ed.) 2011 (4th edn) *Jane Austen's Letters* (Oxford)

Lewis, T. (ed.) 1866 *Extracts from the Journals and Correspondence of Miss Berry from the Year 1783 to 1852* vol. 2 (London)

Macdonald, J. 1790 *Travels in various parts of Europe, Asia, and Africa during a series of thirty years and upwards* (London)

Mackenzie, E. 1827 *A Descriptive and Historical Account of the Town and County of Newcastle upon Tyne including the borough of Gateshead* (Newcastle upon Tyne)

Mackenzie, W.C. 1916 *The War Diary of a London Scot (Alderman G.M. MacAulay) 1796–7 with a review of the year* (Paisley)

McLynn, F. 1989 *Crime and Punishment in Eighteenth-century England* (London)

Maiben, F. 1870 *An Original Collection of Extant Epitaphs Gathered by a Commercial in Spare Moments* (London, published anonymously)

Manners, J.H. 1805 *Journal of a Tour round the southern Coasts of England* (London, published anonymously)

Markham, S. 1990 *A Testimony of Her Times. Based on Penelope Hind's Diaries and Correspondence 1787–1838* (London)

Markham, S. 1997 'A gardener's question for Mrs Leigh Perrot' *Jane Austen Society Collected Reports 1986–1995*, pp. 213–14

Middleton, J. 1807 *View of the Agriculture of Middlesex* (London)

Millard, W.S. 1895 'The Battle of Copenhagen' *Macmillan's Magazine* 72, pp. 81–93

Mingay, G. 2002 'Agriculture and rural life', pp. 141–57 in H.T. Dickinson (ed.) 2002 *A Companion to Eighteenth-Century Britain* (Oxford)

Montague, L. 1785 *The Housewife. Being a Most Useful Assistant in all Domestic Concerns, Whether In a Town or Country Situation* (London)

Moore, W. 2009 *Wedlock: How Georgian Britain's Worst Husband Met His Match* (London)

Moritz, C.P. 1809 'Travels Through Various Parts of England in 1782', pp. 1–120 in W. Mavor 1809 *The British Tourist's, or Traveller's, Pocket Companion* vol. 4 (London)

Mortimer, T. 1810 *A General Dictionary of Commerce, Trade, and Manufactures* (London)

Moss, W. 1781 *An Essay on the Management and Nursing of Children in the earlier periods of infancy* (London)

Nicholson, J. and Burn, R. 1776 *The History and Antiquities of the Counties of Westmorland and Cumberland* vol. 1 (London)

Pasley, T. 1931 (ed. R.M.S. Pasley) *Private Sea Journals 1778–1782* (London, Toronto)

Penhallurick, R.J. 1991 *The Anglo-Welsh Dialects of North Wales* (Frankfurt, Bern, New York, Paris)

Pennant, T. 1776 (4th edn) *A Tour in Scotland* (London)

Percival, R. 1774 'Observations on the State of Population in *Manchester*, and other adjacent Places' *Philosophical Transactions of the Royal Society of London* vol. 64, pp. 54–66

Porter, G.R. 1851 *The Progress of The Nation in its Various Social and Economical Relations from the Beginning of the Nineteenth Century* (London)

Pratt, S.J. 1801 *Gleanings in England* vol. 2 (London)

Pratt, S.J. 1803 *Gleanings in England* vol. 3 (London)

Pratt, S.J. 1804 (3rd edn) *Gleanings in England* vol. 1 (London)

Price, R. 1783 (4th edn) *Observations on Reversionary Payments on schemes for providing annuities for widows, and for persons in old age* vol. 1 (London)

Pugh, J. 1787 *Remarkable Occurrences in the Life of Jonas Hanway, Esq.* (London)

Rattenbury, J. 1837 *Memoirs of a Smuggler, compiled from his diary and journal* (Sidmouth)

Repton, J.A. 1812 'An Account of the Opening of the Great Barrow at Stow-Heath, near Aylsham, in Norfolk, in July 1808. Communicated by John Adey Repton, Esq., F.A.S. in a letter to Craven Ord, Esq. F.R.S. and F.A.S., V.P.' *Archaeologia* vol. 16, pp. 354–5

Ringsted, J. 1774 *The Cattle Keeper's Assistant, or genuine directions for country-gentlemen, sportsmen, farmers, grasiers, farriers, &c.* (London)

Romney, P. 1984 *The Diary of Charles Fothergill 1805. An Itinerary to York, Flamborough and the North-Western Dales of Yorkshire* (Leeds)

Roud, S. and Bishop, J. (eds) 2012 *The New Penguin Book of English Folk Songs* (London)

Rowe, H. 1796 *Poems* vol. 1 (London)

Rubenhold, H. 2005 *The Covent Garden Ladies: Pimp General Jack & The Extraordinary Story of Harris's List* (Stroud)

Rudder, S. 1779 *A New History of Gloucestershire* (Cirencester)

Sandford, H. 1888 *Thomas Poole and his Friends* vol. 2 (London)

Shaw, S. 1808 'A Tour to the West of England, in 1788', pp. 172–335 in J.A. Pinkerton *General Collection of the Best and Most Interesting Voyages and Travels in All Parts of the World* (London)

Sheridan, T. 1762 *A Course of Lectures on Elocution* (London)

Silliman, B. 1810 *A Journal of Travels in England, Holland and Scotland, and of two passages over the Atlantic, in the years 1805 and 1806* vol 1 (New York)

Silliman, B. 1820a (3rd edn) *A Journal of Travels in England, Holland and Scotland, and of two passages over the Atlantic, in the years 1805 and 1806* vol 2 (New Haven)

Silliman, B. 1820b (3rd edn) *A Journal of Travels in England, Holland and Scotland, and of two passages over the Atlantic, in the years 1805 and 1806* vol 3 (New Haven)

Simond, L. 1815 *Journal of a tour and residence in Great Britain, during the years 1810 and 1811, by a French Traveller* vol. 1 (Edinburgh)

Simond, L. 1817 (2nd edn) *Journal of a tour and residence in Great Britain during the years 1810 and 1811* vol. 2 (Edinburgh, London)

Smith, H. 1785 (4th edn) *Letters to Married Women* (London)

Smith, J.T. 1874 *Vagabondiana or, Anecdotes of Mendicant Wanderers Through the Streets of London* (London)

Southey, R. 1814 *Letters from England by Don Manuel Alvarez Espriella* vol. 3 (London)

Spilsbury, F. 1791 *Free Observations on the Scurvy, Gout, Diet and Remedy* (Norwich)

Stevenson, W. 1812 *General View of the Agriculture of the County of Dorset* (London)

Struve, C.A. 1802 *A Familiar View of the Domestic Education of Children* (trans. from the German, with three letters by A.F.M. Willich) (London)

Trusler, J. 1784 *Principles of Politeness and of Knowing the World* (Berlin)

Trusler, J. 1790 (2nd edn) *The London Adviser and Guide* (London)

Vickery, A. 2003 *The Gentleman's Daughter: Women's Lives in Georgian England* (New Haven and London)

Vickery, A. 2009 *Behind Closed Doors: At Home in Georgian England* (New Haven and London)

Walker, A. 1792 *Remarks made in a Tour from London to the Lakes of Westmoreland and Cumberland, in the summer of M,DCC,XCI* (London)

Walker, J. 1791 *A critical pronouncing dictionary and expositor of the English language* (London)

Warner, R. 1801 *Excursions from Bath* (Bath)

Watson, G. 1827 *A Narrative of the Adventures of a Greenwich Pensioner written by himself* (Newcastle)

Wesley, J. 1831 *The Works of the Reverend John Wesley, A.M.* vol. 7 (New York)

West, J.L. 1977 *The Taylors of Lancashire: Bonesetters and Doctors 1750–1890* (Worsley)

White, C. 1773 *A Treatise on the Management of Pregnant and Lying-In Women* (London)

White, G. 1789 *The Natural History and Antiquities of Selborne, in the County of Southampton: with Engravings, and an Appendix* (London)

White, G. 1837 (new edn) *The Natural History and Antiquities of Selborne, in the County of Southampton.* (London)

White, J. 2012 *London in the Eighteenth Century. A Great and Monstrous Thing* (London)

Willan, R. 1801 *Reports on the Diseases in London during the years 1796, 97, 98, 99 and 1800* (London)

Williams, C. (trans.) 1933 *Sophie in London 1786 being the Diary of Sophie v. la Roche* (London)

Wilson, R.G. 2002 'The Landed Elite', pp. 158–71 in H.T. Dickinson (ed.) 2002 *A Companion to Eighteenth-Century Britain* (Oxford)

Winstanley, R.L. 1981 *The Diary of James Woodforde (The first six Norfolk years 1776–1781). Volume 1 1776–1781* (Parson Woodforde Society)

Winstanley, R.L. 1983 *The Diary of James Woodforde (The first six Norfolk years 1776–1781). Volume 2 1778–1779* (Parson Woodforde Society)

Winstanley, R.L. 1984 *The Diary of James Woodforde (The first six Norfolk years 1776–1781). Volume 3 1780–1781* (Parson Woodforde Society)

Winstanley, R.L. 1988 *The Ansford Diary of James Woodforde. Volume 5: 1772–1773* (Parson Woodforde Society)

Winstanley, R.L. 1989 *The Oxford & Somerset Diary of James Woodforde 1774–1775* (Parson Woodforde Society)

Winstanley, R.L. 1996 *Parson Woodforde – The Life & Times of a Country Diarist* (Bungay)

Winstanley, R.L. 1998 *The Diary of James Woodforde. Volume 10 1782–1784* (Castle Cary)

Winstanley, R.L. 2012 'Carl Philipp Moritz – A German Traveller in Georgian England' *Parson Woodforde Society Quarterly Journal* 45, pp. 35–48

Winstanley, R. and Jameson, P. (eds) 1999 *The Diary of James Woodforde. Volume 11 1785–1787* (Castle Cary)

Wordsworth, W. 1815 *Poems by William Wordsworth Including Lyrical Ballads, and the Miscellaneous Pieces of the Author* vol. 1 (London)

Wright, L. 1960 *Clean and Decent. The History of the Bathroom and the W.C.* (London, Boston)

Wright, T. 1867 *Caricature History of the Georges* (London)

Wrigley, E.A. and Schofield, R.S. 1989 *The Population History of England 1541–1871: A Reconstruction* (Cambridge)

# LIST OF MAPS

# LIST OF ILLUSTRATIONS

SECTION ONE

So-called Zoffany portrait (now attributed to the artist Ozias Humphry) of Jane Austen as a young girl. From Austen-Leigh, W. and Austen-Leigh, R. 1913 *Jane Austen: Her Life and Letters. A Family Record* (London), frontispiece

The cottage in Chawton, Hampshire, where Jane Austen lived from 1809 to 1917 (Authors' collection)

Parchment indenture of Richard Cureton, apprenticed in 1783 to William Wakelin (or Wakelen), girdler (Authors' collection)

A view of London and the River Thames in 1814 from Blackfriars Bridge (Authors' collection)

A woman using water from a pump near cottages in Wenlock, Shropshire, in 1815. From Stevens, F. 1815 *Views of the cottages and farm-houses in England and Wales* (London)

Building new terraced houses, with a bricklayer standing on wooden scaffolding while a labourer mixes mortar. From *The Book of English Trades and Library of the Useful Arts* 1818 (new edn) (London)

A 1794 halfpenny token of John Fowler, a London whale oil merchant (Authors' collection)

'Afternoon dress', a fashion plate of 1800 (Authors' collection)

A weaver making worsted stockings on a stocking loom. The print, dated January 1805, is from *The Book of English Trades and Library of the Useful Arts* 1818 (new edn) (London)

A hairdresser cutting and dressing the long hair of a male customer. The print, dated September 1808, is from *The Book of English Trades and Library of the Useful Arts* 1818 (new edn) (London)

St Peter and St Paul church in Over Stowey, Somerset (Authors' collection)

A copper penny token issued at Bath in 1811 (Authors' collection)

Reverse of a copper 'cartwheel' twopence of George III (Authors' collection)

A copper halfpenny of 1791 (obverse and reverse) issued by the copper works of Charles Roe at Macclesfield (Authors' collection)

The obverse and reverse of a halfpenny copper token of the industrialist John Wilkinson (Authors' collection)

A man viewed from the rear seated at a loom, depicted on a 1791 copper halfpenny token (Authors' collection)

A halfpenny token, payable at the warehouse of John Kershaw, a Rochdale mercer and draper (Authors' collection)

Advertisements in the *Morning Chronicle* newspaper for 29 October 1807 (Authors' collection)

Joseph Johnson, a crippled black beggar and former merchant seaman. The print, dated December 1815, is from Smith, J. T. 1874 (first published 1817) *Vagabondiana; or, Anecdotes of Mendicant Wanderers Through the Streets of London* (London)

A workhouse depicted on a copper penny token issued by the Overseers of the Poor at Sheffield (Authors' collection)

A boy selling matches in a London street. The print, dated December 1815, is from Smith, J. T. 1874 (first published 1817) *Vagabondiana; or, Anecdotes of Mendicant Wanderers Through the Streets of London* (London)

A child street hawker selling potatoes from a wooden wheelbarrow. Printed by S. & J. Fuller at the Temple of Fancy, Rathbone Place, London (Authors' collection)

The River Tyne in 1789. From Brand, J. 1789 *The history and antiquities of the town and county of the town of Newcastle upon Tyne vol. 2* (London)

## SECTION TWO

Performances at theatres in London advertised in *The Times* newspaper for 23 May 1808 (Authors' collection)

A state lottery ticket sold in 1808 (Authors' collection)

The latest catalogue of Lackington's bookseller in London advertised in the *St James Chronicle* on 19 June 1817 (Authors' collection)

A bookseller with two customers choosing books. From *The Book of English Trades and Library of the Useful Arts* 1808 (new edn) (London)

Obverse and reverse of a halfpenny token issued in 1795 by Lackington's bookseller (Authors' collection)

A view of Hotwells spa, near Bristol, in 1801. Artist G. Holmes. Engraved by J. Walker, 44 Paternoster Row, London, published 1 June 1801 (Authors' collection)

Front page of the *Morning Chronicle* for 24 October 1807 (Authors' collection)

A road map of January 1785 showing the route from Newbury eastwards along the Bath road from London. From *A New and General view of the direct roads of England & Wales as described in Paterson's British Itinerary* 1785 (London)

William Tomlins, a crossing sweeper and beggar. The print, dated May 1816, is from Smith, J.T. 1874 (first published 1817) *Vagabondiana; or, Anecdotes of Mendicant Wanderers Through the Streets of London* (London)

A coachmaker constructing a post-chaise. The print, dated August 1804, is from *The Book of English Trades and Library of the Useful Arts* 1818 (new edn) (London)

A woman being burned at the stake, illustrating the execution of Christian Bowman in 1789. From Ashton, J. 1882 *Chap-Books of the Eighteenth Century with Facsimiles, Notes, and Introduction* (London), p. 452

An apothecary (or druggist) making his own medicines. From *The Book of English Trades and Library of the Useful Arts* 1818 (new edn) (London)

Ching's Worm Lozenges advertised in the *St James Chronicle* for 19 June 1817 (Authors' collection)

A beggar with a wooden leg and crutches. The print, dated April 1816, is from Smith, J. T. 1874 (first published 1817) *Vagabondiana; or, Anecdotes of Mendicant Wanderers Through the Streets of London* (London)

Newcastle's charitable infirmary, depicted in 1789. From Brand, J. 1789 *The history and antiquities of the town and county of the town of Newcastle upon Tyne vol. 2* (London)

No. 8 College Street in Winchester, Hampshire, where Jane Austen died on 18 July 1817 (Authors' collection)

The memorial tablet to the Reverend ('Parson') James Woodforde inside All Saints church, Weston Longville, Norfolk (Authors' collection)

The cathedral at Winchester in 1809. From Milner, J. 1809 *The History, Civil and Ecclesiastical & survey of the antiquities of Winchester vol. 2* (Winchester)

# ACKNOWLEDGEMENTS

During our research, we have been assisted by several libraries and archives, as well as by various individuals and institutions who have kindly given permission to reproduce quotations or have helped in other ways. We are very grateful to the London Library, especially the Trustees of the London Library Trust for the Carlyle Membership. Thanks are also due to Exeter University's Library, the Devon and Exeter Institution (notably Roger Brien, James Turner and Su Conniff) and the British Library (especially Manuscripts and the Document Supply Service).

As ever, special mention must be made of everyone at the St Thomas branch of the Devon Library Services, including Karen Lee, Judith Prescott and Lee Rawlings, who dealt brilliantly with our constant requests, despite having to operate from temporary premises. Karen's car was written off (though thankfully she was unhurt) while in pursuit of our Jane Austen requests, which was way beyond the call of duty. We are also indebted to Lesley Wiltshire for all her work in the Devon Library Services interlibrary loans department.

We enjoyed working at the Somerset Heritage Centre, where we greatly appreciated the friendly and helpful staff. This archive holds the original copies of the extensive diaries of William Holland, which have yet to be published in their entirety. David Worthy has been incredibly generous in sharing information about the Holland diaries, and his help has been invaluable. We would also like to thank John Upton for kindly allowing us to quote from the Upton-Wilkinson archive; the Trustees of the National Museum of the Royal Navy (NMRN) for the use of their archives; Moretonhampstead History Society for giving permission to use their Treleaven's diary archive; the Yorkshire Archaeological Society for permission to use *The Diary of Charles Fothergill 1805*, and the Thomas Fisher Rare Book Library of the University of Toronto, which holds the original manuscript of the Fothergill Papers.

The Parson Woodforde Society very generously gave us permission to use their wonderful editions of the complete Woodforde diaries. We are also grateful to Jenny Alderson from the society for her help, while Martin Brayne kindly provided much valuable information, as did Peter Jameson. Since Parson Woodforde is usually regarded as a Norfolk man, we were pleased to find that he had deep roots in Ansford and nearby Castle Cary in Somerset. We visit Castle Cary at least twice a year, and everyone at Max Foote Associates there deserves a special mention.

Stephen Lysch (of Palgrave, Ontario, Canada) freely shared information on the Cureton family, which was much appreciated. Many thanks as well to Jane Wickenden, Historic Collections Librarian at the Institute of Naval Medicine for her generous help, as well as to Robin Agnew, Andrew Butcher, Dr Tony Corley, Dr Ian Mortimer, Deirdre Le Faye, Keith Gregson, Dr David Higgins of the Society for Clay Pipe Research, David Warner, Chris Mortimer of Blacksnow Web Design for his constant expertise and support, the Dorset History Centre, Matthew Sheldon of the National Museum of the Royal Navy, Richard Walker of the British Library, Simon Foote of Exeter University library, Professor David Watkin, Liz Egan and Lauren Ryall-Stockton of the Thackray Museum in Leeds and Joan Livesey of Wigan Archives Service. As ever, we have neglected friends and family while writing this book, and we are grateful for their understanding.

Finally, we owe a big vote of thanks to Richard Beswick at Little, Brown (UK) and to Rick Kot at Viking Penguin (US) for taking on this book, and to all those involved in the various publishing processes including Zoe Gullen (indomitable desk editor), Victoria Pepe, Anniina Vuori, Nathalie Morse, John Gilkes (for his maps), Sue Phillpott (copy-editing), Alison Tulett (proofreading) and Sarah Ereira (indexing).

# INDEX

abortion 44
accents 51–4; *see also* dialects
Acland, Hugh 388
Acland, John 326
afterlife 324, 325
agriculture 39, 40, 193–8; child workers 70, 73;
    dairy 105–6; improvements/changes xix,
    194, 203, 208; servants/workers 67, 92, 95,
    140, 176, 189, 193–4; *see also* cattle,
    enclosures, harvests, manure, milk,
    ploughmen, wheat
Aikin, John 312–13, 386
alcohol 31, 111–12, 207, 210, 226, 300, 312; *see
    also* beer, gin, wine
alighting stones 241
Allen, Mrs (*Northanger Abbey*) 130
almanacs 168–9
almshouses 202, 317
Althens, Henry 68
America: beaver imports 129; language 52; *see
    also* Silliman, Simond, slaves,
    transportation, wars
American Revolutionary War (War of
    Independence) xvii, 281, 282
amputation 304, 309, 312–13
amulets 166
anaesthetics 25, 26, 311–12
anatomists/anatomy schools 11, 25, 296, 297,
    309, 318, 319–21, 328; *see also* dissection
Andrews, Harry 153
Andrews, Michael 135
Andrews, Richard 112
animals *see* birds, cats, cattle dogs, farriers,
    horses
Ansford, Somerset xxv, 92, 211
apothecaries (druggists) 12, 293, 295–6, 297,
    304, 305, 308
apples 43, 59, 109, 152
apprentices xxii, 5, 7, 39, 68, 69–73, 76, 77, 78,
    206, 215, 296, 299
Aranson, Pascoe 306–7
archaeology 115, 228
architecture xix, 81–2, 83, 172
Arkwright, Richard 120, 190

Armitage, Joseph 193
army: agents 69, 373; boots 128; career 175;
    casualties 5, 309; hats 129; JA's brother's
    career 69; in JA's work xvii–xviii; medical
    men 297; recruitment 200, 305, 380; *see also*
    militias, wars
ashes 101, 143, 145; potash 138
Ashton-under-Lyne, Lancs 8
Assizes 265–6, 274, 275, 277, 285, 287
Astick, Robert 1–2
Atkins, Thomas 281
Austen, Anna (niece of JA) xx–xxii, 35, 239,
    353
Austen, Cassandra (mother of JA) 20, 27, 32,
    36, 353, 382
Austen, Cassandra (sister of JA): as a baby 32,
    36; birth 32; death of sister-in-law 336;
    destroyed JA's letters 235; education 65;
    executrix of JA's will 337–8; at Gomersham
    195; at JA's death 324; niece of Mrs Leigh-
    Perrot 274; walking 238; in Weymouth 110,
    219
Austen, Charles (brother of JA) 69
Austen, Edward (brother of JA) *see* Knight
Austen, Edward (nephew of JA) 54
Austen, Francis (Frank, brother of JA) 69
Austen, George (nephew of JA) 54
Austen, George (brother of JA) 69
Austen, George (father of JA) 62, 147, 148, 195,
    301
Austen, Henry (brother of JA): banker 69,
    175, 373; career 69, 175, 373; childhood 32;
    homes 78, 145, 380; illness 293; JA's
    memorial 342; in JA's will 337; Oxford
    university 69
Austen, James (brother of JA) 20–1, 69, 90,
    147
Austen, Jane: accent 53; aunt charged with
    theft 274, 275; on ball at Deane 219; birth
    27; on brother's health 293; on brother's
    house 78, 145–6; clothes 122, 123, 129–30,
    133–4; on cousin's career 148; on curate for
    Deane 147; death 324; on deaths 20, 88,
    302, 328; on dentistry 306; on donkey

lace 124–5, 130, 274, 336, 337
Lackington, James 68, 83, 233
Lake District xxv, 4, 60, 88, 123, 126, 127, 144, 190, 193, 227, 302, 329
lamps/lanterns 98, 99, 101, 222, 230, 256; *see also* candles, rushlights
Lancaster, Joseph 66, 361
Lancaster, William 270
land ownership 80, 197, 362
La Roche, Sophie von 101
Latham, Henry 222, 299
Latin 62, 64–5, 360
laundry 36, 134–5, 136–40, 310; *see also* washerwomen
lawns 80, 108
laws: on apothecaries 297; Bloody Code 263–4, 275; on bull-baiting 212; on burial 335; on canals 185; on climbing boys 76, 79; on corpses 321; on education 67; on machine-breaking 193; on madhouses 315; on marriage 5–6, 14, 16; on miners 184; on newspaper postage 231; on nonconformists 161; private Acts of Parliament 16, 171, 197, 251; stamp duty tax 155; on State Lottery 226; on unmarried pregnant women 2; on weights and measures 345
leaping (sport) 214, 218
leeches 301, 302–3
Leeds, Yorks 158, 168, 208, 266, 307
Leggett/Leggatt, Ben 92, 98, 108, 200, 203, 241, 298
Leicester, Lord 228
Leigh-Perrot, Jane 273–5, 382
letters 235–7
libraries xx, 233–5
lice 134
lighting 98–101; *see also* candles, lamps, moon, rushlights
linen 9, 21, 28, 36, 37, 72, 96, 115, 118, 120, 124, 134, 136, 137, 139, 141, 216, 282, 313, 324; smoothers 310
literacy 68, 231–2, 377
Littleworth, Bessy 32
Litton Mill, Derbyshire 71–2
Liverpool xxv, 46; architecture, 83; Beacon's Gutter 87, 138; canals 260; class distinction in church, 158–9; dentists 306–7, 386; housing, 87; Jewish traders 163; Mrs Hemans born 362; Nelly Weeton lived 123, 134; population 40; slave trade 199; stagecoaches 244; theatre 222; windmills 103
livery: carriages 9, 243; servants 91, 243, 266
London: accent 53–4; ballad singers 224; balloon flight 261–2; balls 219–20; Bills of Mortality 39; booksellers 233; burials 335; childbirth 22, 25, 27; chimney sweeps 76–8; clothes shops 122, 126; coachmakers 243; coffee-houses 231; coinage 179; cricket 215; crime 266–7, 271, 291–2; dentistry 305, 306, 309; drapery stores 125–6; education 68; executions 285; eye hospital 313; fog 256–7; Foundling Hospital 36, 43; frost fair 210; funerals 330; Hans Place 77–8, 380; housing 83–4, 85–6, 88–9, 94; ice-houses 110; immigration 203; inns 254; Irish community 42, 85; Jewish community 42; leisure attractions 229–30; linen ordered from 21; manners 129; meat supplies 109; medical centre 296; milk supplies 105; newspapers 231; Old Bailey 265; pedlars 181; police 264; population 40; postal system 235; press-gangs 200; prostitutes 45, 47, 134; public transport 248, 249; riots 289–90; Royal Exchange 191; Season 82; shops 180; size xxiii, 39, 40; smuggled merchandise 291–2; street lighting 256; streets 249; Sundays 159; theatres 221–2; toilets 143–4; umbrellas 130–1; wallpaper suppliers 86–7; water supply 136; weddings 6, 11; workhouses 70, 71; *see also* Bank of England, bodysnatchers, Thames
Lord, Mary 28
Lord, Sarah 143
Lord, Thomas 215; Lord's Cricket Ground 215–16
lottery/lottery clubs 226–7
Loveday *see* Benwell
Lucas, Charlotte (*Pride and Prejudice*) 338
Luddites 192–3
lunatics/lunatic asylums 313–17, 387
lunch 113
Lyme Regis, Dorset xxi, 110, 219
Lyons, G. (optician) 310–11

MacAulay, George 83, 363
Macdonald, John 130–1
McGuigin, Simon 273
Mackey, Brian 41
madhouses 313–17
Magdalen Hospital for Penitent Prostitutes 47
magistrates 179, 193, 214, 245, 265, 266, 271, 290, 291
Magnes, Richard 59, 360
maiden garlands 172
malaria 141, 295, 299
man-midwives *see* midwives
Manchester xxiii, 23, 27–8, 40, 42, 83, 260, 318; *see also* Percival (John), White (Charles)

underwear *see* drawers, shifts, shirts, stays, stockings
Unitarians 161
Upholland, Lancs, 21, 23, 44, 86, 87, 93, 123, 164–5, 277
urine 35, 105, 138, 142, 167, 195

vaccination 299; *see also* inoculation
Valentine's Day 170
Vauxhall gardens 229–30, 370
vegetable: dye 86, 133; oil 101
vegetables (garden stuff) 103, 107–8, 109, 181
vinegar 44, 53, 293, 303, 313

wages: agricultural workers 92; bread prices 104; canal cutters 186; children 69, 72; craftsmen 92; factory workers 189, 190; falling 173, 188, 204; industrial workers 92; manual workers 173, 264; miners 176, 183, 184; servants 23, 61, 91–2, 223; strike over 204; tailors 206; toll collectors 251; *see also* incomes
waggons 184, 195, 240, 242, 247, 259; *see also* carts
waistcoats 2, 27, 117–18, 121, 126, 282, 291
Wakelin, William 69–70
Walker, Adam 52–3, 359
Walker, Alice 281–2
Walker, John 53
walking xxiv, 2, 7, 10, 238–40
wallpaper 86–7, 363
Walpole, Horace xx, 83, 362
Wapshare, Mary 34–5
Ware, Thomas 152, 324–5
Warner, Richard 72, 187, 189–90, 242
wars with France and America: casualties, 5, 308–9; in JA's work xvii–xviii; Napoleonic xvii, 5, 163, 204, 308, 311; Peninsular 210, 308; press-gangs 199–200; prisoners-of-war xviii, 178–9, 280–1; teeth collected after battles 308–9; unemployment, 203; see also army, invasion threat, militias, Royal Navy
washerwomen 137, 138, 250
washing machines 138
watches (pocket)/watchmakers 86, 122, 144, 189, 264, 267
watchmen 189, 211, 265, 268, 339
water: heating 136; supply 97–8, 110–11, 134–6; *see also* pumps, wells
water-closets 144–5
Waterloo, Battle of (1815) 204, 309
Watson, George 46
wax/beeswax 99–100, 179, 235, 326, 364

weather: forecasting 258–9; harsh winters 95, 143, 257; mud 1, 115, 128, 187, 211, 238–9, 250; rain 239, 257; winter temperatures 94–5, 257, 259; *see also* floods, fog, smog, snow
weaving 72, 120, 188, 189, 191
weddings xxii, 1–13, 39, 41, 354; *see also* marriage
Weeton, Nelly: on abortion 44; on canal travel 260; on childbirth 21, 28; on class distinction 158–9; on clergy 151–2, 158–9; on clothes 116, 117, 123, 159, 218; on dentistry 306; description of bedroom 93; on elopement 13; on fair 208; family background 4, 64, 91; on food 106, 260; on ghosts 164–5; governess xxv, 4, 64, 88, 91, 193; on hairstyles 134; on illegitimate children 23; on illness 293, 299; on laundry 138; letters and diaries, xxv–xxvi, 235–6; on library 234–5; on Luddites 193; on manure 144; marriage 15, 16; on marriage 4, 13, 15, 16, 23; on mourning clothes 336; on pupil's death 97, 123, 328, 336; on regatta 218; on renting houses 86, 87, 88; on seduction 46; on servants 46, 91; status xxv; on stockings 116; on suicide case 277; on theatre 222; on women's careers 65
Weeton, Tom 4, 16, 88, 106, 116, 117, 22, 235, 293
Weit, David 144
wells 135, 136
Wesley, John 161–2, 278
Weston, Miss 12
Weston Longville, Norfolk 6, 180, 226, 306; beating the bounds 171–2; church ceremonies 7, 33, 131, 153, 332, 333; entertainments, 152–3; house fire 97–8; parsonage/rectory 1, 87, 92, 143; tithes 152–3; travel 255; weddings 2, 6–7; Weston House 24, 79, 92, 221, 239; Woodforde's parish, xxv, 148
wet-nurses 30, 31, 51, 356
Weymouth, Dorset 51, 110, 218–19, 227
Wharton, Jack 194, 295, 298
wheat xviii, 10, 104, 195, 232, 275, 290
whipping 43, 283–4
White, Charles 23, 26–8, 31, 297
White, Gilbert 29, 100, 109, 158, 164, 250, 334–5
Whitefield, George 161
Whitehaven, Cumberland 73, 74–5
whitewash 86, 208
Whitfield, Susanna 78
Whitworth Doctors 296–7, 302, 304, 305